Legal and Ethical Challenges in Data Privacy Rights and Cybersecurity

Calvin Nobles
https://orcid.org/0000-0003-4002-1108

University of Maryland Global Campus, USA

Kevin Richardson
https://orcid.org/0009-0002-3212-8669

Talladega College, USA

Quatavia McLester
https://orcid.org/0000-0003-1596-0517

Columbus State University, USA

Darrell Norman Burrell
https://orcid.org/0000-0002-4675-9544

Marymount University, USA

IGI Global
Scientific Publishing
Publishing Tomorrow's Research Today

Published in the United States of America by
IGI Global Scientific Publishing
701 East Chocolate Avenue
Hershey, PA, 17033, USA
Tel: 717-533-8845 | Fax: 717-533-7115
Website: https://www.igi-global.com E-mail: cust@igi-global.com

Library of Congress Cataloging-in-Publication Data

Names: Nobles, Calvin - editor | Richardson, Kevin - editor | McLester, Quatavia - editor | Norman Burrell, Darrell - editor
Title: Legal and ethical challenges in data privacy rights and cybersecurity / edited by Calvin Nobles, Kevin Richardson, Quatavia McLester, Darrell Norman Burrell.
Description: Hershey : IGI Global Scientific Publishing, 2026. | Includes bibliographical references and index. | Summary: "This book aims to provide a robust, interdisciplinary foundation for addressing the profound governance challenges emerging at the nexus of law, ethics, and digital innovation"-- Provided by publisher.
Identifiers: LCCN 2025031498 (print) | LCCN 2025031499 (ebook) | ISBN 9798337349671 hardcover | ISBN 9798337349688 paperback | ISBN 9798337349695 ebook
Subjects: LCSH: Privacy, Right of | Privacy, Right of--Moral and ethical aspects | Data protection--Law and legislation | Computer security--Law and legislation
Classification: LCC K3264.C65 L437 2026 (print) | LCC K3264.C65 (ebook) | DDC 323.44/8--dc23/eng/20250902
LC record available at https://lccn.loc.gov/2025031498
LC ebook record available at https://lccn.loc.gov/2025031499

British Cataloguing in Publication Data
A Cataloguing in Publication record for this book is available from the British Library.

Table of Contents

Detailed Table of Contents

concludes with the suggestions to increase legal protection, enforce moral leadership and to make sure that cyber law protects not only electronic systems but also those people who live in a more interconnected world.

This perspective paper explores cybersecurity and information security as critical dimensions of healthcare administration and organizational behavior within Applied Behavior Analysis (ABA) telehealth organizations. As digital platforms become central to clinical delivery, ABA therapists, highly skilled in behavioral science but often under-trained in cybersecurity, face increasing exposure to data breaches and compliance risks. Most security incidents in healthcare stem from preventable human factors such as cognitive overload, automation complacency, and inconsistent adherence to security protocols. Integrating behavioral principles with administrative governance can transform cybersecurity from a technical afterthought into a core element of professional and organizational competence. Embedding cybersecurity within organizational culture ensures sustainable protection of client data while advancing ethical, secure, and high-performing ABA telehealth systems.

This chapter is a study on the ethical and legal issues as presented by biometric surveillance technologies, the interests that the change of human bodily digitization into digital bearers of identity is fundamentally changing the connection between the individual identity, bodily liberty, and institutionalised power. It also reflects on the interdisciplinary understanding of the concept through law analysis, critical theory, and empirical studies to understand how the specificities of biometric datafication introduce a unique vulnerability between biological labels and their biological owners. As the analysis depicts, the lapse in traditional systems of consent is leading to coercive surveillance. The chapter concludes with recommendations on the ethical governance of data minimisation and transparency, but also limitations on high-risk use cases such as emotion recognition, mass surveillance, and postulates that informational privacy is not sufficient to protect human dignity and that the substantive recognition of the right to bodily integrity must extend to the digital realm.

Cyberspace has become a prerequisite for human flourishing in the present century. Almost all human interactions use cyberspace for increased productivity, efficiency, and economic growth. The speed and results of cyber activities are significantly ahead of real-world human interactions. However, cyberspace is not without drawbacks and challenges. Cybersecurity and data privacy have become essential concerns of the present century, as cybercrimes, cyber terrorism, data breaches, and cyber theft have become everyday occurrences. Besides, issues like the digital divide complicate the global march towards sustainability through cyberspace. Many countries have enacted various laws and policies to ensure cybersecurity. However, they are not globally effective as cyberspace is beyond the territorial boundaries. It demands a globally acceptable ethico-legal framework that guarantees a dignified cyberspace. From this perspective, this chapter calls for an international law perspective applicable to all states and some foundational ethical principles that should guide all cyber activities.

Social media platforms collect vast personal data, through lengthy terms and conditions that users accept without understanding. Globally, laws like the General Data Protection Regulation (GDPR), California's CCPA have set high standards for consent and user rights. India, through the Digital Personal Data Protection Act (DPDP) of 2023, has introduced its own framework, recognizing privacy as a fundamental right following the landmark Puttaswamy v. Union of India judgment.

Preface

The accelerating digitization of social, economic, and political life has fundamentally reshaped how data is created, collected, governed, and contested. Across jurisdictions, data now functions simultaneously as a driver of innovation, a tool of governance, and a site of profound vulnerability. As artificial intelligence, biometric systems, social media platforms, and global data infrastructures expand in scope and sophistication, longstanding legal doctrines and ethical frameworks are being tested in unprecedented ways. Questions once confined to technical or sector-specific debates now implicate constitutional rights, human dignity, democratic accountability, and global justice.

Legal and Ethical Challenges in Data Privacy Rights and Cybersecurity emerges from this moment of transition and tension. The chapters in this volume collectively recognize that privacy and cybersecurity are no longer discrete or purely technical concerns. Instead, they represent deeply intertwined legal, ethical, organizational, and human challenges that demand interdisciplinary engagement. The contributors examine how states, institutions, corporations, and individuals navigate competing imperatives—security versus liberty, innovation versus accountability, efficiency versus consent—within rapidly evolving digital ecosystems.

As editors, we have intentionally curated a volume that reflects both global diversity and conceptual breadth. The chapters draw from comparative legal analysis, ethical theory, organizational behavior, and applied case studies, spanning jurisdictions in North America, Europe, and Asia. Together, they demonstrate that while legal regimes and cultural contexts may differ, the underlying challenges of data protection, surveillance, cybersecurity, and human autonomy are shared across borders. This book is therefore designed to serve scholars, practitioners, policymakers, and students seeking a rigorous and holistic understanding of data privacy and cybersecurity in the twenty-first century.

CHAPTER OVERVIEW

Chapter 1 examines the complex relationship between the right to privacy and national cybersecurity imperatives, with a particular focus on India's evolving data protection framework. Through comparative analysis with the European Union and Canada, the authors explore how constitutional values, proportionality, and institutional oversight can be reconciled with AI-driven surveillance and national security concerns.

Chapter 2 expands the discussion by analyzing cybersecurity regulation as a mechanism for protecting individual rights in the face of escalating digital threats. By integrating domestic and international legal perspectives alongside real-world case studies, this chapter highlights the persistent challenge of balancing state security interests with personal privacy and human rights.

Chapter 3 shifts the focus to organizational and human factors in cybersecurity, using healthcare and Applied Behavior Analysis (ABA) telehealth organizations as a case study. This chapter emphasizes that cybersecurity failures are often rooted not in technology, but in behavioral, cultural, and administrative shortcomings, underscoring the need to embed security awareness into professional practice and organizational governance.

Chapter 4 critically interrogates biometric surveillance and the ethical implications of using the human body as a source of data. Drawing on legal analysis and critical theory, this chapter argues that informational privacy alone is insufficient and calls for the recognition of bodily integrity as a digital-era right, particularly in the context of mass surveillance and emotion recognition technologies.

Chapter 5 advances the discussion toward a global ethical and legal framework for cybersecurity and data privacy. Acknowledging the borderless nature of cyberspace, this chapter argues for internationally shared principles capable of safeguarding human dignity while addressing cybercrime, cyber terrorism, and systemic digital inequality.

Chapter 6 offers a critical examination of consent in social media data harvesting under global privacy regimes. By comparing frameworks such as the GDPR, CCPA, and India's Digital Personal Data Protection Act, this chapter exposes the limitations of formal consent mechanisms and highlights the need for stronger enforcement and user-centered protections.

Chapter 7 addresses the growing legal and ethical dilemmas posed by artificial intelligence and big data. The chapter evaluates global regulatory and ethical responses and advocates for a human-centric, multi-level approach grounded in transparency, accountability, and cross-border cooperation.

Chapter 8 provides a comprehensive overview of the fragmented global regulatory landscape governing cybersecurity and data protection. By analyzing major compliance frameworks and emerging technologies, this chapter offers practical guidance for organizations seeking to navigate regulatory complexity while integrating privacy and security by design.

Chapter 9 concludes the substantive contributions by examining corporate data privacy frameworks in the age of emerging technologies. Focusing on AI-driven accountability challenges, this chapter explores the transformation of personal data into an economic asset and critically assesses the adequacy of existing legal mechanisms in assigning responsibility within a globalized digital economy.

CONCLUSION

Taken together, the chapters in this volume reveal that data privacy and cybersecurity challenges cannot be resolved through isolated legal reforms or technological solutions alone. They require sustained engagement with ethical principles, institutional design, organizational behavior, and global cooperation. The contributors consistently demonstrate that effective governance must be anticipatory rather than reactive, embedding privacy, security, and accountability into systems from their inception.

This volume also underscores the importance of centering human dignity and autonomy in digital governance. Whether addressing biometric surveillance, AI-driven decision-making, corporate data practices, or cybersecurity compliance, the chapters highlight the risks of reducing individuals to data subjects without meaningful agency. Protecting privacy in the digital age is not merely about compliance; it is about preserving trust, legitimacy, and the foundational values of democratic and constitutional societies.

As editors, we hope this book serves as both a scholarly contribution and a practical resource. By bringing together diverse perspectives and methodologies, *Legal and Ethical Challenges in Data Privacy Rights and Cybersecurity* invites readers to think critically about the future of data governance and to participate in shaping legal and ethical frameworks that are resilient, inclusive, and responsive to the realities of a rapidly transforming digital world.

Chapter 1
Reconciling the Right to Privacy With National Cyber-Security Imperatives:
A Legal Analysis of Data Protection Laws in the Age of AI-Driven Surveillance

Ramya Krishnappa
https://orcid.org/0000-0001-8900-454X
Christ University, India

Rajiv Gurugopinath
https://orcid.org/0000-0003-3845-6778
Ramaiah College of Law, India

ABSTRACT

The chapter analyses the struggles of privacy and cybersecurity governance in India in comparison with some of the best practices used in other countries and the elements of collision between the core rights and the security needs of the country. Based on the Puttaswamy judgment, and the Digital Personal Data Protection Act, 2023, the paper, by taking comparative lessons of the European Union rights-based GDPR and Canadian malleable, principles-based, PIPEDA/CPPA regulation framework, offers insights into the formulation of the arbitration process under the Digital Personal Data Protection Act, 2023. It offers a hybrid-type policy framework which entails privacy-by-design, proportionality independent oversight and

DOI: 10.4018/979-8-3373-4967-1.ch001

cross-border data adequacy frameworks. It insists on the reinforcement of the Data Protection Board of India making checks on surveillance activity. Its purpose is to achieve protection of the constitutional values and at the same time perform secure, non-innovation-restricting digital governance in the age of transformation driven by AI and international information flows.

INTRODUCTION

The Digital Rights Paradox arises from the conflicting relationship between the expansion of individual digital rights and the growing dominance of state and corporate control in digital spaces. Rights such as internet access, data protection, and the right to be forgotten are increasingly recognized as fundamental (Varlamova, 2019). Yet, when classical principles of sovereignty are applied to the digital environment, states struggle to manage governance while safeguarding individual autonomy and privacy (Ruohonen, 2021). The paradox lies in the dual reality that individuals are empowered by digital rights but simultaneously constrained by mechanisms of surveillance and corporate control. This inability to reconcile rights with sovereignty exacerbates governance dilemmas, producing tensions between freedom and control.

The paradox is further intensified by the commodification of data and surveillance-driven platform economies, where terms of service and social media contracts reflect corporate interests rather than individual rights. Economic contradictions also emerge, as open-data initiatives are undermined by the proprietary power of Big Tech, generating market inefficiencies. Simultaneously, the globality of digital rights challenges territorial boundaries and requires collaborative international governance (Wagner et al., 2023). Thus, while digital technologies expand empowerment, they also reinforce systemic domination, underscoring the urgent need for legal frameworks that balance rights, governance, and financial imperatives.

Momentum toward recognition of privacy as a constitutional right has accelerated with technological innovation and global interconnectedness. In the United States, privacy questions emerged early, shaped by constitutional debates in the twentieth century. India followed with the landmark Justice K.S. Puttaswamy v. Union of India case, which declared privacy a fundamental right under Article 21, embedding it as central to autonomy and dignity in the digital era (Kaur, 2024). Similarly, European initiatives—including reforms in Spain and broader EU directives—demonstrate a global consensus to constitutionalize digital rights and embed them within fundamental legal frameworks. At the international level, human rights law has reinforced privacy as a core principle. European institutions have taken the lead in addressing transnational data transfers, while the UN General Assembly Resolution 68/167 recognized privacy as a digital-era human right and called for safeguards against mass surveillance. Despite this, persistent challenges remain: doctrines like the U.S. third-party doctrine and the Stored Communications Act reflect narrow legal interpretations that fail to capture the realities of digital surveillance. As technologies evolve, constitutional protections must adapt to ensure that privacy remains a cornerstone of individual freedom while balancing security and collective interests (Dhamo & Dhamo, 2024; Chugh, 2023).

THEORETICAL CONTEXTS FOR ARTIFICIAL INTELLIGENCE

Recent literature stresses foundational AI governance principles rooted in constitutional law, political science, and ethics. Constitutional values of privacy, autonomy, proportionality, and transparency have emerged as key benchmarks for assessing AI systems' legitimacy. Jurisprudential analyses—such as the adoption of proportionality tests derived from the European Court of Human Rights—help blend legal theory with practical oversight for surveillance and algorithmic systems. Concepts like surveillance capitalism and digital sovereignty underscore how AI technologies challenge traditional understandings of state power and individual rights, catalyzing new forms of legal reasoning and judicial review. Beyond doctrinal law, socio-technical perspectives draw from political theory and technology studies to frame AI as both an enabler and risk to empowerment. Varlamova (2019) and Wagner et al. (2023) highlight the "paradox of digital rights," reflecting on how technological advancement leads to both greater autonomy and heightened vulnerability for individuals in data-driven societies. The literature critiques the "black box" opacity of complex algorithms, arguing for algorithmic transparency as a fundamental pillar within democratic rule-of-law frameworks (Engelmann 2023).

INTERDISCIPLINARY INSIGHTS: ETHICS, LAW, AND BEYOND

AI governance now draws from diverse disciplines—law, philosophy, political science, computer science, and sociology—to create a more holistic regulatory paradigm. For instance, ethical frameworks emphasize explainability, fairness, and non-discrimination, challenging mere compliance with technical standards and calling for value-sensitive design (Descalzo 2024; Felzmann et al. 2020).

Political science contributes by scrutinizing the roles and legitimacy of oversight bodies, calling for multilayered, multi-stakeholder regulation to combat technocratic overreach (Kniep et al., 2023). Socio-legal research shows predictive policing and algorithmic profiling raise structural risks for minority rights and perpetuate bias when historical datasets remain uncorrected (Singhvi, 2024; Hiller, 2022; Nabil et al., 2025; Machayya 2024). Psychologists and sociologists add insights on behavioral impacts, especially around workers' autonomy in gig economies and privacy under biometric surveillance (Gordon et al., 2021; Newlands, 2022; Alotaibi et al., 2019).

UPDATED INTERNATIONAL COOPERATION MECHANISMS

There is a marked evolution in international approaches to AI and data governance, moving from state-centric regulations to more complex, multilateral, and hybrid models. The European Union's GDPR provides a strict, rights-based regime, with enforcement led by robust authorities like the EDPB, while Canada's CPPA exemplifies a pragmatic, sector-specific, yet flexible approach enforced by the Office of the Privacy Commissioner (Korff, 2023). The report also references new trends such as:

- Adequacy and Reciprocity Agreements: India's alignment with OECD and EU standards through cross-border data transfer pacts—ensuring lawful, reciprocal, and rights-respecting exchanges—strengthens international trust and compliance.
- Reformed Mutual Legal Assistance Treaties (MLATs): Modernization to guarantee more timely, rights-respecting access for cross-border law enforcement, as flagged by recent recommendations.
- Multi-Stakeholder and Layered Oversight: International cooperation increasingly features collaborative models involving civil society, technical experts, and independent regulators alongside state actors for both national and transnational AI governance (Kniep et al. 2023; Graeden et al. 2023).
- Privacy-by-Design as a Statutory Mandate: International consensus is growing around embedding privacy-by-design and explainability into all AI and digital infrastructure by law (Descalzo 2024; Felzmann et al., 2020).
- International Human Rights Frameworks: Recent literature stresses the need for coordinated interpretation of human rights obligations—such as Article 17 of the ICCPR—across AI regulation, supported by transnational precedents and comparative jurisprudence.

The rise of Artificial Intelligence (AI) and datafication has reshaped national security paradigms, amplifying intelligence collection, predictive analytics, and counterintelligence capacities. Machine learning and natural language processing enable agencies to analyze vast datasets and anticipate threats, while in the Global South AI supports surveillance and cybersecurity despite persistent capacity gaps.

Military applications, including autonomous weapons and cyber defense, are altering conflict dynamics and raising profound ethical and geopolitical questions (Chugh, 2023).

The integration of AI into counterintelligence enhances detection of hostile activities but raises parallel concerns over privacy and ethics. Increasingly, predictive and prescriptive analytics are essential for security stability, though they necessitate new governance frameworks to address ethical and strategic risks (Montasari, 2022; Usman et al., 2023). Viewed against a decade of digital rights development, AI exemplifies both the promise of technological innovation and the urgent need to balance efficiency with accountability (Teo, 2024).

The chronology of digital rights reflects this evolving tension. In 2012, scholars identified the paradox of digital access as both empowering and threatening autonomy. By 2015, the UN General Assembly Resolution 68/167 formally recognized the right to privacy in cyberspace, creating a framework for convergence in privacy, data protection, and accountability (Khazanchi & Saxena, 2025; Nyst & Falchetta, 2016).

A turning point came in 2017, when India's Puttaswamy ruling enshrined privacy under Article 21, while Europe advanced the GDPR and complementary reforms, positioning the EU as a global rule-setter in digital governance (Dowd, 2021). By the early 2020s, debates expanded to encompass digital sovereignty, AI-driven datafication, and data geopolitics, with states demanding localized storage, algorithmic transparency, and ethical AI oversight (Hulkó et al., 2025; Coche & Kolk, 2024).

By 2021, growing recognition of surveillance capitalism, misinformation, and automated decision-making confirmed the urgency of comprehensive legal frameworks (Livson et al., 2021). This trajectory underscores an evolution in the very conception of digital rights. No longer treated as extensions of civil liberties, they are increasingly seen as distinct legal entities requiring new jurisprudential paradigms and institutional protections (Kulikova, 2019). National AI strategies, digital constitutions, and transnational regulatory coalitions reflect this reorientation. The EU's proposed AI Act, India's DPDP Act and the OECD's framework on trustworthy AI exemplify efforts to embed binding ethical principles into governance.

These developments highlight the deep interdependence of digital rights, democratic accountability, and socio-technical systems. Going forward, integrating constitutional values such as dignity, autonomy, and non-discrimination into technological design and deployment will be essential to preserve both individual freedoms and the rule of law in an era increasingly defined by automation, surveillance, and datafication (Fornasier, 2022).

The de-territorialized nature of data flows has intensified concerns over digital sovereignty, as information stored in foreign jurisdictions often becomes subject to competing legal frameworks. This raises significant challenges for law enforcement and privacy protections, since traditional mutual legal assistance treaties (MLATs) have proven inadequate for timely and rights-respecting cooperation (Coche & Kolk, 2024). Evidence of this tension can be seen in initiatives such as the U.S. CLOUD Act and the EU's e-Evidence package, both designed to simplify cross-border access to data while incorporating safeguards of proportionality and fundamental rights.

Analysis of these instruments, however, suggests they risk overreach and incompatibility with domestic privacy regimes, prompting criticism from civil society and digital rights advocates. The link between sovereignty and data governance underscores the necessity of developing international legal harmonization that protects individual rights while ensuring legitimate law enforcement access in a globalized digital environment.

The comparative experiences of the EU and Canada provide models for India as it implements the Digital Personal Data Protection Act. The GDPR exemplifies a rights-based, prescriptive framework that enforces strict compliance obligations and empowers independent supervisory authorities to uphold accountability (Dowd, 2021). By contrast, Canada's PIPEDA and proposed CPPA adopt a principles-based and flexible approach, emphasizing fair information practices such as consent, collection limits, accuracy, and safeguards (Livson et al., 2021).

These regimes demonstrate that enforceability and adaptability need not be mutually exclusive; rather, they can be blended into hybrid systems that protect rights without stifling innovation. For India, adopting a dual strategy—strengthening investigatory independence for the Data Protection Board while providing sector-specific guidance inspired by Canada—would build institutional credibility and balance citizen protection with economic competitiveness. Thus, comparative jurisprudence suggests that India's future digital governance will benefit from integrating both GDPR-style rigor and CPPA-style flexibility.

The accelerating role of artificial intelligence in surveillance, defense, and governance has brought urgency to questions of oversight and accountability. Research shows that AI-enabled predictive analytics, while enhancing operational efficiency, also risks entrenching systemic biases and undermining due process if deployed without safeguards (Teo, 2024). European efforts to regulate AI through the proposed AI Act, coupled with OECD's trustworthy AI framework, exemplify attempts to embed ethical principles directly into binding regulatory instruments (Díaz-Rodríguez et al., 2023).

India's DPDP Act, although focused on data protection, could be expanded to mandate privacy-by-design, transparency, and algorithmic accountability across AI systems. Such integration would align with international best practices and help mitigate risks of surveillance capitalism, automated discrimination, and erosion of public trust (Figure 1). Ultimately, the convergence of AI and digital rights highlights the need to link constitutional values such as dignity, autonomy, and non-discrimination with the design and governance of emerging technologies (Fornasier, 2022).

Figure 1. The timeline illustrates the evolution of digital rights from 2012 to 2024, highlighting key global and regional developments that shaped the legal and ethical landscape of the digital age. It begins with the 2012 recognition of the digital rights paradox, where increased connectivity also brought new threats to autonomy and privacy.

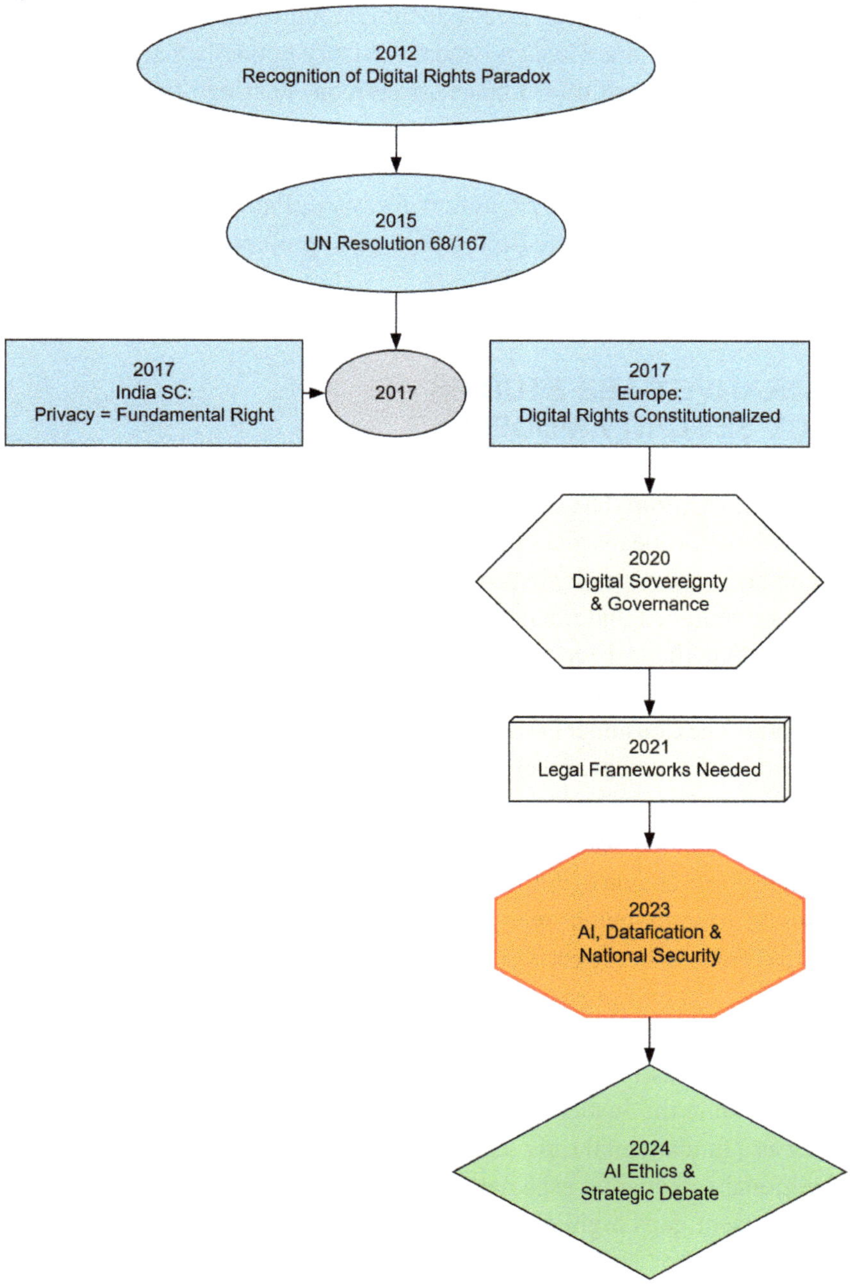

Source: Author Made

MECHANISMS FOR MEANINGFUL PUBLIC PARTICIPATION

Ensuring democratic legitimacy in AI governance systems demands structured opportunities for participation from civil society, technical experts, and affected communities at multiple levels of policy formation and oversight. Kniep et al. (2023) and Criado & Guevara-Gómez (2024) document multi-stakeholder accountability ecosystems in the EU and Canada, where advisory councils, participatory policy consultations, and algorithmic impact assessment hearings enable public input before deployment of high-risk AI systems. India can draw from these by integrating public comment processes into the Data Protection Board's regulatory actions and mandating community consultation for surveillance technologies in urban environments, ensuring marginalized voices are represented and that participatory transparency is not a mere formality.

COMPARATIVE CASE STUDIES OF PRIVACY-SECURITY MODELS

European Union: The GDPR, with its "privacy by design" mandate and independent European Data Protection Board, provides strong procedural rights, requiring proportionality in processing and judicial authorization for intrusive state surveillance. Judgments such as Schrems I & II and Article 17 of ICCPR demonstrate the insistence on fundamental rights even amid national security concerns (Staben & Leisterer, 2017).

Canada: The Consumer Privacy Protection Act (CPPA) features flexible, sector-agnostic enforcement and empowers the Office of the Privacy Commissioner with oversight over both public interest exceptions and security exemptions. Canada's National Security and Intelligence Review Agency (NSIRA) provides specialized oversight of digital surveillance programs, requiring privacy impact assessments and regular reporting (Korff, 2023; Bhushan, 2024).

United States: In the case of Carpenter v. United States, the Supreme Court recognized advanced privacy intrusion risks from real-time location tracking, establishing a higher threshold for law enforcement data access and influencing global standards in AI-driven investigations.

India: While the Justice K.S. Puttaswamy v. Union of India recognized privacy as a fundamental right, the Digital Personal Data Protection Act requires additional safeguards, especially against broad government exemptions and enforcement gaps highlighted in comparative commentary (Bhushan, 2024; Korff, 2023).

China and Global South (Data Localization and Human Rights): China's Personal Information Protection Law (PIPL) requires data localization, influencing global debates about extraterritorial enforcement and the limits of privacy rights in heavily surveilled societies. Similar dilemmas arise in Indonesia, where digital rights frameworks are adapting to both local context and international best practices (Wang, 2023).

Belgium (Algorithmic Police Oversight): Belgium has pioneered democratic oversight mechanisms by integrating multi-stakeholder review of algorithmic police surveillance. Regular audits and civil society participation help check technocratic dominance and reinforce legitimacy (Kniep et al., 2023).

LEGAL EVOLUTION ALONGSIDE TECHNOLOGICAL ADVANCEMENT

Proactive, Adaptive Regulation: Jurisdictions are increasingly adopting "regulatory sandboxes," sunset clauses, and ongoing legislative review to flexibly accommodate emerging technologies such as facial recognition, biometric databases, and emotion-detection AI (Meghwal, 2025; Amingad et al., 2023).

Transparency and Explainability: Laws now mandate explainable AI (XAI) and qualified algorithmic transparency, aiming to resolve black-box risks while balancing technical trade secrets and public accountability (Golovin, 2024; Rane et al., 2024).

Embedding Multidisciplinary and Global Inputs: Global frameworks, notably the OECD and UN Guiding Principles on Business and Human Rights, encourage inclusion of ethics, legal scholarship, technical standards, and social impact assessments in ongoing legislative evolution (Graeden et al., 2023).

FORWARD-LOOKING, MULTIDISCIPLINARY PERSPECTIVE

A comprehensive approach now requires a regular, multidisciplinary algorithmic impact assessments and participatory policy development, integrating technical, legal, and ethical review at all stages (Criado & Guevara-Gómez, 2024). Institutionalizing independent review panels with sectoral expertise to continuously update national and cross-border regulations as technology evolves (NSIRA reports; Korff, 2023). Recognizing and preemptively responding to new risks presented by AI in areas like law enforcement, health, gig work, and national security, ensuring flexible but principled evolution of laws (Newlands, 2022; Montasari, 2022).

OPERATIONALIZING DATA SUBJECT RIGHTS IN AI-DRIVEN NATIONAL SECURITY

Data subjects' rights must be reinforced even within national security and law enforcement frameworks. The GDPR and the Canadian CPPA both allow for certain restrictions in the context of national security, but only with stringent necessity and proportionality tests, independent approvals, and redress mechanisms (NSIRA reports). For practical impact:

- Enshrine rights to access, correction, and deletion, even in security databases, with clear procedural exceptions only as proportionate to demonstrable threats and mandate impact assessments and require notification to oversight bodies for any broad surveillance or AI use in public safety, following EU and Canadian standards (Descalzo, 2024).
- Establish procedures for independent complaint mechanisms and redress for wrongful inclusion in AI-driven surveillance lists and implications of Emerging Technologies and Adaptive Regulation with the rise of facial recognition, emotion detection, and ubiquitous biometric monitoring introduce new risks of discrimination and "black box" opacity, amplifying the need for adaptive, technology-neutral legal standards (Engelmann, 2023; Amingad et al., 2023; Gordon et al., 2021).

ADAPTIVE REGULATORY STRATEGIES SHOULD INCLUDE:

- Incorporating regulatory sandboxes for AI deployment, where provisional safeguards and stakeholder input adapt rules to new technological risks before large-scale implementation and creating periodic sunset clauses for technology-specific exemptions, requiring legislative review of AI surveillance authorities in light of evolving risks (Meghwal, 2025).
- Mandating cross-sectoral technical audits, transparent publication of system architectures, and open records of algorithmic impact assessments for accountability and iterative regulatory update (Felzmann et al., 2020).

PROBLEM STATEMENT

The accelerating integration of artificial intelligence (AI) and algorithmic governance into security, policing, and digital platforms has created a pressing conflict between technological efficiency and the constitutional right to privacy. Evidence shows that AI-powered predictive policing and surveillance tools exacerbate systemic biases and disproportionately target marginalized communities, leading to discrimination, privacy violations, and erosion of trust in public institutions (Nabil et al., 2025). In India, while the landmark Justice K.S. Puttaswamy v. Union of India judgment recognized privacy as a fundamental right, the subsequent rise of AI-based surveillance and mass datafication has strained this constitutional guarantee.

The Digital Personal Data Protection Act, 2023 (DPDP Act) was enacted to address these concerns, yet scholars highlight gaps such as broad government exemptions, weak enforcement mechanisms, and the challenge of balancing privacy with national security imperatives (Bhushan, 2024). Globally, the European Union's GDPR offers a strict rights-based framework, while Canada's CPPA provides a flexible, principles-driven model. However, uneven international protections complicate cross-border data governance (Korff, 2023). This paper therefore investigates how India can develop a hybrid privacy–cybersecurity jurisprudence that embeds proportionality, transparency, and democratic oversight, while mitigating risks from surveillance capitalism and algorithmic bias in public decision-making.

PURPOSE AND METHODOLOGY

Purpose

The purpose of this narrative literature review is to explore the intersection of privacy, cybersecurity, and artificial intelligence (AI), with a focus on how constitutional rights and data protection laws respond to challenges posed by surveillance capitalism, predictive policing, and algorithmic decision-making. Specifically, the review seeks to answer: How can India, informed by comparative insights from the European Union and Canada, develop a hybrid legal framework that balances privacy rights, cyber security needs, and technological innovation in the AI era?

Research Question

- How can constitutional principles of privacy, proportionality, and transparency be effectively embedded into AI-driven governance systems in India while drawing from global best practices?

Methodology

This study adopts a narrative literature review method, systematically synthesizing academic scholarship, policy documents, and legal case studies published within the last ten years. The databases and sources consulted include apart from other sources:

- **Google Scholar**
- **ProQuest**
- **SSRN (Social Science Research Network)**
- **SpringerLink**
- **HeinOnline**
- **JSTOR**

Search Terms and Synonyms

The following search terms and Boolean combinations were used to identify relevant literature:

- *Privacy* ("data protection," "informational privacy," "right to be forgotten")
- *Cybersecurity* ("data security," "digital sovereignty," "cyber governance")
- *Artificial Intelligence* ("AI governance," "algorithmic accountability," "machine learning regulation")
- *Surveillance* ("predictive policing," "algorithmic surveillance," "surveillance capitalism")
- *Comparative law* ("GDPR," "Digital Personal Data Protection Act," "Canadian CPPA," "global privacy frameworks")

Articles were selected based on their relevance, recency (2015–2025), and contribution to understanding the legal, ethical, and governance dimensions of privacy and AI.

SIGNIFICANCE OF THE PAPER

The significance of this study lies in addressing the growing conflict between technological innovation and constitutional safeguards in the digital era. Reports indicate that global data breaches exposed over 22 billion records in 2021 alone, with cybercrime costs projected to reach USD 10.5 trillion annually by 2025. At the same time, the expansion of predictive policing and algorithmic surveillance has raised profound concerns of bias and discrimination, with studies demonstrating that such systems disproportionately target marginalized groups, undermining trust in public institutions (Singhvi, 2024; Nabil et al., 2025). In India, the Digital Personal Data Protection Act, 2023 (DPDP Act) is a landmark legislative development, yet its enforcement challenges, government exemptions, and potential misalignment with international frameworks like the GDPR (Korff, 2023; Bhushan, 2024) highlight the urgent need for jurisprudential clarity. This paper's focus on reconciling privacy, cybersecurity, and AI ethics within a comparative framework is therefore timely and essential.

The knowledge generated from this research has practical relevance for policymakers, legal practitioners, technologists, and civil society organizations. Policymakers can use the findings to design hybrid governance models that safeguard rights while promoting innovation. Legal practitioners and scholars benefit from a deeper understanding of comparative frameworks, enabling stronger litigation and advocacy in privacy-related cases. For technologists and regulators, the study provides a roadmap for embedding privacy-by-design, proportionality, and transparency into AI systems, mitigating risks of surveillance capitalism and algorithmic bias. At a broader level, the results will contribute to the field of constitutional and technology law by bridging theory with applied governance, and offer a global South perspective to the ongoing international dialogue on AI regulation.

By expanding the body of knowledge, this paper also has the potential to improve the world of practice. Embedding constitutional values in AI governance can enhance public trust, ensure fairer law enforcement, and safeguard democratic accountability in the face of rising surveillance. Moreover, the comparative insights from the EU and Canada can help India craft a balanced regulatory regime that avoids the pitfalls of both over-regulation and under-enforcement. Thus, the study not only advances academic discourse but also serves as a foundation for policy reform, institutional strengthening, and rights-respecting AI adoption, ensuring that technological transformation remains aligned with constitutional morality and global human rights standards.

RESEARCH QUESTIONS

This study is guided by the overarching question:

- How can India develop a hybrid privacy–cybersecurity jurisprudence that balances constitutional rights, technological innovation, and national security in the era of AI-driven governance?

To address this broad inquiry, the following sub-questions are posed:

1. What are the legal and ethical challenges posed by AI-enabled surveillance, predictive policing, and algorithmic decision-making to the right to privacy?
2. How have global frameworks, particularly the EU's General Data Protection Regulation (GDPR) and Canada's Consumer Privacy Protection Act (CPPA), responded to similar challenges?
3. What lessons can India draw from these comparative frameworks to strengthen the Digital Personal Data Protection Act, 2023 (DPDP Act), and related cyber-security laws?
4. In what ways can proportionality, transparency, and democratic oversight be embedded into AI regulation to ensure alignment with constitutional principles?
5. What practical governance models can balance the imperatives of innovation, privacy protection, and national security in India's digital ecosystem?

NATURE OF THE STUDY / METHODS

This study adopts a qualitative research approach, specifically a narrative literature review situated within the field of constitutional and technology law. The narrative review method is appropriate because the research problem concerns the evolving legal, ethical, and policy challenges posed by artificial intelligence (AI), predictive policing, and digital surveillance—issues that require conceptual synthesis rather than empirical measurement. The philosophical orientation of this study draws on jurisprudential analysis and comparative legal methodology, emphasizing constitutional principles such as proportionality, transparency, and autonomy, while situating them within global debates on digital rights and AI governance.

The literature for this review was systematically identified through academic databases including Google Scholar, ProQuest, SpringerLink, HeinOnline, JSTOR, and SSRN, focusing on publications from 2015–2025 to ensure relevance. Search terms included: *privacy* ("data protection," "right to be forgotten"), *cybersecurity* ("digital sovereignty," "cyber governance"), *artificial intelligence* ("algorithmic accountability," "AI regulation"), *surveillance* ("predictive policing," "surveillance capitalism"), and *comparative law* ("GDPR," "Digital Personal Data Protection Act" "CPPA," "global privacy frameworks"). Inclusion criteria were peer-reviewed journal articles, books, policy documents, and case law addressing privacy, AI ethics, and digital governance; exclusion criteria involved sources lacking scholarly rigor or predating the transformative shifts in AI regulation.

The analysis followed a thematic synthesis approach, organizing findings under key dimensions: (1) AI-enabled surveillance and privacy risks; (2) predictive policing and minority rights; (3) jurisprudential responses in India, EU, US, and Canada; and (4) emerging principles such as privacy-by-design, proportionality, and accountability. Case law such as *Justice K.S. Puttaswamy v. Union of India, Carpenter v. United States*, *Schrems I & II*, and *R. v. Spencer* was analyzed alongside statutory frameworks like the GDPR and DPDP Act, 2023, to extract comparative insights.

This methodological orientation is justified because it allows for a multi-disciplinary synthesis—drawing on law, ethics, political science, and technology studies—to develop a coherent perspective on how India can build a hybrid privacy–cybersecurity jurisprudence informed by global best practices. By combining doctrinal legal analysis with thematic review, the study ensures both conceptual depth and policy relevance.

LITERATURE REVIEW

1. Introduction to Digital Rights and AI Governance

The last decade has witnessed a rapid evolution in the understanding of digital rights, with privacy, autonomy, and informational self-determination emerging as central to constitutional democracies. The paradox of digital rights, described by Varlamova (2019) and Wagner et al. (2023), lies in the simultaneous empowerment and vulnerability of individuals in a data-driven society. While digital technologies enable connectivity and access, they also expose users to surveillance, commodification, and algorithmic profiling. This paradox underscores the tension between technological innovation and constitutional guarantees, particularly as AI becomes embedded in governance, law enforcement, and everyday life.

2. The Rise of AI-Enabled Surveillance

AI technologies such as machine learning and natural language processing have revolutionized state surveillance. Studies by Singhvi (2024) and Sultana (2024) show how governments are increasingly using predictive analytics to identify threats, while private corporations commodify user data for profit. In urban contexts, AI-enabled surveillance systems can track individuals in real time, raising concerns over proportionality and consent. Globally, surveillance capitalism represents a structural risk where personal data becomes a traded asset, often without meaningful oversight. This trend compromises autonomy and creates an environment where individuals are constantly monitored, reducing trust in institutions.

3. Predictive Policing and Minority Rights

Predictive policing has emerged as one of the most contested uses of AI in governance. While proponents argue it improves efficiency, research shows it exacerbates systemic bias. Hiller (2022) and Singhvi (2024) demonstrate how predictive policing disproportionately targets minority communities due to historically biased datasets. Nabil et al. (2025) caution that predictive algorithms undermine the right to non-discrimination and erode public trust in law enforcement. This parallels earlier discriminatory practices such as "stop and frisk" in the U.S. International human rights frameworks, including Article 17 of the ICCPR, emphasize privacy and dignity, yet predictive policing practices often conflict with these principles.

4. Algorithmic Surveillance and Behavioral Profiling

Behavioral profiling has become ubiquitous in both public and private sectors. AI-driven facial recognition, geolocation tracking, and activity monitoring raise serious privacy risks. Amingad et al. (2023) demonstrate how convolutional neural networks (CNNs) can classify emotions in real-time, while Kahla (2024) highlights their application in crime prevention. However, Machayya (2024) warns that algorithmic bias and profiling can reinforce stereotypes, producing harmful outcomes. In the gig economy, Newlands (2022) shows how algorithmic surveillance affects workers' autonomy, leading to constant productivity monitoring. This surveillance extends to biometric systems (Gordon et al., 2021) and mobile authentication models (Alotaibi et al., 2019), creating a pervasive environment of monitoring.

5. Constitutional and Jurisprudential Developments in India

India has emerged as a significant case study in constitutionalizing digital rights. The *Justice K.S. Puttaswamy v. Union of India* decision recognized privacy as a fundamental right under Article 21. This landmark ruling laid the foundation for subsequent laws, particularly the Digital Personal Data Protection Act, 2023 (DPDP Act). Bhushan (2024) and Kaur (2024) note that the DPDP Act represents a rights-based approach aligned with international norms but suffers from weaknesses such as broad government exemptions and weak enforcement. Cases such as the Pegasus spyware scandal underscore the fragility of privacy protections in the face of national security concerns.

6. Comparative Perspectives: EU and Canada

The General Data Protection Regulation (GDPR) remains the most comprehensive framework globally. Emphasize is laid on its strict enforcement mechanisms, cross-border applicability, and embedding of privacy-by-design. Similarly, the Consumer Privacy Protection Act (CPPA) in Canada offers a principles-based but flexible approach, with oversight by the Office of the Privacy Commissioner. Scholars argue that India could adopt a hybrid model, blending the GDPR's strict rights-based standards with Canada's pragmatic, sector-specific flexibility (Korff, 2023). This comparative perspective reveals that both over-regulation and under-regulation have drawbacks, and India requires a balanced path.

7. The Black Box Problem in AI Decision-Making

Opaque AI models, particularly deep learning systems, create what scholars call the black box problem. Engelmann (2023) argues that the opacity of algorithmic reasoning erodes transparency and accountability in public decision-making. This is especially problematic in law enforcement, where decisions affect fundamental rights. Explainable AI (XAI) techniques such as SHAP and LIME have been proposed but cautions that full transparency may compromise sensitive data. Golovin (2024) advocates for qualified transparency, balancing openness with security. This debate highlights the urgent need for regulatory intervention to safeguard democratic legitimacy in algorithmic governance.

8. Privacy-by-Design and Emerging Governance Models

The concept of privacy-by-design (PbD) is gaining traction as a legal and technological mandate. Descalzo (2024) and Felzmann et al. (2020) highlight how PbD embeds privacy safeguards into AI systems from inception rather than as an afterthought. Internationally, the GDPR, Canada's CPPA, and India's DPDP Act all integrate PbD principles, though enforcement varies and argue for proactive legal design to embed values into technology, while emphasizing federated learning and differential privacy as tools for compliance. Embedding PbD into governance frameworks enhances both accountability and innovation.

9. Democratic Oversight and Accountability

Oversight remains a critical gap in global AI governance. Kniep et al. (2023) highlight the importance of democratizing intelligence oversight to counter technocratic dominance and describe multi-stakeholder accountability ecosystems as essential for algorithmic governance. In India, a potential reform lies in strengthening the Data Protection Board of India to ensure independence, technical competence, and sector-specific oversight. Comparative insights from Canada's NSIRA and the EU's EDPB illustrate institutional pathways for ensuring both accountability and legitimacy in AI governance.

10. Synthesis of Literature

The reviewed literature reveals a common theme: privacy rights, cybersecurity imperatives, and AI innovation must be reconciled within a balanced governance framework. India stands at a crossroads, with the DPDP Act providing a foundational step but requiring significant strengthening. Comparative insights from the EU and Canada offer models of strict enforcement and flexible pragmatism, respectively. Ultimately, embedding constitutional principles—proportionality, transparency, and oversight—into AI governance is not only a legal necessity but also a democratic imperative.

RECOMMENDATIONS FROM THE LITERATURE

Based on the review, the following actionable recommendations are proposed:

1. **Adopt a Hybrid Regulatory Model** – India should integrate the strict rights-based standards of the GDPR with the flexible, sector-specific approach of Canada's CPPA to balance innovation with accountability.
2. **Strengthen the Data Protection Board of India (DPB)** – Ensure independence, technical capacity, and investigatory powers to enforce the DPDP Act effectively.
3. **Mandate Privacy-by-Design in AI Systems** – Require all AI systems, particularly those used in law enforcement, to undergo privacy impact assessments and embed privacy safeguards from inception.
4. **Regulate Predictive Policing** – Establish strict oversight, data quality requirements, and fairness audits to prevent algorithmic bias against minority communities.
5. **Enhance Algorithmic Transparency** – Introduce legal obligations for explainable AI (XAI) in high-stakes decision-making while safeguarding sensitive information.
6. **Ensure Proportionality in Surveillance** – Implement judicial oversight and proportionality tests for all state surveillance measures, modeled on European Court of Human Rights standards.

7. **Strengthen Cross-Border Data Governance** – Negotiate adequacy and reciprocity agreements with the EU and other jurisdictions to facilitate lawful, rights-based data transfers.
8. **Promote Multi-Stakeholder Oversight** – Involve civil society, technical experts, and parliament in AI governance, ensuring democratic accountability.
9. **Address Surveillance Capitalism** – Introduce regulations that limit corporate commodification of personal data and mandate transparency in data monetization practices.
10. **Invest in Public Awareness and Education** – Launch national campaigns to enhance digital literacy, emphasizing privacy rights and responsible AI use.

SURVEILLANCE CAPITALISM, PREDICTIVE POLICING, AND AI RISKS

There are essential ethical, legal, and social concerns with the relation between surveillance capitalism, predictive policing and AI risks, which are inextricably linked. Joseph Paul Jones referred to it as surveillance capitalism; that is, the commodification of personal information, trespass of privacy and moral agency, and the enemy to democracy due to the way it operationalizes human psychology against corporate interest. This form of capitalism is directly connected with predictive policing, which is based on the idea of using AI to predict the appearance of criminal acts with the purpose of increasing the efficiency of the law enforcers.

The adoption of predictive policing, however, poses unethical issues, and among them one will find the infringement of the fundamental right to privacy, as well as algorithmically unfair decision making, and the absence of accountability and transparency (Nabil et al., 2025). Such problems can be seen in the example offered by the NYPD when dealing with predictive policing, as critics accuse the department of privacy violation and labelling people and neighborhoods. Moreover, they may result in even more dehumanizing processes of policing, as a shift towards the algorithmic predictions can make decisions purely data-based as opposed to community-based ones. The wider implication of such technologies can be seen through the concept of pre-crime society in which a country is subject to constant surveillance and control as a potential criminal and encompasses a mix of surveillance and regulatory capital. These systems can make existing biases even greater, and since they especially affect the underprivileged groups, inequalities exist in the system today.

This trend of shifting to an algorithmic form of governance, not only hurts the value of democratic responsibility but also introduces the risks of permanent establishment of a neoliberal regime of security where efficiency is sold as the core virtue. To overcome these issues, it is demanded to provide radical advances in AI development and application with an accent on social justice and equity that requires AI to be a means of positive change in society but not a factor deepening infrastructural disparities. Finally, the combining of AI in policing and surveillance capitalism has come to a point where it is necessary to reconsider the principles of the value of technological inventions, concentrating on the support of human rights and democracies (Nabil et al., 2025).

ALGORITHMIC SURVEILLANCE AND BEHAVIOURAL PROFILING

Behavioural profiling and algorithmic surveillance are becoming an essential part of present-day security and management technologies, utilizing the sophisticated technology to improve operations effectiveness and promote the safety of the population. Among them, AI intelligent surveillance systems employing deep learning, i.e., convolutional neural networks (CNNs), can easily recognize faces and classify their emotional expressions and analyse them in real-time, thus surveillance of the people in urban environments (Amingad et al., 2023). This is further advanced on crime detection and prevention where the AI systems can go through the video surveillance systems and generate prediction as a way to stop crimes hence given the law enforcement community ways to early act on crimes (Kahla, 2024).

Nevertheless, the implementation of these technologies also presents a considerable number of ethical issues namely, privacy and algorithmic biases. Roshan Machayya points out the possible prejudice transported by algorithmic profiling and can produce harmful effects in case they are not treated with understanding, making the popularization of legal instruments that would help diminish the potential impact of algorithmic prejudice crucial (Machayya, 2024). Algorithmic surveillance of connection data may facilitate the identification of practices that are potentially influential between terrorist threats in the setting of counter-terrorism, but, at the same time, it represents significant privacy problems (Figure 2) (Labbay, 2023). With the gig economy, the examples of the algorithmic surveillance are ubiquitous, as employees are constantly put under the geolocation and activity tracking, which distracts them and affects how they perform in the workplace (Newlands, 2022).

In addition, surveillance with the help of biometric data, as discussed by Gordon et al., demonstrates that such systems put restrains on the levels of privacy, and people consistently fail to conceal their activities correctly based on predictive models (Gordon et al., 2021). Continuous authentication is also done through behavioral profiling in mobile applications, with the approach being more secure as it identifies a user by their interaction, but has the information privacy potential downside (Alotaibi et al., 2019). Lastly, with regards to road safety, driver behaviors are profiled through AI methods and deep learning which provides knowledge towards effective traffic safety and potential accidents (Oban et al., 2024). Combined, these studies reveal that the effects of algorithmic surveillance and behavioral profiling are as double-sided as a sword, as they can bring greater safety and enhanced efficiency and, at the same time, require more serious attention when talking about ethical and privacy concerns.

Figure 2. The Analysis of AI Surveillance and its intensity and its risk of Privacy across the Sectors

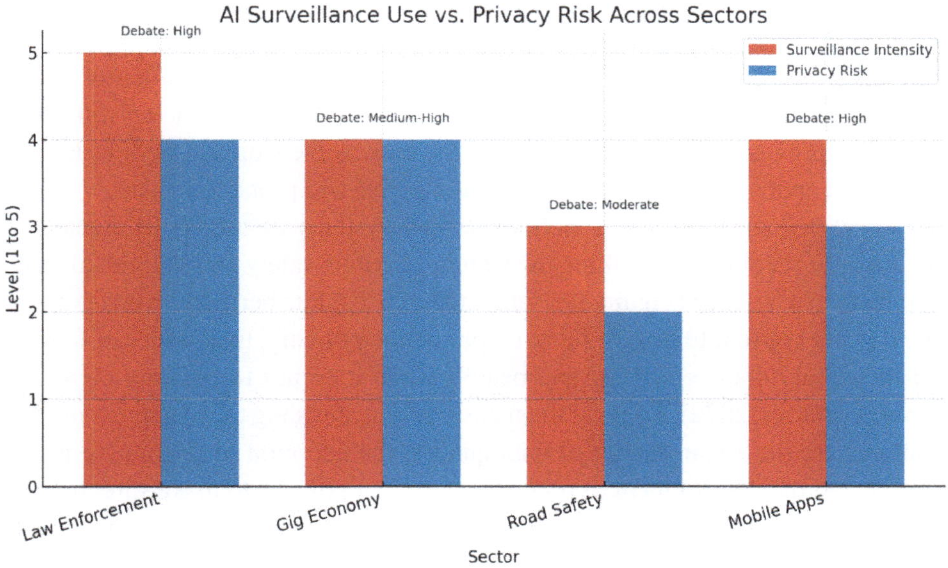

In this chart, the relative amount of surveillance facilitated by AI and the privacy threats posed by it have been highlighted in four sectors: Law Enforcement, Gig Economy, Road Safety and Mobile Applications. Although the law enforcement and gig jobs marketplaces present the greatest level of surveillance intensity and thus the resultant privacy risks, mobile apps also showcase high magnitudes of ethical complexities. The road safety applications are a comparatively lesser privacy risk even though they are technologically advanced. The figure emphasizes the differences in the level of ethical controversy that each industry represents as a result of using behavioural profiling and algorithm monitoring.

PREDICTIVE POLICING AND MINORITY RIGHTS

Predictive policing, the use of algorithms assuming that past crime is predictive of future crime, has been associated with a serious issue of minority rights and the targets of prejudice. Although the technology is touted as a promising means to increase efficiency in the area of law enforcement, it is accused of reinforcing systemic prejudices against minority groups. The bias in the training data, a by-product of historical over-policing in these communities, will unreasonably result in greater targeting of minorities and will contribute to socio-economic inequalities (Hiller, 2022) (Singhvi, 2024). Such bias is not merely a technical deficiency but a legal and ethical one because predictive policing will yield erroneous detainments and undermine rights, including the rights under s. 9 of the Canadian Charter, which safeguards against arbitrary detention (Hiller, 2022). Predictive policing still exhibits its concerning parallels with its predecessors, such as the stop and frisk technique, which are condemned by people as both ineffective and prone to racism.

Ethical consequences are deep, because such systems are usually ill-transparent and not very accountable, making the weight of public safety and individual rights even harder to balance (Figure 3) (Nabil et al., 2025). Furthermore, when communities do not consent to or give input on predictive policing, then issues of fairness and the equal allocation of lag and benefit when it comes to policing come into question (Purves, 2022). Some of the measures that are being taken to prevent these problems are the enhancement of data quality, the adoption of restorative justice aspects, and the development of powerful oversight policies to make sure that predictive technologies are used to the benefit of all communities fairly (Singhvi, 2024). Moreover, such systems have proved to work towards eliminating biases, increasing trust, and treating everyone more fairly when domain knowledge is integrated into them (Downey et al., 2024).

Nevertheless, the main problem still lies in the necessity to reconcile the practices of predictive policing with the both basic rights of humans including right to privacy and non-discrimination as it has been outlined in several international settings. The outstanding threat of the rise of predictive policing to violate minority rights will also be a relevant factor unless radical changes and multi-stakeholder cooperation among policymakers, technologists, and the civil society would voice itself in a meaningful manner (Nabil et al., 2025).

Figure 3. This shows how the issue of the black box in AI-intensive public decision-making is a complex issue that reduces transparency, trust, and legitimacy because deep learning algorithms are essentially opaque. It compares challenges of a black box system known as diminished citizen confidence and the feeling of bias with possible mitigation methods such as Explainable Artificial Intelligence (e.g. SHAP, LIME) conditioned transparency, the rule of law measures such as the right to explanation, and alternative technology, e.g. blockchain. The figure reveals the constant conflict between the readability and safeguarding of sensitive data and justifies the importance of regulatory frameworks and interdisciplinary studies in the aspect of democratic accountability in the governance of AI.

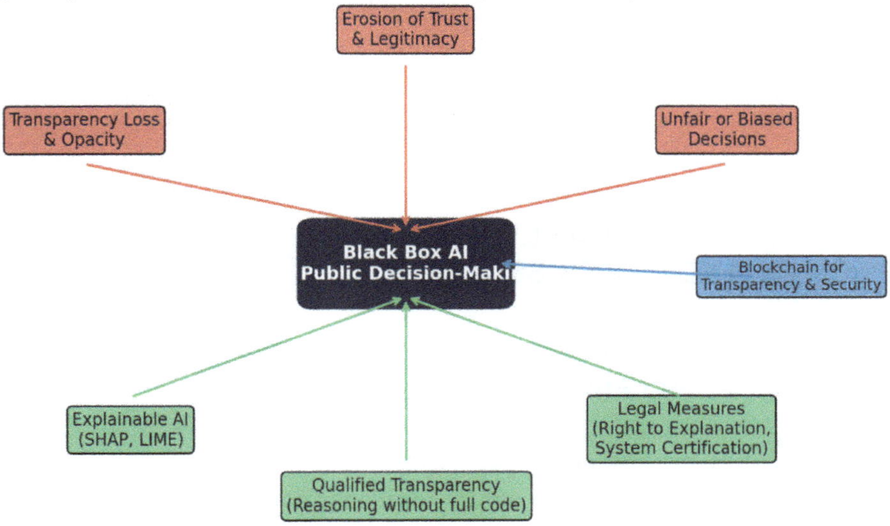

Source: Author Made

The black box challenge in AI especially as regards the area of public decision-making poses immense challenges that concern transparency, trust and legitimacy. The level of AI systems, particularly those deploying deep learning, makes it hard to comprehend and trust the decision of such systems by the consumers and stakeholders, which is important in the governmental operations, where citizens are directly affected. Transparency issues in AI algorithms may erode the legitimacy of the decisions because the people do not perceive them as fair and responsible to hold a democratic society.

In response to such issues, several approaches have been suggested, and one of them involves the creation of Explainable AI (XAI) methodologies like SHAP and LIME that promote the interpretability and transparency of the AI decision making process (Rane et al., 2024). These methods aid in recognizing biases and the requirement to follow the standards of ethics thus creating trust and responsibility (Rane et al., 2024).

Nonetheless, full transparency is not always possible or desirable and cannot be achieved easily because sensitive information may be disclosed as a result (Nešpor, 2024). Rather, a compromise is offered in the form of so-called qualified transparency or presenting the reasoning behind the decisions but maintaining a secrecy of underlying algorithms (Nešpor, 2024). The law or regulatory action such as the right to explanation, and system certification is also significant in regard to the question of providing accountability and transparency in AI (Golovin, 2024).

Besides, AI, and other new innovations, such as blockchain can optimize decision-making procedures in terms of increased transparency and safety (Sultana, 2024). Even in the face of these developments, the black box issue continues to be the major development in the way AI is currently deployed unethically and ineffectively in making government decisions, and it continues to require interdisciplinary research and policy in alignment with democratic principles and trustworthiness (Sultana, 2024).

GLOBAL LEGAL FRAMEWORKS ON PRIVACY AND CYBER SECURITY

Indian Context: Exploring the Puttaswamy Judgement, IT Act, DPDP Act and other provisions

The field of privacy and cyber security has greatly developed over time in India, through the view of the judicial decisions and changes in legislation. The land mark case Justice K.S. Puttaswamy, the right to privacy was classified under the fundamental right under Article 21 of the Constitution in the judgement by the Supreme Court. The ruling became the constitutional marker in the establishment of an all-encompassing data protection and cyber security regulation that embraces proportionality, legality, and necessity as key components in the action of the state interfering with privacy.

The Information Technology Act, 2000 (IT Act) continues to be the most important law on cyber security in India and has created a framework of regulating electronic transactions, prevention of cybercrime along with penalties. Through amendments especially the IT (Amendment) Act 2008, data protection was included as an addendum to Section 43A and Section 43 of IT (Reasonable Security Practices and Procedures and Sensitive Personal Data or Information) Rules, 2011 which included reasonable security practices. These regulations formalized the responsibility that the data controllers had on protecting sensitive personal data.

The year 2023 brings a breakthrough in the Indian regulatory landscape of data protection as the country adopts the Digital Personal Data Protection Act (DPDP

Act) that is being viewed as an extension of the privacy foundations enshrined by the Supreme Court through its Puttaswamy ruling in 2017, which categorized privacy as a fundamental right in India (Bhushan, 2024) (Kaur, 2024). The Digital Personal Data Protection Act, 2023 (DPDP Act) reflects a paradigm of a rights-based system of management of data, in part complying with international recommendations such as the GDPR in the EU (Table 1). It negates rules of lawful processing, data minimization, and purpose limitation and proposes a data fiduciary framework and framework of consent and non-consent fines.

It also constitutes such a Data protection board of India to implement and resolve the disputes. Along with these key tools, industry-specific policies on cyber security protocols, aspects of data protection in the telecommunications industry, and elsewhere support the bedrock of the law. Notwithstanding, issues are still present in balancing privacy and national security interests, enforcing the free flow of cross-border data, and countering growing AI-based monitoring and hacking risks.

This Act is consistent with the international standards, being compared with the one in the European Union, General Data Protection Regulation (GDPR), and is intended to bring power on the side of individuals by providing them with the control over their own data through a well-considered approach to consent and remarkable rights of access, rectification, erasure, and data portability (Bhushan, 2024). The DPDP Act lays strict burdens on data fiduciaries of data collection and processing, storage, security, and disclosure, and under the supervision of the Data Protection Board (DPB). But the Act also has its difficulties, which include overloading businesses with compliance demands and possible uncertainties as to how the Act is supposed to work.

The influence of the Act on the digital economy and innovations in India indicates the possibilities of both advantages and issues since it is necessary to find the right balance to develop the industry and provide data security. Other privacy related issues that have been sensitized by technology as well as the digitization era and include the breach of data, including that of mass surveillance, new forms of privacy violations, like in Pegasus spyware scandal (Kaur, 2024) have also been the concern of the DPDP Act.

In spite of its strengths, the Act has been criticised because of government exemptions, issues of data localisation and the lack of effective establishment of a strong data protection authority. Also, the DPDP Act can be considered inadequate in the terms of the GDPR, which means that European requirements require particular attention when it comes to data flows between the EU/EEA and India (Korff, 2023).

Such implementations of the Act as the right to be forgotten and data portability are considered to be vital in ensuring the existence of a structured and machine-readable data ecosystem (Bisht & Sreenivasulu, 2024). On the whole, though the DPDP Act is a good measure to enhance privacy in the digital era, it still needs to be refined and equipped with strong enforcement measures to enhance privacy and guard the rights of individuals to privacy of their information (Malhotra & Malhotra, 2024) (Bisht & Sreenivasulu, 2024).

Table 1. Privacy and Cybersecurity Framework- India

Aspect	India
Foundational Right	Right to Privacy (Puttaswamy, 2017)
Primary Legislation	IT Act 2000 (as amended), DPDP Act 2023
Regulatory Authority	Data Protection Board of India
Scope of Protection	Digital personal data; sector-specific rules
Core Principles	Lawfulness, consent, purpose limitation, data minimization
Penalties	Up to ₹250 crore under DPDP Act
Cross-Border Data Flow	Conditional transfer; adequacy-based and consent-based

Source: Author Made

This table outlines India's privacy and cyber security regime, anchored in the constitutional recognition of privacy as a fundamental right. It highlights the IT Act, 2000 (as amended) and the Digital Personal Data Protection Act, 2023 as the primary legislative instruments, with the Data Protection Board of India as the key enforcement authority. The framework emphasizes lawful processing, consent, purpose limitation, and data minimization, with significant penalties for non-compliance and conditional cross-border transfer mechanisms.

UNITED STATES, EUROPEAN UNION AND CANADIAN CONTEXT

Regulatory environment Data protection laws in the European Union, United States and Canada are different and exert different influences as they are shaped by legal systems and values of their cultures. The GDPR and the proposed ePrivacy Regulation are an ambitious measure of data protection of the EU, in which privacy is regarded as a fundamental human right and in which data subjects are inflicted with strict obligations on data controllers and processors to promote transparency and security so that data can be handled. The extraterritorial application given by the GDPR and its harmonization trends is meant to ensure the safety of the information of EU citizens worldwide, which creates an impact on the international data protection frameworks (Table 2).

Table 2. Privacy and Cybersecurity Framework- EU (GDPR)

Aspect	EU (GDPR)
Foundational Right	Charter of Fundamental Rights of the EU, Art. 8
Primary Legislation	General Data Protection Regulation (GDPR)
Regulatory Authority	National Data Protection Authorities + EDPB
Scope of Protection	All personal data (digital and physical)
Core Principles	Lawfulness, fairness, transparency, purpose limitation, data minimization, accuracy
Penalties	Up to €20 million or 4% of global turnover
Cross-Border Data Flow	Restricted unless adequate protection or safeguards

Source: Author Made

This table captures the EU's robust, rights-based approach under the General Data Protection Regulation, grounded in Article 8 of the Charter of Fundamental Rights of the EU. It provides comprehensive protection for all personal data, enforced by national Data Protection Authorities and coordinated by the European Data Protection Board. The GDPR mandates principles such as fairness, transparency, and accuracy, enforces strict cross-border transfer conditions, and imposes some of the world's heaviest penalties for violations.

On the contrary, the American sectoral approach follows, where legislations such as the CLOUD Act and the California Consumer Privacy Act (CCPA) tackle certain spheres of data privacy. The CLOUD Act makes international access to data available by police, and it raises the possibility of invasion of privacy under the EU-US Privacy Shield scheme (Thiele, 2018). Even though similar to the GDPR in one way or another, the CCPA is less stringent and has carve outs to federal laws, as well as certain limits on implementing it. This is a decentralized system because there are gaps in terms of data protection in the U.S. sector wise as compared to the integrated system within the EU jurisdiction (Table 3).

Table 3. Privacy and Cybersecurity Framework- US (Sectoral Laws)

Aspect	US (Sectoral Laws)
Foundational Right	No explicit constitutional privacy right (sectoral protections)
Primary Legislation	CCPA, HIPAA, GLBA, COPPA, etc.
Regulatory Authority	Sectoral regulators (FTC, HHS, etc.)
Scope of Protection	Sector-specific data (health, finance, children, consumers)
Core Principles	Transparency, notice, consent (varies by sector)
Penalties	Varies by law; e.g., CCPA up to $7,500 per violation
Cross-Border Data Flow	No comprehensive regime; contractual or sector-based rules

Source: Author Made

This table reflects the United States' fragmented, sector-specific privacy framework, which lacks an overarching constitutional privacy right but relies on targeted laws such as CCPA, HIPAA, GLBA, and COPPA. Enforcement is decentralized across sectoral regulators like the FTC and HHS, with rules and penalties varying by domain. The US model focuses on transparency, notice, and consent within specific sectors and has no unified cross-border data protection regime, relying instead on contractual or sector-based arrangements.

In the meantime, the Personal Information Protection and Electronic Documents Act (PIPEDA) and the proposed Consumer Privacy Protection Act (CPPA) of Canada place Canada somewhere in the middle, the PIPEDA and CPPA having much the same core principles of privacy, but looser regulation process including and towards cloud computing. CPPA is in the shift to update Canada into more modern privacy framework more fitting into the international benchmarks and catching up with new technological issues . Taken altogether, these regulatory regimes demonstrate a wide range of approaches used by EU, US, and Canada in finding the golden mean between the protection of privacy and technological and economic interests against the unique challenges to the global data economy (Table 4).

Table 4. Privacy and Cybersecurity Framework- US (Sectoral Laws)

Aspect	Canada (PIPEDA/CPPA)
Foundational Right	Implicit under Charter rights
Primary Legislation	PIPEDA (soon CPPA)
Regulatory Authority	Office of the Privacy Commissioner of Canada
Scope of Protection	Personal information in commercial activities
Core Principles	Consent, limiting collection, accuracy, safeguards
Penalties	Up to CAD $25 million under CPPA
Cross-Border Data Flow	Allowed with adequate protection or consent

Source: Author Made

This table presents Canada's privacy framework, currently under PIPEDA and transitioning to the Consumer Privacy Protection Act (CPPA). Rooted in implied Charter rights, it applies to personal information in commercial activities, with oversight by the Office of the Privacy Commissioner of Canada. The framework emphasizes consent, limited collection, and safeguards, with substantial penalties under CPPA. Cross-border transfers are permitted where adequate protection or explicit consent is ensured, aligning closely with EU adequacy standards.

Deepening the discussion on ethical oversight and transparent AI, incorporating advanced privacy-preserving technologies, broadening comparative legal perspectives, and anticipating future technological and legal developments strengthens the chapter's analytical and policy contributions. The following synthesis leverages cited sources to provide a comprehensive, forward-looking analysis.

ETHICAL OVERSIGHT AND TRANSPARENT AI PRACTICES

Ethical oversight in AI governance requires institutionalizing multi-layered accountability frameworks that incorporate legal mandates, technical audits, and civil society scrutiny to address algorithmic bias, discrimination, and surveillance excesses (Kniep et al., 2023; Criado & Guevara-Gómez, 2024). Transparency is a core principle, not only about algorithmic decision-making but also about data provenance and consent mechanisms. XAI (Explainable AI) tools such as SHAP and LIME provide pathways for qualified transparency, enabling stakeholders to understand AI outcomes without compromising sensitive security or trade secrets (Engelmann, 2023; Bolovin, 2024). Legal frameworks like the GDPR and Canada's CPPA embed obligations for transparency and fairness by design, which India's legislation may emulate with sectoral adaptations (Korff, 2023; Bhushan, 2024).

ADVANCED PRIVACY-PRESERVING TECHNOLOGIES

Emerging technical methods such as federated learning, differential privacy, and homomorphic encryption offer critical tools for minimizing data exposure during AI model training and deployment, aligning with the principle of privacy-by-design (Descalzo, 2024; Felzmann et al., 2020). These technologies enable AI systems to learn from distributed data sources without centralizing sensitive personal information, substantially lowering risks of data breaches and unauthorized surveillance. Legislation mandating the usage of these privacy-enhancing technologies coupled with effective enforcement mechanisms could position India at the forefront of responsible AI innovation (Okon et al., 2024; Blix et al., 2017).

BROADENED COMPARATIVE LEGAL PERSPECTIVES

European Union: The GDPR's strict enforcement, cross-border data transfer restrictions, and data protection impact assessments illustrate a rights-centric governance approach that extends beyond mere compliance into proactive prevention.

Canada: Its oversight body, the Office of the Privacy Commissioner, employs participatory assessments and rigorous enforcement paired with flexible principles, balancing innovation and protection effectively (Korff, 2023; Bhushan, 2024).

United States: Landmark cases such as Carpenter v. United States introduce judicial checks against indiscriminate data collection while the CLOUD Act navigates transnational data accessibility tensions, highlighting ongoing legal adaptation challenges (Thiele, 2018).

Belgium: Democratic oversight of police algorithmic surveillance sets a global example of embedding civil society and technical expertise as standard components of AI accountability frameworks (Kniep et al., 2023).

Emerging Jurisdictions: Countries like Indonesia and China innovate varied data localization and privacy rules, indicating jurisdiction-specific calibrations of privacy and security balance in the global South and East (Wang, 2023).

Anticipating Future Technological and Legal Developments - Regulatory systems must be inherently adaptive, incorporating:

Regulatory Sandboxes: Controlled environments where new AI technologies are deployed under supervision to gather data on risks and benefits before full-scale implementation (Meghwal, 2025).

Sunset Clauses and Periodic Reviews: Time-bound powers and legislative checks to ensure outdated or overly broad surveillance authorities are curtailed or renewed only when justified.

Cross-Disciplinary and Cross-Jurisdictional Collaboration: Legal frameworks must integrate ethics, computer science, and social sciences insights, while facilitating international jurisdictions to cooperate on dynamic, emerging risks (Graeden et al., 2023).

Embedding Ethics into AI Lifecycle: Moving beyond post hoc audits to embedding ethical review and human rights impact assessments at every stage of AI system design, deployment, and decommissioning.

POLICY IMPLICATIONS AND LEGAL FRAMEWORKS

Together, these considerations imply that India's hybrid privacy-cybersecurity regime should:

Mandate and enforce privacy-by-design using advanced privacy-preserving technologies.

Institutionalize layered, multidisciplinary oversight including civil society and technical expertise.

Evolve legislatively with technology, supported by empirical oversight data from sandboxes and audits.

Advance global compatibility through adequacy agreements and harmonized cross-border data rules.

Strengthen judicial and parliamentary checks on AI-enabled security and surveillance systems.

This multidimensional, adaptive, and comparative framework offers a durable legal foundation that balances privacy, national security, and innovation effectively within India's socio-legal context while drawing from international best practices.

JURISPRUDENTIAL DEVELOPMENTS AND COMPARATIVE CASE LAW

Figure 4. The chart presents the doctrinal cross-over and cross-under between four landmark cases relating to privacy and surveillance law and policy-Justice K.S. Puttaswamy v. UOI, Carpenter v. US, Schrems I & II and that of R. v. Spencer. There are three fundamental factors supposed to map each of them (1) the doctrinal type or criterion taken up, including, proportionality, modified reasonable expectation of privacy, or essential equivalence; (2) the constitutional or legal basis on which the ruling was grounded in, using domestic constitutions or supranational charters; (3) and technological context that influenced the legal thinking of judges, from bio-metrics identification systems to transnational data transfer and metadata security. The visualization draws attention to a common tendency of global judicial systems to find solutions to concretize the theoretical aspects of understanding the privacy rules in view of the contemporary practices of digital monitoring, still maintaining the jurisdiction-related differences in addressing the privacy regulations

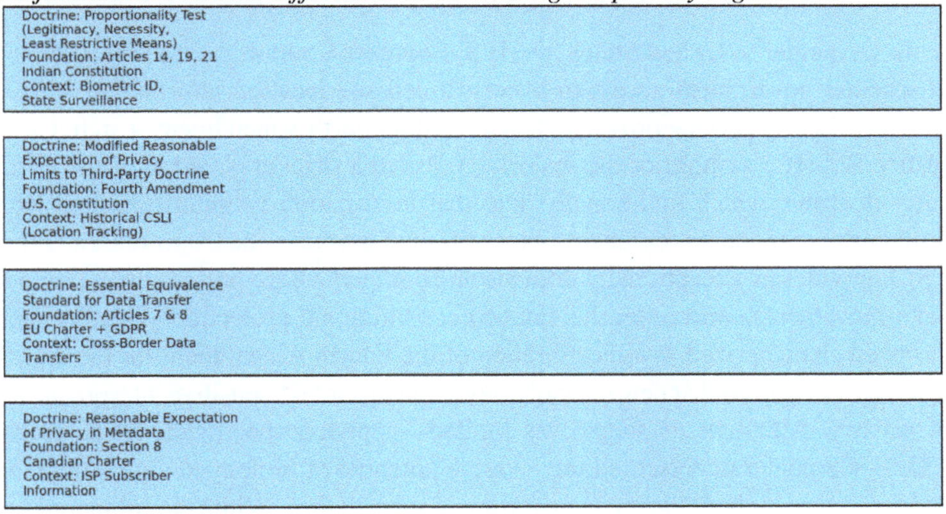

Source: Author Made

Justice K.S. Puttaswamy v. India (Union of India)

The landmark case of Justice K.S. Puttaswamy (Retd.) v. Union of India marked a philosophical and jurisprudential shift in Indian constitutional law, affirming privacy as a fundamental right. Delivered unanimously by a nine-judge bench, the ruling overturned earlier precedents such as M.P. Sharma v. Satish Chandra and Kharak Singh v. State of Uttar Pradesh, which had denied or narrowly construed the right to privacy. The Court grounded its reasoning in Articles 14 (equality), 19 (freedom), and 21 (life and personal liberty), emphasizing that privacy is intrinsic to dignity, autonomy, and constitutional morality (Bhandari et al., 2017). It also introduced a proportionality test to evaluate state interference with privacy, requiring legitimacy, necessity, and minimal intrusion—standards that now guide the scrutiny of digital governance tools, biometric databases, and surveillance measures (Figure 4). Beyond doctrinal development, Puttaswamy aligned India with international human rights norms, notably Article 17 of the International Covenant on Civil and Political Rights (ICCPR), and laid the foundation for critiques of state programs such as Aadhaar's authentication and mandatory linkages. The judgment further acknowledged the dynamic nature of privacy in a digital era where state power and technology may overshadow individual freedoms, thereby shaping both subsequent legislation—such as the Digital Personal Data Protection Act, 2023—and evolving judicial interpretations of informational self-determination (Kaur, 2025)

Carpenter v. United States (USA)

In Carpenter v. United States, the U.S. Supreme Court addressed the question of whether government access to historical cell-site location information (CSLI) from third-party service providers constituted a Fourth Amendment search. Chief Justice Roberts, writing for the majority, rejected a strict application of the third-party doctrine, which traditionally held that information voluntarily shared with third parties carried no reasonable expectation of privacy. The Court reasoned that CSLI provides an exceptionally intimate and comprehensive portrait of an individual's movements, warranting heightened constitutional protection. This decision has been characterized as a recalibration of the Fourth Amendment for the digital age, as it recognized that new technologies demand context-sensitive interpretations of privacy. Although its scope was limited—applying specifically to historical CSLI—Carpenter underscored the invasive potential of prolonged digital tracking and set important boundaries on government surveillance. While the ruling did not completely discard the third-party doctrine, it affirmed that constitutional privacy cannot be eroded simply by technological advancements, influencing later debates on geolocation warrants, metadata collection, and access to smart-device data.

Schrems I and II (EU)

In Schrems I (C-362/14, 2015), the Court of Justice of the European Union (CJEU) invalidated the EU–U.S. Safe Harbor framework, finding that U.S. law permitted mass surveillance without adequate safeguards, thereby violating Articles 7 and 8 of the EU Charter of Fundamental Rights. The case, initiated by Austrian activist Max Schrems, challenged Facebook Ireland's transfer of personal data to the United States under frameworks vulnerable to surveillance regimes such as the Foreign Intelligence Surveillance Act (FISA) (Chander, 2020). The CJEU established the "essential equivalence" test, requiring that third-country legal regimes provide protections substantively equivalent to those within the EU. This reasoning was reaffirmed in Schrems II (C-311/18, 2020), which struck down the successor EU–U.S. Privacy Shield while allowing the continued use of Standard Contractual Clauses (SCCs), albeit with enhanced compliance obligations for data exporters. Together, these rulings not only reshaped global data transfer law but also reinforced the extraterritorial reach of the GDPR, insisting that fundamental rights protections cannot be compromised for commercial expediency (Bradford et al., 2021). Despite this new framework, ongoing legal challenges and privacy concerns persist regarding the sufficiency of U.S. safeguards against government access to data, indicating that the fundamental tension between data transfer needs and fundamental rights protection remains unresolved.

R v Spencer (Canada)

In R. v. Spencer, the Supreme Court of Canada considered whether police could obtain subscriber information from an Internet Service Provider (ISP) without a warrant. The Court ruled that such data carries a reasonable expectation of privacy because it can directly link individuals to their online activities, thereby exposing highly intimate aspects of their lives. Applying Section 8 of the Canadian Charter of Rights and Freedoms—which protects against unreasonable search and seizure—the Court rejected the view that contractual agreements with ISPs negate privacy expectations (Ferencz et al., 2022). Instead, it emphasized the "biographical core" of subscriber information, recognizing its capacity to be as revealing as content data in the digital context. While acknowledging statutory provisions that allow information-sharing with law enforcement, the Court held that such actions must still comply with Charter protections. Spencer thus marked an important expansion of Canadian privacy law, aligning it with international recognition of metadata's sensitivity and influencing lower courts as they balance investigative needs with robust privacy safeguards (Conrad & Heggie, 2024).

CHALLENGES IN HARMONIZING CYBER SECURITY AND PRIVACY

The competing arguments of proportionality and necessity in national surveillance and the legal jurisdiction issues of cross-border data access is complex in nature and brings in to the equation legal, ethical, and practical issues. Proportionality in surveillance is the orderliness of data gathering or monitoring by the security agencies and is not extravagant in relation to the purposeful security goals. The principle plays a pivotal role in preserving a balance between national security and individual privacy rights as pointed out by the European Court of Human rights and other courts of law, which note that any surveillance activity must be justified by a warrant under law, and proportional in the threat being countered (Kugelmann & Kosin, 2018).

Nevertheless, the indispensability of monitoring usually prompts states to take expansive steps (in some cases even transgressing proportionality), particularly when international IT surveillance arbitrage comes into play, where the state can gain access to more data than it is legally allowed to do under domestic legislation(Staben & Leisterer, 2017).

The use of data across borders attracts jurisdictional dilemmas particularly when data territoriality is rendered more insignificant since data are stored and communicated across the globe (Berman, 2018). The de-territorialization of data presents complex jurisdictional challenges, as information stored in one country may fall under the legislative authority of another, creating conflicts in enforcement and accountability. To address such difficulties, instruments like the U.S. CLOUD Act and the EU's proposed e-Evidence package have sought to simplify cross-border data access while ensuring compliance with principles of fundamental rights and proportionality (Ruohonen, 2023). However, these initiatives have raised concerns about potential overreach and inconsistency with existing legal frameworks. The challenges are particularly acute in India, where reliance on mutual legal assistance treaties (MLATs) has proven inadequate, and divergent data disclosure policies of technology companies have further obstructed cooperation (Meghwal, 2025). These gaps highlight the urgent need for clearer legislation and stronger mechanisms of international collaboration to reconcile privacy protections with effective law enforcement. Ultimately, the central dilemma remains how to balance surveillance for security purposes against the proportional requirement to safeguard individual rights, a tension that continues to evolve alongside the rapid transformations of the digital age (Kukava, 2023).

Democratic accountability and control of intelligence activities, consent, autonomy, and due process in algorithmic systems, are little-understood issues that have ethical, legal and social ramifications of technology. The management of intelligence activity has long been liberal (and technocratic): it is assumed that intelligence activity is not biased in favor of a certain side and relies more on technical knowledge to mediate between equal risks to the individual and security to all individuals. Nevertheless, this method of thinking tends to narrow down the meaning of oversight since it is usually an expert-led, institutionalized system that might not embrace the full involvement of the democratic way. Rather, oversight must be more transparent, international, and controversial, as we can securely observe in the conflicts in Germany and the UK as well as the US, as these are forceful indicators of a more open and democratic oversight system (Kniep et al., 2023).

The subject of accountability in the context of the algorithmic system is also as important as it is in various sectors in the presence of negative implications of AI. Algorithmic accountability is a form of collaboration among multi-stakeholders, regulation by the public and the involvement of citizens which works against these issues. The concept of human rights is offered as one of the models of AI governance that focuses on transparency, accountability, and explicability to guarantee the sensible usages of AI. Oversight of the algorithmic systems, like the police surveillance, is important since most of the technologies have the potential to have a significant impact on policing and bargaining on powers and thus requires judicial oversight to consider socio-technical harms.

Moreover, the ethical use of AI systems must be transparent and have due process as evidenced by the legislative actions in the US, Europe, and Brazil, which intend to provide systems to govern them to enable ethical and safe implementation of AI (Engelmann, 2023). It is proposed that democratic control should be incorporated into the operation of AI systems so that they will not serve to subvert democracy and that AI systems can be employed in a proper manner in politics and society (Bogiatzis-Gibbons, 2024). In sum, any intelligence surveillance as well as algorithmic responsibility would necessitate a re-envisioning of democratic practices which would involve transparent, ethical practices and dynamics driven by democratic imperatives and principles.

The OECD AI Principles provide a globally recognized framework that balances innovation with human-centered values such as fairness, transparency, accountability, and respect for human rights. These principles emphasize the responsible stewardship of AI through proactive governance mechanisms that encourage inclusive growth, social justice, and environmental sustainability. Their updated guidance on transparency and explainability particularly aligns with the need for regulatory frameworks to ensure AI systems can be understood and challenged by affected individuals, reinforcing democratic oversight (Kniep et al., 2023; Engelmann, 2023).

United Nations reports on digital rights frame privacy and informational self-determination as fundamental human rights in the digital era, especially as AI-driven systems permeate governance, law enforcement, and the economy. This rights-based approach demands continuous impact assessments, safeguards against bias and discrimination, and global cooperation for consistent enforcement across jurisdictions. The UN's emphasis on dignity and non-discrimination resonates with the evolving privacy-security paradigms under India's DPDP Act and international frameworks such as the GDPR and CPPA (Wagner et al., 2023; Varlamova, 2019; Korff, 2023).

Scholars like Kate Crawford deepen the discourse on algorithmic accountability by revealing the socio-political underpinnings and power asymmetries embedded in AI systems. Crawford's work stresses that transparency and technical explainability must be supplemented by public engagement, robust liability rules, and auditor independence to guard against systemic harms. Incorporating her insights into India's AI governance model encourages embedding ethical principles throughout AI lifecycles and establishing participatory oversight that integrates diverse social perspectives (Bogiatzis-Gibbons, 2024; Criado & Guevara-Gómez, 2024).

Advanced privacy-preserving technologies such as federated learning, differential privacy, and homomorphic encryption offer promising tools for minimizing data exposure while enabling effective AI development and security applications. Legal mandates to deploy these techniques, mandated via privacy-by-design principles, improve compliance with constitutional privacy guarantees amidst increasingly pervasive algorithmic surveillance. India's regulatory frameworks can benefit by integrating these privacy safeguards to address emerging risks from black-box AI models and ubiquitous biometric data collection (Descalzo, 2024; Felzmann et al., 2020; Okon et al., 2024).

Anticipating future developments, AI governance must adopt flexible regulatory mechanisms such as regulatory sandboxes and sunset clauses to adapt laws alongside technological innovation and evolving societal norms. Multidisciplinary and cross-jurisdictional collaborations are critical for harmonizing standards and managing risks posed by generative AI, predictive analytics, and automated decision-making. Institutionalizing periodic ethical and technological reviews will ensure that legal frameworks remain robust, inclusive, and reflective of fast-changing AI landscapes (Graeden et al., 2023; Meghwal, 2025).

Together, these international standards and scholarly perspectives enrich the chapter's legal and ethical foundation, offering India a pathway to balance constitutional rights, cybersecurity, and innovation through informed, dynamic, and rights-respecting AI governance that resonates globally (Korff, 2023; Bhushan, 2024; Kniep et al., 2023).

TOWARD A PRIVACY-CENTRIC CYBER SECURITY JURISPRUDENCE

Privacy-by-design implementation in AI systems can be considered a tricky responsibility that involves meeting demands stipulated by such provisions of law as necessity, proportionality, and design transparency. Privacy by design (PbD) is a forward-looking strategy aimed at incorporating the privacy aspect into the design and functioning of AI systems so that it is the default mode and not an added feature (Descalzo, 2024).

That requirement in principle (grounded in the necessity principle) is that AI should only transmit or store data that is necessary to it, that is, data that it must receive or store in order to achieve its purpose but no more than is necessary, with data collection and data storage being limited to that extent that is strictly necessary (Nonju & Ihua-Maduenyi, 2024).

Proportionality, which has been considered in the context of the trade secrets and privacy balancing, represents the act of incorporating that the purpose of data processing of AI systems is peculiar and not superfluous relative to the goal of such actions (Popowicz-Pazdej, 2023). The essential part of trust and accountability of AI is transparency; transparency is the ability to interpret data processing operations of AI systems and to make them accessible to the users. Transparency by Design principles can govern the evolution of AI systems that default to transparent conditions, which alleviates the situation of the automated decision-making environment (Felzmann et al., 2020). Not only is the nature of integration of these principles is a mandate under the law of numerous jurisdictions but also it is a solution that serves as a strategic step in reducing the risk of privacy and increasing the adherence to privacy laws that are globally accepted like the GDPR, CCPA and PIPL (Mbah, 2024) (Blix et al., 2017).

The PbD would involve sufficient privacy impact assessment, the involvement of stakeholders in the implementation of such, and the financing of privacy-enhancing technologies like federated learning and differential privacy (Okon et al., 2024). The integration of these principles in AI systems allows organizations to make their way in the complicated environment of regulatory work, safeguard the most basic institutional right to privacy, and innovation in a manner that is privacy-sensitive.

The experiences of the European Union (EU) and Canada provide valuable lessons for strengthening privacy and cybersecurity jurisprudence in India, particularly as the Digital Personal Data Protection Act, 2023 (DPDP Act) seeks alignment with global best practices. The EU's General Data Protection Regulation (GDPR) represents the most comprehensive rights-based data protection framework, emphasizing principles of lawfulness, fairness, transparency, purpose limitation, data minimization, and accountability. It grants robust rights to individuals, including the right to be forgotten, data portability, and the right to object to automated decision-making, while embedding privacy-by-design and privacy-by-default directly into its legal architecture to ensure that privacy is treated as foundational rather than ancillary (Graeden et al., 2023).

Its enforcement model, though decentralized, relies on national Data Protection Authorities (DPAs) coordinated by the European Data Protection Board (EDPB) to promote consistency across member states. Drawing from this model, India can enhance its DPDP Act by empowering the Data Protection Board of India with strong investigatory and enforcement powers, ensuring its functional independence, and embedding statutory obligations for privacy-by-design in the regulation of emerging technologies such as AI (Roy, 2025).

Canada's Personal Information Protection and Electronic Documents Act (PIPEDA) and the proposed Consumer Privacy Protection Act (CPPA) reflect a principles-based model of privacy law, guided by ten fair information practices including consent, collection limits, accuracy, safeguards, and accountability. Unlike the prescriptive approach of the GDPR, the Canadian framework is more flexible, relying on the Office of the Privacy Commissioner (OPC) for interpretive guidance, while the CPPA introduces stronger enforcement tools such as administrative fines, an appeals tribunal, and cross-border data safeguards (Birrell et al., 2024). For India, this pragmatic and situational enforcement approach could complement the Digital Personal Data Protection Act, 2023 (DPDP Act) by offering industry-specific guidance and collaborative compliance mechanisms, thereby balancing consumer protection with business innovation. A hybrid model, combining the rights-based rigor of GDPR with Canada's commercial orientation, could help India bridge the gap between individual rights and economic growth (Shekar et al., 2023).

To achieve this, India must anchor its framework on four key principles—necessity, proportionality, transparency, and oversight—drawing on European Court of Human Rights jurisprudence and Canadian proportionality tests to restrict surveillance practices in scope, duration, and intrusiveness. Embedding privacy-by-design measures such as minimization, anonymization, and storage security into AI and surveillance systems—enforced through mandatory Privacy Impact Assessments (PIAs)—would further mitigate risks without undermining operational efficiency (Ardabili et al., 2023).

Accountability could be strengthened through multi-tier oversight involving the Data Protection Board of India, parliamentary committees, and independent auditing bodies, echoing Canada's National Security and Intelligence Review Agency (NSIRA) and EU supervisory authorities. Finally, given the deterritorialized nature of cyber threats, India must adopt transparent mechanisms for lawful cross-border data access and exchange, grounded in adequacy and reciprocity principles of the GDPR while advancing MLAT reforms to ensure faster yet rights-respecting international cooperation.

CONCLUSION AND POLICY RECOMMENDATIONS

The history of India's privacy and cybersecurity regulation reflects a dramatic shift in global data protection regimes, elevating privacy from a peripheral concern to both a constitutional right and an economic necessity. Landmark judicial recognition, particularly the Justice K.S. Puttaswamy case, provided the normative foundation for the Digital Personal Data Protection Act, 2023 (DPDP Act). Yet, the legislative trajectory also exposes critical gaps in institutional design, cross-border data regulation, and the reconciliation of privacy with national security. The central challenge is constructing a governance framework that balances individual rights with the operational demands of state security and the innovation needs of an AI-driven economy marked by surveillance technologies, predictive analytics, and algorithmic decision-making.

Comparative experiences offer valuable guidance as the European Union's GDPR enshrines a rights-based, enforceable framework characterized by strict compliance, privacy-by-design and by-default, and powerful oversight authorities. Canada, by contrast, has developed a more principles-based and flexible regime under PIPEDA and the proposed CPPA, emphasizing context-sensitive enforcement and participatory oversight through the Office of the Privacy Commissioner. For India, a hybrid model could provide the best path forward—adopting the EU's enforceability and clarity while incorporating Canada's flexibility and sectoral adaptability. Such an approach would be especially useful in governing AI applications, where rigid compliance could stifle innovation while weak frameworks risk eroding public trust.

ACTIONABLE STEPS FOR AI GOVERNANCE

Adopt a Hybrid Regulatory Model - India should synthesize the strict, rights-based approach of the EU's GDPR with the flexible, sector-specific enforcement of Canada's CPPA to balance accountability and innovation. This hybrid model is well-suited for a rapidly evolving digital ecosystem and offers a middle path between over-regulation and regulatory gaps, as supported by comparative scholarship (Korff, 2023).

- Strengthen the Data Protection Board of India - Enhancing the functional independence, investigatory authority, and technical expertise of the Data Protection Board of India (DPB) is essential for credible enforcement and sectoral oversight. Institutional reforms should empower the DPB with robust audit and sanctioning powers, modeled on leading global authorities like the EDPB (Bhushan, 2024; Kniep et al., 2023).
- Mandate Privacy-by-Design in AI Systems - Legal requirements for Privacy-by-Design (PbD) must be enforced across all AI deployments, emphasizing impact assessments before system rollout. Proactive integration of privacy and data minimization strengthens both accountability and compliance (Descalzo, 2024; Felzmann et al., 2020).

- Regulate Predictive Policing and Algorithmic Profiling - Regulatory frameworks should embed strict data quality requirements, fairness audits, and regular impact reviews to guard against algorithmic bias, especially in criminal justice and surveillance contexts (Singhvi, 2024; Hiller, 2022; Nabil et al., 2025.
- Enhance Algorithmic Transparency and Explainability - Implement legal mandates for explainable AI, particularly for "black box" or high-stakes decision-making systems. Qualified transparency, supported by judicial standards, can help protect sensitive information while maintaining oversight (Engelmann, 2023).
- Ensure Proportionality and Judicial Oversight in State Surveillance - All AI-enabled state surveillance should be subject to proportionality review and independent judicial authorization, taking cues from European Court of Human Rights standards (Staben & Leisterer, 2017; Kukava, 2023).
- Negotiate and Update Cross-Border Data Governance - India should advance modern adequacy and reciprocity agreements for international data transfers, aligning with OECD and EU safeguards, and update Mutual Legal Assistance Treaties (MLATs) for time-sensitive, rights-respecting cooperation (Graeden et al., 2023; Das & Sagar, 2024).
- Promote Multi-Stakeholder Oversight - Broaden oversight to include civil society, technical experts, and parliamentary actors to ensure democratic accountability and legitimacy in regulatory processes (Kniep et al., 2023; Criado & Guevara-Gómez, 2024).
- Regulate Surveillance Capitalism - Introduce statutory controls over the commercialization of personal data, requiring robust transparency and consent mechanisms in corporate data monetization.
- Public Awareness and Education - Invest in nationwide digital literacy campaigns highlighting privacy rights and ethical AI use to build a rights-aware, resilient digital society (Singh & Anusha, 2024).

These steps, jointly embedded in domestic legislative reform and comparative international experience, provide a robust, actionable agenda for bridging privacy, cybersecurity, and AI innovation in India's governance landscape.

Policy reform must begin with strengthening the Data Protection Board of India (DPB). Granting the DPB functional independence from executive control, robust investigatory and audit powers comparable to EU Data Protection Authorities, and technical expertise in AI, cybersecurity, and international data governance is essential. The DPB could also establish sector-specific oversight mechanisms—covering fintech, healthtech, edtech, and public surveillance—inspired by Canada's specialized regulatory interaction model. Alongside institutional strengthening, India must legislate a National Security–Privacy Balance Framework grounded in the principles of necessity, proportionality, and transparency. Drawing from European Court of Human Rights jurisprudence and Canadian oversight practices (e.g., NSIRA), such a framework should require judicial authorization for intrusive surveillance, mandatory Privacy Impact Assessments (PIAs) for AI-driven security systems, and transparent, multi-stakeholder oversight involving parliamentary committees, independent auditors, civil society, and technical experts.

Equally important is embedding privacy-by-design as a statutory requirement for all AI systems and public digital infrastructure, backed by sanctioning powers comparable to the GDPR. On cross-border data flows, India should pursue an adequacy-and-reciprocity regime, ensuring data transfers only to jurisdictions with comparable protections and modernizing Mutual Legal Assistance Treaties (MLATs) to secure timely, rights-respecting access to extraterritorial data. Alignment with OECD and EU adequacy standards would enhance India's credibility in global data governance. Complementary measures, including regulator-led capacity-building and public awareness initiatives, would reinforce institutional legitimacy and citizen trust.

Altogether, India's path forward demands a layered and flexible governance system—anchored in constitutional rights, informed by international best practices, and adaptive to fast-changing technological risks. At this intersection of privacy, cybersecurity, AI governance, and national security, India must balance individual sovereignty in the digital realm with lawful, proportionate tools for addressing legitimate security threats. A hybrid approach, synthesizing the EU's rights-based rigor with Canada's flexible enforcement model, offers the most promising pathway for India to secure both innovation and accountability in the coming decade.

REFERENCES

Alotaibi, S., Alruban, A., Furnell, S., & Clarke, N. (2019). A Novel Behaviour Profiling Approach to Continuous Authentication for Mobile Applications. 246. DOI: 10.5220/0007313302460251

Amingad, S. C., Rahul, M., Sathvik Reddy, P. S., & Gupta, N. S. (2023). Enhancing Public Safety with AI-Powered Intelligent Surveillance: An Examination of Immediate Incident Detection and Rapid Response in Urban Settings. *2023 International Conference on Advances in Computation, Communication and Information Technology (ICAICCIT)*, 205. DOI: 10.1109/ICAICCIT60255.2023.10465690

Ardabili, B. R., Pazho, A. D., Noghre, G. A., Neff, C., Bhaskararayuni, S. D., Ravindran, A., Reid, S., & Tabkhi, H. (2023). Understanding Policy and Technical Aspects of AI-enabled Smart Video Surveillance to Address Public Safety. *Computational Urban Science*, *3*(1), 21. Advance online publication. DOI: 10.1007/s43762-023-00097-8

Berman, P. S. (2018). Legal Jurisdiction and the Deterritorialization of Data. SSRN Electronic Journal. DOI: 10.2139/ssrn.3134782

Bhandari, V., Kak, A., Parsheera, S., & Rahman, F. (2017). An Analysis of Puttaswamy: The Supreme Court's Privacy Verdict. IndraStra Global, 11, https://www.ssoar.info/ssoar/handle/document/54766

Bhushan, V. (2024). EMPOWERING INDIVIDUALS: A DEEP DIVE INTO THE DIGITAL PERSONAL DATA PROTECTION ACT, 2023. *International Journal of Advanced Research*, *12*(5), 891–902. DOI: 10.21474/IJAR01/18799

Birrell, E., Rodolitz, J., Ding, A. A., Lee, J., McReynolds, E., Hutson, J., & Lerner, A. (2024). SoK: Technical Implementation and Human Impact of Internet Privacy Regulations. *2022 IEEE Symposium on Security and Privacy (SP)*, 673. DOI: 10.1109/SP54263.2024.00206

Kumar Bisht, A., & Shanmukha Sreenivasulu, N. S. (2024). Information Privacy Rights in India: A Study of the Digital Personal Data Protection Act, 2023. In IntechOpen eBooks. IntechOpen. DOI: 10.5772/intechopen.1007353

Blix, F., Elshekeil, S. A., & Laoyookhong, S. (2017). Data protection by design in systems development: From legal requirements to technical solutions. 2017 12th International Conference for Internet Technology and Secured Transactions (ICITST), 98. DOI: 10.23919/ICITST.2017.8356355

Bogiatzis-Gibbons, D. J. (2024). Beyond Individual Accountability: (Re-)Asserting Democratic Control of AI. *2022 ACM Conference on Fairness, Accountability, and Transparency*, 2017, 74. DOI: 10.1145/3630106.3658541

Bradford, L., Aboy, M., & Liddell, K. (2021). Standard contractual clauses for cross-border transfers of health data after Schrems II. *Journal of Law and the Biosciences*, *8*(1), lsab007. Advance online publication. DOI: 10.1093/jlb/lsab007

Chander, A. (2020). Is Data Localization a Solution for Schrems II? SSRN Electronic Journal. DOI: 10.2139/ssrn.3662626

Chugh, U. (2023). The Evolution of Privacy Laws in the Digital Age: Challenges and Solutions. *Indian Journal of Law.*, *1*(1), 51–60. DOI: 10.36676/ijl.2023-v1i1-07

Coche, E., & Kolk, A. (2024). When Digitalization Meets Regulation across Borders: An Explainer with Actionable Insights. *AIB Insights*, *24*(3). Advance online publication. DOI: 10.46697/001c.122505

Conrad, C., & Heggie, C. (2024). Legal and Ethical Challenges Raised by Advances in Brain-Computer Interface Technology. DOI: 10.2139/ssrn.4872064

Criado, J. I., & Guevara-Gómez, A. (2024). Who evaluates the algorithms? An overview of the algorithmic accountability ecosystem. 19. DOI: 10.1145/3657054.3657247

Descalzo, F. (2024). Designing Artificial Intelligence with Privacy at the Center. *2024 IEEE Biennial Congress of Argentina (ARGENCON)*, DOI: 10.1109/ARGENCON62399.2024.10735892

Dhamo, A., & Dhamo, I. (2024). Right to Privacy and Constitution: An In-Depth Analysis. *Interdisciplinary Journal of Research and Development*, *11*(1 S1), 190. DOI: 10.56345/ijrdv11n1s128

Dowd, R. (2022). Digitized Data Protection as a Fundamental Human Right. In *Springer eBooks* (p. 27). Springer Nature., DOI: 10.1007/978-3-030-82969-8_2

Downey, A., Islam, S. R., & Sarker, M. K. (2024). Predictive Policing: A Fairness-aware Approach. *International Journal of Artificial Intelligence Tools*, *33*(3), 2460005. Advance online publication. DOI: 10.1142/S0218213024600054

Engelmann, A. G. (2023). Algorithmic transparency as a fundamental right in the democratic rule of law. *Brazilian Journal of Law Technology and Innovation*, *1*(2), 169–188. doi:10.59224/bjlti.v1i2.169-188

Felzmann, H., Fosch-Villaronga, E., Lutz, C., & Tamò-Larrieux, A. (2020). Towards Transparency by Design for Artificial Intelligence [Review of Towards Transparency by Design for Artificial Intelligence]. Science and Engineering Ethics, 26(6), 3333. Springer Science+Business Media. DOI: 10.1007/s11948-020-00276-4

Ferencz, S., Blomley, N., Flynn, A., & Sylvestre, M.-È. (2022). Are Tents a "Home"? Extending Section 8 Privacy Rights for the Precariously Housed. *McGill Law Journal. Revue de Droit de McGill, 67*(4), 369. DOI: 10.7202/1098591ar

Fornasier, M. de O. (2022). Artificial Intelligence and Democratic Rule of Law. *Revista de Estudos Constitucionais Hermenêutica e Teoria Do Direito, 13*(3), 351–369. DOI: 10.4013/rechtd.2021.133.06

Golovin, K. S. (2024). THE NEED FOR LEGAL REGULATION OF THE "BLACK BOX" OF ARTIFICIAL INTELLIGENCE. *Vestnik of Kostroma State University, 30*(3), 290–297. DOI: 10.34216/1998-0817-2024-30-3-290-297

Gordon, J., Curran, M. T., Chuang, J., & Cheshire, C. (2021). Covert Embodied Choice: Decision-Making and the Limits of Privacy Under Biometric Surveillance. DOI: 10.1145/3411764.3445309

Graeden, E., Rosado, D. P., Stevens, T., Knodel, M., Hendricks-Sturrup, R., Reiskind, A., Bennett, A., Leitner, J., Lekas, P., & DeMooy, M. (2023). A new framework for global data regulation. arXiv (Cornell University). https://doi.org/10.48550/arxiv.2308.12955

Hiller, K. (2022). Predictive Policing and the Charter. *Manitoba Law Journal, 44*(6), 224–245. DOI: 10.29173/mlj1303

Hulkó, G., Kálmán, J., & Lapsánszky, A. (2025). The politics of digital sovereignty and the European Union's legislation: Navigating crises. *Frontiers in Political Science, 7*, 1548562. Advance online publication. DOI: 10.3389/fpos.2025.1548562

Kahla, L. Z. (2024). Leveraging Artificial Intelligence for Crime Detection and Prevention. *INTERANTIONAL JOURNAL OF SCIENTIFIC RESEARCH IN ENGINEERING AND MANAGEMENT, 8*(5), 1–5. Advance online publication. DOI: 10.55041/IJSREM34207

Kaur, K. (2025). DIGITAL SURVEILLANCE AND INDIAN PRIVACY LAWS. *LawFoyer International Journal of Doctrinal Legal Research., 3*(1), 61–77. DOI: 10.70183/lijdlr.2024.v03.4

Kaur, T. (2024). Right To Privacy in Digital Age: A Study with Indian Context. [EEL]. *European Economic Letters, 14*(4), 1744–1752. DOI: 10.52783/eel.v14i4.2307

Khazanchi, D., & Saxena, M. (2025). Navigating digital human rights in the age of AI: challenges, theoretical perspectives, and research implications. Journal of Information Technology Case and Application Research, DOI: 10.1080/15228053.2025.2452028

Kniep, R., Ewert, L., Reyes, B. L., Tréguer, F., Cluskey, E. M., & Aradau, C. (2024). Towards democratic intelligence oversight: Limits, practices, struggles. *Review of International Studies, 50*(1), 209–229. DOI: 10.1017/S0260210523000013

Korff, D. (2023). The Indian Digital Personal Data Protection Act, 2023, viewed from a European Perspective. SSRN Electronic Journal. DOI: 10.2139/ssrn.4614984

Kukava, K. (2023). Balancing the Right to Privacy and National Security Interests in the Digital Age. *Journal of Law, 2*(2). Advance online publication. DOI: 10.60131/jlaw.2.2023.7711

Kulikova, A. A. (2019). Digital law as a nascent branch of Russian law. Proceedings of the 1st International Scientific Conference "Modern Management Trends and the Digital Economy: From Regional Development to Global Economic Growth" (MTDE 2019). DOI: 10.2991/mtde-19.2019.86

Labbay, A. (2023). La surveillance algorithmique des données de connexion dans le cadre de la lutte contre le terrorisme. *Cahiers de La Recherche Sur Les Droits Fondamentaux, 21*, 117–124. DOI: 10.4000/crdf.8874

Livson, M., Eshtokin, S., Vasyukov, V., Yudina, E., Baybarin, A., & Pivneva, S. (2021). Impact of Digitalization on Legal Regulation: Formation of new legal practices. *Journal of Law and Sustainable Development, 9*(2), e0749. Advance online publication. DOI: 10.37497/sdgs.v9i2.28

Machayya, C. R. (2024). Strategic approaches to bias and variance in algorithmic profiling. In *Routledge eBooks* (p. 726). Informa., DOI: 10.4324/9781003606642-157

Malhotra, C., & Malhotra, U. (2024). Putting Interests of Digital Nagriks First: Digital Personal Data Protection (DPDP) Act 2023 of India. *The Indian Journal of Public Administration, 70*(3), 516–531. DOI: 10.1177/00195561241271575

Mbah, G. O.Geraldine O Mbah. (2024). Data privacy in the era of AI: Navigating regulatory landscapes for global businesses. *International Journal of Science and Research Archive, 13*(2), 2040–2058. DOI: 10.30574/ijsra.2024.13.2.2396

Meghwal, T. (2025). Emerging Challenges in Regulating Artificial Intelligence Under Cyber Security Laws in India. DOI: 10.2139/ssrn.5030258

Montasari, R. (2022). Artificial Intelligence and National Security. In *Springer eBooks*. Springer Nature., DOI: 10.1007/978-3-031-06709-9

Nabil, A. R., Tusher, M., Akther, M. N., & Rayhan, R. U. (2025). Ethical Implications Of Ai- Powered Predictive Policing. Ethical Implications Of Ai- Powered Predictive Policing: Balancing Public Safety With Privacy Concerns.., *2*(1), 47–58. DOI: 10.70937/itej.v2i01.54

Nešpor, J. (2024). Automated Administrative Decision-Making: What is the Black Box Hiding? *AUC IURIDICA*, *70*(2), 69–83. DOI: 10.14712/23366478.2024.23

Newlands, G. (2022). The algorithmic surveillance of gig workers. In *Routledge eBooks* (p. 64). Informa., DOI: 10.4324/9781003161875-6

Nonju, K. D. S., & Ihua-Maduenyi, A. B. (2024). The Impact of Artificial Intelligence on Privacy Laws. *International Journal of Research and Innovation in Social Science*, *2150*. Advance online publication. DOI: 10.47772/IJRISS.2024.8090178

Nyst, C., & Falchetta, T. (2017). The Right to Privacy in the Digital Age. *Journal of Human Rights Practice*, *9*(1), 104–118. DOI: 10.1093/jhuman/huw026

Oban, V., Kaya, M., Safi, G., Çimen, İ. N., Çatak, T., Karadağ, B., Görmüs, G., Çandir, A., & Alagöz, F. (2024). Profiling Driver Behaviors Using AI-Based Methods and Deep Learning Techniques for Improving Road Safety: A Comparative Study of Algorithms. 2024 9th International Conference on Computer Science and Engineering (UBMK), 955. DOI: 10.1109/UBMK63289.2024.10773587

Okon, S. U., Olateju, O. O., Ogungbemi, O. S., Joseph, S. A., Olisa, A. O., & Olaniyi, O. O. (2024). Incorporating Privacy by Design Principles in the Modification of AI Systems in Preventing Breaches across Multiple Environments, Including Public Cloud, Private Cloud, and On-prem. *Journal of Engineering Research and Reports*, *26*(9), 136–158. DOI: 10.9734/jerr/2024/v26i91269

Popowicz-Pazdej, A. (2023). The proportionality between trade secret and privacy protection: How to strike the right balance when designing generative AI tools. *Journal of Data Protection & Privacy.*, *6*(2), 153. DOI: 10.69554/ILGY4235

Purves, D. (2022). Fairness in Algorithmic Policing. *Journal of the American Philosophical Association*, *8*(4), 741–761. DOI: 10.1017/apa.2021.39

Rane, J., Kaya, Ö., Mallick, S. K., & Rane, N. L. (2024). Enhancing black-box models: Advances in explainable artificial intelligence for ethical decision-making. DOI: 10.70593/978-81-981271-0-5_4

Roy, S. (2025). Inside India's Draft Digital Personal Data Protection Act. DOI: 10.2139/ssrn.5082157

Ruohonen, J. (2021). The Treachery of Images in the Digital Sovereignty Debate. *Minds and Machines*, *31*(3), 439–456. DOI: 10.1007/s11023-021-09566-7

Ruohonen, J. (2023). Recent Trends in Cross-Border Data Access by Law Enforcement Agencies. arXiv (Cornell University). https://doi.org/10.48550/arXiv.2302.09942

Shekar, K., Tripathi, A., & Birla, B. (2023). Principle-based Framework towards Cross-Border Data Transfers. SSRN Electronic Journal. DOI: 10.2139/ssrn.4527681

Singh, A., & Anusha, A. (2024). The Digital Personal Data Protection Act, 2023: An Ambitious Government Step Towards Ensuring Its Wide Reach. *The Indian Journal of Public Administration*, *70*(3), 502–515. DOI: 10.1177/00195561241271533

Singhvi, H. (2024). Socio-Economic Impacts of Predictive Policing on Minority Communities and Potential Solutions. DOI: 10.58445/rars.2024

Staben, J., & Leisterer, H. (2017). International Cross-Surveillance: Global IT Surveillance Arbitrage and the Principle of Proportionality as a Counterargument. *Surveillance & Society*, *15*(1), 108–122. DOI: 10.24908/ss.v15i1.5277

Sultana, R. (2024). Artificial Intelligence For Decision Making In The Era Of Big Data Evolution. *Non Human Journal.*, *1*(1), 17–40. DOI: 10.70008/jbimisr.v1i01.59

Teo, S. A. (2025, June). Artificial intelligence and its 'slow violence' to human rights. *AI and Ethics*, *5*(3), 2265–2280.DOI: 10.1007/s43681-024-00547-x

Thiele, C. (2018). U.S. CLOUD Act - Danaergeschenk für den Europäischen Datenschutz. *Zeitschrift Für Informationsrecht*, *6*(2), 128–132. DOI: 10.33196/ziir201802012801

Usman, H., Tariq, I., & Nawaz, B. (2023). IN THE REALM OF THE MACHINES: AI'S INFLUENCE UPON INTERNATIONAL LAW AND POLICY. *Journal of Social Research Development*, *4*(2), 383–399. DOI: 10.53664/JSRD/04-02-2023-13-383-399

Varlamova, N. V. (2019). DIGITAL RIGHTS — NEW GENERATION OF HUMAN RIGHTS? *Proceedings of the Institute of State and Law of the RAS*, *14*(5), 141–167. DOI: 10.35427/2073-4522-2019-14-5-varlamova

Wagner, B., Sanchez, A., Sekwenz, M., Dideriksen, S., & Murray-Rust, D. (2023, Dec. 13). The Politics of Digital (Human) Rights. Oxford Research Encyclopedia of International Studies. Retrieved 24 Feb. 2026, from https://oxfordre.com/internationalstudies/view/10.1093/acrefore/9780190846626.001.0001/acrefore-9780190846626-e-694DOI: 10.1093/acrefore/9780190846626.013.694

Wang, G. (2023). The Necessity of Extraterritorial Application of the Personal Information Protection Law and Suggestions for Its Improvement. *International Journal of Frontiers in Sociology*, *5*(16). Advance online publication. DOI: 10.25236/IJFS.2023.051616

Chapter 2
Cybersecurity Regulation and Individual Rights:
Legal Responses to Digital Threats

Azamat Ali
https://orcid.org/0000-0003-2931-2166
Lovely Professional University, Punjab, India

Ankit Dixit
Lovely Professional University, Punjab, India

ABSTRACT

Digital technologies have become highly popular in the modern world, which has added more risk to cyber threats, and it becomes a major concern regarding human rights and data safety. The chapter discusses the reaction of law to digital threats in the perspective of cybersecurity regulation. It discusses the role that the national and international legal systems play in safeguarding personal data, protecting digital security and defending the rights of individuals. It also dwells on the issues of keeping a balance between national security and the rights of individual privacy. Case studies and some law cases that refer to the real life are also provided to demonstrate the tendencies of governments and institutions reacting to cyber offences. The chapter concludes with the suggestions to increase legal protection, enforce moral leadership and to make sure that cyber law protects not only electronic systems but also those people who live in a more interconnected world.

DOI: 10.4018/979-8-3373-4967-1.ch002

1. INTRODUCTION

Digital technologies are growing rapidly, and the results of this process already affected nearly every aspect of life. Regardless of communication and trade, education or governance, digital platforms have become the foundation on which people and institutions are working. This increasing reliance on digital infrastructure has however also caused a lot of vulnerabilities. The cyber threats have become way much complex and sophisticated because the world has become global. Those threats not only pose risks to maintaining the level of security of information systems but also the personal data and the rights and freedoms of the individuals in general (Montasari, 2024). The list of cyber threats is extensive e.g. unauthorized access to personal data, identity theft, financial fraud, ransomware attack, state-sponsored cyber-espionage. Such threats pose a challenge on people and companies, as well as states. As digital gadget use, online space, and cloud computing expands, cyber-attackers continuously think of new ways of exploring available system weaknesses. What was once viewed as a problem of an IT department is now a matter of policy makers, legal expert and concerns of human rights activists. Cybersecurity does not only mean protection of machines or networks; it is also protecting humans and their human rights in the digital age (Schmitt, 2023).

Cybersecurity has therefore become the national concern and interest. Info which was stored in the form of physical files has now been stored and sent in electronic forms. Government and private institutions continue to collect and process the health records, bank data and even personal communications and biometric identifiers. This digital spine, although convenient and efficient in the delivery of various services, exposes people to more vulnerability to misuse of their data. After a system is breached, its effects can be long-term and far reaching, damaging personal image, personal security and they can be even insulting (Tabaghdehi, 2024). Cybersecurity as such is related to safeguarding the rights of the individual. One of the core rights of privacy is endangered by a cyber-intrusion. Privacy rights are an essential part of both personal autonomy and personal freedom of expression that people can reach each other, think and share information without being afraid of being spied at or otherwise discovered. Such rights are violated by hacking personal information by cybercriminals or the government or other bodies, which compromises the principles of the democratic society (Romaniuk & Hattiangady, 2023).

Another right that is being compromised in the internet is the freedom of expression. By attacking journalists, human rights defenders or any political dissidents, one can frighten those who are in possession of this freedom of speech, silence potential critics, discourage critiques, and reduce the terms within which the general speech is exercised. Similarly, cyberbullying and Internet bullying may have catastrophic psychological outcomes, particularly the underprivileged populations.

They do not lead to physical assault, but they trample upon the right to personal security and mental well-being (Rawaqa, 2025). It is noteworthy that human rights concerns have taken the center stage in discussions on cybersecurity following the advent of cyber threats. Traditionally, cybersecurity policies used to dwell on the technical challenges, as well as on the national security concerns. Conversely, the human element of digital security has increased in the importance of the past few years. Human rights-based approaches to cybersecurity are becoming of interest in international organizations, in courts, and within the civil society. It is implied that the laws and policies ought not only to protect systems against attacks but also serve to make sure that they observe the rights of individuals in the process (Madnick et al., 2024).

The improper utilization of the huge quantities of information gathered by digital surveillance is one of the obvious ones. In as much as the same may be warranted to the name of the national security or counterterrorism, some fundamental laws like due process, movement, and equality under the law may be infringed where there lacks proper regulation of the same surveillance. In the same vein, such practices by companies when they obtain data on their users without prior and well-informed consent and without adequate measures to ensure data protection undermines the right to make informed decisions and the necessity of data protection (Bayer, 2022). These problems were brought to the fore more during the COVID-19 pandemic. There was an expansion of telework, online learning, and online medical practices because all of this shifted online together with digital contact tracing, remote monitoring, and data sharing, all of which predisposed them to cyber risks (Saleous et al., 2023). This time brought about the vulnerabilities of existing cybersecurity measures and demonstrated the necessity to reinforce them to guarantee the rights of individuals as well as social and technological advancements.

2. PROBLEM STATEMENT

The problem of cybersecurity threats is an alarming issue because it threatens human rights, which can be considered as one of the most fundamental ones in the context of the digital age. There are more complex and common cyber-attacks and they not only attack personal information but also attack fundamental rights, including privacy and freedom of expression (Montasari, 2024). Hacking, data breaches, and identity theft are only a part of the bigger issues that violate personal integrity, democracy, and human liberation (Romaniuk & Hattiangady, 2023). Also, the use of online harassment and cyberbullying may silence other individuals inflicting psychological harm and breaching not only the right of free expression but also the right of personal security as well (Rawaqa, 2025).

Cybersecurity is a national or technical security problem which has traditionally been referred to as a technical security problem. However, the digital threats are growing in their dimension and scope that creates an urgent need to ensure protection of human rights in cyberspace. Existing laws have a hard time adjusting to a new threat and provide inconsistent security based on local jurisdiction. Freedom of democracy, civil liberties, and the rule of law are at the risk of being exploited as a result of the absence of effective and coordinated actions on the part of the government. Simply put, the difficulty is in finding the way to remedy the twofold issue of protecting internal systems and data, as well as fundamental human rights in the more complicated and intricate digital world.

3. SIGNIFICANCE OF THE CHAPTER

In this chapter, the author brings to attention the issue of cybersecurity in human rights, stating that the assurance of digital rights is one of the global priorities. With the changing digital outlook, global frameworks also enforce the notion that the same offline rights which are enjoyed by citizens, including privacy and freedom to express oneself, must be afforded online. The resolution of the United Nations Human Rights Council (2012) confirms the statement that the rights are universal no matter what medium is used. The most notable of the universal rules, enshrined in the Universal Declaration of Human Rights, is the right to privacy (Article 12), the freedom of speech (Article 19) that are also applicable to the internet (Ayalew, 2022).

The UN Guiding Principles on Business and Human Rights also emphasize that human rights have to be supported in the digital terrain by the activities of the companies, which are recognized as private (McVey, 2022). It is represented, for instance, by the European Union General Data Protection Regulation (GDPR), which focuses on the protection of data and personal freedom and tries to balance all the security and rights (Bayer, 2022). With the help of the comparative analysis of India, the United States, the European Union, and international norms, this chapter reveals the gaps in the law and outlines the best practices in aligning the technical and legal approaches to our consummate practice. It represents a connection between policy, law, and technology and gives principles that can be used to develop solid frameworks of cybersecurity that secure digital rights, facilitate innovation, and enshrine democratic principles.

4. METHODOLOGY

This chapter accepts the qualitative, doctrinal type of research studies on the basis of legal analysis and literature review. It analyses laws, regulations, policies and courts cases on cybersecurity and digital rights. It is both descriptive and analytical in nature, which focuses on evaluating the way in which the existing models of legal frameworks deal with the situation in cybersecurity, as well as the way it affects the basic rights. The analysis of all Indian, the United States and European Union cybersecurity legislations and regulatory strategies is provided by comparison. This term of comparison assists in determining the best practices, deficiencies and areas that require redress to further protect the digital rights. The literature review made in the chapter also encompasses scholarly articles, international conventions, policy reports as well as landmark judicial cases. The examples of real-life cyber-attacks, surveillance scandals, and other influential cases of the court are examined in order to provide a picture of how legal and theoretical ideas apply in practice. The combination of doctrinal legal research, comparative analysis and examination of case studies (in other words mixed method approach) will give an in-depth and encompassing reply to the question of how cybersecurity practices can operate in line with the protection of human rights. Such an approach guarantees the comprehensive examination and provides the chapter with conclusions and proposals.

5. LITERATURE REVIEW

Definition and Scope of Cybersecurity Law

Cybersecurity law is a group of regulations and precepts that grant control over the practices of people, organizations, and governments within the space of the Internet. It deals with prevention and method of punishments to cybercrimes like hacking, exchange of malware, unauthorized access to data and spies. Due to the explosive increase in digital technologies in such spheres as healthcare, finance, defense, and public administration, cybersecurity legislation has become a large field (Lukings & Lashkari, 2022). The majority of the countries implement the mix of sectorial regulations, national cybersecurity policies, and administrative standards. In India, the existing law that is used to handle cybercrimes and protect personal information is the Information Technology Act, 2000.

In the US, there are several laws stipulating the actions of federal agencies like the Cybersecurity Information Sharing Act (CISA, 2015) and Federal Information Security Management Act (FISMA) that encourages information sharing. Regional conventions are forming on cybersecurity harmonization and transnational cooperation globally. The laws on cybersecurity also place duties on the shoulders of the non-public operators especially those dealing with critical infrastructure or personal data. These involve the presence of risk assessment, breach reporting and execution of technical safety measures, such as encryption and multi-factor authentication. Failure to comply normally leads to the legal consequences, monetary sanctions, and reputational damage (Toledano, 2024). But with the current speed of the developing technology, these laws have to be regularly amended and interpreted to deal with newly occurring threats.

Fundamental Rights Affected by Digital Threats

Cyber threats are a threat to digital systems and basic human rights. The internet has created a situation where exercising the civil, political and socio-economic rights is vital. Some fundamental rights are likely to fail because of cybersecurity breaches and include:

- Right to Privacy: The right of privacy is the most threatened thing in the digital era. This right can be badly hampered by hackers, corporations, or states collecting, using, or sharing their personal data without their consent. Of note are medical records, financial systems, and biometric information that are at risk. Justice K.S. Puttaswamy v. Privacy as a right not only in itself but as a legal liberty under the Article 21 of the Indian Supreme Court states that the Indian Supreme Court acknowledged privacy as a fundamental right of life and liberty (Aswathy & Tyagi, 2022).
- Freedom of Expression: Free speech is under threat owing to cyberattacks of journalists, activists, and media houses. The laws that govern cybersecurity in other nations are also used to monitor the digital landscape, silence information, or silence those that oppose them. The self-censorship is another way that mass surveillance encourages when people are afraid that they may be tracked twenty-four hours a day and seven days a week (Orgeret et al., 2024).
- Right of Access to Information: The digital infrastructure plays an important role in gaining access to government services, education, health and employment. Hackers attacking government records or ISPs can interfere with the access of citizens to the basic services. Shutdown of the internet or limited access based on discrimination completely contradicts the principle of digital inclusion and increases the state of social inequalities (Toledano, 2024).
- Right to Due Process: The victims of cybercrimes should be offered due process of the law. The challenge with cross-border cybercrimes though is that the crimes are difficult to investigate and prosecute. Jurisdiction dispute and

non-existing extradition treaties often slow the process of justice, violating the right to due process and fair redress to law (Kulshrestha et al., 2022).

International Human Rights Law in the Digital Context

The rights of human beings worldwide drive the optimization of cybersecurity and fundamental rights. Examples of rights enshrined in the Universal Declaration of Human Rights (UDHR, 1948) and operative in cyberspace include privacy (Article 12) and the freedom of freedom of expression (Article 19) (Ayalew, 2022). Such protections are reinforced by treaties, such as the International Covenant on Civil and Political Rights (ICCPR) and regional instruments, such as the European Convention of Human Rights (ECHR). ICCPR provides that lawful, necessary and proportional state interventions such as surveillance should be conducted. According to the General Comment No. 16 of the UN Human Rights Committee, communication interception has to be controlled to the greatest extent (Ventura, 2022). As attested by the UN Human Rights Council (UNHRC) in 2012, rights should apply online or offline. Business and human rights are also under the scrutiny of the UN Guiding Principles on Business and Human Rights, which requires the transition of the human rights principles to the digital landscape even by private enterprises (McVey, 2022). European Union General Data Protection Regulation (GDPR) is a benchmark privacy protection in the world. It dictates its strident regulations when it comes to data processing, breach notification and user consent. GDPR is proving that privacy and digital innovation do not have to be mutually exclusive on the basis of a rights-based framework.

Role of Constitutional Protections and Legal Doctrines

The constitutions of the countries greatly influence the security of cyberspace. Privacy, freedom of speech and access to information is acknowledged in a large number of countries as constitutional rights. In India, Article 21 was understood by the Supreme Court to entail a right to privacy. In the United States, digital surveillance is covered under the Fourth Amendment as it places restraints against unreasonable searches and seizures (Di Nuzzo, 2022).

One principle that is often used in assessing cybersecurity policies by courts is:

- Lawfulness: It is the provision of the fact that the action taken has a definite legal authority to support it.
- Necessity: Determining whether or not the measure is aimed at receiving a noble need such as national security.

- Proportionality: That the scope of surveillance or data collection is narrow to the required.

The Latin American and European equivalent is the right of habeas data that gives a person authority to obtain and revise personal data. Courts monitor such policy measures so that cybersecurity does not violate essential freedoms. Mass Surveillance and data retention laws have been overturned by courts across the world because they are too broad or discriminatory (Helberger, 2025). Transparency and law reforms have been advanced by judicial activism in most instances.

National Regulatory Frameworks and Cybersecurity Laws

India

The key legislation on cybersecurity in India is the Information Technology Act, 2000 followed by amendment in 2008. It classifies crime like hacking, identity theft, and cyber terrorism. Section 43 counts the unauthorized access, whereas the Section 66 determines the punishment likely to be obtained as a result of hacking. Section 66E in the Act criminalizes the unauthorized publishing of personal images, too. CERTI-In: is the Indian Computer Emergency Response Team, which provides coordination in cases of computer security incidents and issues warnings (Amal Chandra, 2024).

United States

The U.S does not use a comprehensive cybersecurity law but a sectoral approach. The Act on Cybersecurity Information Sharing (CISA, 2015) promotes sharing information on threats, and the Federal Information Security Modernization Act (FISMA) helps to implement the security requirements within federal agencies. Unlawful access is criminalized by acts such as Computer Fraud and Abuse Act (CFAA) and health-related data are secured by HIPAA (McConomy & Leber, 2022). Additional regulatory controls on the state level contribute to this tangled structure.

European Union

The first law to emerge by the EU on its security in cyberspace was the Network and Information Systems (NIS) Directive, 2016. It demands the states that are members to safeguard their key infrastructure in terms of energy, healthcare and transport. Those distributing critical services should have the security strategies and report attacks. This is supported by the GDPR (2018), which introduces severe data protection provisions, such as a 72-hour response to breaches, and a practice of privacy by design (Schutze, 2022). The extraterritorial scope of GDPR urges companies across the world to abide by its rules when dealing with the personal data of EU residents.

Table 1. Comparison of Key National Cybersecurity Laws

Aspect	India (IT Act)	USA (CISA, CFAA, FISMA, etc.)	EU (NIS Directive & GDPR)
Primary Law(s)	IT Act, 2000 (amended 2008)	CISA (2015); CFAA (1986); FISMA (2014); HIPAA (1996)	NIS Directive (2016); GDPR (2018)
Focus Area	Cybercrimes; personal data protection	Critical infrastructure security; public-private info-sharing	Infrastructure security; data protection (breach response)
Breach Notification	Limited requirements (sector-specific, e.g. certain financial sectors)	Largely voluntary under CISA; sector-specific mandates	Mandatory reporting within 72 hours (GDPR)
Enforcement Body	CERT-In; State Police; Judiciary	Department of Homeland Security (DHS); FBI; Secret Service; sectoral regulators (FTC, etc.)	National cybersecurity agencies; European Union Agency for Cybersecurity (ENISA); Data Protection Authorities
Penalties	Fines and imprisonment (varying by offense)	Civil and criminal penalties (fines, imprisonment, etc.)	Administrative fines up to €20 million or 4% of global turnover (GDPR); other penalties under national laws
Incident Reporting	Encouraged but not uniform or comprehensive	Voluntary in many cases; mandatory in some sectors/ states	Mandatory for operators of essential services (NIS Directive) and data controllers (GDPR)
Strengths	Covers a wide range of cyber offenses; updated in 2008 for new threats	Multiple laws targeting specific issues; involvement of various agencies and public-private programs	Strong rights-based approach (especially GDPR); cross-border consistency across member states (to some extent)
Challenges	Some provisions outdated; enforcement can be weak; lack of comprehensive data protection law (until recently)	No single national framework; patchwork can create gaps; inconsistent state laws	Varied implementation by member states; enforcement and uniform application can differ; constant need to update definitions of emerging threats

Legal Provisions for Data Breaches, Hacking, and Identity Theft

The national legislation on cybersecurity covers the typical crimes that endanger cybersecurity and the human rights.

- Data Breaches: A data breach is when some personal or sensitive information is disclosed without any authorization. Due to laws, organizations must ensure that they prevent breaches and in cases that it does, the law demands that it is reported. In India a criminal offence is laid down in section 72A of the IT Act which addresses the deliberate publicizing of personal information which has been acquired illegitimately. GDPR (Article 33) of the EU, a data controller must, within 72 hours, report specific cases of breach to the authorities. In the US, no single federal law has been enforced, with more than 50 state laws implementing breach notice and requirements and regulations by different sectors like the healthcare industry, which has established HIPAA (McConomy & Leber, 2022).
- Hacking: Hacking refers to unauthorized access to a computer system or a computer network. The IT Act of India (Section 66) renders punishment of up to three years in prison to be slapped on a person guilty of hacking. The U.S. computer fraud and abuse act (CFAA) criminalizes the act of accessing the information stored in so-called protected computers without authorization and gives the option of civil and criminal recourse. In EU, EU provides directives where member states criminalise unlawful access to information systems and impose punishment (Harkin & Panagiotopoulos, 2025). There is still debate about the issue of separating malicious hacking and ethical security research.
- Identity Theft: Identity theft also refers to the use of personal information of a person to commit fraud or any other form of crime. In India, identity theft and impersonation via computer resources are penalized by the Sec. 66C and Sec. 66D of the IT Act. The Identity Theft and Assumption Deterrence Act and state statute in the U.S. prevents the use of an identifying data of another individual in illegal applications. In the EU, misuse of the availability created is not prevented by dedicated instance law, but instead mitigated by data minimization and consent requirements established by GDPR (Sivakumar et al., 2024).

Enforcement Mechanisms, Penalties, and Challenges

The implementation of cybersecurity entails tracking of the offences, exploration of the cybercrimes and administering of the relevant penalizations. The punishment normally awarded to cybercrimes is harsh in terms of fines as well as jail times. As an example, the IT Act by India provides fines of up to 50 million rupees and up to 7 years in jail in case of serious offenses in the field of cyber terrorism. GDPR fines that are imposed by the European Union go up to 20 million euros or 4 percent of the worldwide revenue of the company whichever is higher. The Computer Fraud and Abuse Act (CFAA) is even more punitive in the United States, as the penalties can become a lifetime in prison or even several decades (Arnell & Faturoti, 2023). Further, there is prevalence of civil damages and litigations, where organizations are charged on breach or negligence.

A number of challenges are however working against effective enforcement of cybersecurity laws. Jurisdictional concerns emerge due to the fact that the attacks occur on lawful territory which may be in different geographical locations hence it is difficult to see which law to adopt. Most law enforcement agencies do not have availed expertise and resources that can be capacitated to tackle advanced cyber-attacks. Firms tend to under-report or rather hide infringements fearing to hamper on image of its core business. Moreover, development of technology is fast than the legal system thus there are loopholes through which some of the bad practices are not dealt with directly. The low quality of international cooperation, which is based on different legal standards and cross-border proceedings speed, also complicates the enforcement process. These obstacles demonstrate that effective cybersecurity can be achieved not only due to current and strong laws but better international cooperation and harmonized enforcement systems.

Role of Cybercrime Units and Law Enforcement

Cybercrime rules impact is significant and special cybercrime forces are a feature that enhances enforcement of the statutes and to respond to online threats. Most states in India have to Cyber Crime Cells and national-level entities such as the Central Bureau of Investigation (CBI) have separate cyber divisions. Indian Cyber Crime Coordination Centre (I4C) which was initiated in 2020 is concentrated on the central response mechanism, capacity building, and digital forensics though still some subunits are struggling with the lack of resources and even technical knowledge (Chandra, 2025). In America, the federal governments head cyber enforcement. Major Cyberattacks are managed by the Federal Bureau of Investigation (FBI), which has the Cyber Division and Critical Infrastructure agency is managed by the Cybersecurity and Infrastructure Security Agency (CISA). A Cyber Fraud Task Force is managed by the United States Secret Service, and the National Cyber Investigative Joint Task Force targets multi-agency responses to serious cyber threats (Salomon, 2022). In the European Union, a member country has its own cybercrime units, which are assisted by the European Cybercrime Centre (EC3), a department at the Europol. Next to this, the EU Agency for Cybersecurity (ENISA) supports the exchange of intelligence and the conduct of common law-enforcement operations that are frequently aimed at transnational cybercrime gangs (Mueck & Gaie, 2025). Globally, the international cooperation between different countries including intelligence sharing and aligned operations is facilitated by an institution like the INTERPOL Global Complex for Innovation in Singapore.

Global Governance and International Legal Instruments

Role of International Organizations

International institutions are also essential towards the establishment of global norms in cybersecurity and interstate cooperation. The United Nations (UN) has made the steps towards providing principals that should guide the state in cyberspace with the development of the Group of Governmental Experts (UN GGE) and the Open-Ended Working Group (OEWG). The 2013, 2015, and 2021 GGE reports also stipulated that international law governs the cyberspace, including the UN Charter, and proposed to voluntarily embrace some norms, including no attack to critical infrastructure in peacetime (Baram, 2024). The OEWG also encourages transparency, capacity building and inclusiveness in discussions that can enhance cyber governance (Moynihan, 2021). The Global Cybersecurity Agenda (GCA) by the International Telecommunication Union (ITU) assists countries to have cybersecurity strategies, technical standards and the development of capacity building programs, with a specific concentration on increasing the resilience of the developing world.

Council of Europe has been the major source of contributing to the international cyber law and one of them is the Budapest convention on cybercrime which was adopted in year 2001 and are usually used to unify national legal systems and so allow cooperation across jurisdictions and criminalize crime acts like hacking of data, interference of data as well as child exploitation on the internet. More than 70 countries have accepted this treaty or adopted them in the form of a model (Polyzoidou, 2021). Regional structures are also likely to be involved in cybersecurity governance, within the EU, the GDPR and the NIS Directive is advanced regulations. Likewise, Malabo Convention of the African Union (2014), as well as Organization of American States (OAS) initiatives contributes to cyber confidence-building and the development of cybersecurity systems in the region.

Key Legal Frameworks for International Cybersecurity

Among the most notable global treaties is the Budapest Convention on Cybercrime (2001) that has demanded signatories to criminalize a wide range of cybercrimes and to offer cooperation on investigations and extraditions. Although not all countries are in the treaty with some exemplified by India, it still remains to be considered as the most important system in combatting cybercrime in the world (Polyzoidou, 2021). The European Union has a strict regulation known as the

General Data Protection Regulation (GDPR, 2018) that defines how personal data should be gathered, notifications in case of data theft, and the consent of the user. Its international applicability to the organizations that process data of EU citizens has played a major role in governing the formulation of data protection legislation in all parts of the world (Stepenko et al., 2022). The UN Group of Governmental Experts (GGE) has published reports that present crucial elements of liable state conduct in cyberspace, such as advertence of cyberattacks against construction infrastructures and growth of international collaboration in averting unlawful usage of the information and correspondence technologies (ICTs) (Baram, 2024). Furthermore, the UN Open-Ended working Group (OEWG) upholds principles of inclusivity and capacity building where all countries have chances to engage the crafting of International Cybersecurity (Moynihan, 2021).

Table 2. Key Global Cybersecurity Frameworks and Instruments

Framework / Instrument	Institution	Focus Area	Status / Scope
Budapest Convention	Council of Europe	Cybercrime laws and cooperation	Open to global adoption; ~70+ countries involved
GDPR	European Union	Data protection and privacy	Extraterritorial reach (global impact on companies)
UN GGE Reports	United Nations (UN)	Norms of state behavior in cyberspace	Non-binding but influential consensus norms
UN OEWG	United Nations (UN)	Inclusive dialogue on cyber governance	Ongoing, open to all UN member states (global participation)
ITU Global Cybersecurity Agenda	International Telecommunication Union	Technical support and global collaboration	Focus on capacity-building (esp. in developing countries); non-binding guidelines

Cross-Border Data Flows and Jurisdictional Challenges

The transport of data cross-nationally without anything holding it back poses immense legal dilemmas to the fields of cybersecurity and law enforcement. Others have enacted laws that mandate storage of personal information of natives in the national servers known as data localization. The notable examples are the draft data protection law in India and the Cybersecurity Law in China. Holding back, analysts debate that the localization enhances a nation, making it strong in terms of national security and also facilitates law enforcement, but on the other side, opponents say that localization means higher price tags on infrastructures, break international trade and causes security threats by silos. International agreements like the EUUS Data

Privacy Framework seek to enable cross-border data flows with the high protection of privacy but the conflicts remain.

As an example, the Schrems II court decision of the European Court of Justice declared the EU-U.S. Privacy Shield invalid because of the insufficient surveillance safeguards in the United States (Corrales Compagnucci, 2025). Strike the right balance between national data control and the advantages of global data flow is a challenge yet. The fact that investigating cybercrimes involves cross-national factors tends to make it even more difficult as far as jurisdictional complexities are concerned. Though Mutual Legal Assistance Treaties (MLATs) help cooperation between the countries, they are cumbersome and time-consuming. The Budapest convention enables quicker cooperation among signatories, but this is rather narrow. There are no universal regulations regarding cyber jurisdiction and sovereignty, so the former abusers are free to use states with poor enforcement (Polyzoidou, 2021).

Gaps in Global Cooperation and Need for Harmonization

There is no form of international cybersecurity governance, with different legal and policy frameworks remaining partitioned. No international agreement has been reached on the issue of online application of international law with Russia and China suggest reconciliation of the UN in the form of a new international cyber treaty focusing on digital sovereignty whilst the west seems content with the present framework like the Budapest Convention. Varying national data-protection, surveillance and cybercrime laws leave gaps to criminals and burden leaders of multinational businesses with unnecessary costs to meet compliance. Most of the developing countries do not have comfort features of good law and technical systems hence do not have the ability to engage in international cybersecurity programs. Moreover, not all actors in the sphere of technology fall under international law (especially given the fact that private technology firms are global in nature, for instance they are not directly subject to international law) and voluntary industry programs such as the Paris Call are incoherent. In response to such gaps, scholars suggest that drafting international agreements that would help harmonize cybercrime definitions, evidence, and enforcement are necessary. Model cyber laws have been able to assist countries to harmonise their local legislations with the international best practices. Training, technical aid and capacity building in the developing countries is the key to enhancing their law enforcing and responding abilities. Lastly, there should be good collaboration among all parties which include business, civil society and governments to exchange threat intelligence and in the development of effective standards.

Digital Surveillance, Consent, and Privacy Security Dilemma

Governments often justify surveillance programs in the name of national security, but these initiatives frequently involve the mass collection of data from ordinary citizens, including emails, call logs, browsing histories, and biometric details. Such practices risk infringing on the right to privacy, which is protected by Article 12 of the Universal Declaration of Human Rights (UDHR) and various national constitutions (Vaghri, 2022). To prevent misuse, surveillance must adhere to legal safeguards such as judicial warrants, legislative oversight, and independent supervisory bodies (Gohdes, 2024). Legal standards require that surveillance follow due process, with clear authorization and court supervision. It must also meet the tests of necessity, being used only when strictly required, and proportionality, ensuring the scope of surveillance is not excessive. Courts in the U.S., Europe, and other regions have invalidated mass surveillance and data retention laws that fail to comply with these principles.

Informed Digital Consent

In the online world, there is a practice of sharing personal information with little or no knowledge about what will be done with the data because online privacy policies are usually longwinded and technical. Valid consent should not be implicit, vague and irreversible. The GDPR introduced in the EU has high regulations on consent, that is, strong positive actions, and in India, the Digital Personal Data Protection Act (2023) has also attached importance to transparency and user rights (Kumar et al., 2025). In government-based surveillance though, consent is not secured and it is therefore imperative that the oversight and regulatory checks occur. To secure digital rights, it is necessary to tighten their consent mechanisms, streamline privacy notices, and guarantee the user control over information.

Case Studies

In 2013 in what came to be known as the Snowden revelations, U.S. National Security Agency (NSA) mass surveillance programs such as PRISM and XKeyscore were revealed having been run by the agency. Such leaks changed the world and triggered worldwide discussions of the privacy and ensuing reforms like passing the USA FREEDOM Act (2015), which limited governmental mass gathering of information (Gioe & Hatfield, 2021). The 2021 Pegasus spyware crisis case 1 in 2021, the misuse of powerful surveillance software created by NSO Group to track journalists, activists, and political leaders across the globe became known, raising concerns about the unregulated use of states as spies. The Aadhaar verdict of the Supreme Court in India in 2018 held the biometric identification program constitutional but did not allow its compulsory use when accessing services such as banking and telecommunication, further committing to privacy as a natural right (Sadhya & Sahu, 2024).

Landmark Digital Rights Cases

The Carpenter v. United States (2018), case represented a highly important change in the constitutional law of the United States where the U.S. Supreme Court made a decision that the historical data of cell phone location is supposed to be obtained via warrant because it is sensitive (Mattson, 2022). In India, the Justice K.S. Puttaswamy V., The ruling of Union of India (2017) acknowledged the privacy as a fundamental right under Article 21 of the Constitution, which affected the data protection mechanism of the country (Gautam, 2022). In Europe, there is the case of Digital Rights Ireland v. The judgment of Minister for Communications (2014) declared the EU Data Retention Directive incompatible and disproportionate with the rights to privacy (King, 2022).

Government and Institutional Responses

National strategies securing cyberspace have been formulated by governments to enhance cybersecurity and incident response strategies. In India, the CERT-In, the U.S. Cybersecurity and Infrastructure Security Agency (CISA), and the EU ENISA are critical in organizing national activities as well as protecting crucial infrastructure. The notification of breaching has increasingly become sturdy, with GDPR reporting 72 hours after and India law of 2023 and state acts requiring immediate reporting of breaching information. There have been a rising number of judicial oversights as well, with the courts heavily investigating state surveillance and hackings, such as investigations into the Pegasus spyware scandal in India (Halis Kasap, 2024).

Trends in Judicial Interpretation

Privacy is being viewed as one of the fundamental rights by courts all over the world since digital information is sensitive. The principles of proportionality and necessity are extensively deployed and the courts are resisting sweeping surveillance measures that do not carry sufficient safeguards. Court decisions focus on the autonomy of the user, as a matter of demands of clearly and knowingly agreeing to process of data. Important themes also include transparency and accountability, and governments and corporations must demonstrate that their operations on handling data are needed. Also, the courts are dealing with the new dangers of implementing

AI-based profiling, facial recognition, and spyware, demanding stringent measures and controls (Payton & Claypoole, 2023).

6. RESULTS, RECOMMENDATIONS, CONCLUSIONS, AND SOLUTIONS

Results and Conclusions

The discussion in this chapter indicates that the advancement of digital technologies has posed new legal and ethical issues of cybersecurity with high levels of complexity. To one hand, our growing dependency on cyberspace and use of it as the medium of communication and business has only served to highlight the weaknesses of privacy, data security, and other fundamental freedoms, and to the other hand, challenged the flexibility of our legal systems. A variety of key problems become evident in the course of this study: the possibility of unauthorized tracking and analytical activities, the fact of uninformed digital consent, incompleteness or ageing of particular acts that regulate the data security, the discrepancies in global terms in the management of cyber threats. These issues are not just technical, they have the potential of seriously eroding what are considered to be fundamental values of democracy, civil liberties and the rule of law. Legal systems across the globe have until recently offered mixed reactions to digital threats and in most instances, in an uncoordinated manner. Some jurisdictions (such as the European Union) have devoted much effort to developing a comprehensive system of data protection and cybersecurity, with examples that include the GDPR and joint strategies of response to cyber incidents.

The developing nations, however, are yet to reach a mature cyber legal regime with some countries missing unified policies or current sovereign laws. These decisions on landmark cases (both in the U.S. and the EU, and in India, etc.) have, over time, slowly built up what can be called the law of digital rights. Courts have aided in both confirming the right to privacy as a fundamental right, have required governments and corporations to restrict their surveillance to proportional and justifiable ones, and have demanded transparency and accountability. However, considerable loopholes are left. The issue of laws enforcement is constant- the number of bad actors is high, and they have a tendency to utilize cross-border gaps and areas where the jurisdiction is grey. Although there is an increasing international cooperation, they are still not on the level which would efficiently address the global cyber threats. Moreover, some of the most exposed people (human rights defenders, journalists, minority groups, etc.) are not being properly guarded against cyber harassment or specific cyberattacks, which implies that some narrower intervention is necessary.

Based on these findings, it would be clear that more advanced and effective cybersecurity laws and policies will be required in the future. These legal regimes must be user-driven where the users are given control over their own data and the aim is to protect rights of the individuals. They ought to also have clear things to say on sensitive concerns such as the monitoring scope of the government, patterns of information sharing, and what legal information can be considered as a valid obtainment of digital consent. Broader or inexplicit laws are also susceptible to abuse to violate freedoms (e.g. laws that can be applied in a way to suppress free communication on the Internet or to torment the individual privacy). Thus our laws should be very carefully prepared and justified based on the idea of necessity, proportionality, and due process. What it means in practice is that any restriction of the digital rights needs to be defined in the law in a clear manner, obviously necessary due to a good aim, and be narrowly tailored in a way that does not stretch it out.

Policy Recommendations and Solutions

Following the detailed overview and discussion, the following policy recommendations appear that would help balance cybersecurity demands and safeguarding digital rights:

- Revert to Rights-Based Cybersecurity Guidelines: Cybersecurity plans and national laws must clearly address human rights as one of the main priorities. This will involve integration of legal protection of privacy, freedom of expression, and autonomy of personal data to the legal foundations and policies of cybersecurity. As an illustration, in case of the adoption of cybercrimes or surveillance acts, legislators ought to encompass provisions that safeguard or secure the privacy of confidential communications, as well as ensure some form of control to eliminate the likelihood of misuse. By having a rights-based approach, it also implies that human rights experts should be involved in the development of a cybersecurity framework and proposing a human rights impact assessment of new cyber measures.
- Implement Data Security Laws: Governments should consider implementing and strictly enforcing certain laws that are solely governing how personal data is collected, used and stored. Public and private sectors should be required through these laws to have a robust data security. It would be essential to have definite regulations on encryption of sensitive data, frequent security checks, and timely notification and reaction to disclosure of confidential information. When a data breach occurs there must be not only the duties to notify but also remedies to the individuals who were impacted (credit monitoring or compensation funds) and punishment to the entities that had the means to prevent

the problem but did not because it was not reasonable. Strong enforcement will create the motivation to motivate organizations to regard data protection as an issue of compliance and corporate responsibility.

- Ramp Up Judicial and Regulatory Scrutiny: Good oversight is a key to avoiding an abuse of cybersecurity and surveillance authorities. External regulatory agencies (such as the data protection authorities, or the telecom regulators) should be provided statutory powers to review and audit government and corporate conducts with regard to personal data use and surveillance. These agencies must have the right to measure, demand betterments, and issue punishment for noncompliance. Along the line, the judiciary must also be involved in sanctioning and examining obtrusive actions. As an example, a warrant preceded by the court should be used normally in surveillance laws on communications. Compounding the checks and balances by accretion of check institutions and judiciary review will facilitate the removal of abuses and hold the government agencies and the privately operated companies accountable.
- Promote International Cooperation: The threats seen in cyberattacks are international and solutions must be international as well. States ought to strive to achieve stronger global accords and common lawyering procedures. This would be the entry into frameworks such as the Budapest Convention or the creation of new conventions supporting sharing of evidence and the harmonization of laws concerning computer crime to a worldwide level. It is essential to enhance the time and efficiency of the mutual legal assistance in the events of a cybercrime. Regional or international cooperative cyber security units or cyber intelligence sharing centers could be formed to address problems such as botnets, international-fraud rings and state-sponsored attacks. There should also be international support when it comes to capacity building, enabling the poor nations to develop the required lawful and technological tools to tackle cyber threats thus constituting international security.
- Put heavy accent on Ethics and Transparency in Technology: There should be a heavy focus on ethics of digital governance. Both technology companies and public institutions ought to incorporate such principles as transparency, accountability, and e-trust into their businesses. In practice, it implies greater transparency in how companies manage their data and assesses their decisions based on algorithms, and how governments explain the laws and orders according to which they carry out surveillance or demand the information of the user. Some guidance on the ethical use of emerging technologies (such as AI, big data analytics and IoT devices) can be formulated, either as industry codes of conduct or as tightened regulations that would constrain the design and use of those technologies so that they do not infringe on privacy and pro-

mote discrimination. The establishment of digital ethics culture will restore and uphold the confidence of people in government programs, as well as the technology sector.

To sum it up, the future of cybersecurity will be when both safety of a system and person are maintained and respected. The dynamic of law and policy should be moving along with the changing technology with the democracy principles and the vision of the creation of the safer and inclusive online world. Cybersecurity approaches that embrace human rights considerations promise being more viable and useful since they will have legitimacy and confidence of those they are meant to serve.

7. RECOMMENDATIONS FOR FUTURE RESEARCH

Future research might investigate a variety of valuable research topics to further reinforce the nexus between cybersecurity and digital rights:

- Global Legal Harmonization: The development of global legal harmonization by comparing the legal systems of various jurisdictions in terms of their ability to coordinate their legislation on cybersecurity and data protection would be useful. One area where research could be used is in developing guidelines towards an international cybercrime convention and enhancement of the current conventions so as to deal with jurisdictional issues and cooperation in criminal law enforcement across borders.
- Emerging Technologies and Human Rights: More legal analysis needs to be done as to the human rights implications of emerging technologies (artificial intelligence in cybersecurity, facial recognition surveillance, and quantum computing). This would involve discussing how we can design cyber defense tools based on AI ethically, or how legislation ought to act early on things such as deepfakes and algorithmic bias, and so on, and so forth, making sure that using new technologies will not violate privacy or equality or due process.
- Surveillance Oversight Mechanisms: There should be studies that would examine good models of oversight on government surveillance programs. This could be in form of case studies of the checks and balances in other countries, critiques of transparency reports or providing suggestions on how to enhance the protection of whistleblowers and oversight within intelligence operations. The purpose would be to define the best practices to find balance between state security demands and human rights.

- Online Rights of Vulnerable Groups: Targeted studies on the perpetration of the digital rights of marginalized or vulnerable population are essential. This could be looking at how to better defend human rights defenders and journalists against targeted spyware, preventing online harassment and hate speech against minorities and protecting freedom of expression, or how to secure the rights of children in a highly-digitized world (including cyber bullying, online exploitation, and children data privacy).
- Cyber Laws Impact Assessment: Longitudinal studies of the actual world effects of significant cybersecurity and data protection laws (including the GDPR, the emerging data protection law in India or the California Consumer Privacy Act) can provide valuable answers. These studies would allow quantifying the effect of such laws on security, breaches, or user confidence and whether there have been unintended effects and implementation issues. The results would provide policymakers with the information on which parts of these regulations are effective and which part of them should be adjusted or synchronized on a global scale.

Following the directions described, researchers and practitioners will be able to inform and improve the policies that will control the safe-but-rights-respecting digital future. Future research that cuts across law, technology and human rights will be particularly necessary as new risks and opportunities unfold on cyberspace.

REFERENCES

Amal Chandra, C. (2024). Strengthening India's Cybersecurity and Data Privacy Landscape: A Comprehensive Overview. *The Indian Journal of Public Administration, 70*(3), 466–478. DOI: 10.1177/00195561241271616

Arnell, P., & Faturoti, B. (2023). The prosecution of cybercrime – why transnational and extraterritorial jurisdiction should be resisted. *International Review of Law Computers & Technology, 37*(1), 29–51. DOI: 10.1080/13600869.2022.2061888

Aswathy, S. U., & Tyagi, A. K. (2022). Privacy breaches through cyber vulnerabilities: Critical issues, open challenges, and possible countermeasures for the future. In *Security and Privacy-Preserving Techniques in Wireless Robotics* (pp. 163–210). CRC Press. DOI: 10.1201/9781003156406-14

Ayalew, Y. E. (2022). Untrodden paths towards the right to privacy in the digital era under African human rights law. *International Data Privacy Law, 12*(1), 16–32. DOI: 10.1093/idpl/ipab027

Baram, G. (2024). Cyber diplomacy through official public attribution: Paving the way for global norms. *International Studies Perspectives, 22*(?),(ekae022). DOI: 10.1093/isp/ekae022

Bayer, J. (2022). Procedural rights as safeguard for human rights in platform regulation. *Policy and Internet, 14*(4), 755–771. DOI: 10.1002/poi3.298

Chandra, D. (2025). Examining the Contours and Challenges of National Cybercrime Reporting Portal in Countering Digital Financial Frauds. *Journal of Victimology and Victim Justice, 8*(1), 65–83. DOI: 10.1177/25166069241306546

Corrales Compagnucci, M. (2025). The EU–US Data Privacy Framework: Is the Dragon Eating Its Own Tail? In *International Transfers of Health Data: A Global Perspective* (pp. 17–39). Singapore: Springer Nature. DOI: 10.1007/978-981-97-9983-1_2

Di Nuzzo, V. (2022). Search and seizure of digital evidence: human rights concerns and new safeguards. In *Investigating and Preventing Crime in the Digital Era: New Safeguards, New Rights* (pp. 119–149). Springer International Publishing., DOI: 10.1007/978-3-031-13952-9_6

Gautam, P. (2022). Right to privacy as a fundamental right – extension of Article 21 of the Indian Constitution? *Revista de Drept Constitu ional, 1*(01), 95–98. Retrieved from https://www.ceeol.com/search/article-detail?id=1058906

Gioe, D. V., & Hatfield, J. M. (2021). A damage assessment framework for insider threats to national security information: Edward Snowden and the Cambridge Five in comparative historical perspective. *Cambridge Review of International Affairs, 34*(5), 704–738. DOI: 10.1080/09557571.2020.1853053

Gohdes, A. R. (2024). *Repression in the Digital Age: Surveillance, Censorship, and the Dynamics of State Violence*. Oxford University Press. DOI: 10.1093/oso/9780197743577.001.0001

Halis Kasap, G. (2024). Defending privacy across borders: Public interest litigation in the fight against data exploitation. *Netherlands International Law Review, 71*(3), 427–460. DOI: 10.1007/s40802-024-00273-5

Harkin, D., & Panagiotopoulos, V. (2025). Regulating tools for hacking: Limitations, challenges and possibilities. *Policy and Internet, 17*(2), e70004. DOI: 10.1002/poi3.70004

Helberger, N. (2025). The rise of technology courts, or: How technology companies reinvent adjudication for a digital world. *Computer Law & Security Review, 56*, 106118. DOI: 10.1016/j.clsr.2025.106118

King, M. (2022). Doing the Right Thing: It Is in Our Power to Act and Not to Act. In *Leadership and Business Ethics* (pp. 441–464). Springer Netherlands. DOI: 10.1007/978-94-024-2111-8_26

Kulshrestha, P., Gautam, R., & Singh, A. (Eds.). (2022). *Cyber Crime, Regulation and Security: Contemporary Issues and Challenges*. Libertatem Media Private Limited. DOI: 10.55662/CCRSbook.2022

Kumar, D., Kaur, G., Srivastava, A., Ghosh, A., & Ghosh, S. (2025). The Ethical and Regulatory Challenges of Consumer Privacy in the Digital Era. In *AI Marketing and Ethical Considerations in Consumer Engagement* (pp. 173–194). IGI Global Scientific Publishing., DOI: 10.4018/979-8-3373-3476-9.ch009

Lukings, M., & Lashkari, A. H. (2022). *Understanding Cybersecurity Law and Digital Privacy*. Springer International Publishing. DOI: 10.1007/978-3-030-88704-9

Madnick, B., Huang, K., & Madnick, S. (2024). The evolution of global cybersecurity norms in the digital age: A longitudinal study of the cybersecurity norm development process. *Information Security Journal: A Global Perspective, 33*(3), 204–225. DOI: 10.1080/19393555.2023.2201482

Mattson, L. (2022). *The Carpenter Shift: The Evolution of Fourth Amendment Jurisprudence in the Digital Age*. [White paper/Working paper]. Retrieved from JSTOR: https://www.jstor.org/stable/pdf/community.34031526.pdf

McConomy, B. C., & Leber, D. E. (2022). Cybersecurity in healthcare. In *Clinical Informatics Study Guide: Text and Review* (pp. 241–253). Springer International Publishing., DOI: 10.1007/978-3-030-93765-2_17

McVey, M. (2022). Untangling the authority of external experts in the corporate implementation of the UN Guiding Principles on Business and Human Rights. *Journal of Human Rights, 21*(5), 620–638. DOI: 10.1080/14754835.2022.2105646

Montasari, R. (2024). *Cyberspace, Cyberterrorism and International Security in the Fourth Industrial Revolution: Threats, Assessment and Responses*. Springer Nature. DOI: 10.1007/978-3-031-50454-9

Moynihan, H. (2021). The vital role of international law in the framework for responsible state behaviour in cyberspace. *Journal of Cyber Policy*, *6*(3), 394–410. DOI: 10.1080/23738871.2020.1832550

Mueck, M., & Gaie, C. (2025). Introduction to the European Cybersecurity Act. In *European Digital Regulations* (pp. 229–247). Springer Nature Switzerland., DOI: 10.1007/978-3-031-80809-8_10

Orgeret, K. S., Westlund, O., & Krøvel, R. (Eds.). (2024). *Journalism and Safety: Digital Threats, Professional Fragilities, and Safety Cultures*. Taylor & Francis. DOI: 10.4324/9781003544517

Payton, T., & Claypoole, T. (2023). *Privacy in the Age of Big Data: Recognizing Threats, Defending Your Rights, and Protecting Your Family*. Bloomsbury Publishing PLC. DOI: 10.5771/9781538167830

Polyzoidou, V. (2021). Combatting cybercrime: Thoughts based on the Second Additional Protocol (Draft) to the Budapest Convention on Cybercrime. In *EU Internet Law in the Digital Single Market* (pp. 355–375). Cham: Springer International Publishing. DOI: 10.1007/978-3-030-69583-5_15

Rawaqa, S. (2025). Identifying and regulating human rights defenders (HRDs). *The International Journal of Human Rights, 29*(?), 1–31. DOI: 10.1080/13642987.2025.2517571

Romaniuk, S. N., & Hattiangady, P. (2023). Cybercrime, national security, and internet governance. In *The Handbook of Homeland Security* (pp. 211–230). CRC Press. DOI: 10.4324/9781315144511

Sadhya, D., & Sahu, T. (2024). A critical survey of the security and privacy aspects of the Aadhaar framework. *Computers & Security*, *140*, 103782. DOI: 10.1016/j.cose.2024.103782

Saleous, H., Ismail, M., AlDaajeh, S. H., Madathil, N., Alrabaee, S., Choo, K. K. R., & Al-Qirim, N. (2023). COVID-19 pandemic and the cyberthreat landscape: Research challenges and opportunities. *Digital Communications and Networks*, *9*(1), 211–222. DOI: 10.1016/j.dcan.2022.06.005 PMID: 35765301

Salomon, J. M. (2022, May). Public-private partnerships and collective cyber defence. In *2022 14th International Conference on Cyber Conflict: Keep Moving! (CyCon)* (Vol. 700, pp. 45–63). IEEE. DOI: 10.23919/CyCon55549.2022.9810912

Schmitt, M. (2023). Securing the digital world: Protecting smart infrastructures and digital industries with artificial intelligence (AI)-enabled malware and intrusion detection. *Journal of Industrial Information Integration*, *36*, 100520. DOI: 10.1016/j.jii.2023.100520

Schutze, B. (2022). Data protection and data security in the EU: the European General Data Protection Regulation. In *Nursing Informatics: A Health Informatics, Interprofessional and Global Perspective* (pp. 437–451). Springer International Publishing., DOI: 10.1007/978-3-030-91237-6_29

Sivakumar, C. L. V., Mone, V., & Abdumukhtor, R. (2024). Addressing privacy concerns with wearable health monitoring technology. *Wiley Interdisciplinary Reviews. Data Mining and Knowledge Discovery*, *14*(3), e1535. DOI: 10.1002/widm.1535

Stepenko, V., Dreval, L., Chernov, S., & Shestak, V. (2022). EU personal data protection standards and regulatory framework. *Journal of Applied Security Research*, *17*(2), 190–207. DOI: 10.1080/19361610.2020.1868928

Tabaghdehi, S. A. H. (2024). Ethical governance of digital footprint data: a journey towards a responsible society. In *Business Strategies and Ethical Challenges in the Digital Ecosystem* (pp. 369–379). Emerald Publishing Limited., DOI: 10.1108/978-1-80455-069-420241017

Toledano, S. A. (2024). *Critical Infrastructure Security: Cybersecurity Lessons Learned from Real-World Breaches*. Packt Publishing Ltd.

Vaghri, Z. (2022, January). Article 16: The Right to Protection of Privacy. In *Monitoring State Compliance with the UN Convention on the Rights of the Child: An Analysis of Attributes* (Vol. 25, p. 93). Springer Nature. DOI: 10.1007/978-3-030-84647-3

Ventura, D. (2022). Democracy through the lens of digital surveillance: An assessment of the legitimacy of general principles of law. In *Democracy and Sovereignty* (pp. 291–321). Brill Nijhoff., DOI: 10.1163/9789004508712_013

Chapter 3

Human Factors:
Organizational Behavioral Perspectives in Healthcare Cybersecurity for Applied Behavior Analysis (ABA) Therapists

Adina Lundy
https://orcid.org/0000-0001-7564-2110
University of Rhode Island, USA

Quatavia McLester
https://orcid.org/0000-0003-1596-0517
Columbus State University, USA

Darrell Norman Burrell
https://orcid.org/0000-0002-4675-9544
Marymount University, USA

Calvin Nobles
https://orcid.org/0000-0003-4002-1108
University of Maryland Global Campus, USA

Sharon Burton
https://orcid.org/0000-0003-1653-9783
Embry-Riddle Aeronautical University, USA

Amina I. Ayodeji-Ogundiran
https://orcid.org/0009-0004-6020-5742
Bowie State University, USA

Kim L. Brown-Jackson
https://orcid.org/0000-0001-9231-2076
Capitol Technology University, USA

Terrence D. Duncan
https://orcid.org/0000-0002-5456-6013
Liberty University, USA

Marlena Daryousef
https://orcid.org/0000-0001-9513-501X
Colorado Technical University, USA

Jorja Wright Stokes
https://orcid.org/0000-0002-7028-995X
University of Charleston, USA

Won Kang Song
https://orcid.org/0009-0004-8644-4987
Capitol Technology University, USA

DOI: 10.4018/979-8-3373-4967-1.ch003

ABSTRACT

This perspective paper explores cybersecurity and information security as critical dimensions of healthcare administration and organizational behavior within Applied Behavior Analysis (ABA) telehealth organizations. As digital platforms become central to clinical delivery, ABA therapists, highly skilled in behavioral science but often under-trained in cybersecurity, face increasing exposure to data breaches and compliance risks. Most security incidents in healthcare stem from preventable human factors such as cognitive overload, automation complacency, and inconsistent adherence to security protocols. Integrating behavioral principles with administrative governance can transform cybersecurity from a technical afterthought into a core element of professional and organizational competence. Embedding cybersecurity within organizational culture ensures sustainable protection of client data while advancing ethical, secure, and high-performing ABA telehealth systems.

INTRODUCTION

Applied Behavior Analysis (ABA) therapy is a scientifically grounded discipline that applies the principles of behavioral psychology to understand and improve socially significant behaviors through systematic observation, measurement, and reinforcement (Zoder-Martell et al., 2020; Cavalari et al., 2015; Haymes et al., 2015). As a leading evidence-based practice, ABA interventions are widely recognized as the gold standard for supporting individuals with autism spectrum disorder (ASD), intellectual disabilities, and other developmental or behavioral challenges (Zoder-Martell et al., 2020; Cavalari et al., 2015; Haymes et al., 2015). Through targeted intervention strategies, ABA therapists help clients acquire essential communication, social, and adaptive life skills that enhance long-term independence and family well-being. Beyond autism intervention, ABA principles are increasingly applied to education, behavioral health, and organizational performance management, highlighting the discipline's relevance across multiple domains of human and organizational functioning.

The rapid expansion of telehealth has transformed the delivery and administration of ABA services, expanding access to rural and underserved populations while improving flexibility and continuity of care (Zoder-Martell et al., 2020; Cavalari et al., 2015; Haymes et al., 2015). From a healthcare administration perspective, telehealth integration enables more efficient scheduling, cross-disciplinary coordination, and digital documentation. However, it also requires organizations to manage complex information systems and data-governance responsibilities traditionally handled by hospital-level IT departments. As ABA organizations, many of them small or mid-sized, adopt electronic health records (EHRs), cloud-based data systems, and mobile devices for clinical operations, their cybersecurity exposure increases substantially. Sensitive client data, including behavioral assessments, session recordings, and personally identifiable information (PII), has become a lucrative target for cybercriminals. Even a minor lapse, such as accessing client data through unsecured Wi-Fi or storing notes on a personal laptop, can create systemic vulnerabilities that jeopardize both client confidentiality and organizational compliance.

In today's digitized healthcare ecosystem, cybersecurity has evolved from a technical specialization into a fundamental component of healthcare administration, ethical governance, and organizational culture. The healthcare sector's increasing reliance on automation, telecommunication, and interconnected systems has yielded remarkable efficiencies but also new forms of organizational risk. Automation enhances clinical documentation, data accuracy, and administrative efficiency; yet, without sufficient human oversight, it can also foster cognitive complacency, a behavioral condition where excessive trust in automated systems replaces critical thinking and vigilance (Nobles & Burrell, 2024). Within ABA telehealth organizations, this complacency may manifest as habitual security oversights, such as therapists saving data on personal devices, neglecting logout protocols after virtual sessions, or assuming that HIPAA-compliant software automatically guarantees full compliance.

These risks are compounded by the human factors that account for many cybersecurity breaches across healthcare. Research consistently demonstrates that over 70 percent of security incidents result not from system flaws but from preventable human errors, weak passwords, phishing susceptibility, or neglected updates (Yeo et al., 2022; Jones & Burrell, 2025; Burrell, 2024; Burrell et al., 2021; Burrell et al., 2022; Wright, 2023). For telehealth-based ABA practitioners, additional contextual pressures, home-office distractions, multitasking, and blurred boundaries between professional and personal technology use, further heighten these vulnerabilities (Nobles, 2022).

From an organizational behavior standpoint, cybersecurity failures often reflect deficits in culture and leadership rather than technical infrastructure. When clinicians perceive cybersecurity as an administrative burden rather than an ethical responsibility, compliance becomes reactive and inconsistent. In contrast, healthcare organizations that frame information security as part of their organizational mission and culture of care demonstrate higher adherence to protocols and fewer incidents of negligence. Leadership engagement is central to this process: clinical directors and administrators who model secure telehealth practices, communicate the rationale behind security measures, and foster psychological safety in error reporting create a learning-oriented climate that reduces risk. Conversely, punitive or siloed administrative approaches discourage reporting and inhibit the open communication essential to cybersecurity resilience (Edmondson, 2018).

The ethical and administrative implications of cybersecurity failures in ABA organizations are profound. A single data breach can compromise client privacy, erode trust with families, and expose organizations to violations under the Health Insurance Portability and Accountability Act (HIPAA), leading to legal penalties, reputational damage, and therapeutic disruption (Jones & Burrell, 2025; Burrell, 2024; Burrell et al., 2021; Burrell et al., 2022; Wright, 2023). Beyond compliance, insecure practices undermine the fundamental ethical precept of nonmaleficence, to "do no harm," extending professional responsibility from clinical interactions to digital stewardship.

Consequently, cybersecurity within ABA telehealth must be understood as an extension of professional and organizational conduct, not merely an IT function. Healthcare administrators and ABA leaders play a crucial role in shaping environments where secure digital behavior is reinforced, normalized, and embedded within the culture of care. Just as ABA therapists use reinforcement and modeling to strengthen adaptive behaviors in clients, organizations can apply the same behavioral principles, feedback, recognition, and contingency management, to sustain secure practices among staff. Cultivating cybersecurity as an organizational competency requires continuous learning, leadership modeling, and systemic reinforcement. In this perspective, the integrity of ABA practice in telehealth depends on aligning clinical excellence with information-security maturity, ensuring that ethical care and data protection remain inseparable pillars of modern healthcare administration.

PROBLEM STATEMENT

While comprehensive frameworks such as the Health Industry Cybersecurity Practices (HICP) and the National Institute of Standards and Technology (NIST) Cybersecurity Framework provide detailed technical and procedural guidance, small and medium-sized Applied Behavior Analysis (ABA) organizations often lack the administrative capacity, trained personnel, and financial resources to implement these frameworks effectively. From a healthcare administration perspective, cybersecurity compliance represents not only a technological challenge but also an organizational governance issue that requires leadership engagement, policy enforcement, and the alignment of clinical and administrative processes. Research indicates that up to 73 percent of healthcare breaches result from human error or negligence rather than from system-level failures (Yeo et al., 2022).

Within ABA telehealth settings, the complexity of the digital ecosystem amplifies these vulnerabilities. Clinicians often rely on multiple devices, tablets for virtual sessions, smartphones for caregiver communication, and laptops for documentation or billing, all of which may connect through unsecured personal or public networks.

Without a clearly defined cybersecurity governance structure, each endpoint, user, and process becomes a potential risk vector (Jones & Burrell, 2025; Burrell, 2024; Burrell et al., 2021; Burrell et al., 2022; Wright, 2023). Administrative oversight is frequently decentralized, leaving responsibility for secure practices to individual clinicians who may lack the technical knowledge or behavioral conditioning to maintain consistent security hygiene.

Organizational culture and behavior significantly influence how cybersecurity is enacted within these small healthcare systems. In many ABA practices, cybersecurity is perceived as a secondary administrative burden or an external IT concern unrelated to the therapeutic mission. When this perception prevails, clinicians are less likely to comply with best practices or to view data protection as a shared organizational responsibility. Moreover, punitive administrative responses, such as reprimanding therapists for accidental misdirection of client information, can erode psychological safety and discourage reporting of near misses (Edmondson, 2018). This suppression of open communication undermines organizational learning and prevents the identification of systemic issues.

Thus, the problem extends beyond technological inadequacy to include organizational culture, leadership behavior, and administrative modeling. ABA telehealth organizations require more than secure infrastructure, they need a leadership-driven culture that embeds cybersecurity into daily workflows, reinforces positive behavior through recognition and training, and fosters psychological safety that encourages transparency and collective accountability. The absence of such behavioral and administrative alignment leaves these organizations exposed not only to data breaches but also to reputational, ethical, and legal consequences.

PURPOSE OF THE INQUIRY

The purpose of this perspective paper is to explore how human factors, organizational culture, and behavioral training strategies influence cybersecurity resilience in Applied Behavior Analysis (ABA) telehealth organizations. This inquiry positions cybersecurity as both a clinical ethics issue and an administrative responsibility requiring leadership engagement, staff empowerment, and system-level behavioral reinforcement. As a perspective-style academic paper, this study synthesizes insights from peer-reviewed research and professional practice literature to bridge theory and applied practice. Unlike empirical research, it does not generate new data but instead integrates concepts from behavioral science, cybersecurity governance, and healthcare management to construct a conceptual model that can guide future empirical inquiry and administrative practice. Such perspective papers play an essential role in academic discourse by translating interdisciplinary theory into actionable frameworks that inform leadership, policy development, and professional education.

Sustainable cybersecurity in ABA telehealth practice requires more than technical compliance; it demands a cultural transformation in which secure behavior is embedded within clinical professionalism and administrative governance. This involves cultivating shared ethical values, consistent administrative modeling, and observable secure practices among therapists, supervisors, and organizational leadership. For example, a therapist conducting a virtual session must manage competing priorities, maintaining therapeutic engagement, ensuring confidentiality, and preventing unauthorized observation. These competing demands illustrate the need for a sociotechnical and behavioral model in which cybersecurity practices, such as verifying client identity, using encrypted telehealth platforms, and maintaining screen privacy, are supported and reinforced by leadership and organizational systems. Ultimately, the paper's purpose is to frame cybersecurity in ABA organizations as a core component of healthcare administration and professional culture, emphasizing the interconnectedness of human behavior, leadership, and system design in sustaining ethical, secure, and efficient digital care delivery.

SIGNIFICANCE OF THE INQUIRY

The integration of applied behavioral science, healthcare administration, and cybersecurity governance offers a transformative opportunity to enhance data protection and reduce human error across healthcare organizations. ABA therapists are uniquely positioned to contribute to this interdisciplinary effort because they specialize in modifying human behavior through reinforcement, feedback, and environmental structuring, mechanisms that are equally effective in shaping secure digital conduct within organizational settings. Translating these clinical competencies into administrative strategies can strengthen an organization's overall cybersecurity posture and resilience (Nifakos et al., 2021; Burrell, 2024; Wright, 2023; Jones & Burrell, 2025).

From an organizational behavioral perspective, the creation of a cybersecurity-conscious culture depends on how leadership communicates values, models secure behavior, and reinforces positive performance. Administrative leaders in ABA organizations, clinical directors, operations managers, and compliance officers, serve as the primary agents of culture formation. When these leaders consistently emphasize cybersecurity during supervision, staff meetings, and performance evaluations, they embed secure behavior into the organizational identity. Reinforcement-based strategies used in ABA practice, such as immediate feedback and recognition of compliance successes, can be repurposed for cybersecurity training. For instance, acknowledging therapists who correctly identify phishing attempts or who model secure telehealth behavior in staff meetings helps normalize cybersecurity as a component of professional excellence.

Furthermore, the ethical and regulatory frameworks guiding ABA practice—the Behavior Analyst Certification Board (BACB) Ethics Code and the Health Insurance Portability and Accountability Act (HIPAA), align closely with the core principles of cybersecurity: confidentiality, integrity, and availability. Protecting client data, therefore, transcends compliance; it represents an ethical expression of the therapeutic commitment to "do no harm." By merging behavioral science, ethical governance, and healthcare administration, ABA organizations can operationalize data protection as both a cultural value and an administrative priority. In sum, this inquiry underscores the importance of integrating behavioral principles with organizational leadership and administrative systems to cultivate a culture of cybersecurity competence. When ABA organizations align clinical expertise, administrative leadership, and behavioral reinforcement within their cybersecurity strategies, they not only comply with technical standards but also advance the ethical, cultural, and organizational integrity of healthcare delivery in the digital age.

LITERATURE CONTEXT AND THEORETICAL FRAMEWORK

Cybersecurity in healthcare is best understood as a socio-technical phenomenon shaped by human behavior, organizational learning, and technological infrastructure. The HICP guidelines developed by the U.S. Department of Health and Human Services emphasize "cyber hygiene" as a universal precaution comparable to clinical hygiene, a set of habits practiced by all staff to prevent systemic vulnerabilities (HHS, 2022). Similarly, the NIST Cybersecurity Framework advocates for leadership engagement, risk assessment, and continuous improvement as integral to security maturity.

Organizational learning theory (Argyris & Schön, 1996) explains that safety emerges from reflection, feedback, and adaptation. In telehealth ABA organizations, this means integrating security debriefs into supervision and staff meetings. Discussing small incidents, such as an unencrypted file accidentally sent via email, helps identify systemic issues and prevents recurrence. The Job Demands–Resources (JD–R) model (Bakker & Demerouti, 2017) further illustrates that excessive workload without supportive resources increases error rates. Therapists balancing multiple clients and administrative tasks may experience "security fatigue," leading to shortcuts such as storing client data locally rather than uploading it to a secure cloud system. Providing sufficient resources, streamlined tools, and management support mitigates this fatigue.

Another relevant concept is "trust in automation complacency," a cognitive bias in which individuals over-rely on automated systems such as spam filters or antivirus software. In telehealth ABA settings, therapists may assume that the video-conferencing platform is automatically HIPAA-compliant and fail to check updates or permissions. Calibrated trust, maintaining awareness while leveraging automation, requires explicit training, role-based accountability, and ongoing human oversight (Lee & See, 2004).

Finally, psychological safety, the shared belief that it is safe to speak up about mistakes, plays a crucial role in cybersecurity governance (Edmondson, 2018). Telehealth therapists must feel comfortable reporting incidents such as a misdirected email or unauthorized screen recording without fear of reprisal. Organizations that cultivate psychological safety foster transparency, timely reporting, and organizational learning, thereby strengthening cybersecurity resilience.

HUMAN FACTORS AND ORGANIZATIONAL DYNAMICS IN TELEHEALTH ABA CYBERSECURITY

In telehealth ABA practice, human behavior directly influences cybersecurity outcomes. Therapists frequently conduct sessions from home environments where family members, shared networks, and personal devices increase exposure risks. A therapist might, for instance, use a household laptop for both personal and professional activities. If that device lacks encryption or up-to-date antivirus protection, client data may be compromised by malware or accidental file sharing.

Leadership behavior is the antecedent of secure practice. When clinical directors model cybersecurity vigilance by conducting telehealth sessions in private, using secure connections, and emphasizing confidentiality during team meetings, they establish clear expectations for staff. Conversely, when leaders neglect such practices, it signals that security is optional, promoting complacency. As HHS guidance emphasizes, leadership engagement and resource allocation are essential for developing resilient cybersecurity programs (HHS, 2022).

Behavior-based training is also vital. Telehealth organizations can apply principles of Applied Behavior Analysis, reinforcement, shaping, and immediate feedback to cybersecurity learning. For example, monthly simulated phishing exercises teach staff to recognize deceptive emails masquerading as updates to the telehealth platform. Immediate feedback following each simulation, thanking those who report and coaching those who err, creates a feedback loop that shapes secure digital habits over time (CISA, 2020).

Telehealth therapists also face unique cognitive demands: managing child behavior on screen, monitoring parental engagement, and ensuring technical stability.

Under stress and time pressure, cognitive load can cause lapses such as leaving a session window open after ending a meeting. Regular micro-trainings integrated into supervision sessions can counteract this effect by reinforcing small, repeatable security behaviors, logging out, clearing session notes, and encrypting reports.

A supportive organizational culture complements individual training. Research on high-reliability organizations shows that transparent, learning-oriented cultures outperform punitive ones in safety outcomes (Weick & Sutcliffe, 2015). In a telehealth ABA context, open reporting of security concerns, such as a glitch in teleconferencing software, enables quick remediation and system improvements. Conversely, fear of punishment suppresses this feedback, allowing minor errors to evolve into major breaches.

THE THEORY OF PLANNED BEHAVIOR (TPB)

The Theory of Planned Behavior (TPB) provides an essential framework for understanding why highly trained Applied Behavior Analysis (ABA) therapists, experts in behavioral modification, may nonetheless struggle to enact consistent cybersecurity behaviors in digital practice. TPB posits that human behavior arises from the interaction of attitudes, subjective norms, and perceived behavioral control, which together shape an individual's intentions and actions (Ajzen, 1991, 2020; Bosnjak et al., 2020; Sussman & Gifford, 2019). For ABA therapists working within telehealth and data-driven environments, these factors profoundly influence whether they safeguard client information or inadvertently expose vulnerabilities.

ABA clinicians are extensively trained in data collection, ethical practice, and treatment fidelity, but rarely receive formal education in information security principles. Consequently, attitudes toward cybersecurity may range from cautious curiosity to mild resistance. Many therapists view encryption protocols, multifactor authentication, or password management as administrative hurdles that detract from client-focused care. For example, a telehealth therapist juggling multiple virtual sessions may reuse weak passwords or store progress notes on a personal laptop to save time. According to TPB, such attitudes diminish behavioral intention even when clinicians cognitively recognize the importance of security.

Subjective norms within ABA organizations also play a pivotal role. When leadership emphasizes compliance metrics, session completion, billing accuracy, and client progress but neglects digital-safety modeling, clinicians infer that security is peripheral. Conversely, when supervisors routinely discuss cybersecurity during team meetings, report near misses transparently, and praise therapists who demonstrate secure practices (e.g., verifying telehealth identities or encrypting shared documents), secure behavior becomes socially reinforced. This dynamic aligns with Nobles's

(2022) observation that automation failure in healthcare often stems from cultural rather than technical breakdowns, negative social norms, or the absence of visible role models that suppress secure practice even amid robust technical infrastructure.

Perceived behavioral control further shapes cybersecurity conduct (Nobles, 2018; Nobles, 2022). Therapists often perceive data-protection measures as beyond their expertise, assuming that the organization's IT department is responsible for ensuring compliance. Without adequate cybersecurity literacy, clinicians may lack the confidence to evaluate software permissions, identify phishing attempts, or implement HIPAA-compliant telehealth settings. A targeted training intervention, a brief, behavior-analytic workshop using shaping and reinforcement to teach password hygiene and phishing recognition, can significantly improve perceived control and reduce risky behavior. Showing a commitment to employee engagement demonstrates TPB's assertion that when individuals feel competent and supported, they are more likely to engage in protective digital practices (Ajzen, 2020; Bosnjak et al., 2020).

In ABA telehealth contexts, TPB reveals a paradox: therapists possess an advanced understanding of behavior modification, yet underapply these same principles to their own digital conduct. Bridging this gap requires reframing cybersecurity not as a technical task but as an ethical extension of client confidentiality and professional responsibility.

THE ICEBERG MODEL OF ORGANIZATIONAL CULTURE

The Iceberg Model of Organizational Culture illuminates why cybersecurity training and compliance efforts in ABA organizations often fail to yield durable behavior change. The model suggests that most cultural elements, values, beliefs, and assumptions lie beneath the visible surface of policies and procedures (Biewendt et al., 2021; Haider, 2009; Mahringer et al., 2025; Sasu, 2016). In many ABA practices, visible artifacts include HIPAA compliance binders, telehealth consent forms, and periodic data-security reminders. Nevertheless, beneath these visible layers, implicit beliefs persist: that "clinical work takes priority over technology" or that "security is the IT team's responsibility."

When leadership addresses only surface-level compliance, mandating password updates or issuing policy memos, without reshaping the underlying culture, cybersecurity initiatives often collapse under routine pressure. For example, one mid-sized ABA agency introduced encrypted data-sharing software for home-based therapists. Despite technical upgrades, staff continued emailing session notes through unsecured accounts because they perceived the new system as burdensome and unaligned with organizational priorities. Only after leadership reframed cybersecurity as a collective clinical ethic, integral to protecting clients' dignity, did compliance improve.

Nobles (2018, 2022) observed that automation and security initiatives falter when organizations attempt to modify only the visible layer while neglecting the deeper cultural substrata. In ABA telehealth settings, this might manifest as clinicians perceiving electronic-supervision software as punitive oversight rather than a collaborative safeguard. When organizations explicitly connect technology to invisible values, collaboration, ethical accountability, and client safety, the technology becomes a trusted partner rather than a source of anxiety.

Thus, the Iceberg Model demonstrates that meaningful cybersecurity transformation in ABA practices requires harmonizing the visible artifacts of security (encryption systems, checklists, audits) with invisible drivers, values that define how clinicians perceive control, accountability, and ethical care. For highly trained therapists who already operate under strict behavioral ethics, aligning cybersecurity with professional identity is key to achieving sustainable trust and compliance.

DENISON'S ORGANIZATIONAL CULTURE MODEL

Denison's Organizational Culture Model offers a pragmatic structure for linking cultural traits, involvement, consistency, adaptability, and mission to cybersecurity performance in ABA organizations (Denison & Spreitzer, 1991; Denison, 1990; Denison et al., 2014). It illustrates how the same cultural mechanisms that sustain effective clinical operations can also enhance information-security maturity.

Involvement encourages participatory design and shared ownership. In many ABA practices, clinicians have minimal input into technology selection, leading to resentment or avoidance. When leadership includes therapists in decisions about electronic data-collection tools, telehealth platforms, and record-keeping systems, buy-in increases and misuse declines. For example, an ABA agency that convened a clinician-led "security advisory panel" to evaluate telehealth platforms saw higher adherence to encryption protocols and lower rates of accidental data exposure.

Consistency promotes alignment between stated policies and actual practice. ABA clinicians operate across varied environments, such as home, clinic, and telehealth, often blending personal and organizational technology. Inconsistent security expectations (e.g., different password rules for supervisors and technicians) create confusion and noncompliance. Establishing uniform, clear cybersecurity policies, such as standardized VPN use and data-retention intervals, supports predictable, secure behavior across all roles (Jones & Burrell, 2025; Burrell, 2024; Burrell et al, 2021; Burrell et al, 2022; Wright, 2023).

Adaptability reflects an organization's capacity to learn from security incidents. After a minor breach, one ABA telehealth provider conducted a "cyber incident debrief," inviting clinicians to analyze antecedents, behaviors, and consequences, an ABA-style functional analysis of security failure. This participatory reflection transformed the event into a learning opportunity, reinforcing proactive reporting and environmental redesign.

Mission anchors cybersecurity within the ethical commitment to client welfare. ABA's guiding principles, beneficence, confidentiality, and professional integrity, parallel cybersecurity's aims of protecting data and privacy. When leaders explicitly link data security to client safety, therapists perceive compliance not as bureaucratic but as central to therapeutic ethics. Denison's framework, therefore, translates the abstract values of clinical professionalism into concrete, secure behaviors.

TECHNOLOGICAL DETERMINISM

Technological determinism, the belief that technology itself drives progress, poses distinct risks in ABA telehealth organizations (Nobles, 2015; Burrell et al., 2018; Burton et al., 2023). This perspective leads clinicians and administrators to assume that purchasing a "HIPAA-compliant" telehealth platform automatically guarantees data protection. Such overconfidence fosters automation bias, in which users over-trust digital systems and disengage from critical oversight (Lee & See, 2004; Robinson, 2023).

For instance, a therapist using automated electronic-signature software might believe client consent forms are securely archived, neglecting to verify encryption settings or file permissions. Similarly, when organizations delegate all data security responsibility to their EHR vendor, they overlook human factors, such as device misuse or unmonitored screen recordings, that often precipitate breaches. Deterministic thinking obscures the relational dimension of cybersecurity, where technology's safety depends on ongoing human vigilance and contextual judgment (Jones & Burrell, 2025; Burrell, 2024; Burrell et al, 2021; Burrell et al, 2022; Wright, 2023).

Human-factors research argues for trust calibration, a balanced relationship in which a technology user trusts technology's capabilities while remaining alert to its limitations (Nobles, 2022; Robinson, 2023). ABA telehealth teams can operationalize this by pairing technological safeguards with human checkpoints. For example, after an automated session recording upload, the supervising clinician verifies the encryption status before final approval. This simple behavioral contingency reinforces active engagement and ethical accountability.

Technological determinism also risks eroding clinicians' professional confidence. When systems are portrayed as infallible, therapists may feel their judgment is secondary to algorithmic outputs, reducing perceived behavioral control. Counteracting this requires transparent communication about system design, error rates, and human oversight responsibilities. By teaching therapists to view technology as a collaborative aid rather than a substitute for professional judgment, organizations preserve autonomy while enhancing vigilance. Rejecting technological determinism allows ABA practices to embrace a socio-technical balance: technology supports, but does not replace, human ethics, reflection, and responsibility.

RECOMMENDATIONS AND BEST PRACTICES

1. Cultivate Leadership-Driven Cybersecurity Culture

Leadership should integrate cybersecurity into the fabric of organizational ethics. Directors and supervisors can model proper telehealth practices, using secure connections, verifying client identities, and ensuring privacy during sessions. Recognizing therapists who demonstrate consistent security compliance fosters social learning and reinforces desired behavior (Bandura, 1986).

2. Apply Behavioral Principles to Security Training

Cybersecurity education should mirror the behavioral methods ABA therapists use with clients. Scenario-based phishing simulations, role-play exercises, and immediate feedback transform abstract rules into observable behaviors. For instance, after a simulated attack, a brief coaching conversation can help therapists analyze the antecedent and consequence of their actions, promoting active learning.

3. Foster Psychological Safety in Reporting

Therapists must feel empowered to disclose near misses without fear. Establishing non-punitive reporting systems and regular debriefings encourages openness. A virtual “security huddle” can be incorporated into weekly supervision, where staff anonymously share lessons learned from potential incidents. This environment promotes accountability and mutual support.

4. Align Policies with Ethical and Regulatory Standards

Cybersecurity policies should be clearly tied to BACB ethical guidelines and HIPAA requirements. Each telehealth clinician should receive a concise “data-security checklist” before initiating sessions, verifying encrypted connections, ensuring recordings are securely stored, and restricting access to digital notes. Policies written in plain language ensure comprehension across all staff levels.

5. Promote Continuous Learning and System Feedback

Cybersecurity must evolve alongside technology. Regular audits, after-action reviews, and system update briefings reinforce continuous improvement. For example, after a software update, leadership can host a brief webinar to highlight new security features and common errors. Integrating feedback loops ensure cybersecurity remains dynamic, adaptive, and behaviorally informed.

BURRELL/NOBLES TRUST IN AUTOMATION COMPLACENCY (TAC) MODEL

Overview

The Trust in Automation Complacency (TAC) Model explains how human factors, cognitive load, psychological safety, organizational culture, and feedback mechanisms interact to shape trust and mitigate complacency in automated systems and potential cybersecurity lapses. It conceptualizes trust not as a fixed psychological state but as a dynamic human process that evolves through perception, experience, and context. The model emphasizes that sustainable trust arises when human–machine relationships are grounded in transparency, critical engagement, and shared responsibility rather than blind reliance or defensive skepticism.

Step 1: Perceptual Framing and Cognitive Orientation

Trust formation begins with the human perception of automation, how individuals interpret system intent, reliability, information security protocols, and purpose. If automation is viewed as a surveillance or control mechanism, users experience cognitive dissonance and distrust; when seen as a supportive cognitive aid, trust becomes possible. Human factors such as mental workload, attention, and prior experience shape these perceptions. Training and communication should therefore frame automation as a cognitive partner, a tool designed to extend human judgment rather than constrain it.

Step 2: Psychological Safety and Emotional Regulation

The second stage centers on psychological safety, the emotional condition enabling individuals to question, report, and interact openly with automation without fear of reprisal. Psychological safety allows for the expression of uncertainty and the recognition of errors, both of which are essential to preventing complacency.

Leaders play a pivotal human-factor role here by establishing emotional trust climates, modeling transparency, and reframing human overrides or interventions not as failure, but as responsible vigilance.

Step 3: Cognitive Engagement and Active Trust Calibration

At this stage, users move from passive acceptance to active trust calibration, continuously evaluating when to rely on automation and when to intervene. This process engages higher-order cognitive functions such as judgment, situation awareness, and risk assessment. Structured exercises (e.g., scenario-based training or simulated failures) help users experience both automation's capabilities and limitations, reinforcing the balance between over-trust and under-trust. Trust calibration is therefore a metacognitive process, sustained through feedback, reflection, and adaptive learning.

Step 4: Human–System Feedback and Learning Integration

Trust stability depends on bi-directional feedback loops between humans and systems. Human factors engineering emphasizes that users must have intuitive channels to report anomalies, inconsistencies, or contextual mismatches. Simultaneously, automation should provide interpretable explanations for its outputs. This reciprocal learning dynamic, in which the system adapts to human input and humans adjust their expectations based on system transparency, creates a resilient trust ecosystem that prevents vigilance decay and automation bias.

Step 5: Organizational and Ethical Embedding

Human factors extend beyond individual cognition to the broader organizational and ethical environment that governs the use of automation. Policies and governance structures must reinforce accountability, transparency, and inclusivity in decision-making. Cross-disciplinary committees and ethical oversight processes ensure that human perspectives remain central in automation governance. At this level, ethical reflection and participatory design institutionalize trust as a shared moral and operational responsibility, reducing the likelihood of silent compliance or moral deskilling.

Step 6: Adaptive Resilience and Complacency Prevention

The final stage represents adaptive trust maturity, where humans and automation operate in a state of balanced reciprocity. Users maintain confidence in the system's functionality while remaining cognitively vigilant and emotionally engaged. Organizational culture reinforces this equilibrium through continuous learning, scenario testing, and transparent communication about the limits of automation. Complacency is prevented not through tighter control but through sustained human adaptability, empathy, and critical inquiry, ensuring that automation remains a dynamic partner in complex decision-making rather than a passive authority.

Summary

The Trust in Automation Complacency (TAC) Model situates trust as a human-centered, adaptive process shaped by psychological safety, cognitive engagement, feedback integration, and ethical governance. By addressing both the cognitive (thinking and decision-making) and affective (emotional and cultural) dimensions of automation interaction, the model offers a comprehensive human-factors framework for cultivating appropriate trust, cybersecurity awareness, and preventing complacency. It underscores that automation achieves its fullest potential only when humans are empowered to think critically, question constructively, and participate continuously in the evolution of the systems they use.

CLINICAL IMPLICATIONS

The integration of cybersecurity into telehealth-based Applied Behavior Analysis (ABA) practice transforms data protection from a purely administrative duty into a clinical competency that directly impacts client welfare. Therapists' digital behaviors, such as securely transmitting data, verifying telehealth identities, and maintaining encrypted records, become expressions of ethical and clinical responsibility. Embedding cybersecurity training within clinical supervision ensures that secure practices are reinforced through feedback, modeling, and reinforcement, consistent with ABA principles. By conceptualizing cybersecurity as a form of professional behavior shaping, clinicians learn to identify vulnerabilities, respond to near misses, and cultivate habits that protect client confidentiality. Psychological safety is essential: when clinicians can report digital errors without fear of reprisal, organizations foster transparency and continuous learning, thereby preventing normalization of risky practices. Ultimately, clinical cybersecurity competency protects not only client data but also therapeutic integrity, affirming that ethical care extends into the digital domain.

ORGANIZATIONAL IMPLICATIONS

At the organizational level, cybersecurity represents a socio-technical challenge requiring leadership commitment, cultural alignment, and system-level learning. Leaders must model secure behavior, allocate time and resources for training, and create structures, such as regular debriefs and "security huddles," that integrate cybersecurity into organizational routines. Denison's and the Iceberg Models highlight that sustainable cybersecurity culture emerges when visible artifacts, such as policies and audits, align with underlying values of ethical responsibility and collaboration. Organizations that cultivate involvement, consistency, adaptability, and mission integration create an environment where staff view cybersecurity not as bureaucratic constraint but as a collective clinical ethic. Moreover, the Job Demands–Resources (JD–R) framework underscores that excessive workload without adequate support increases security fatigue and error rates. To mitigate this, organizations must provide streamlined tools, IT support, and opportunities for feedback, reinforcing that cybersecurity is everyone's responsibility. Over time, this alignment between structure, culture, and leadership transforms cybersecurity into a hallmark of organizational maturity and resilience.

POLICY IMPLICATIONS

Policy development must move beyond technical compliance toward embedding behavioral and cultural principles into cybersecurity governance. Effective policies should integrate behavioral-science insights from the Theory of Planned Behavior (TPB) and organizational learning theory, ensuring that clinicians have not only the knowledge but also the motivation and perceived control to act securely. Policies must explicitly link cybersecurity with professional ethics, emphasizing that safeguarding data is integral to protecting client welfare. Regulatory frameworks such as HIPAA and HICP should be operationalized through clear, behaviorally anchored checklists and role-based accountability structures. Moreover, policies should promote calibrated trust in automation by mandating human oversight and interpretability in digital systems, aligning with the Trust in Automation Complacency (TAC) model. By institutionalizing feedback mechanisms, ethical oversight committees, and participatory policy design, healthcare organizations ensure adaptive governance that evolves with emerging technologies and threats. In this model, cybersecurity policy is not static regulation but a living ethical framework that bridges technology, human behavior, and healthcare justice.

CONCLUSION

Cybersecurity within Applied Behavior Analysis (ABA) and telehealth-based behavioral healthcare is no longer a peripheral administrative task; it is a central pillar of ethical, professional, and organizational practice. As healthcare delivery becomes increasingly digitized, cybersecurity emerges as a core component of healthcare administration and governance, demanding attention not only to technology but to the human systems that sustain it. The majority of vulnerabilities in healthcare organizations, including ABA practices, stem from human behavior, misjudgments, habitual shortcuts, or insufficient situational awareness, rather than from technological failures (Yeo et al., 2022; Jones & Burrell, 2025; Burrell, 2024; Wright, 2023). Addressing these vulnerabilities requires a coordinated strategy that integrates behavioral science with organizational leadership and administrative oversight.

By applying behavioral-science principles such as reinforcement, feedback, and environmental structuring, ABA organizations can transform cybersecurity from a compliance obligation into a culture of ethical and professional responsibility. Leadership engagement and healthcare administrative structures play a crucial role in embedding these principles into everyday practice. When administrators model secure digital behavior, allocate time for cybersecurity training, and integrate data protection goals into performance evaluations, they communicate that cybersecurity is integral to organizational identity and patient safety. In such environments, cybersecurity becomes a collective organizational competency, shaped and maintained through consistent training, participatory leadership, and the cultivation of psychological safety (Edmondson, 2018).

A culture of psychological safety, where clinicians can report errors, ask questions, or disclose near misses without fear of reprisal, encourages transparency and organizational learning (Edmondson, 2018). Within healthcare administration, this cultural feature is essential for preventing the normalization of deviance, a phenomenon in which small, tolerated lapses accumulate into systemic risk. When leaders reinforce open communication, mistakes become data for improvement rather than grounds for punishment, allowing organizations to learn adaptively from incidents and to strengthen resilience.

For ABA telehealth organizations, this transformation requires intentional alignment between clinical culture and administrative systems. Highly trained in behavioral assessment but often under-trained in information security, ABA therapists inhabit a professional paradox: they are expected to safeguard client data using digital systems that often exceed their formal preparation. This challenge is not purely technical, it is behavioral, cultural, and ethical. Secure data management in ABA telehealth should thus be conceptualized as a form of applied behavior change, influenced by attitudes, shaped by social norms, and sustained by perceived behavioral control (Ajzen, 1991; Nobles, 2022).

Organizational behavior and leadership are the linking mechanisms that translate cybersecurity policies into consistent human performance. Leaders who articulate clear expectations, model secure conduct, and reinforce compliance through positive feedback create an environment in which cybersecurity is internalized as part of professional ethics rather than externalized as an IT function. Organizational culture, expressed through shared values, symbols, and routines, determines whether cybersecurity behaviors are perceived as meaningful contributions to client welfare or as bureaucratic distractions. When the administrative mission aligns with ethical care, staff view cybersecurity not as compliance but as compassion in digital form.

Incorporating principles of organizational behavior and healthcare administration, ABA organizations can use participatory design and continuous learning systems to close the gap between policy and practice. This includes involving clinicians in decision-making about telehealth platforms, ensuring equitable access to training resources, and embedding behavioral reinforcement systems that recognize secure practices in real time. Calibrated trust in automation, balanced with human vigilance, ensures that technology remains a tool for therapeutic extension rather than a source of systemic vulnerability (Nobles & Burrell, 2024).

Ultimately, protecting client data is more than a technical necessity; it is an ethical act that reflects an organization's cultural maturity and administrative integrity. When ABA organizations apply the same behavioral principles they use to teach adaptive skills, clear contingencies, reinforcement, and feedback, to cybersecurity training and governance, they cultivate not only compliance but enduring professional integrity. In this way, data protection becomes inseparable from client protection, affirming that in healthcare administration, to safeguard information is to safeguard human welfare, the shared moral foundation of both behavioral science and cybersecurity ethics.

RECOMMENDATIONS FOR FUTURE RESEARCH

Future research should adopt action research methodologies to translate the theoretical insights presented in this paper into applied, evidence-based strategies for strengthening cybersecurity in Applied Behavior Analysis (ABA) telehealth organizations. Action research, characterized by its cyclical process of planning, acting, observing, and reflecting, provides an ideal framework for studying the intersection of human factors, organizational culture, and cybersecurity behavior within real-world practice environments. Unlike purely observational or experimental designs, action research enables practitioner collaboration, contextual problem-solving, and iterative learning, qualities essential to behavioral healthcare organizations that must balance clinical service delivery with regulatory and technological demands.

Given the consideration that small and medium-sized ABA organizations often lack dedicated cybersecurity infrastructure and formal training (Jones & Burrell, 2025; Burrell, 2024; Wright, 2023), future studies should focus on participatory interventions in which ABA practitioners, administrators, and IT professionals co-develop, implement, and refine cybersecurity initiatives. This approach aligns with the applied ethos of ABA itself, which prioritizes data-driven decision-making, direct observation, and reinforcement of behavior change. For instance, an action research study might examine the impact of behavioral reinforcement strategies on therapists' adherence to secure telehealth practices, such as verifying encryption settings, maintaining strong passwords, and properly storing client data. Data collected through iterative cycles could reveal which forms of feedback and reinforcement most effectively sustain secure digital behavior over time.

In addition, researchers should evaluate the effectiveness of behaviorally informed cybersecurity training models within ABA organizations. These studies could integrate ABA-based learning principles such as shaping, immediate reinforcement, and functional analysis into cybersecurity education, testing whether these approaches outperform traditional didactic training methods in producing durable behavioral change. The outcomes of such research would provide empirically grounded best practices for designing security programs that align with the professional competencies of behavior analysts.

In summary, action research offers a pragmatic, ethically grounded, and participatory pathway for advancing cybersecurity resilience in ABA telehealth settings. By engaging practitioners as co-researchers and applying behavioral-science methodologies to cybersecurity challenges, future research can generate actionable knowledge that strengthens both the ethical and operational integrity of ABA organizations. This translational approach will not only enhance digital safety for vulnerable client populations but also establish a replicable framework for integrating human factors psychology into cybersecurity practices across healthcare disciplines.

REFERENCES

Ajzen, I. (1991). The theory of planned behavior. *Organizational Behavior and Human Decision Processes*, *50*(2), 179–211. DOI: 10.1016/0749-5978(91)90020-T

Ajzen, I. (2020). The theory of planned behavior: Frequently asked questions. *Human Behavior and Emerging Technologies*, *2*(4), 314–324. DOI: 10.1002/hbe2.195

Argyris, C., & Schön, D. A. (1996). *Organizational learning II: Theory, method, and practice*. Addison-Wesley.

Bakker, A. B., & Demerouti, E. (2017). Job demands–resources theory: Taking stock and looking forward. *Journal of Occupational Health Psychology*, *22*(3), 273–285. DOI: 10.1037/ocp0000056 PMID: 27732008

Bandura, A. (1986). *Social foundations of thought and action: A social cognitive theory*. Prentice-Hall.

Biewendt, M., Blaschke, F., & Böhnert, A. (2021). A review of contemporary challenges in business culture. *International Journal of Applied Research in Business and Management*, *2*(1), 1–12. DOI: 10.51137/ijarbm.2021.2.1.1

Bosnjak, M., Ajzen, I., & Schmidt, P. (2020). The theory of planned behavior: Selected recent advances and applications. *Europe's Journal of Psychology*, *16*(3), 352–356. DOI: 10.5964/ejop.v16i3.3107 PMID: 33680187

Burrell, D. N. (2024). Understanding Cognitive and Behavioral Psychological Factors that Lead to Cybersecurity Breaches in Healthcare. *RAIS Journal for Social Sciences*, *8*(2), 43–53.

Burrell, D. N., Aridi, A. S., McLester, Q., Shufutinsky, A., Nobles, C., Dawson, M., & Muller, S. R. (2021). Exploring system thinking leadership approaches to the healthcare cybersecurity environment. [IJEACH]. *International Journal of Extreme Automation and Connectivity in Healthcare*, *3*(2), 20–32. DOI: 10.4018/IJEACH.2021070103

Burrell, D. N., Nobles, C., Cusak, A., Omar, M., & Gillesania, L. (2022). Cybercrime and the nature of insider threat complexities in healthcare and biotechnology engineering organizations. *Journal of Crime and Criminal Behavior*, *2*(2), 131–144. DOI: 10.47509/JCCB.2022.v02i02.04

Cavalari, R. N., Gillis, J. M., Kruser, N., & Romanczyk, R. G. (2015). Digital communication and records in service provision and supervision: Regulation and practice. *Behavior Analysis in Practice*, *8*(2), 176–189. DOI: 10.1007/s40617-014-0030-3 PMID: 27703917

Cybersecurity and Infrastructure Security Agency (CISA). (2020). *Phishing campaign assessment guidance.* https://www.cisa.gov

Denison, D. (1990). Corporate culture and organizational. *New York: Wiley. Dike, P.(2013). The impact of workplace diversity on organizations. Dobbin, F., & Jung, J.(2010). Corporate board gender diversity and stock performance: The competence gap or institutional investor bias. NCL Rev, 89*, 809.

Denison, D., Nieminen, L., & Kotrba, L. (2014). Diagnosing organizational cultures: A conceptual and empirical review of culture effectiveness surveys. *European Journal of Work and Organizational Psychology*, *23*(1), 145–161. DOI: 10.1080/1359432X.2012.713173

Denison, D. R., & Spreitzer, G. M. (1991). Organizational culture and organizational development: A competing values approach. *Research in Organizational Change and Development*, *5*(1), 1–21.

Edmondson, A. C. (2018). *The fearless organization: Creating psychological safety in the workplace for learning, innovation, and growth.* Wiley.

Haider, S. (2009). The organizational knowledge iceberg: An empirical investigation. *Knowledge and Process Management*, *16*(2), 74–84. DOI: 10.1002/kpm.326

Haymes, L. K., Storey, K., Maldonado, A., Post, M., & Montgomery, J. (2015). Using applied behavior analysis and smart technology for meeting the health needs of individuals with intellectual disabilities. *Developmental Neurorehabilitation*, *18*(6), 407–419. DOI: 10.3109/17518423.2013.850750 PMID: 24304093

Jones, L. A., & Burrell, D. N. (2025). Illegal Cybersecurity Threats Created by Organizational Arsonists in Healthcare Organizations. *Law. Economics and Society*, *1*(1), 93–p93.

Lee, J. D., & See, K. A. (2004). Trust in automation: Designing for appropriate reliance. *Human Factors*, *46*(1), 50–80. DOI: 10.1518/hfes.46.1.50.30392 PMID: 15151155

Mahringer, C. A., Schmiedle, L., Albicker, L., & Mayer, S. (2025). The Iceberg Model of Change: A taxonomy differentiating approaches to change. *Heliyon*, *11*(2), e41952. DOI: 10.1016/j.heliyon.2025.e41952 PMID: 39911443

Nifakos, S., Chandramouli, K., Nikolaou, C. K., Papachristou, P., Koch, S., Panaousis, E., & Bonacina, S. (2021). Influence of human factors on cyber security within healthcare organisations: A systematic review. *Sensors (Basel), 21*(15), 5119. DOI: 10.3390/s21155119 PMID: 34372354

Nobles, C. (2015). *Exploring pilots' experiences of integrating technologically advanced aircraft within general aviation: A case study*. Northcentral University.

Nobles, C. (2018). Botching human factors in cybersecurity in business organizations. *Holistica Journal of Business and Public Administration*, *9*(3), 71–88. DOI: 10.2478/hjbpa-2018-0024

Nobles, C. (2022). Stress, burnout, and security fatigue in cybersecurity: A human factors perspective. *Holistica Journal of Business and Public Administration, 13*(2), 201–232. DOI: 10.2478/hjbpa-2022-0003

Nobles, C., & Burrell, D. (2024). Exploring the variability of human factors definitions in cybersecurity literature. In *Proceedings of the 19th Midwest Association for Information Systems Conference*. Peoria, IL.

Robinson, N. (2023). Human factors security engineering: The future of cybersecurity teams. *EDPACS, 67*(5), 1–17. DOI: 10.1080/07366981.2023.2211429

. Sasu, A. (2016). The cultural iceberg and other cultural models. *Buletinul tiin ific al Universită ii Tehnice de Construc ii Bucure ti Seria: Limbi Străine i Comunicare,* 9(2), 79-87.

Sussman, R., & Gifford, R. (2019). Causality in the theory of planned behavior. *Personality and Social Psychology Bulletin, 45*(6), 920–933. DOI: 10.1177/0146167218801363 PMID: 30264655

U.S. Department of Health and Human Services (HHS). (2022). *Health Industry Cybersecurity Practices: Managing threats and protecting patients.* https://405d.hhs.gov/Documents/HICP-Main-508.pdf

Weick, K. E., & Sutcliffe, K. M. (2015). *Managing the unexpected: Sustained performance in a complex world* (3rd ed.). Wiley. DOI: 10.1002/9781119175834

Wright, J. (2023). Healthcare cybersecurity and cybercrime supply chain risk management. *Health Economics and Management Review*, *4*(4), 17–27. DOI: 10.61093/hem.2023.4-02

Yeo, L. H.. (2022). Human factors in electronic health-records cybersecurity: An exploratory analysis of healthcare breach incidents in the United States. *JMIR Human Factors*, *9*(2), e35457. DOI: 10.2196/35457

Zoder-Martell, K. A., Markelz, A. M., Floress, M. T., Skriba, H. A., & Sayyah, L. E. (2020). Technology to facilitate telehealth in applied behavior analysis. *Behavior Analysis in Practice, 13*(3), 596–603. DOI: 10.1007/s40617-020-00449-4 PMID: 32837699

Chapter 4
The Ethics of Using Our Bodies as Data:
Biometric Surveillance and Personal Freedom

Nathaniel Akande
https://orcid.org/0009-0001-5930-3116
University of Bradford, UK

ABSTRACT

This chapter is a study on the ethical and legal issues as presented by biometric surveillance technologies, the interests that the change of human bodily digitization into digital bearers of identity is fundamentally changing the connection between the individual identity, bodily liberty, and institutionalised power. It also reflects on the interdisciplinary understanding of the concept through law analysis, critical theory, and empirical studies to understand how the specificities of biometric datafication introduce a unique vulnerability between biological labels and their biological owners. As the analysis depicts, the lapse in traditional systems of consent is leading to coercive surveillance. The chapter concludes with recommendations on the ethical governance of data minimisation and transparency, but also limitations on high-risk use cases such as emotion recognition, mass surveillance, and postulates that informational privacy is not sufficient to protect human dignity and that the substantive recognition of the right to bodily integrity must extend to the digital realm.

INTRODUCTION

The human body is already a primary source of information collection in our increasingly digitalized society. Facial-recognition checkpoints at the airports, smart-

DOI: 10.4018/979-8-3373-4967-1.ch004

phones unlocked by simply gazing at their screen, automated passport control kiosks at transit centres: With a shocking pace, biometric technologies, which identify people through physiological and/or behavioural characteristics, have entered our lives and have frequently done so without a significant public discussion. Biometrics, an area that transcends government and corporate usage to utilize at home (PR Newswire, 2018) is predicted to grow at 14.6% through 2030, surpassing the 40-billion-dollar mark in 2023 it rose to in 2023 (Grand View Research, 2018). The rapid implementation of biometric technologies demonstrates the potential normalization of invasive surveillance in society without public debate, which poses direct threats to autonomy, privacy, and the integrity of our bodily data. By regarding biological features solely as data points, these technologies alter essential power relations and engender irrevocable ethical difficulties. Understanding these risks sets the stage for examining specific ethical and legal tensions, showing why bodily privacy must remain a central concern in a digitalized society.

The question of 'What will it be when our deepest biological traits become the data points of enormous, interconnected surveillance systems?' is too urgent nowadays when biometric systems are used in identification, emotion sensing, and predictive acts (Yeap et al., 2024). The irreversibility of risks to biometric datafication is uncovered in high-profile breaches, including the leaking of the Aadhaar database of India used to identify individuals based on biometric data of all 1.3 billion citizens, with the biometric details of each person being sold at only seven bucks (Khera, 2019). Unlike passwords or credit cards that may be changed once they have been compromised, fingerprints or iris patterns cannot be replaced; hence, a biological truth that needs to be under scrutiny before it transforms fundamental notions of autonomy, privacy, and power (Cohen, 2019).

Emerging applications add these concerns. In the U.S., schools are now using gait recognition to keep an eye on students (Lurye, 2025), and Chinese factories use brainwave-sensing headbands to track fatigue in workers (Cole, 2018). The new EU ban on emotion recognition technology in workplaces recognises the pseudoscientific basis and discriminatory potential of these technologies, failing to offer a unified approach to protecting against them. With biometric surveillance becoming socially acceptable, where Zuboff (2023) has coined the term surveillance capitalism, we have to challenge how existing legal findings can safeguard bodily integrity when our biology is a product of a data market.

In this chapter, the author considers the ethical and legal dilemmas of biometric surveillance and three critical tensions:

1. **Autonomy vs. coercion**: Illusion of consent where refusal typically implies being locked out of necessities (e.g., in the case of workplaces or borders).

2. **Discrimination and inequality**: Members of discriminated minorities are often not recognised in biometric algorithms by race, gender, or disability.
3. **Cybersecurity and irreversibility**: Traditional data breaches can be contained, but once biometrics have been appropriated, the victim remains vulnerable permanently.

Regulatory fragmentation is another source of the problem. Although the EU in GDPR (2013) categorizes biometric data as a special category of information, there is no federal regulation in the U.S., and the Social Credit System in China is using biometrics as a state weapon in the hands of the government (Zuboff, 2023). This causes a surveillance arbitrage in which corporations and unfriendly governments exploit jurisdictional loopholes (Aho & Duffield, 2020).

Methodology and Scope

This chapter takes an interdisciplinary approach where the threads of legal analysis, critical theory, and empirical case studies are combined to deconstruct the society-wide effects of biometric surveillance. Solove (2022) unveils deficiencies in consent patterns, whereas theorists such as Deleuze and Foucault (1977) and Zuboff (2023) attempt to diversify the overview of surveillance as the instrument of institutional authority. Case studies range from facial recognition leak data that Clearview AI scrapes (Clayton & Derico, 2023) to the palm scanners that play out in Amazon stores, locating workers. The above works reveal that biometric systems are not only neutral technologies, but also create conditions that can exploit individuals' biological data. It also underscores the urgency of evaluating regulatory gaps and ethical considerations by situating these technologies within legal, philosophical, and empirical frameworks. This approach lays the foundation for exploring bodily integrity, global governance, and emerging threats as core priorities in safeguarding personal autonomy in digital environments.

The focus in this chapter is on bodily integrity, global governance, and the emerging technological threats as central lenses for analyzing biometric surveillance. While Cheney-Lippold (2017) was used to illustrate how biometrics commodify human biology, the global governance, which centres on the divergence of regulatory responses and their consequences, as well as the emerging threats following the emotional recognition and predictive policing, were all examined. All these reveal the impact that biometric systems have on affecting personal freedom, institutional power, and societal equity, thereby creating layered ethical and legal challenges. In this chapter, we have argued that the right to bodily privacy is not a speciality but a necessity of the democratic condition now under the digital environment. These systems are a path toward applying the body as a digital key and running the risk of turning personhood into algorithmic representations, making it urgent to put ethical checks in place.

LITERATURE REVIEW

The advancement in biometric surveillance has resulted in debates among scholars, industrial leaders, and experts. While some critics argue that biometric surveillance erodes collective safety, decency, and autonomy, others believe that the efficiencies and securities provided by this initiative outweigh its demerits. These views, though contrasted, are not only available among scholars but reflect the broader societal struggle over whether technologies such as this should prioritize human dignity or administrative control. Linking these positions back to the central concern of this chapter, the debate ultimately reveals how surveillance reshapes the meaning of freedom in democratic societies. Through these dimensions, a middle ground insight will be provided in a manner that the system of biometric surveillance is transforming the nature of social relations and power in the 21st century.

Theoretical Foundations

Scholarly debate on biometric surveillance has been crystallizing into two mutually exclusive theoretical camps. On the one hand, critics such as Zuboff (2023) present biometric technologies as leading the way to a new form of capitalism based on human bodies being transformed into data streams to increase corporate profits and state power. Zuboff's concept of "behavioural surplus" shows how intimate traits are harvested as tradeable properties that deepen institutional asymmetries. Similarly, since compromised biometrics cannot be revoked, this was described as a "lifetime vulnerability," since compromised biometrics cannot be revoked (Cohen, 2019). This further shows that hat biometric systems are not just neutral technologies but infrastructures that fundamentally reshape how people perceive their bodies in relation to power and autonomy. In other words, the surveillance economy is not an accessory to democracy but a direct challenge to it.

Another essential building block lies in the theory of contextual integrity proposed by Nissenbaum (2017), which demonstrates that biometric systems habitually transgress norms of information flow. Empirical work by Büchi et al. (2022) illustrates how such intrusions alter behaviour and produce chilling effects. These findings matter because they show that the harms of biometric surveillance extend beyond data misuse; they restructure how people think, act, and self-regulate in democratic societies. When trust collapses under constant surveillance, democratic freedoms are eroded in everyday life.

Conversely, advocates such as Das (2017) emphasize security and efficiency, situating biometric surveillance within rational-choice theory (Becker, 1968). Although efficiency gains such as reducing welfare fraud or improving border control are acknowledged in this perspective, they often ignore the wider social cost. Deleuze and Foucault's (1977) notion of disciplinary power illustrates this tension: when surveillance becomes environmental rather than exceptional, it changes how citizens behave. These clash between security and freedom further confirms that debates around biometrics are not only technical but also moral, as this has revealed the enduring conflicts about whose dignity is protected and whose autonomy is sacrificed.

Historical Evolution

Modern biometrics originated in the late 19th century with fingerprint classification (Galton, 1892). Early uses were limited and often consensual, focusing on criminal identification and border control (Jain et al., 2016). The post-September 11 attack on the U.S., however, shifted the scale of surveillance dramatically. Laws such as the U.S. Patriot Act (2001) and EU biometric passport requirements (2004) normalised mass collection of bodily data. Consumer adoption, for example, through Apple's Face ID (2017), rebranded surveillance as convenience. This trajectory illustrates a more profound shift: biometric technologies have moved from targeted identification to population-wide monitoring.

According to Ajana (2012), the concept of "biometric citizenship" captures this transformation, which shows how bodily autonomy, such as states and corporations, works in co-designing a new definition of bodily autonomy as a commodity of exchange, is reframed as a commodity in exchange for access to services. A case study involving India's Aadhaar system highlights this paradox, which initially was promoted as a fraud-reduction tool, and the Aadhaar system eventually exposed millions to unprecedented risks (Khera, 2019). These examples reveal more than historical change; they show that the spread of biometrics reflects an ideology of inevitability, where efficiency is prioritized over dignity. Without deliberate safeguards, biometric surveillance risks embedding systemic vulnerabilities into the very definition of citizenship.

Critical Gaps in the Current Scholarship

The existing literature leaves major blind spots. While scholars such as Browne (2012) and Magnet (2011) document racial bias in facial recognition, there is limited attention to intersectional harms. Misgendering of trans individuals, exclusion of people with disabilities, and errors with children or the elderly remain underexplored. These gaps matter because they show how biometrics reproduce social inequalities, raising urgent ethical questions about whose bodies are deemed "legible" by technology.

Second, research has disproportionately focused on state surveillance while overlooking corporate commodification. Companies such as Clearview AI and Meta have pioneered exploitative uses of biometric data (Clayton & Derico, 2023; Patel v. Facebook, 2021). Retailers and education platforms now deploy emotion recognition or biometric proctoring with little oversight (Stylios et al., 2022). This corporate turn demonstrates that surveillance capitalism is not only a state project but also a market-driven process that commodifies dignity itself.

Finally, there is insufficient exploration of alternatives such as homomorphic encryption and decentralized identities (Finck & Biega, 2021; Fischli, 2024). While these innovations have proven that biometric surveillance is not inevitable, there has been little engagement and research among scholars to build on his gap, which has reinforced the false binary of "security versus freedom" while ignoring solutions that could safeguard both. Addressing these gaps is vital, as more work on this aspect will afford the researchers and scholars the opportunity to advise the relevant ethical governance bodies on their findings, focusing on the protection of bodily privacy and democratic integrity.

Toward an Integrated Research Agenda

The current literature is doing an impeccable job deconstructing the moral questions raised by biometric surveillance technology; however, it remains a frustrating exercise in terms of interdisciplinary boundaries. For example, feminist and disability law critiques offer critical insights but often fail to inform legal analyses such as GDPR compliance. Similarly, technical research on algorithm development (e.g., Jain et al., 2016) rarely addresses the social and power imbalances inherent in implementing biometric systems. This disconnect shows that while each discipline advances knowledge in its domain, the lack of cross-disciplinary dialogue limits our understanding of how biometric technologies affect real people, particularly marginalized populations. Future research must integrate these perspectives, create frameworks that combine legal, technical, and ethical analyses, and thoroughly interrogate the implications of biometric surveillance, as this will protect human dignity in an increasingly quantified world.

The ethical stakes of biometric surveillance are high, as technology increasingly quantifies human life. Cheney-Lippold (2017) warns that data-driven systems challenge our understanding of what it means to be human, emphasizing that legal or technical fixes alone are insufficient. This literature review thus ends on a call to action to such research, research that brings technical analysis in dialogue with humanistic criticism, that foregrounds marginal experience, and that considers in earnest how technological futures are possible otherwise. It is only with this kind of integrative scholarship that we are likely to find a way forward through this complicated ethical landscape of biometric surveillance in a manner that will safeguard human dignity.

The Nature of Biometric Data: Embodied Identity in the Digital Age

Biometrics technologies have redefined the human body as a digital-identification place, eroding the distinctions between people and data. In contrast to more conventional forms of identification, whose truth can be verified by a single use of a password or ID card, biometric data is uniquely linked to the body it belongs to, raising particular moral and safety concerns. In this section, the process of defining biometric data is discussed, and the risks that an inevitable irreversibility brings are revealed, as well as the implications of this biometric data are examined using the example of the Aadhaar system of India, with special focus on the issue of cybersecurity vulnerabilities. The deployment of biometric surveillance, such as the Aadhaar system, further illustrates how irreversible digital identifiers can mitigate privacy and cybersecurity risks. This further underscores the ethical tension between technological efficiency and personal security, and emphasizes the need for robust policy frameworks that protect biometric data while enabling digital identification.

Types of Biometric Data

There are two major biometric data categories: physiological and behavioural markers. Physiological identifiers, meaning fingerprints, iris patterns, and DNA, are fixed because they are based on fixed biological features that can be expected to persist for much of an individual's life. Such characteristics have been employed in forensic studies since the 19th century, when fingerprints were used (Jain et al., 2016). However, technological advancement has seen them applied in other areas besides criminal identification, such as daily authentication, unlocking smartphones, and border control. Behavioural biometrics record more dynamic identities like gait, voice, and keystroke dynamics. On the one hand, these markers have the possibility of continuous authentication. On the second, they present new complexities, since such markers can vary depending on the context, health, or even emotional status (Stylios et al., 2022).

Inseparability & Risks

The characteristic that comes with biometric data is that it is inseparable from the physical body. The biometric identifiers cannot be revoked or altered compared with the stolen passwords or credit card numbers, which can be changed or cancelled. This permanence, Cohen (2019) calls lifetime vulnerability; When biometric data is compromised, one is always at risk of identity theft, stalking, and abusive use. The so-called surveillance even further exacerbates this (Buchi et al., 2022), meaning that biometric regimes accumulate and process individual information in several different contexts by combining a large amount of data into a single person profile, which is further defined beyond the institutional context. For example, facial recognition technology may be used in the open environment, whereby the presence of the given individual in a mass protest may be connected to their medical or working experience, violating the contextual integrity of privacy that Nissenbaum (2017) claims to be the core of the privacy issue. It further implies that its misuse can lead to persistent threats to personal autonomy and dignity, highlighting the broader societal implications of emerging biometric regimes.

There are also serious biometric security risks due to the non-reversibility of biometrics. Conventional security breaches cause harms that can be cured, but biometric breaches cause protracted and non-measurable injuries. As an example of how weak biometric technologies are abused, such as spoofing, when a biometric system is fooled with synthetic IDs (e.g. fingerprint prints in silicone or high-quality photographs) (Kumar et al., 2024). The ineffectiveness of the existing measures is illustrated by more advanced types of threats to security, including replay attacks wherein information taken off the network is reused to place unauthorized calls, as people and biometrics were intercepted. Consequently, the exploitation of these vulnerabilities further underscores the urgency of rethinking biometric security strategies to ensure personal data information is protected and trust is maintained in digital identity systems.

Case Study

An example of such risks is the Aadhaar system, a biometric identification program in India. Billed as an inclusive governance system, Aadhaar registered more than 1.3 billion people by associating their biometric details with most necessary resources (Shahin & Zheng, 2018). Nevertheless, law enforcement agencies discovered that unauthorized actors could access the database for only $7, and this sensitive data includes fingerprints and iris scans at risk of misuse (Khera, 2019). The vulnerabilities highlighted the flawed technical aspects, including poor encryption and a lack of appropriate authentication schemes, yet highlighted more significant ethical issues. The loss of biometrics, unlike financial data, cannot be reissued, which puts the victims in an unfavourable position. Improper behaviour disproportionately affects marginalized groups, as seen in the Aadhaar case. Primarily, digitally illiterate rural populations were forced into joining without knowing the dangers involved, with technical problems excluding individuals with mismatched fingerprints due to wear on their print (Singh, 2021).

This Aadhaar debacle highlights a paradoxical reality that biometric technologies present themselves as an assurance of security by generating a different order of insecurity. Although the supporters of using biometrics are sure it will decrease fraud, there is more to it. The same permanence that leads to successful identification using biometrics turns out to be risky when the identification fails, leading to easy compilation of liabilities (Cavoukian, 2009). These risks are further compounded by the lack of any real consent mechanism, especially in systems such as Aadhaar, where opting out is the equivalent of losing access to basic services.

In the future, biometric data discourse should address the problem of its two-fold character: empowerment and oppression. As seen by the example of Aadhaar, unless strong guardrails are in place, biometric systems may be used to create a mechanism of exclusion and control. In future structures, not just technical security like the anti-spoofing protocols and decentralized storage are essential, but also ethical considerations like voluntariness and keeping data collection to a minimum. With the development of biometric technologies, their control has to understand that the body is not only a source of information but the root of human identity, which needs protection within other privacy paradigms.

AUTONOMY, CONSENT, AND POWER IMBALANCES IN BIOMETRIC SURVEILLANCE

Illusion of Consent

Despite its critical status, the ethical basis of biometric systems is highly shaky as it is built upon the concept of informed consent. This notion tends to turn into what researchers call the consent theatre. An especially acute illustration of this dynamic is in the workplace, leaving workers with the dilemma between complying with biometrics and staying afloat. This coercive climate can be typified by the palm-scanning time clocks that Amazon introduced into its warehouses in 2021. Without providing their biometric data, the workers risk losing access to jobs, meaning that the given consent forms are another ritual (Bryant, 2021). This so-called consent is window dressing that conceals what Bok (2022) calls structural coercion, in which the institutionally imposed power situation makes opposition virtually impractical.

The delusion of the option proves especially pernicious as biometric systems spread into healthcare, education, and social services, developing, what Deleuze and Foucault (1977) would call a society-wide "disciplinary apparatus." This widespread deployment thus reinforces the illusion of choice, showing that 'consent' often masks systemic coercion rather than protecting individual autonomy.

Power Asymmetries

The imbalances of power in the biometric uptake are further highlighted as one would analyze state-corporate surveillance collaboration. The Social Credit System of China exemplifies how biometric technologies become an even more sophisticated social regulation system when implemented by authoritarian governments (U.S.-China Economic and Security Review Commission, 2020). Their facial scans are taken in the street without their consent, and their biometrics are algorithmically categorized to dictate whether they can travel, work, or even use dating apps. This is where instrumental power takes the form of a system, as Zuboff (2023) exemplifies 2023, meaning that the behavioural remodeling is ongoing instead of open repressions. This absence of effective opt-out methods establishes societies of control where the veneers between institutions dissolve and surveillance is made environmental instead of institutional, which demonstrates the broader ethical and societal implications of biometric technologies, highlighting the urgent need for regulatory oversight.

Intersectional Harms

Such disparities in the power play out with a specific intensity on the axis of intersectional identities and expose the extent to which biometric systems contribute to reinforcing social inequality. Facial recognition AI practices universally misgender transgender and non-binary people and subject them to the bureaucracy of fighting to change the algorithm in both air travel security systems and banks (Keyes, 2018). According to disability rights activists, gait recognition mechanisms do not consider the use of mobility aids, and speech-impaired individuals have problems with voice authentication (Setiawan, 2024). Older populations are doubly discriminated against in the face of an ageing population, as their dynamics and expressivity challenge courtroom facial recognition algorithms, and in biometric recognition systems, behaviours such as keystroke dynamics are distorted by age-related tremors. Racial prejudices, which are already widely investigated in the context of facial analysis algorithms (Buolamwini & Gebru, 2018), take a new turn due to their combination with predictive police technology. Following this shortcomings, not only the existing societal inequities are reflected, it also actively perpetuate exclusion, reinforcing systemic barriers across multiple dimensions of identity. Consequently, biometric systems are not neutral tools as they embed and magnify social hierarchies, demanding critical scrutiny of their design and deployment.

Case Study

The example of the deployment of Clearview AI by U.S police departments exemplifies the dynamic of how such intersectional harms work in production. The enterprise collected billions of facial images without their consent on social media. It formed a database where communities of colour were over-policed and over-represented on mugshot databases (Clayton & Derico, 2023). In this way, when such imperfect identifications enter the pretrial risk assessment toolboxes, they give rise to what Shaheen (2024) defines as the automating inequality - wherein the biometric technologies do not eradicate discrimination but systematize it. It does not just stop at misidentification; the confines of the psychological experience of all-time surveillance have established a digital epidermalization through which skin colour is a tag that displays increased suspicion.

These forces indicate a paradox in biometric governance. Although European regulations such as GDPR view consent as the primary pillar of data protection, the power imbalance makes this practice mostly abstract. Workers would not have any significant choice to make when their refusal to be checked would most likely result in unemployment, and the same is true for citizens when governments want to introduce biometric authentication in service provision. The resultant, so-called surveillance creep, standardizes what had previously existed as exceptional intrusions into personal bodies, especially those already over-examined because of marginalization.

The solution is to stop getting people to sign consent forms and get substantive protection. According to Kuflik (1984), it is not absolute autonomy, as it is necessary to reorganize the power structure that impedes refusal. This could include blanket bans on some of the uses of biometrics, such as emotion recognition, in the work environment, instead of referring to implementation at the individual consent level. It cannot evade placing vulnerable populations at the centre of emphasis when considering the design of systems and the need to ensure that all technology takes into account the entire human diversity, before implementation and consideration, as opposed to later.

The way forward is to understand that there can never be a neutral approach to using biometrics where inequality prevails in a given society, whereby consent is tainted with structural power. Studies show that in workplaces using biometric surveillance, employees from marginalized groups experience higher stress and scrutiny, confirming that structural inequality amplifies risks despite purportedly neutral technology (Nguyen et al., 2022). Ethical governance thus needs to constrain the usage of biometric information and where it is used, especially in areas where saying no comes at intolerable costs. Only by addressing these issues of power imbalance can we ensure that biometric technologies do not become instruments of oppression. Instead, we use them as convenient measures.

SECURITY VS. LIBERTY: THE BIOMETRIC SURVEILLANCE DILEMMA

Mission Creep

The tension between civil liberty and public safety is at its highest when biometric surveillance debates are concerned, as the slippery slope of mission creep has recently been developed. It is often seen how a specific security assistance, initially implemented at airports in the form of a highly tailored solution, quickly spreads to all aspects of society by permeating social tracking, such as the spread of facial recognition on both the southwestern border and the school lunchroom and the retail shop. This tendency towards excesses in functionality characterizes facial recognition software, which is why the 2019 law that prohibits using this type of technology by the government of San Francisco directly reacted to this very tendency (Conger et al., 2019). The decision of the city authorities demonstrated a critical paradox: the technologies that were explained as counterposing terrorism were secretly shifting to policing the homeless and schoolchildren, but there was no discussion as to why this radical change in use was justified democratically. Koops (2021) calls this the surveillance ratchet effect, whereby emergency measures become permanent, but widen their orbit via bureaucratic inertia instead of any deliberate policy decision.

Ethical Proportionality

Considering its social costs, the proportionality test of ethics standards, which requires the necessity and proportionality of measures applied by surveillance, is especially problematic in biometrics. An example of this imbalance is machine-learning policing systems that assess risk based on algorithmically driven facial recognition. These systems are sold and positioned as crime-neutral deterrence measures, yet they are disproportionately placed into minority neighbourhoods, generating their systems of suspicion and surveillance (Benjamin, 2023). The opacity of the technology provides an excess to this issue. When police departments cannot comment on how their algorithms produce what are referred to as risk scores, citizens cannot effectively contradict unfair surveillance (Ferguson, 2017). This adopts the definition of Habermas (1987), and breaches what he would describe as the legitimation conditions of democratic governance, whereby state power must bind itself to reveal itself through justifiable means to win the people's continued trust. The paradigm the resultant security generates turns existing legal precedents inside out--gone is the mantra of "innocent till proven guilty" and in its place is the world of citizens under increasing suspicion based on algorithmic association in the heavily surveyed geographies.

Cybersecurity Risks

Biometric systems present novel cybersecurity weaknesses that shift the risk calculus of surveillance in some fundamental ways. As shown in the 2018 Aadhaar breach in which hackers stole biometric information of more than a billion Indians (Khera, 2019), the importance of treating bodily identifiers as replaceable passwords is devastatingly costly. Fraud cannot be cancelled in the case of credit card numbers, unlike fingerprints or iris scan examples, where the compromised fingerprint or iris scan subjects one to identity theft permanently. Spoofing also compromises the security justification of biometrics; biometrics is susceptible to 3D printed fingerprints (Tolosana et al., 2020) or deepfake videos (Mirsky & Lee, 2021), testing shows that even advanced systems can be deceitful (Tolosana et al., 2020). Such flaws contribute to forming a so-called security theatre where people feel safe, but they put their systems at greater risk (Schneier, 2015). Once the security risk of a single biometric database compromise threatens to compromise millions permanently, this justification of massive data collection defeats itself.

Case Study

The San Francisco case study demonstrates what local opposition can and cannot do when the world is networked surveillance. Although the ban in the city alone did not allow municipal agencies to use facial recognition, it did not stop the federal government from using this technology deployed in the San Francisco International Airport, or enable retailers to install it in stores, even when it was and still is privately owned (Roy, 2022). This jurisdictional patchwork results in what Papadopoulos (2023) calls accountability voids in which the totality of surveillance assemblages navigate with impunity the interstices between legal jurisdiction and circumvent the scope of meaningful oversight. What is achieved is a lose situation, where no strengthened security will exist, and no safeguarded liberties, but instead a regime with a lean and hollow Frankenstein appearance. This San Francisco case underscores how fragmented oversight undermines both security and liberty, highlighting the need for coherent surveillance governance.

Such tensions are expressed in a more fundamental philosophical debate concerning the meaning of security within democratic societies. The advocates of expansive biometric surveillance use the utilitarian calculus operationalized by Bentham (2020) to justify the sacrifice of privacy because it would lead to a much higher level of public safety. Nevertheless, as shown by Kazansky (2021), such anticipatory logic used by biometrics systems merely compromises security since resources meant to search for real crimes are redirected to interpolate and investigate hypothetical ones. This effect of reducing the psychological impact of constant surveillance, which Marx (2016) refers to as the chilling effect, might become more socially corrosive than the crime being prevented by these systems. The tension between privacy and security shows that unchecked biometric surveillance can erode democratic freedoms, calling for more balanced approaches.

In the future, there is also a need to balance security and liberty by considering that even the basic architecture of a biometric system needs redesign. Technical solutions to achieve the reconciliation of these conflicting values, such as on-device processing (viewing biometric data never leaves the phone of a user) or zero-knowledge proofs (in which identity can be proved without raw data being visible), have the potential to offer solutions to any conflict between competitive values (Finck & Biega, 2021). Lawfully, the strongest possible use of the principle of proportionality would demand that surveillance technologies have sunset provisions and an independent review of their effectiveness. Democratic communities need more than ballot-box access to veto surveillance, which does not pass this test, as demonstrated in the San Francisco experiment, in the policy and infrastructural shaping of the technologies.

THE DATAFICATION OF THE BODY AND THE EROSION OF BODILY PRIVACY

Commodification

One of the most significant changes in the bonding between technology and identity is the conversion of human body physiology into digital data. Biometric systems not only keep a record of what is going on with our bodies but make bodies into an algorithmic abstraction that can be sold, bought, and manipulated like any other commodity. The $650 million settlement that Facebook signed with Patel v. This commodification process was exposed by the Facebook case (2021), which has shown how the facial geometry system of the company automatically tagged people in pictures without their actual consent, turning their faces into corporate property. As Cheney-Lippold (2017) postulates, this is the introduction of the so-called algorithmic identity, where the most intimate biological peculiarities can be viewed as raw material for the so-called surveillance capitalism described by Zuboff (2023). This has implications that are bigger than the invasion of privacy. When firms such as Clearview AI sell facial recognition databases as baseball cards (Hill, 2021), they practice what Marxist thinkers would call the alienation of the body belonging to oneself, transforming physiological individuality into exchange value. This exploitation of bodily data underscores how algorithmic identities erode human dignity and personal autonomy globally.

Legal Protections

The current legal systems can hardly tackle this paradigm shift. Currently used by the EU, the General Data Protection Regulation (GDPR) considers biometric data a special category subject to explicit consent. Yet, in practice, this law has its limitations. The exemptions on Article 9 of "substantial public interest" have enabled governments to exploit lax security arguments to install mass surveillance systems. More importantly, the informational privacy extended by the GDPR cannot possibly reflect the visceral wrong committed against the datification of the body, considered by feminist thinkers such as Bordo (2023), who highlights how biometric technologies enforce a machine-readable surface on the body, alienating it from the experience. The Illinois Biometric Information Privacy Act (BIPA) is even more extreme in declaring biometric data irreversibly personal. However, it does so through procedural protections that still overlook the body as more than another data set. The privacy law cannot reverse the ontological injury of turning fingers, faces, and heartbeats into proprietary algorithms, such as written consent and a data destruction schedule required in their law (ACLU Illinois, 2021). Current legal frameworks inadequately safeguard bodies, highlighting persistent gaps in protecting privacy and human integrity.

Emerging Threats

New biometrics technologies are pushing the law's boundaries in disturbing forms. Emotion I.D. technologies allegedly reveal the inner psychological condition based on micro-expressions and other physiologic signs and resemble what is now recognized in the EU AI Act as an unacceptable risk technology. The systems are already being applied in job interviews and classroom surveillance in China (US-China Commission, 2020) and assume an appearance of transparency of affect that is unacceptable to the psychologists as scientifically untenable (Barrett et al., 2019). Wearable biometrics also present similar risks, as wearable devices, such as the Amazon Palm Scanner and the Apple Watch, allow the constant collection of physiological data to be used to monitor health and as a means of surveillance among consumers. According to Hornborg (2021), these technologies exercise a spinning sociometabolic control over stunning body functions that can fall under the optimization of a corporation. The dangers of emotional surveillance in the workplace are reflected in the recent prohibition on emotion recognition in the EU that took effect on February 2025 but with a regulatory patchwork at the global level, these submarines will continue to move to those jurisdictions with laxer protection, a phenomenon which researchers refer to as surveillance arbitrage. Emerging biometric technologies amplify surveillance risks, threatening bodily autonomy and undermining ethical standards worldwide.

Case Study

The Facebook settlement is a good example of an ineffective existing remedy. Although the sum of 650 million may sound a lot, it is equivalent to less than 0.3% of the company's income in 2020, which is closer to a licensing fee in itself than a deterrent (Pester, 2020). More essentially, payment is of no help to the ontological violence of biometric commodification. When the tremors of Parkinson patients and facial expressions of people with autism evolve into units of calculation by corporate algorithms, they form a new type of digital objectification that does not even refer to traditional harm to privacy.

Such a changing context produces an urgent need to radically reconsider the rights of the body in the digital era. Cohen (2019), a legal scholar, suggests adopting a similar legal framework of biometric data through the doctrine of bodily integrity, utilised during physical violation, such as surgery without consent. This would understand that the game algorithmic dismemberment of the body is a form of harm in and of itself, independent of its data misuse. Partial solutions could be technological solutions such as homomorphic encryption (Finck & Biega, 2021), whereby biometric data can be manipulated without exposing raw data. However, as the bans in the EU AI Act imply, other kinds of biometric surveillance might be incompatible with human dignity--not in the sense that they are also an abuse of privacy but in the sense that they reduce persons to products.

GLOBAL REGULATORY LANDSCAPES: DIVERGENT VISIONS OF BIOMETRIC GOVERNANCE

EU (GDPR's Rights-Based Approach)

Regulating biometric surveillance indicates deep philosophical schisms concerning how people see the relationship between people, technology, and the state's power. The GDPR of the European Union is the most adventurous effort to set up a rights-based regime where they deem the biometric data as a special category under Article 9, requiring explicit consent and limitation of purposes (GDPR, 2016). Such a method is pegged on what Lubbe-Wolff (2014) referred to as informational self-determination, which theoretically enables citizens to establish dominance over their biological data. Nonetheless, its application outlines some critical inconsistencies- where the GDPR forbids companies to process biometric data without the user consent, Article 23 of the same regulation gives the member states the authority to suspend the GDPR protocol under the pretext of national security reasons. Such a workaround has allowed the implementation of systems such as the German automated facial recognition in train stations, illustrating how even strong structures fall victim to security exceptionalism. These regulatory mismatches reveal more than technical flaws; they expose a global governance failure where bodies are treated as data assets rather than as the basis of human dignity. Without harmonized safeguards, biometric surveillance entrenches inequalities across borders and normalizes practices that corrode democratic accountability. Thus, the regulatory landscape is not just fragmented but also complicit in redefining bodily privacy as negotiable. This inconsistency highlights how human dignity becomes negotiable, proving that even rights-based systems struggle to protect bodily privacy fully.

U.S. (Patchwork Laws Like BIPA)

Across the Atlantic, the decentralized model in the United States has given rise to a patchwork of regulations that leaves most of the citizens unprotected. The Biometric Information Privacy Act (BIPA) in Illinois is considered the gold standard in the nation since it requires informed written consent, and even the monetization of biometric data is prohibited (ACLU Illinois, 2021). However, its success is limited to the territory, as residents of Illinois could sue Facebook over violations of facial recognition at $650 million (Patel v. According to Facebook, 2021), Texans have no such remedy permitted by their less powerful 2009 biometric statute. As McGraw and Mandl (2021) call it, such a federalist process, privacy federalism, creates compliance anarchy for various multinational enterprises and allows surveillance arbitrage. Lack of federal outlawing implies that police forces with a ban on facial recognition can collaborate with the nearby jurisdiction to receive the device, rendering any accountability gaps (Papadopoulos, 2023). The fragmented framework undermines bodily autonomy, leaving dignity and privacy unprotected, where state boundaries weaken citizens' biometric safeguards.

China (State-Controlled Surveillance)

The Chinese example fails to follow the Western paradigm by completely assimilating biometrics into government domination structures. Facial recognition, gait analysis, and mobile payment data are integrated to formulate algorithmic risk profiling of citizen trustworthiness within the Social Credit System (U.S.-China Commission, 2020). With the Personal Information Protection Law of 2021, China openly subordinates any individual rights to national security priorities, obligating businesses to submit to the authorities without question biometric data when needed (Gulyamov & Raimberdiyev, 2023). What it creates, Zuboff (2023) calls instrumentarian power: a mode of governance where surveillance is the invisible infrastructural facet of social control. The fact that one cannot go without the system to receive healthcare, receive transport services, or even attend education makes the notion of consent moot (Aho & Duffield, 2020). China's biometric regime dissolves consent, showing how dignity is displaced when the body is entirely subsumed under state power.

Gaps

These regulatory mismatches impose perilous loopholes on the interdependent globe. Including national security exemptions, which are standard in all three systems, has become a black box of rights abuses. The EU law enforcement directive permits cross-border sharing of biometric data with little control (Shepherd, 2021). In contrast, the U.S. allows the federal agencies to retrieve data stored anywhere worldwide by an American company (Tschider, 2020). The Cybersecurity Law of China requires that biometrics of Chinese citizens be stored in their country; however, it does not address the data of foreigners being processed by Chinese corporations such as Huawei (Creemers, 2020). Such regulatory incoherency supports what Lindner (2019) terms surveillance globalisation, with data transiting across territorial boundaries to avoid protection, in examples from facial recognition: European faces captured by Chinese cameras in African airports and processed with Israeli algorithms in the cloud by American corporations.

It is especially disastrous to vulnerable populations. By delivering iris scans to UNHCR databases, refugees can contribute to databases with access via authoritarian governments at home, without suspicion (Madianou, 2021). There is practically zero transparency in such cross-border police agreements as INTERPOL's facial recognition system, even though programs are known to cause serious misidentification of political dissidents through algorithms. These processes present us with an ugly paradox, namely that the very technologies that are being lauded as the answer to global security issues, border control, human trafficking, and terrorism are themselves establishing transnational surveillance infrastructures that exert undue pressure upon the already socially marginalised.

New ideas about governance hint at minor reforms that only attempt to correct the balance of power. The AI Act adopted by the EU is trying to categorise some of the biometric applications as an unacceptable risk, whereas sectoral bills in the U.S. focus on individual abuses, such as facial recognition by police. Neither addresses the root cause: the fact that bodies have now become data has not been met with adjustments to current structures, where biometric surveillance can still be viewed as an exception, rather than the threat to autonomy critics like Cohen (2019) describe it to be. The world biometric marketplace will take a toll on human dignity until the regulatory framework treats the body as a contested terrain. These loopholes erode bodily privacy, proving that without harmonised safeguards, dignity and autonomy collapse under global biometric surveillance regimes.

ETHICAL GOVERNANCE IN THE AGE OF BIOMETRIC SURVEILLANCE

Core Principles

The fast spread of biometric technologies requires a system of governance that not only considers their technological risks but also pays attention to the severe implications of these technologies to the dignity of humanity. This controversy has reached the crux of identifying the nature of the tension or dilemma, namely, how the potential positive impacts of biometric identification can be reaped without making it the tool of oppression. For instance, the collection of biometric data for photo tagging, which was not used for its intended purpose and without the data owner's consent, raises profound questions about user autonomy and dignity as seen in the case of *Patel v. Facebook*. Any ethical approach should be anchored on three core principles: data minimisation, purpose limitation, and transparency; however, there is a need to go beyond procedural compliance into substantive protections.

The GDPR concept of data minimization is fundamental in biometrics because data privacy and security are personal. Following Cavoukian (2009) in her position paper about Privacy by Design, it can be stated that systems must not collect more biometric data than is needed to perform the intended operation: a fingerprint to access the workplace, and not all facial scans, to give an example. The need to apply this concept is acute, especially when it comes to novel technologies such as the application of vein pattern recognition, where the temptation to store data just in case tends to prevail over need (Finck & Biega, 2021). Purpose limitation should also be coupled with this strategy, so that biometric information collected to assure security in airports is not used later to fuel specific advertising, which is a line that should not be crossed; furthermore, this aspect could be pinpointed with Nissenbaum's (2017) contextual integrity theory. The Patel v. The case of Facebook revealed the effect of disregarding this principle as the company used a facial recognition system to repurpose profile pictures to tagging algorithms whose purpose was unnamed.

Biometric systems' transparency needs to go past mere notifications to contain real accountability of algorithms. This is because the current black box systems, in which even the operators do not understand how they make their decisions, contravene what Hildebrandt (2020) refers to as the right to reasonable inferences. The guidelines of the EU AI Act on high-risk AI systems start solving this issue by demanding documentation of training data and decision logic. Yet, more must be done without independent mechanisms to audit the system. Controversies like the issue of the ShotSpotter, where acoustic sensors and biased algorithms create an inaccurate gunshot recording by the police, express just how risky opaque technology is when presented by the proponents as an objective and neutral system (Ferguson, 2017).

Prohibitions

Some biometrics are too risky to accept under any other possible condition. An especially objectionable form of pseudoscientific monitoring, which is currently prohibited in EU workplaces by the AI Act, is emotion recognition technology. Psychological research (e.g., Fridlund et al., 2014; Barrett et al., 2019) has clarified that facial expressions do not reliably reflect internal states. However, companies are selling such systems to monitor students in their classrooms and screen people at borders. Equally, mass surveillance systems such as the Chinese Social Credit System or the real-time facial recognition cameras in London establish a scenario wherein even the perceived state of being monitored is enough to alter the behaviour at the population level. Systems like that must be categorically banned, like chemical weapons, known to be destructive to the democratic world.

Innovations

Technological solutions can partly solve such moral dilemmas. Privacy-preserving architectures such as homomorphic encryption encourage biometric matching with a user not having to produce raw data- a hospital would check a patient's identity against encrypted templates without having to access real fingerprints (Prakasha & Sumalatha, 2025). Decentralized identity schemes like those that rely on blockchain-based zero-knowledge proofs allow one to authenticate without a centralized database that can risk being hacked (Fischli, 2024). The National Digital Identity program in Singapore illustrates how the national government systems can apply these principles, as they store the biometric data on personal devices and not servers (Cooper et al., 2022). Nevertheless, according to Tschider (2020), even with high-security cryptography, it might be impossible to eliminate power imbalances in the mandatory use of cryptography in the required services.

Technical safeguards must then be offered, along with institutional reforms for effective governance. Replacing the medical review committees, independent biometric ethics boards may screen future uses before putting them into practice (Metcalf & Crawford, 2016). The automatic expiry of Sunset clauses on surveillance programs is unless there is an ongoing re-evaluation of the necessity of the same, hence, a control mechanism of mission creep. However, most importantly and urgently, marginalised groups must be meaningfully involved in the design and oversight procedures because their lived experience exposes the evils that even the privileged designers fail to see (Benjamin, 2023).

The way forward acknowledges that biometric technologies are political decisions in drag as technical necessities. Although inclusion of ethical considerations into the law and the systems themselves could still invert their inevitable application toward liberation over domination, we are quickly reaching the point of no return as monitoring systems become permanent.

CONCLUSION

The emergence of biometric surveillance and the ensuing shifts in the interaction of human identity and digital systems have compromised the nature of the former to the point of revealing cracks in our ethical and legal foundations. As shown in this chapter, the same qualities that lead biometric technologies to be potent, their permanence, intimacy, and inseparability with the body, make them particularly dangerous. The semblance of consent in coercive extremes, the scaling up of social inequalities by biased algorithms, and the irrevocable dangers of the biometric data hack have outlined one commonality: the belief that the body as information is consumable will predispose the prerequisite premises of individual sovereignty and liberal society.

Even new trends are likely to inflate such conflicts in the future. When paired with the application of AI to specific behavioural analyses, predictive profiling also runs the danger of reducing people to algorithmic predictions of criminality or productivity, thereby strengthening systemic discrimination. The growing ubiquity of wearable biometrics, such as smartwatches that track stress levels, to augmented reality glasses and headsets that can actively perform facial recognition, breaks down the distinction between willingly using such a device and ambient surveillance. The scrutiny of these developments must be urgent, because of their technical implications, of course, but also due to their corrosive effect on human agency. As the core of our bodies is turned into endless sources of data collection, the concept itself, that of privacy, would be migrated into a more privileged domain, available only to those who can afford not to use basic services or avoid the industry of being watched.

The way ahead has to start with a paradigm shift: human decency, not efficiency or safety alone, should guide whether biometrics are used in governance. This means transitioning to proactive protections beyond reactive regulation and taking the form of categorical prohibition of inherently exploitative technology such as emotion recognition, conversive restrictions in data storage, and seeking effective oversight of the involved stakeholders, ensuring that the marginalized population takes centre stage. Legal systems need to change and consider biometric information no longer to be such sensitive data as the achievement of a favour, but instead include it in the physical integrity of the self, with protections no less than those against physical assault. Technological innovation is a necessary condition but not a sufficient one without utilizing parallel changes in power; to the extent that systems decentralize and designs are privacy-friendly, such systems will only cause less harm when implemented in a framework more concerned with equity than control.

Those stakes go beyond policy arguments--they are in the marrow of what it means to be human in an age of quantification. To repel the reductive trend of personhood to biometric profiles, we need to affirm that the body is not a set of data points; the body is the container of lived experience, dignity, and self-organization. The difficulty of the situation does not lie in regulating biometric surveillance but in the necessity to reshape its presence in society so that people can use these technologies to their advantage instead of enslaving themselves by them. That reckoning has come before our surveillance infrastructures are too firmly established to break. It is what our freedom will be based upon.

REFERENCES

ACLU of Illinois. (2021). Biometric Information Privacy Act (BIPA). https://www.aclu-il.org/campaigns-initiatives/biometric-information-privacy-act-bipa

Aho, B., & Duffield, R. (2020). Beyond surveillance capitalism: Privacy, regulation and big data in Europe and China. *Economy and Society*, *49*(2), 187–212. DOI: 10.1080/03085147.2019.1690275

Ajana, B. (2012). Biometric citizenship. *Citizenship Studies*, *16*(7), 851–870. DOI: 10.1080/13621025.2012.669962

Barrett, L. F., Adolphs, R., Marsella, S., Martinez, A. M., & Pollak, S. D. (2019). Emotional expressions reconsidered: Challenges to inferring emotion from human facial movements. *Psychological Science in the Public Interest*, *20*(1), 1–68. DOI: 10.1177/1529100619832930 PMID: 31313636

Becker, G. S. (1968). Crime and punishment: An economic approach. *Journal of Political Economy*, *76*(2), 169–217. DOI: 10.1086/259394

Benjamin, R. (2023). Race after technology. In *Social Theory Re-Wired* (pp. 405–415). Routledge. DOI: 10.4324/9781003320609-52

Bok, H. (2022). *Freedom and responsibility*. Princeton University Press. DOI: 10.2307/j.ctt7s9q6

Browne, S. (2012). Race and surveillance. In *Routledge handbook of surveillance studies* (pp. 72–79). Routledge. DOI: 10.4324/9780203814949.ch1_2_d

Bryant, J. (2021, March 5). *Facebook's $650M BIPA settlement 'a make-or-break moment.* IAPP. https://iapp.org/news/a/facebooks-650m-bipa-settlement-a-make-or-break-moment

Büchi, M., Festic, N., & Latzer, M. (2022). The chilling effects of digital dataveillance: A theoretical model and an empirical research agenda. *Big Data & Society*, *9*(1), 20539517211065368. DOI: 10.1177/20539517211065368

Buolamwini, J., & Gebru, T. (2018, January). Gender shades: Intersectional accuracy disparities in commercial gender classification. In *Conference on fairness, accountability and transparency* (pp. 77-91). PMLR.

Cavoukian, A. (2009). *Privacy by Design: Taking on the Challenge*, Canadian Electronic Library. Canada. Retrieved from https://coilink.org/20.500.12592/9965z2 on 15 Jul 2025. COI: 20.500.12592/9965z2.

Cheney-Lippold, J. (2017). We are data: Algorithms and the making of our digital selves. In *We are data*. New York University Press. DOI: 10.18574/nyu/9781479888702.001.0001

Clayton, J., & Derico, B. (2023, March 27). Clearview AI used nearly 1m times by US police, it tells the BBC. *BBC News*. https://www.bbc.com/news/technology-65057011

Cohen, J. E. (2019). Review of Zuboff's the age of surveillance capitalism. *Surveillance & Society*, *17*(1/2), 240–245. DOI: 10.24908/ss.v17i1/2.13144

Cole, S. (2018). *China Claims It's Scanning Workers' Brainwaves to Increase Efficiency and Profits*. [online] VICE. Available at: https://www.vice.com/en/article/china-brain-wave-hats-helmets-productivity/ [Accessed 10 Aug. 2025].

Conger, K., Fausset, R., & Kovaleski, S. F. (2019, May 14). San Francisco Bans Facial Recognition Technology. *The New York Times*. https://www.nytimes.com/2019/05/14/us/facial-recognition-ban-san-francisco.html

Cooper, A. K., Marskell, J. D., & Chan, C. H. (2022). National Digital Identity and Government Data Sharing in Singapore: A Case Study of Singpass and APEX.

Deleuze, G., & Foucault, M. (1977). Intellectuals and power. *Language, counter-memory, practice*, 205-17.

Deleuze, G., & Foucault, M. (1977). Intellectuals and power. *Language, counter-memory, practice*, 205-17.

Ferguson, A. G. (2017). The rise of big data policing: Surveillance, race, and the future of law enforcement. In *The rise of big data policing*. New York University Press.

Finck, M., & Biega, A. J. (2021). Reviving purpose limitation and data minimisation in data-driven systems. *Technology and Regulation*, *2021*, 44–61. DOI: 10.71265/z7r0t122

Fischli, R. (2024). Data-owning democracy: Citizen empowerment through data ownership. *European Journal of Political Theory*, *23*(2), 204–223. DOI: 10.1177/14748851221110316

Fischli, R. (2024). Data-owning democracy: Citizen empowerment through data ownership. *European Journal of Political Theory*, *23*(2), 204–223. DOI: 10.1177/14748851221110316

Fridlund, A. J., Ekman, P., & Oster, H. (2014). Facial expressions of emotion: Review of literature, 1970–1983. *Nonverbal behavior and communication*, 143-224.

Galton, F. (1892). *Finger prints (No. 57490-57492)*. Cosimo Classics.

GDPR. (2013a). *General Data Protection Regulation (GDPR) – Final text neatly arranged*. General Data Protection Regulation (GDPR). https://gdpr-info.eu/art-9-gdpr/

Grand View Research. (2018). *Global Biometrics Technology Market Share | Industry Report 2018-2025*. [online] Grandviewresearch.com. Available at: https://www.grandviewresearch.com/industry-analysis/biometrics-industry

Hill, K. (2021, July 21). Clearview AI raises $30 million from investors despite legal troubles. The New York Times. https://www.nytimes.com/2021/07/21/technology/clearview-ai-facial-recognition.html

Jain, A. K., Nandakumar, K., & Ross, A. (2016). 50 years of biometric research: Accomplishments, challenges, and opportunities. *Pattern Recognition Letters*, *79*, 80–105. DOI: 10.1016/j.patrec.2015.12.013

Keyes, O. (2018). The misgendering machines: Trans/HCI implications of automatic gender recognition. *Proceedings of the ACM on human-computer interaction*, *2*(CSCW), 1-22. DOI: 10.1145/3274357

Khera, R. (2019). *Dissent on Aadhaar: Big Data meets Big Brother*. Orient BlackSwan.

Koops, B. J. (2021). The concept of function creep. *Law, Innovation and Technology*, *13*(1), 29–56. DOI: 10.1080/17579961.2021.1898299

Kuflik, A. (1984). The inalienability of autonomy. *Philosophy & Public Affairs*, •••, 271–298.

Kumar, T., Bhushan, S., Sharma, P., & Garg, V. (2024). Examining the vulnerabilities of biometric systems: Privacy and security perspectives. In *Leveraging Computer Vision to Biometric Applications* (pp. 34–67). Chapman and Hall/CRC. DOI: 10.1201/9781032614663-3

Lurye, S. (2025). *Schools are using AI to protect students. It also leads to false alarms — and arrests*. [online] ABC News. Available at: https://abcnews.go.com/Technology/wireStory/schools-ai-surveillance-protect-students-leads-false-alarms-124440368

Magnet, S. A. (2011). When biometrics fail: Gender, race, and the technology of identity. In *When Biometrics Fail*. Duke University Press.

Metcalf, J., & Crawford, K. (2016). Where are human subjects in big data research? The emerging ethics divide. *Big Data & Society*, *3*(1), 2053951716650211. DOI: 10.1177/2053951716650211

Newswire, P. R. (2018). *Global $40+ Billion Biometric System Market 2018-2023 - Analysis & Forecasts by by Authentication Type, Functionality, Component, Application, and Geography*. [online] Prnewswire.com. Available at: https://www.prnewswire.com/news-releases/global-40-billion-biometric-system-market-2018-2023----analysis--forecasts-by-by-authentication-type-functionality-component-application-and-geography-300695999.html

Nissenbaum, H. (2017). Deregulating collection: must privacy give way to use regulation? *Available at SSRN* 3092282. DOI: 10.2139/ssrn.3092282

Patel v. Facebook, Inc., 932 F.3d 1264 (9th Cir. 2019)

Prakasha, K. K., & Sumalatha, U. (2025). Privacy-preserving techniques in biometric systems: Approaches and challenges. *IEEE Access : Practical Innovations, Open Solutions.*

Setiawan, A. (2024). Intelligent systems for disabilities technology for a more inclusive life. *Available at SSRN* 5062273.

Shaheen, R. (2024). Gender and Surveillance: The Implications of Biometric Technologies for Privacy and Equity. *Journal of Gender, Power, and Social Transformation, 1*(3), 29–35.

Shahin, S., & Zheng, P. (2018). Big Data and the Illusion of Choice: Comparing the Evolution of India's Aadhaar and China's Social Credit System as Technosocial Discourses. *Social Science Computer Review, 38*(1), 25–41. DOI: 10.1177/0894439318789343

Singh, P. (2021). Aadhaar and data privacy: Biometric identification and anxieties of recognition in India. *Information Communication and Society, 24*(7), 978–993. DOI: 10.1080/1369118X.2019.1668459

Solove, D. J. (2022). The limitations of privacy rights. *The Notre Dame Law Review, 98*, 975.

Stylios, I., Kokolakis, S., Thanou, O., & Chatzis, S. (2022). Key factors driving the adoption of behavioral biometrics and continuous authentication technology: An empirical research. *Information and Computer Security, 30*(4), 562–582. DOI: 10.1108/ICS-08-2021-0124

Tschider, C. A. (2020). Beyond the" black box. *Denv. L. Rev., 98*, 683.

U.S.- China Economic and Security Review Commission. (2020). *China's Corporate Social Credit System: Context, Competition, Technology and Geopolitics*. Www.uscc .gov. https://www.uscc.gov/research/chinas-corporate-social-credit-system-context -competition-technology-and-geopolitics

Yeap, K. H., Chow, C. T., Low, H. T., & Nisar, H. (2024). *Enhanced Biometric Identification Using Photoplethysmography Signals*. Cambridge Scholars Publishing.

Zuboff, S. (2023). The age of surveillance capitalism. In *Social theory re-wired* (pp. 203–213). Routledge. DOI: 10.4324/9781003320609-27

Chapter 5
Cybersecurity vis-à-vis Data Privacy:
An Ethico-Legal Framework for a Dignified Cyberspace

Jipson Joseph
https://orcid.org/0009-0005-1795-5051
Christ University, India

ABSTRACT

Cyberspace has become a prerequisite for human flourishing in the present century. Almost all human interactions use cyberspace for increased productivity, efficiency, and economic growth. The speed and results of cyber activities are significantly ahead of real-world human interactions. However, cyberspace is not without drawbacks and challenges. Cybersecurity and data privacy have become essential concerns of the present century, as cybercrimes, cyber terrorism, data breaches, and cyber theft have become everyday occurrences. Besides, issues like the digital divide complicate the global march towards sustainability through cyberspace. Many countries have enacted various laws and policies to ensure cybersecurity. However, they are not globally effective as cyberspace is beyond the territorial boundaries. It demands a globally acceptable ethico-legal framework that guarantees a dignified cyberspace. From this perspective, this chapter calls for an international law perspective applicable to all states and some foundational ethical principles that should guide all cyber activities.

DOI: 10.4018/979-8-3373-4967-1.ch005

1 INTRODUCTION

The evolution of the term, space, over the last two centuries is quite interesting. It has extended to an unlimited and unimaginable area of discussion with the evolution of cyberspace. Although cyberspace must have originated with the evolution of computers and network systems, the word was first used in fiction in the 1980s. Cyberspace points to a digital environment, where digits are the guiding principles (Haefner & Sternberg, 2020). Many equate cyberspace with a virtual world, claiming it is unreal. Although the chapter does not intend to engage with this controversy, it affirms that cyberspace has become more influential in human lives compared to the real world. The contemporary world underlines the importance of cyberspace for a meaningful existence, as it is essential for economic growth, commercial activities, education, healthcare, research, and global interconnection (Lambach, 2020). Cyberspace has become increasingly intermingled with the various activities of the present generation, as it cannot think of a meaningful existence without cyberspace (Tick et al., 2021; Osler & Zahavi, 2023).

The influence of cyberspace in the present time is beyond our imagination. Individuals, organizations, state actors, and international institutions require cyberspace to function effectively. Just like an ordinary human flourishing requires a secure environment, people's cyber interactions cannot reap good results without secure cyber settings (Haefner & Sternberg, 2020). Security and privacy are the most cherished human rights in cyberspace. However, several instances of cybercrimes, data privacy violations, cyber attacks, hacking activities, data breaches, and cyberterrorism have been reported in the 21st century. These instances underline that cyber insecurities are the most complex concerns of the present century. Although people cannot survive and flourish without cyberspace and cyber activities, the increased cyber insecurities and privacy violations confuse and jeopardize their engagement in cyberspace (Admass et al., 2024). Compared to the previous century, when people were worried about poverty, unemployment, environmental degradation, and lack of healthcare facilities, the present generation is most concerned about cybersecurity and data privacy, as their absence can cause massive harm to critical infrastructure facilities (Plotnek & Slay, 2021).

1.1 Statement of Problem and Methodology

Digitalization has broadened its ambit to include almost all areas of human interactions. Accordingly, cyberspace, cybersecurity, data privacy, data protection, and networking have become significant concerns of the present discussions (Ari et al., 2024). People always prioritize a standard of living regardless of the cyber or real world. To lead a dignified and secure life, free from insecurity and encroachment, is the aspiration of all individuals (Adhikari, 2024). However, the present experiences underline that cyber insecurities and data privacy violations are increasing uncontrollably, causing severe damage to human interactions (Quach et al., 2022). Statista (2024) notes that cybercrimes are increasingly growing globally, and the total cost of cybercrimes is US$9.22 trillion, which is expected to escalate to US$13.82 trillion in 2028. It shows how widely cybercrimes have been harming people and causing financial loss. Cyber threats that cause serious security and privacy concerns include AI-powered cyber attacks, deepfake technology, malware threats, cryptojacking, phishing variants, supply chain attacks, etc. (Moore, 2025). Cyberattacks have become daily, with an average of 2200/day. It is estimated that a cyberattack happens every 39 seconds, causing severe security and privacy concerns. From this perspective, the World Economic Forum (2019) stated that cyberattacks would be one of the five most significant risks the global community will face in the next ten years. Continuous cyber attacks and privacy violations jeopardize people's engagement in cyberspace. Since everything has become digital and AI-powered, people cannot help but use digital technologies. However, they also have fear and anxiety even when they increasingly interact in cyberspace (Siddiqi et al., 2022).

The main challenge is that society requires a significant amount of time to understand the drawbacks of a technological advancement. It creates confusion in addressing such issues, which cybercriminals take advantage of (Brown & Fazal, 2021). Countries like the US, the European Union (EU), India, Australia, and Canada have enacted cybersecurity and data privacy laws to ensure a dignified cyberspace (Mishra et al., 2022). Besides, the problem is that cyberspace is not limited to any territorial space. It is beyond the territorial space of a country. The infiltrators may initiate their cybercrime from a country where cyberlaws are not rigid. This causes many problems for the prosecution of offenders. Justice delivery becomes difficult in such a situation. Besides, the ethical principles that should guide cyber activities are not universally accepted. This necessitates an effective ethico-legal framework that is globally applicable to ensure a dignified cyberspace (Savaş & Karataş 2022). However, many countries use hackers to track the activities of other countries and people, create issues in foreign countries, and attack their infrastructure facilities. It poses questions concerning the ethicality and legality of those activities (Dhirani et al., 2023). Who decides what is legal/ethical regarding cyber activity? Should these apply only to individuals and private organizations? If states are not committed to following the ethical principles and laws, how can they demand that people follow those mandates? This chapter thus examines the various challenges to cybersecurity and data privacy from this perspective and proposes the ethical and legal principles that should guide cyberspace. The chapter uses the critical, analytical, comparative, and exploratory methods of doctrinal methodology to enhance the discussions on cybersecurity vis-à-vis data privacy and advance the ethico-legal framework for a dignified cyberspace.

2 THEORETICAL FRAMEWORK

Cyberspace has become one of the most discussed terms in the contemporary world. The definitions of cyberspace point to a setting where communications over computer networks occur (Kitchin, 1998). The current society has become increasingly digital and cannot think of existing without communication over computer networks. It has entered almost all fields, covering the interactions between persons, institutions, societies, and states (Haefner & Sternberg, 2020). The differentiation between domestic and international has become insignificant with the evolution of cyberspace. It provided many opportunities for people to become actively interconnected with various cultures, people, and societies, leading to a fast-growing virtual world. Such an increased interconnectedness became more vibrant with the theoretical support of globalization, liberalization, and an open economy (Lambach, 2020). Cyberspace empowers humans with many possibilities to improve the standard of living and ensure a progressive realization of the fundamentals of human lives by increasingly interconnecting with one another. For instance, during the COVID-19 pandemic, cyberspace provided online education (Tick et al., 2021), telehealth (Brown-Jackson, 2022), e-commerce (Xiao et al., 2022), online communication (Osler & Zahavi, 2023), and work-from-home (Daneshfar et al., 2023) options that helped people revive their potential, social and economic engagement, and interactions. However, cyberspace is not without challenges and drawbacks. Since the potential of cyberspace is beyond human imagination, its challenges are also beyond human thinking (Haefner & Sternberg, 2020). Security and privacy are the two most essential terms concerning people's dignified lives in cyberspace.

Security is equated with safety, protection from fear, absence of risks, or resilience. It is a dynamic and relational term (Porcedda, 2017). It changes along with time and circumstances. Security is mainly associated with the protection of the territorial borders of a state. The idea of national security evolved in such a perspective, which became the center of security discussions in the aftermath of the two World Wars (Zelikow, 2003). It received a broader perspective with the increased number of nuclear powers around the globe. The national security perspective thus became an international security paradigm (Adhikari, 2024). However, in 1994, the United Nations Development Program (UNDP) initiated another shift in security studies by proposing the human security paradigm. It affirmed that the individual is the reference point for the security concerns (Gilder, 2021). All these discussions on security revolve around the real-world problems and issues. However, the evolution of cyberspace and its increased interaction with human lives and society have raised questions on security in cyberspace (Admass et al., 2024). The globe has realized the potential of cyberthreats, which are more dangerous than conventional insecurities. Accordingly, the present world focuses more on cybersecurity discussions. Cybersecurity is "a set of security concepts, policies, tools, guidelines, risk management techniques, best practices, and training that may be utilized to secure an organization's cyber environment and assets" (Mishra et al., 2022). The security perspective is not restricted to the Westphalian state. It moves beyond the Westphalian state to the international community, the state territories to an individual human being, and the real-world issues to cyberspace complexities and threats. Although the dialectic between the state and the individual is at the heart of security discussions (Porcedda, 2017), cybersecurity concerns affirm that they adversely affect both the state and the individual. Compared to national and international insecurities, which primarily endanger the institutional settings of the states, cyber insecurities harm both states and individuals simultaneously.

Security and privacy are closely interconnected. Absolute security guarantees enhanced claims of privacy, and *vice versa*. Privacy is the most sacred space in which a person enjoys maximum freedom and assertion of individuality. Privacy refers to the unique right of an individual to be free from external interference and controls (Ari et al., 2024). One's words, actions, decisions, and living patterns should result from complete freedom. However, privacy cannot be absolute. The state has the power to restrict the right to privacy of its citizens legitimately (Rubenfeld, 1989). In contrast, illegitimate control over people's privacy violates the fundamental right guaranteed by the UDHR, international covenants, and several national constitutions. Compared to many other rights, the right to privacy first became an international human right, even before most national constitutions had incorporated this unique right (Diggelmann & Cleis, 2014). Article 12 of the UDHR functions as a torchlight for the entire discussion on the right to privacy across the globe. Article 17 of the International Covenant on Civil and Political Rights (ICCPR) broadened the ambit of Article 12 of the UDHR and underlines that "no one shall be subjected to arbitrary or unlawful interference with his privacy, family, home, or correspondence, nor to unlawful attacks on his honor and reputation." The right to privacy guards against arbitrary and unlawful attacks, interference, or encroachment into people's private lives. It insists on protecting the honor and reputation of each person. Privacy includes distancing oneself from society and protecting one's elementary community norms, such as intimate relationships and public reputation (Diggelmann & Cleis, 2014). It aims at preserving the dignity of oneself and one's family.

The right to privacy also includes data privacy, a foremost concern of the digital world. International law has interpreted the provisions of the UDHR and ICCPR concerning the right to privacy, including data privacy. Although data protection (data privacy) appears to be an offspring of the right to privacy, it has started to make its way in contemporary society (Tzanou, 2013). Data privacy primarily focuses on protecting personal information in all stages of its processing (Bygrave, 2002). Personal/institutional information protection is the central element of data privacy concerns. Personal information is any information relating to an identified or identifiable person (Tzanou, 2013). Article 8 of the Charter of Fundamental Rights of the European Union places data protection along with the right to privacy, affirming their interconnection. Scholars have discussed the nature of the relationship between data protection and privacy. Some argued that they are separate and distinct (Scandamis et al., 2007), whereas others argued that they closely interact in various ways (Tzanou, 2013). At the same time, it should be noted that data protection and privacy are not identical. The right to privacy is a broader concept that includes many vital elements under personal information and relationships (Westin, 1970). In contrast, data protection or privacy refers to protecting personal/institutional information in cyberspace. Data privacy thus evolves from the right to privacy and is its subset. Not all personal data breaches amount to violations of the right to privacy. Nevertheless, privacy is the "one—if not the—major" value that data protection discussions prioritize to safeguard (Bygrave, 2002). Although data protection laws have many vital concerns and interests, they promote the importance of protecting data privacy, which is closely associated with the right to privacy (Tzanou, 2013).

3 LITERATURE REVIEW

Several recent studies have been undertaken concerning cybersecurity and digital privacy, as digital technologies increasingly influence global interactions. Hasal et al. (2021) examine the question of security and privacy within the ambit of chatbots. Since chatbots are widely used in almost all fields of human interaction, the security and privacy concerns about their use have become a central discussion point in contemporary society. They also suggest some measures to ensure the security of the users and protect their personal information. However, their focus is limited to the use of chatbots. Murdoch (2021) explores the challenges in the new era of digital technologies concerning protecting crucial health information. The nature of AI has increased the possibilities of data breaches, security threats, and privacy violations by both public and private actors, which require effective rules and regulations. The article fails to make significant suggestions concerning the laws and regulations. Quach et al. (2022) examine the privacy and data protection concerns in the increased digitalization context of consumer-firm relationships. Savaş and Karataş (2022) affirm that the unprecedented increase of digital data in cyberspace has raised serious security concerns. National governments and international institutions face an increased rate of cybersecurity threats daily, which demands a well-designed cybersecurity strategy. Cyber governance must be systematically designed to address various cyber insecurities affecting people, institutions, national governments, and international agencies. They affirm the importance of a global framework, which is also the focus of this chapter. Using evidence from seven countries, such as the EU, the US, Canada, Australia, China, India, and Malaysia, Mishra et al. (2022) investigated the cybersecurity attributes and identified fourteen common attributes. These seven countries are chosen as they have a strong legal framework to ensure cybersecurity and data privacy. They state that cybersecurity is more robust in some countries than in others. For instance, while the US has efficient E-banking policies, Canada has priority concerning E-Commerce and spam policies. The differences in the prioritization show the need for a globally accepted framework.

AlDaajeh et al. (2022) state that digital information and telecommunication have transformed the lives of people as well as the economic growth of nations. The increased adoption of cyberspace in national and international economic, political, social, and cultural interactions also forces countries to focus on cyber sovereignty. The present society cannot undermine cybersecurity as it has become similar to protecting territorial integrity to promote national interests. People and institutions should be more aware of the importance of cybersecurity. National cybersecurity laws and policies should be systematically communicated to people to ensure they know about such mechanisms. Paul et al. (2023) specifically focus on the digitalization of the healthcare sector and critically evaluate its security and privacy concerns. Incorporating digital technology in the healthcare sector has contributed to its growth. However, it also raises crucial security and privacy concerns. Dhirani et al. (2023) note that Industry 5.0 has outweighed the limitations of Industry 4.0 through its increased adoption of digital technologies. These technologies should adhere to specific ethical and regulatory guidelines. Users' privacy and security are affected when such policies are not adequately implemented. Bakare et al. (2024) compare the data privacy laws and their compliance between the European Union and the US. They state that the EU's General Data Protection Regulation (GDPR), which came into force in 2018, is a comprehensive framework covering the European Union and its economic interactions. In contrast, a comprehensive federal data privacy law does not exist in the US. The GDPR promotes a rights-based data protection and privacy approach, but the US system has a fragmented regulatory landscape. Saleh (2024) discusses the role of blockchain in addressing cyber insecurities and privacy violations. It affirms that blockchain can potentially increase the security and privacy of the digital space and AI systems because of its decentralized functioning.

Cybersecurity and data privacy point to the same reality. They affirm the importance of a secure cyberspace. The studies mentioned above underline the insecurities addressed by various sectors with digitalization. They emphasize the importance of a legal framework for ensuring a safe cyberspace. However, except for Savaş and Karataş (2022), none argue for a global legal framework. The ethical principles are also poorly dealt with. From this perspective, this study calls for a global framework and strong ethical principles for a dignified cyberspace.

4 DIGNIFIED CYBERSPACE: MEANING AND IMPLICATIONS

Various terms, like cyber environment, cyber field, and cyber area, refer to cyberspace (Savaş & Karataş, 2022). It is also understood as a virtual world created by linking "computers, Internet-enabled devices, servers, routers, and other components of the Internet's infrastructure." It cannot be equated with the Internet. While the Internet is the physical infrastructure of interconnected computers, cyberspace exists because of the Internet network, but not in physical space. It exists only in the virtual space (Bussell, 2025). It points to the information systems spread across the globe and space and the networks that connect them (Savaş & Karataş, 2022). It affirms that there is no specific boundary for cyberspace. The word cyberspace was first coined by William Gibson in 1982 in a science fiction novel. He identified cyberspace as the creation of a computer network that exists in a world of artificially intelligent beings. In the 1990s, cyberspace was used to refer to the interaction between people using the Internet. Slowly, it has become a space of active socioeconomic, political, literary, cultural, national, and international interactions. At the beginning of the evolution of cyberspace, many believed it should be free from the involvement and restrictions of national governments and international regulations (Bussell, 2025). However, the globe immediately realized the potential harm and insecurities it could cause without effective measures and rules to control its use and activities. Just as people's dignified lives can be maintained with well-designed policies and enactments, a dignified cyberspace also requires appropriate guidelines and laws. Balancing the ethical, legal, technical, and expectations framework is essential for a dignified cyberspace (Dhirani et al., 2023).

4.1 Access to the Internet

The current global society depends heavily on the digital space. The Internet and cyber-based technologies are increasingly used in almost all societal interactions for increased efficiency and productivity. Citizens, organizations, and governments require the Internet to improve efficiency and economic growth (Mishra et al., 2022). Access to the Internet thus becomes a crucial concern for attempts toward a dignified cyberspace. Access to the Internet is not yet explicitly acknowledged as a fundamental human right in international law. However, it is implicitly recognized as evolving from the right to freedom of expression (Tully, 2014). Several countries, like India, have recognized it as a fundamental right evolving from Article 19(1)(a) and Article 21 of the Constitution (Sabu Mathew George vs. Union of India, 2018; Anuradha Bhasin vs. Union of India, 2020). Internet access has become a basic requirement for social inclusion, economic participation, and enhanced communication (Powell et al., 2012). Realizing this necessity, SDG9.c states that the globe should "significantly increase access to information and communications technology and strive to provide universal and affordable access to the Internet in least developed countries by 2020." However, the International Telecommunication Union report (2021) states that almost 2.9 billion people are still offline. Although there has been a significant increase in the number of people with Internet access, the globe has not fully become digital with universal and affordable Internet access. The freedom to connect through the Internet has been widely propagated as everyone requires it for increased productivity and efficiency (Tully, 2014).

4.2 Addressing the Digital Divide

The digital divide is a critical obstacle to achieving a dignified cyberspace. Although the globe boasts of technological advancements, digitalization, and economic growth, its many regions have not yet been able to enjoy the fruits of these advancements. The difference between developed and developing countries, rich and poor, educated and uneducated, and men and women is evident concerning the involvement and interactions in the digital space. The inclusion and exclusion tactics complicate global Internet access (Powell et al., 2012). Since affordable Internet access is essential for education, healthcare, e-commerce, e-governance, and political engagement, its unavailability to some sections leads to socioeconomic inequality. It is against the demands of the right to equality and justice. Cyberspace interactions help people advance in economic interactions. However, denying some sections of society access to cyberspace is a new method of division and social exclusion. The digital divide is widely experienced in many fields (Saeed & Masters, 2021; Mubarak & Suomi, 2022; Acilar & Sæbø, 2023). The increasing digital divide is a significant challenge to the sustainable future of the globe. SDG5.b demands to "enhance the use of enabling technology, in particular information and communications technology, to promote the empowerment of women" and to address the gender digital divide.

4.3 Achieving Sustainability

Sustainability is the catchword of the 21st century, which has become so popular with the Millennium Development Goals (MDGs) and the Sustainable Development

Goals (SDGs). Sustainability refers to maintainability. However, with the evolution of sustainable development (WCED, 1987), sustainability has become a broader term that stands for meeting the needs of the present generation without compromising that of future generations. It is understood in terms of social, economic, and environmental pillars. These three pillars could be adequately achieved in the present century only through a systematic use of cyberspace. SDG5.b and SDG9.c have focused on increasing people's Internet access capacity to accomplish the global sustainability objective. No society in the present time can achieve sustainability without dignified cyberspace interactions. People's access to cyberspace and secure interactions allow them to achieve a sustainable future.

4.4 Affirming Interconnectedness

Emerging digital technologies have transformed the nature and quality of cyberspace. It has become increasingly interconnected, dependent, collaborative, and effective (Dhirani et al., 2023). A society's existence depends on thousands of human interactions. Similarly, cyberspace also underscores interconnectedness. It points to a global network of interconnected users and objects. Such global networks increase and intensify the networking of people and things, empower the management of human communities, and promote the potential of businesses and services, producing better results (Đurđević & Stevanović, 2016).

4.5 Alleviating Challenges

The increased networking capacity of cyberspace is beyond the scope of the users of computers and mobile phones. The evolution of Artificial Intelligence (AI), Internet of Things (IoT), and Machine Learning (ML) has provided immense scope for activities in cyberspace. Such advancements increase economic growth, sustainability drive, and social inclusion. However, these are not without any challenges and drawbacks. Protection of personal rights and ethical principles like transparency and accountability is a prime challenge in cyberspace. This is mainly due to the lack of an international regulatory system and legal framework applicable to all, regardless of territorial differences. Protection of democratic institutions and state values and the implementation of network security are also complex tasks in cyberspace (Đurđević & Stevanović, 2016). There are instances of allegations against some states, arguing that they have funded hackers and cybercriminals to create tensions and confusion in other states. Addressing such complex cases of state-sponsored espionage is a herculean task in cyberspace (Brown & Fazal, 2021). Cyberspace promotes decentralized communication in which the state has no specific control. Most cyber insecurities and data privacy violations report that the offenders operate from a different country than the victim's. It reduces the state's capacity to address such threats and violations. Besides, the security measures that are available today are mostly inadequate to address the challenges (Đurđević & Stevanović, 2016). The most challenging issues concerning cyberspace are security and data privacy. The latest reports underline that cybercrimes and data privacy violations increase substantially with the increased number of cyberspace users. Such an increase poses a considerable concern for the globe as it will adversely affect people's interactions in cyberspace, ultimately leading to economic disadvantages and national insecurity (Plotnek & Slay, 2021; Mishra et al., 2022). The sections below will explain the means to alleviate these challenges that complicate the functioning of cyberspace.

5 CYBERSECURITY VIS-À-VIS DATA PRIVACY: COMPLEX QUESTIONS OF CYBERSPACE

As examined above, security refers to the absence of threats and harms; privacy underlines protecting crucial personal information. Both security and privacy point to free and secure societal interactions. Similarly, cybersecurity and data privacy also underline the importance of security and privacy in the digital space. These have become vital concerns due to the growing dependency on cyberspace. Cyberthreats and privacy violations in the digital world have become so common. Cybercriminals actively engage in cyberspace to exploit people's personal information, property, and operations for their economic advantage and personal gains. Data breaches are the main challenge faced by cyberspace. Many people tend to believe that data breaches affect only the financial sector. However, the examples from various fields, like the entertainment sector, supply chain management, the food delivery sector, the educational institutions, the healthcare industry, government agencies, and international institutions, affirm that it affects all crucial fields of human life (Dalal et al., 2022). Most international institutions and national governments actively incorporate cyberspace into their daily activities and critical services to people. Although it increases the efficiency of their services, it also makes them vulnerable to cybercrimes, causing more harm to people, society, and the nation (Mishra et al. 2022). Many believe that data breaches and cyber insecurities are primarily causing problems for international agencies, national governments, multinational corporations, and well-functioning firms and institutions. However, the latest data states it is a serious concern for small-scale industries, businesses, and individuals (Dalal et al., 2022). The size of the firm/organization is not a concern for cybercriminals. They prioritize squeezing individuals' and organizations' personal information and assets for their gain. Besides, cyberterrorism is on the rise, and it poses more dangerous threats to a country's critical infrastructure facilities than conventional terrorist attacks (Plotnek & Slay, 2021).

Cybercriminals use various methods to attack individuals, organizations, and state authorities in cyberspace. These include spam, phishing, malware, spoofing, Denial of service attacks, ransomware, and password attacks (Dalal et al., 2022). Most cybercriminal activities target the sensitive customer information of organizations and institutions that work in education, healthcare, social security, insurance, e-commerce, banking, and telecommunication sectors. They also encroach on people's intellectual property rights and other valuables (Posey et al., 2017). At present, they exploit people and organizations by not relying solely on computers but also using social engineering tactics (Dalal et al. 2022). Social engineering is nothing other than a process of masking the real intention of the attacker to get access to vital information. Cybercrimes occur easily when users become victims of the attackers' manipulation, deception, and persuasion. This necessitates that people's involvement in the digital space should be cautious, following the timely guidelines of national governments and international institutions. More than system and security failures, human susceptibility to these types of cyberattacks is the main reason for the rapid growth of cybercrimes. The latest cyberattackers' modus operandi underlines that they target people's financial and psychological vulnerability (Posey et al., 2017). Greed is not a prime reason for such susceptibility (Siddiqui et al., 2022). People often do not understand that they are becoming victims of social engineering and cyberattacks. Before fully realizing the impact of a cyberattack, they would have become its victims.

Cybersecurity is no longer an individual or institutional problem alone. It has become an international concern as the issues in cyber environments are more common, complex, and deeper in the present times. Since cyber environments make the globe a single unit without any territorial differentiations, it is essential to have a global perspective towards cybersecurity (Savaş & Karataş, 2022). However, biased national security concerns, political ideologies, and economic disparity between the countries have become hindrances to achieving this objective.

5.1 Cybersecurity: A Desired Protection

Closely observing the present society informs us that it lives more in cyberspace than in the real world. All the conventional activities and services that were part of face-to-face communication have now shifted to the digital world. For instance, when buying a product (e.g., a watch), most people visit a shop, interact with the shopkeeper, and make the choice. However, it is now done through the online store, where the product specifications and reviews are evaluated. People also use online platforms to buy essential grocery items, toilet articles, vegetables, fruits, and vital services like healthcare. When people, government, and institutions increasingly engage in cyberspace for various activities, the ultimate objective is to ensure security in the transactions. However, constant cyberattacks complicate the cybersecurity aspirations. Most cyberattacks aim at critical infrastructure facilities of a society, as they can cause more damage to its meaningful living. They can also cause unpredictable harm to national security (Mishra et al., 2022).

Notable cyber attacks have already occurred in 2025, causing security tensions in many countries. In January, the Taiwan National Security Bureau claimed that Chinese hackers targeted its government systems and telecommunication firms. It stated that the hackers had a 20% higher success rate in their attempts compared to 2023. Ukraine's cybersecurity agency claims that the Russian cyberattacks have rapidly increased in 2024. The attackers targeted the energy sector and defense-related systems through malware distribution and phishing. In February, the North Korean hackers stole almost US$1.5 billion in cryptocurrency from a Dubai-based exchange, which is the largest cryptocurrency heist. The Chinese government claims it is becoming a constant target of foreign cyber attackers, adversely affecting government agencies, education, healthcare, defense, research, and transportation sectors. In March, serious allegations were raised against Iranian hackers for spreading espionage against the governments of Iraq and Yemen. In April, Algeria-linked cyberattackers targeted Morocco's National Social Security Fund, exposing almost two million people's personal and financial data. In May, the UK's National Cyber Security Center named China a dominant national security threat (CSIS, 2025). The latest trends show that countries prefer to encroach on each other's cyberspace rather than encroaching on their territorial boundaries, as it can cause more harm to people's dignified lives. Whether national, terrorist, or private actors, cyberattacks cause widespread complexities, causing significant economic loss, distress, and loss of life (Plotnek & Slay, 2021).

5.2 Data Privacy: A Guarantee for the Future

Although there has been difficulty in defining privacy, data privacy is a more understandable concept. Justice Brandeis in *Olmstead v. United States* (277 US 438 (1928)) affirmed that privacy is the most celebrated right of the civilized man, and its value is rarely questioned (Solove, 2008). The same applies to data privacy. The right to data privacy is the most valued right of contemporary society, where data is the wealth valued. However, privacy concerns were not monolithic across cultures, societies, countries, and individuals. The philosophical foundation upon which a society was built also influenced its perspectives on privacy (Posey et al., 2017). Such a scenario and a biased approach towards privacy gradually changed with the influence of globalization and liberalization. Although breaches of personal information are a global phenomenon, all people have a negative impression of the system's functioning, as it violates their right to privacy. People who live in countries with more liberal thoughts might feel more concerned when such breaches happen, compared to those in restrictive settings. Due to the widespread use of social media and other online platforms, there is now a greater possibility for spreading such news within a limited period. Instances of data breaches and privacy violations may erode public trust (Goel & Shawky, 2009).

Hackers have become a standard term in the present century. Regardless of ethical/unethical, public/private, and legitimate/illegitimate, they target the crucial information of individuals, organizations, or countries. The world of hackers has become so broad, depending on the nature of their activity. Terms like green hat, blue hat, black hat, white hat, gray hat, and red hat refer to the nature of hackers' service (Dhirani et al., 2023). Most countries use the help of hackers or employ them as active agents to hack vital information from other countries. Sometimes, these hackers are also used to harm other countries' security systems and critical infrastructure facilities (CSIS, 2025). This shows that states, which are responsible for protecting the right to privacy of their citizens, violate the right to privacy of other nationals. This would be a violation of Article 12 of the UDHR. The protection of the right to privacy in Article 12 of the UDHR argues that "no one shall be subjected to arbitrary interference with his privacy." The provisions of the UDHR can be realized only when all state parties take up the responsibility to protect and promote them. This responsibility cannot be limited to their commitment towards their citizens alone. It is a global responsibility. Suppose any state authorities fund hackers to attack the critical infrastructure facilities of other countries and steal information about other nationals. In that case, it violates its responsibility towards the fundamental human rights enshrined in the UDHR. Privacy is an acclaimed human right, which is universal, inalienable, indivisible, and interdependent. It applies equally to all people on Earth, regardless of any differentiating parameters. These unique characteristics of privacy as a human right argue that state parties should respect it without differentiating between citizens and other nationals. Only then can the globe realize its aspirations for a sustainable future.

5.3 Cybersecurity and Data Privacy: Challenges

Although cybersecurity and data privacy are the desired objectives for a dignified cyberspace, these are not adequately realized. Several fragmented efforts to ensure cybersecurity and data privacy can be seen worldwide. However, the lack of coordinated and collaborative effort is the biggest drawback to achieving these objectives. Since cyberspace cannot be equated with any country's territorial space, the laws applicable to a specific country's cyber interactions may not be applicable in another country. This creates confusion and complexity. The global nature of cyberspace should be visible in the laws and policies framed for its protection. When cyberlaws change along with state territories, it creates more possibilities for cybercriminals' free movement and involvement. They might be situated in a country where cybersecurity and data protection laws are not strictly implemented, but they cause harm in other countries where these violations are serious legal concerns. It creates a paradoxical situation. Besides, these differences also cause problems for organizations, as they face issues in following the applicable guidelines and laws. They may be forced to modify their applications' ethical and legal framework depending on the policies and regulations of each state (Mishra et al., 2022). If a globally recognized cybersecurity and data privacy enactment and policy existed, its implementation and practice would have been more straightforward. A general agreement or an international covenant among the states is required to confront the increasing cybersecurity issues.

Another crucial challenge concerning implementing cybersecurity and data privacy is the financial burden involved. It involves substantial costs, which may not be easily manageable for many institutions. When the costs for such a significant protective framework increase, many firms try to compromise, ultimately affecting the value and safety of cyberspace (Bakare et al., 2024). This is particularly evident in the case of institutions in developing and underdeveloped countries. It can be addressed only when there is an effective, supportive system from the developed world and the international institutions. However, this may remain an unrealizable dream in the present age of tariff wars between countries.

6 AN ETHICO-LEGAL FRAMEWORK

The latest trends show that cyberattacks and cybercrimes have become so common. This precarious situation forced many national governments to design laws and policies that regulate cyber interactions and guarantee cybersecurity and data privacy. The EU's GDPR is a significant example of such attempts. Many international institutions and national governments followed the model of GDPR to frame their specific policies and enactments for maintaining cybersecurity. However, the latest data shows that cyber insecurities and data breaches are rising yearly (Dalal et al., 2022). The most notable concern of cyberspace is its anonymity. It is notoriously difficult to identify the specific actors of cybercrimes accurately. It is also not easy to definitely locate their place and involvement. These problems make prosecuting cybercriminals a herculean task, prompting them to actively engage in more criminal activities (Plotnek & Slay, 2021). Ethical considerations are essential for meaningful interactions in real or cyber lives. Although ethical perspectives cannot be definitively proved or concluded like mathematical problems, the cultural capital of any society affirms that certain well-designed ethical principles are required for society's march towards a sustainable future (Reiss, 2010).

The society cannot think that if there are no specific ethical guidelines and principles, everyone will behave in a dignified manner. People's specific prejudice and bias will influence their behavior patterns, which may cause harm and insecurity to others. This human tendency is also visible in cyberspace. Since cyberspace provides the possibility for free, accessible, and worldwide service to its users, it may not be easy to ensure security and privacy without some ethical principles and legal mandates (Pawlicka et al., 2023). Digital technologies and cyberspace interactions widely require following ethical principles and values, as they have already significantly impacted almost all areas of human interaction. Wherever human actors are involved, some ethical principles are also required. It underlines how humans should behave in such an area, explains why they should not be used as mere means, and challenges any attempts that demean their dignity. Cybersecurity aims to help cyberspace users mitigate the risks and vulnerabilities associated with their systems, networks, and data (Dhirani et al., 2023). It can be effectively done only with the help of a well-designed ethical and legal framework. Discussions on the required ethical and legal principles are increasing as cybercrimes and data privacy violations increase. However, the ethical domain and the legal framework are not growing as quickly as digitalization. Several cyber firms have designed ethical codes for their professionals and users. They affirm that they prioritize protecting the "safety and welfare of society and the common good" (ISC2 Code of Ethics, n.d.). However, they all face implementation complexities, adversely affecting cyberspace's security aspirations.

6.1 Accountability

Cyberspace now handles millions of personal data, educational records, e-commerce details, health records, bank account details, biometric information, infrastructure coordination, and national security records (Dhirani et al., 2023). Cyberspace witnesses millions of recorded unauthorized access, data misuse, and privacy violations (Bakare et al., 2024). This necessitates that cyber interactions and the decision-making process should be auditable. Cyberspace's accountability evolves from the accountability of its users and professionals. Each user, hacker (regardless of their difference in hacking activity), professional, organization, state, and international institution has to show accountability towards each other by taking responsibility for their cyberspace activities. It is easy to put a burden on others. For instance, the Russian hackers easily blame the Ukrainian hackers and vice versa for the misuse of cyberspace (CSIS, 2025). The primary ethical principle (golden rule) underlines that "do not do unto others what you would not have them do unto you." Accountability insists that service providers collaborate with other cyberspace actors to ensure an efficient cybersecurity and privacy network (Murdoch, 2021).

6.2 Transparency

Transparency is openness and honesty in interactions in the real or cyber world. However, the present globe testifies to many examples where openness and transparency are ignored or undervalued. Several cyberactivities, like unauthorized access, data interference, illegal interception, ID theft, system interference, and electronic fraud, point to the transparency issues in cyberspace (Pawlicka et al., 2023). Chatbots are increasingly employed in cyberspace (Hasal et al., 2021). Human actors often interact with chatbots without realizing they are interacting with machines. It may sometimes cause 'emotional reliance' and addiction to chatbots (Samuel, 2024). Although most chatbots' descriptions state that they are machines, people may neglect to read such descriptions or may not understand them. Even though the service providers cannot be blamed for a lack of transparency, it poses specific ethical concerns. Most service providers do not explain such details in plain and simple language and prioritize confusing the users rather than supporting them. Any malicious intention of the service providers or the professionals in the field is against the demands of transparency. Sometimes, the users will be asked to accept the cookies to access a cyberspace service. However, some service providers may use it to infiltrate our system with malicious intent (Hasel et al., 2021). In a recent Australian survey, the consumer respondents stated that they are unaware of what the firms do with the collected data. They expressed their inability to protect their data due to a lack of time and knowledge. They also criticized the data protection process as complex and challenging (Quach et al., 2022). The GDPR states that organizations can collect data only for the intended purpose and the collected data cannot be stored permanently (Bakare et al., 2024). It emphasizes the required transparency in cyber activities. No institution can collect personal data without clearly stating its motive. The collected data should be used only for the already stated purpose. Any step contravening its affirmation is considered a violation of data privacy. The permanent storage of data can also cause privacy violations. The GDPR provision, in this regard, is very progressive, as it systematically controls the possibilities for data privacy violations.

6.3 A Human Rights-Protected Cyberspace

Cyberspace is the creation of humans for the benefit of humans. They are the source and ends of cyberspace. They use it for their dignified living. Cyberspace thus should be designed in such a way as to protect human values and claims (Dhirani et al., 2023). Since ethics and ethical behavior are profound considerations of cybersecurity policies and plans, it is closely associated with human rights (Pawlicka et al., 2023). Protecting individual rights is given predominance in the digital era across the globe. Security and privacy are fundamental human rights enshrined in the UDHR (Articles 3 & 12) and all other international covenants. These rights are people's basic claims that should be realizable in both the cyber and real worlds. The human rights approach claims that people have explicit rights over their data in cyberspace. People have the right to know what personal information is collected and how it is used. They have the right to access, the right to be informed, the right to erasure, and the right to rectification. These rights oblige other actors to adhere to lawfulness, fairness, and transparency (Bakare et al., 2024). At the same time, people should be aware of these rights; otherwise, they will not be able to ensure their implementation in daily life. This requires people to be adequately conscientized about cyber rights.

6.4 People-Centered Approach

The ultimate aim of cyberspace should be to promote human well-being and societal welfare. Any technological advancement should be focused on increasing human potential and capabilities. The confusion between national and human security is the main issue in adequately addressing the impact of many innovations, including cyberspace. The increased use of cyberspace, which has no territorial limits, for national security has caused tensions in cybersecurity discussions. Cybersecurity and data privacy are paid more attention from the national security perspective. However, the human security element is neglected (Rajaretnam, 2019). Cybersecurity and data privacy should concentrate on protecting individuals' personal information and vital needs. Such an attempt can help expand cyberspace's security and privacy concerns globally (Mishra et al., 2022). If all the countries change their attitude towards cybersecurity and data privacy, from a national security perspective to a human security perspective, they can easily address cyberattacks and data breaches through systematic collaboration. Furthermore, a critical analysis of data breaches and cybercrimes states that most cyber insecurities are due to human errors. Humans are the weakest link in cybersecurity. When they make a mistake, it causes adverse repercussions on themselves and the security of their organization (Savaş & Karataş, 2022). Such a situation necessitates that national and international agents concentrate on capacity-building. Efficient human capital creation is essential for confronting various cybercrimes and data breaches.

6.5 Legal Framework

Several countries have already enacted laws to address cyberattacks and ensure cybersecurity. Mishra et al. (2022) explain the legal frameworks for cybersecurity and data privacy in the USA, the EU, Canada, Australia, China, India, and Malaysia. These countries have enacted various laws to guarantee their citizens a dignified cyberspace. They cover telecommunication, network, cloud computing, e-commerce, online banking, smart grid, consumer rights, cybercrime, national encryption, privacy, identity theft, digital theft, data security, and spam. It underlines that the cyberlaws must be broad enough to address all possible cyberattacks and data privacy violations. The EU's GDPR is considered the most prominent legal framework and an example for other countries about cybersecurity and data privacy provisions (Hasel et al., 2021). Pawlicka et al. (2023) give a significant example to argue that cyberspace requires an efficient legal framework. In July 2020, the Gramin fitness tracking company faced a cyberattack (ransomware) from a Russian organization. Since the Gramin company lost access to its products and services, it could not satisfy its clients by providing meaningful service. It forced the company to pay US$10 million as ransom to regain access. Although many discussions occurred concerning the legality and ethicality of cyberattacks, the company had to compromise with the hackers to safeguard its reputation. Such incidents have occurred frequently across the globe, adversely affecting individuals, organizations, and states. Such a scenario demands a globally accepted legal framework under the initiative of the UN. Since the globe increasingly utilizes cyberspace for various activities, it cannot flourish with compromises alone. It requires effective policies and laws that apply to all. There are various national and regional enactments other than the GDPR. Some examples include the Australian Privacy Act, the California Privacy Rights Act, and the Digital Personal Data Protection Act (India). Although these enactments benefit customers, they are too costly for firms (Quach et al., 2022). Obviously, violations of cybersecurity and data privacy should be strictly handled. Nevertheless, the globe requires cooperation between different actors rather than creating tension to become more effective in ensuring cybersecurity.

7 FUTURE DIRECTIONS

While cyberattacks were a rare phenomenon in the past, they have become routine activities that happen almost every minute. Cyberattacks and privacy violations are increasing in number and magnitude. The nature and forms of cyberattacks vary from time to time. The scope of cyber insecurities has become so broad that it encompasses almost all areas of human interactions that utilize cyberspace. Realizing the severity of cyber insecurities forces the national government and international institutions to frame appropriate policies and prompt responses. Although the nature and magnitude of cyberattacks have significantly changed, most institutions and people still use traditional malware defensive systems. They were effective in the beginning. However, in the present times, the globe requires more robust and effective defensive systems as cyber interactions are comparatively much higher than in the previous decades (Mishra et al., 2022). Compromises in cybersecurity may damage the entire system of functioning across the globe. Internet outages are more complicated and costly for the entire globe. The instances of Facebook outage (2021), Microsoft 365 outage (2023, 2024), and CrowdStrike (2024) showed the world how vital cyberspace has become in human lives. Accordingly, the globe must take adequate measures to handle such insecurities and collapses.

Dalal et al. (2022) note a significant lack of qualified personnel who can efficiently address cybersecurity and data privacy issues. Many countries have initiated academic programs and research support systems to promote more human capital. As cyberattacks are increasing daily, the availability and active engagement of qualified personnel can support national and international attempts to confront such threats. Cybercriminals utilize people's lack of knowledge about cyberspace interactions and their vulnerabilities (Savaş & Karataş, 2022). The qualified personnel and various agencies should advance awareness generation among ordinary people to empower them to face cyber insecurities prudently. Besides, not all countries face the same degree of cyberattacks and privacy violations (Mishra et al., 2022). Economic growth, technological advancements, and a strict legal framework are various factors that influence a country's vulnerability to such kinds of attacks. Some countries have already made successful efforts to address cyber insecurities. They should support other countries in devising adequate strategies, policies, and laws promoting efficient cybersecurity networks. The increased occurrence of cybercrimes demands that the globe needs more efficient policies that apply to all individuals, institutions, and devices in cyberspace. Cybersecurity is not an individual competition area; it should be an internationally recognized standard for enhancing the security of all cyber interactions. Therefore, the designed policies should be adaptive, participatory, and inclusive. It should include public and private, as well as national and international actors. The policies should cover all areas and users, and must be binding on everyone (Savaş & Karataş, 2022).

8 CONCLUSION

Cyberspace has permeated every aspect of human life. The broader the cyberspace perspectives, the stronger the cybersecurity and privacy concerns. The 21st

century world has become more vulnerable to cybercrimes and insecurities than conventional wars. Data privacy violations are so frequent that people face confusion and anxiety concerning the effectiveness of cyberspace. Data privacy and cybersecurity laws and policies are thus essential for a dignified cyberspace (Bakare et al., 2024). The above analysis underlined that cybersecurity and data privacy are not two distinct terms but are intimately linked. Mostly, they are inseparable. Both terms emphasize the importance of protecting people's personal information and cyber activities, respecting their dignity and rights. Cybersecurity and data protection, regardless of territorial differences, should become the most desired objective of the world. The UN and other international institutions should coordinate with various states and public and private actors to encourage and ensure security and privacy in cyberspace. Cybersecurity violations and data privacy breaches should be addressed seriously. Even if state actors do these, they should be liable to the global community based on the Golden Rule of ethics. Even when this chapter proposes some specific ethical principles required for a dignified cyberspace, it should be acknowledged that there is no single universally accepted ethical framework (Reiss, 2010). Besides, the evolving nature of cyberspace argues that the ethical framework, which should guide cyberspace, may change with time. However, this chapter argues that some principles can be universally and indefinitely accepted. The chapter does not state that the ethico-legal framework explained is universally acceptable, but all can value the principles included in this framework. Some may add other principles, extending the depth of the framework. The basic objective of all those who frame policies, principles, and enactments concerning cybersecurity and data privacy should be to ensure a dignified cyberspace for people to grow and improve their standard of living.

REFERENCES

Đurđević, D., & Stevanović, M. (2016). The Value Challenge of Interconnectedness in Cyberspace for National Security. *Sinteza*, 15-23. https://portal.sinteza.singidunum.ac.rs/paper/391

Acilar, A., & Sæbø, Ø. (2023). Towards Understanding the Gender Digital Divide: A Systematic Literature Review. *Global Knowledge, Memory and Communication*, *72*(3), 233–249. DOI: 10.1108/GKMC-09-2021-0147

Adhikari, A. S. (2024). The Concept of International Security. *Hasanuddin Journal of International Affairs*, 4(2), 78-89. https://journal.unhas.ac.id/index.php/hujia/article/view/34797

Admass, W. S., Munaye, Y. Y., & Diro, A. A. (2024). Cyber Security: State of the Art, Challenges, and Future Directions. *Cyber Security and Application*, *2*, 100031. DOI: 10.1016/j.csa.2023.100031

AlDaajeh, S., Saleous, H., Alrabaee, S., Barka, E., Breitinger, F., & Choo, K.-K. R. (2022). The Role of National Cybersecurity Strategies on the Improvement of Cybersecurity Education. *Computers & Security*, *119*, 102754. DOI: 10.1016/j.cose.2022.102754

Ari, A. A. A., Ngangmo, O. K., Titouna, C., & Thiare, O. Kolyang, Mohamadou, A., & Gueroui, A.M. (2024). Enabling Privacy and Security in Cloud of Things: Architecture, Applications, Security & Privacy Challenges. *Applied Computing and Informatics*, 20(1-2), 119-141. https://www.emerald.com/aci/article/20/1-2/119/1223199

Bakare, S. S., Adeniyi, A. O., Akpoukwe, C. U., & Ench, N. E. (2024). Data Privacy Law and Compliance: A Comparative Review of the EU GDPR and USA Regulations. *Computer Science & IT Research Journal*, 5(3), 528-543. https://www.fepbl.com/index.php/csitrj/article/view/859

Brown, J. M., & Fazal, T. M. (2021). #SorryNotSorry: Why States Neither Confirm Nor Deny Responsibility for Cyber Operations. *European Journal of International Security*, *6*(4), 401–417. DOI: 10.1017/eis.2021.18

Brown-Jackson, K. L. (2022). Intersections of Telemedicine/Telehealth and Cybersecurity: The Age of Resilience and COVID-19. *Science Bulletin*, *27*(1), 1–11. https://sciendo.com/article/10.2478/bsaft-2022-0001 PMID: 36545951

Bussell, J. (2025). Cyberspace. *Britannica*. https://www.britannica.com/topic/cyberspace

Bygrave, L. (2002). *Data Protection Law: Approaching Its Rationale, Logic, and Limits*. Kluwer Law International.

CSIS (Center for Strategic & International Studies). (2025). *Significant Cyber Incidents*. https://www.csis.org/programs/strategic-technologies-program/significant-cyber-incidents

Dalal, R. S., Howard, D. J., Bennett, R. J., Posey, C., Zaccaro, S. J., & Brummel, B. J. (2022). Organizational Science and Cybersecurity: Abundant Opportunities for Research at the Interface. *Journal of Business and Psychology*, *37*(1), 1–29. https://link.springer.com/article/10.1007/s10869-021-09732-9. DOI: 10.1007/s10869-021-09732-9 PMID: 33564206

Daneshfar, Z., Asokan-Ajitha, A., Sharma, P., & Malik, A. (2023). Work-from-home (WFH) During COVID-19 Pandemic – A Netnographic Investigation Using Twitter Data. *Information Technology & People*, *36*(5), 2161–2186. DOI: 10.1108/ITP-01-2021-0020

Dhirani, L. L., Mukhtiar, N., Chowdhury, B. S., & Newe, T. (2023). Ethical Dilemmas and Privacy Issues in Emerging Technologies: A Review. *Sensors (Basel)*, *23*(3), 1151. https://www.mdpi.com/1424-8220/23/3/1151. DOI: 10.3390/s23031151 PMID: 36772190

Diggelmann, O., & Cleis, M. N. (2014). How the Right to Privacy became a Human Right. *Human Rights Law Review*, *14*(3), 441–458. DOI: 10.1093/hrlr/ngu014

Gilder, A. (2021). International Law and Human Security in a Kaleidoscopic World. *Indian Journal of International Law*, *59*(1-4), 111–137. https://link.springer.com/article/10.1007/s40901-020-00109-w. DOI: 10.1007/s40901-020-00109-w

Goel, S., & Shawky, H. A. (2009). Estimating the Market Impact of Security Breach Announcements on Firm Values. *Information & Management*, *46*(7), 404–410. DOI: 10.1016/j.im.2009.06.005

Haefner, L., & Sternberg, R. (2020). Spatial Implications of Digitalization: State of the Field and Research Agenda. *Geography Compass*, *14*(12), e12544. https://compass.onlinelibrary.wiley.com/doi/full/10.1111/gec3.12544. DOI: 10.1111/gec3.12544

Hasal, M., Nowaková, J., Saghair, K. A., Abdulla, H., Snášel, V., & Ogiela, L. (2021). Chatbots: Security, Privacy, Data Protection, and Social Aspects. *Concurrency and Computation*, *33*(19), e6425. https://onlinelibrary.wiley.com/doi/full/10.1002/cpe.6426. DOI: 10.1002/cpe.6426

ISC2 Code of Ethics. (n.d.). https://www.isc2.org/Ethics

Kitchin, R. M. (1998). Towards Geographies of Cyberspace. *Progress in Human Geography*, *22*(3), 385–406. https://journals.sagepub.com/doi/abs/10.1191/030913298668331585. DOI: 10.1191/030913298668331585

Lambach, D. (2020). The Territorialization of Cyberspace. *International Studies Review*, *22*(3), 482–506. DOI: 10.1093/isr/viz022

Mishra, A., Alzoubi, Y. I., Anwar, M. J., & Gill, A. Q. (2022). Attributes Impacting Cybersecurity Policy Development: An Evidence from Seven Nations. *Computers & Security*, *120*, 102820. https://www.sciencedirect.com/science/article/pii/S0167404822002140. DOI: 10.1016/j.cose.2022.102820

Moore, M. (2025). Top Cybersecurity Threats to Watch in 2025. University of San Diego. https://onlinedegrees.sandiego.edu/top-cyber-security-threats/#:~:text=Types%20of%20Cyber%20Threats,fostering%20a%20secure%20digital%20environment

Mubarak, F., & Suomi, R. (2022). Elderly Forgotten? Digital Exclusion in the Information Age and the Rising Grey Digital Divide. *Inquiry: The Journal of Health Care Organization, Provision, and Financing*, 59. https://journals.sagepub.com/doi/full/10.1177/00469580221096272

Murdoch, B. (2021). Privacy and Artificial Intelligence: Challenges for Protecting Health Information in a New Era. *BMC Medical Ethics*, *22*(1), 122. https://link.springer.com/article/10.1186/s12910-021-00687-3. DOI: 10.1186/s12910-021-00687-3 PMID: 34525993

Osler, L., & Zahavi, D. (2023). Sociality and Embodiment: Online Communication During and After COVID-19. *Foundations of Science*, *28*(4), 1125–1142. https://link.springer.com/article/10.1007/S10699-022-09861-1. DOI: 10.1007/s10699-022-09861-1 PMID: 36212516

Paul, M., Maglaras, L., Ferrag, M. A., & Almomani, I. (2023). Digitalization of Healthcare Sector: A Study on Privacy and Security Concerns. *IT Express*, *9*(1), 571–588. DOI: 10.1016/j.icte.2023.02.007

Pawlicka, A., Choraś, M., Kozik, R., & Pawlicki, M. (2023). First Broad and Systematic Horizon Scanning Campaign and Study to Detect Societal and Ethical Dilemmas and Emerging Issues Spanning Over Cybersecurity Solutions. *Personal and Ubiquitous Computing*, *27*(2), 193–202. https://link.springer.com/article/10.1007/s00779-020-01510-3. DOI: 10.1007/s00779-020-01510-3

Plotnek, J. J., & Slay, J. (2021). Cyber Terrorism: A Homogenized Taxonomy and Definition. *Computers & Security*, *102*, 102145. DOI: 10.1016/j.cose.2020.102145

Porcedda, M. G. (2017). *Cybersecurity and Privacy Rights in EU Law: Moving Beyond the Trade-off Model to Appraise the Role of Technology*. European University Institute. https://cadmus.eui.eu/entities/publication/24cc89f2-609c-5722-ad9f-b6080ebf1718

Posey, C., Raja, U., Crossler, R. E., & Burns, A. J. (2017). Taking Stock of Organizations' Protection of Privacy: Categorizing and Assessing Threats to Personally Identifiable Information in the USA. *European Journal of Information Systems*, *26*(6), 585–604. https://www.tandfonline.com/doi/epdf/10.1057/s41303-017-0065-y?needAccess=true. DOI: 10.1057/s41303-017-0065-y

Powell, A., Bryne, A., & Dailey, D. (2012). The Essential Internet: Digital Exclusion in Low-Income American Communities. *Policy and Internet*, *2*(2), 161–192. https://onlinelibrary.wiley.com/doi/10.2202/1944-2866.1058. DOI: 10.2202/1944-2866.1058

Quach, S., Thaichon, P., Martin, K. D., Weaven, S., & Palmatier, R. W. (2022). Digital Technologies: Tensions in Privacy and Data. *Journal of the Academy of Marketing Science*, *50*(6), 1299–1323. https://link.springer.com/article/10.1007/s11747-022-00845-y. DOI: 10.1007/s11747-022-00845-y PMID: 35281634

Rajaretnam, T. (2019). A Review of Data Governance, Regulation, Practices and Cybersecurity Strategies for Businesses: An Australian Perspective. In *International Conference on Education, Technology, Business, and Social Science* (pp. 6-21). Academia Industry Networks.

Reiss, M. (2010). Ethical Thinking. In Jone, A., McKim, A., & Reiss, M. (Eds.), *Ethics in the Science and Technology Classroom: A New Approach to Teaching and Learning* (pp. 7–17). Sense Publishers., https://brill.com/display/book/9789460910715/BP000003.xml DOI: 10.1163/9789460910715_003

Rubenfeld, J. (1989). The Right to Privacy. *Harvard Law Review*, *102*(4), 737–807. https://www.jstor.org/stable/1341305. DOI: 10.2307/1341305

Saeed, S. A., & Masters, R. M. (2021). Disparities in Health Care and the Digital Divide. *Current Psychiatry Reports*, *23*(9), 61. https://link.springer.com/article/10.1007/s11920-021-01274-4. DOI: 10.1007/s11920-021-01274-4 PMID: 34297202

Saleh, A. M. S. (2024). Blockchain for Secure and Decentralized Artificial Intelligence in Cybersecurity: A Comprehensive Review. *Blockchain: Research and Applications*, *5*(3), 100193. DOI: 10.1016/j.bcra.2024.100193

Samuel, S. (2024). People are Falling in Love with — and Getting Addicted to — AI Voices. *Vox*. https://www.vox.com/future-perfect/367188/love-addicted-ai-voice-human-gpt4-emotion

Savaş, S., & Karataş, S. (2022). Cyber Governance Studies in Ensuring Cybersecurity: An Overview of Cybersecurity Governance. *International Cybersecurity Law Review*, *3*(1), 7–34. https://link.springer.com/article/10.1365/s43439-021-00045-4. DOI: 10.1365/s43439-021-00045-4 PMID: 37521508

Scandamis, N., Sigalas, F., & Stratakis, S. (2007). Rival Freedoms in (Terms of) Security: The Case of Data Protection and (the Criterion of) Connexity. *Research Paper No. 7, Challenge, Liberty, & Security*. https://www.files.ethz.ch/isn/45974/CP007%20Rival%20Freedoms%20in%20terms%20of%20security.pdf

Siddiqi, M. A., Pak, W., & Siddiqi, M. A. (2022). A Study on the Psychology of Social Engineering-Based Cyberattacks and Existing Countermeasures. *Applied Sciences (Basel, Switzerland)*, *12*(12), 6042. https://www.mdpi.com/2076-3417/12/12/6042. DOI: 10.3390/app12126042

Solove, D. (2008). *Understanding Privacy*. Harvard University Press.

Tick, A., Cranfield, D. J., Venter, I. M., Renaud, K. V., & Blignaut, R. J. (2021). Comparing Three Countries' Higher Education Students' Cyber-Related Perceptions and Behaviors During COVID-19. *Electronics (Basel)*, *10*(22), 2865. https://www.mdpi.com/2079-9292/10/22/2865. DOI: 10.3390/electronics10222865

Tully, S. (2014). A Human Right to Access the Internet? Problems and Prospects. *Human Rights Law Review*, *14*(2), 175–195. DOI: 10.1093/hrlr/ngu011

Tzanou, M. (2013). Data Protection as a Fundamental Right Next to Privacy? 'Reconstructing' a Not so New Right. *International Data Privacy Law*, *3*(2), 88–99. DOI: 10.1093/idpl/ipt004

UNDP. (1994). *Human Development Report*. https://hdr.undp.org/content/human-development-report-1994

Westin, A. (1970). *Privacy and Freedom*. Bodley Head.

Xiao, L., Cheng, X., & Mou, J. (2022). Understanding Global E-Commerce Development During the COVID-19 Pandemic: Technology-Organization-Environment Perspective. *Journal of Global Information Technology Management*, *25*(1), 1–6. DOI: 10.1080/1097198X.2022.2026658

Zelikow, P. (2003). The Transformation of National Security: Five Redefinitions. *National Interest*, *71*, 17–28. https://www.jstor.org/stable/42895592

KEY TERMS AND DEFINITIONS

Cyberworld: Cyberworld refers to the world of the Internet, the network, and the digital environment wherein the interactions are mostly virtual. In contrast to the physical world, the cyberworld is famous for its speed, productivity, and efficiency.

Data Protection: Data protection is an umbrella term that includes various methods and processes to safeguard the vital information of cyberspace users. It ensures security against all unauthorized attempts to corrupt or steal sensitive information.

Digital Divide: The digital divide refers to the existing inequality concerning cyberspace access, availability, and affordability in different societal sectors. It exists between developed and developing countries, rich and poor people, urban and rural sections of society, and men and women.

GDPR: The General Data Protection Regulation is a historic legislation of the European Union that aimed to protect people's sensitive information in the digital space. It is primarily a consumer-friendly legislation. Although it was adopted in 2016, it came into force on May 25, 2018.

Right to Internet Access: The right to access the Internet is a fundamental digital right that helps people advance in cyberactivities, ensuring economic growth and societal welfare. Although the right to Internet access is not formally declared in any international covenants, it is considered part of the freedom of expression.

SDGs: SDGs are the UN-designed and internationally accepted seventeen goals to ensure a sustainable future for global society. These goals aim to promote sustainability in every field of human interaction.

Sustainability: Sustainability is the capacity of a system to maintain its value for generations. However, from the second half of the 20th century, it has primarily been understood regarding environmental protection. It insists that society, economy, and environment should be able to satisfy the needs of both the present and future generations.

Chapter 6

Scroll, Click, Surrender:
A Critical Study of Consent in Social Media Data Harvesting Under Global Privacy Laws

Sunidhi Setia
https://orcid.org/0000-0001-9174-0458
Jindal Global Law School, O.P. Jindal Global University, India

Yogita Bangar
Jindal Global Law School, O.P. Jindal Global University, India

Harsh Manohar
Jindal Global Law School, O.P. Jindal Global University, India

ABSTRACT

Social media platforms collect vast personal data, through lengthy terms and conditions that users accept without understanding. Globally, laws like the General Data Protection Regulation (GDPR), California's CCPA have set high standards for consent and user rights. India, through the Digital Personal Data Protection Act (DPDP) of 2023, has introduced its own framework, recognizing privacy as a fundamental right following the landmark Puttaswamy v. Union of India judgment. It highlights how Indian law addresses challenges of meaningful consent, dark patterns, and data collection practices in comparison to global norms. It shows that while the DPDP Act introduces requirements for notice, limitation, and user control, gaps remain in enforcement. The paper argues that India's privacy framework is at a crossroads: it must strengthen safeguards against exploitative practices while aligning with global best practices. The paper concludes that clearer rules, stronger accountability, and user-friendly consent mechanisms are essential for protecting autonomy in India's social media ecosystem.

DOI: 10.4018/979-8-3373-4967-1.ch006

1. INTRODUCTION: CONSENT IN THE DIGITAL AGE

Social media platforms have not only transformed human communication, public discourse, and commercial ecosystems but have also gone beyond the role of a technological tool for entertainment and communication. With users from all genders, ages, and communities, social media platforms are a central part of our everyday life (Chidiac et al., 2022). It is important to note that beneath engaging interfaces of these social media platforms lies a powerful and opaque engine of data extraction enabled by a complex interplay of algorithms, behavioural nudging, and often ambiguous consent mechanisms (Guggenberger, 2025). Almost everyone has experienced seeing ads for products moments after mentioning them out loud, bringing into focus the mechanisms through which ads are targeted.

Social media users of all ages, while using these platforms as a form of entertainment, unknowingly end up sharing information while scrolling, clicking, and liking the content. User consent is supposed to be the legal gateway enabling this data collection; in theory, users agree to let platforms harvest and use their personal information. In practice, however, this consent is often an illusion of choice. People typically 'agree' by scrolling through lengthy terms and clicking 'Accept' without real negotiation or understanding, effectively surrendering their data (Goodin, 2023). The result is largely passive, bundled, non-negotiable consent that raises serious ethical and legal questions about how 'informed' or 'free' such consent truly is (Richards & Hartzog, 2018).

In the early days, social media platforms were designed primarily for social connection or dating, mostly with simple banner advertising. Platforms like Facebook changed this simple business model through the introduction of algorithmic content curation and engagement tools, such as the 'Like' button. (Boyd and Nicole, 2007) Engagement with posts became a data point about the users' preferences and interests. With the collection of these data points in mind, the user's role subtly changed from customer to product. (Gerlitz & Helmond, 2013) This evolution has rendered the traditional 'notice and consent' framework obsolete for social media. Simple terms of service have ballooned into gigantic legal documents, enabling the broadest possible permissions for data harvesting.

This study employs a qualitative, doctrinal, and comparative legal methodology to critically examine the concept of user consent in the context of social media data harvesting. The research undertakes a doctrinal analysis of primary legal sources, including India's Digital Personal Data Protection Act (DPDP), 2023, and the preceding Information Technology Act, 2000. The paper further incorporates a critical review of existing academic literature, regulatory enforcement actions, and case law to deconstruct the legal and ethical dimensions of consent, exploring related concepts. Through this multi-faceted approach, the study synthesizes legal interpretation with critical theory to evaluate the practical effectiveness of India's new law and propose recommendations for a more robust privacy framework.

The authors in this paper critically examine the concept of 'consent' in the context of data harvesting by social media platforms, using India as the focal point, while also conducting a comparative analysis with global privacy regimes, notably the European Union (GDPR), the United States (sectoral model), and Brazil (LGPD). The chapter interrogates whether the consent mechanisms employed by social media companies, typically embedded within lengthy and legally dense privacy policies, can be deemed meaningful, informed, and freely given in the true sense of the term. It evaluates how existing legal frameworks protect (or fail to protect) individual autonomy and privacy, especially in jurisdictions like India that are in the process of evolving comprehensive data protection laws. The chapter discusses important legal features of various legal systems around the world and provides critically tailored suggestions for India, which is still at a very nascent stage.

It is paramount to understand the concept of user consent in the architecture of digital privacy laws to analyse how it plays a crucial role in day-to-day scrolling on social media platforms. Consent serves as the legal gateway that permits companies to collect, process, and monetise user data (David, 2023). However, in the realm of social media, as Kovacs and Jain (2020) argue, this consent is often passive, bundled, and non-negotiable. The illusion of choice 'scroll, click, and surrender' is a widespread phenomenon, raising serious ethical and legal questions.

The rise of data-driven social media has eroded the traditional "notice and consent" approach over time. Early internet privacy frameworks assumed that providing users notice (privacy policies) and getting their consent would empower individuals (Nissenbaum, 2011). But modern platforms deploy sophisticated algorithms, behavioural nudges, and ambiguous consent flows that make genuine informed consent elusive (Saetra, 2021). The literature gap exists in the comparative analysis of the DPDP Act's practical ability to overcome the well-documented failures of consent-based models elsewhere. While existing scholarship has extensively detailed the shortcomings of consent under GDPR or has described the features of the new Indian law, there is insufficient research that critically interrogates whether the DPDP Act's provisions are sufficiently robust to address the systemic power imbalances and manipulative designs in the specific socio-technical context of India, which is characterized by vast linguistic diversity and varying levels of digital literacy.

This introduction lays out the problem: are the consent mechanisms used by social media companies typically buried in dense privacy policies, or are one-click 'I Agree' buttons meaningful, informed, and freely given? And how effectively do current laws protect user autonomy and privacy in this environment? Thus, the authors aim to introduce and discuss the rise of data-driven business models in social media. This part will focus on the historical development of social media platforms and the concept of 'notice and consent' and its erosion by these platforms over the period. The chapter centrally focuses on evaluating the legal validity and effectiveness of consent, especially in India, and recommends more user-centric regulatory responses in consideration of yet-developing data privacy laws in India.

2. INDIAN LEGAL LANDSCAPE: CURRENT AND EMERGING FRAMEWORKS

India's privacy law regime has undergone a dramatic evolution in recent years. For much of the internet era, India lacked a dedicated data protection law (Duraiswami, 2017). The primary legal provisions can be found in the Information Technology Act 2000 and the Government of India (2011) Information Technology (Reasonable Security Practices and Procedures and Sensitive Personal Data or Information) Rules, 2011 (the "SPDI Rules"). These rules required companies (termed "body corporates") to have privacy policies and to obtain consent for disclosing sensitive personal data to third parties. However, 'consent' under this regime was not clearly defined; businesses treated it largely as a matter of contract law (Joseph et al., 2020). As long as a user ostensibly agreed (e.g., by accepting terms of service) without coercion or undue influence, it counted as consent, and standard form contracts were generally enforceable so long as they were not grossly unfair. In other words, Indian law acknowledged consent but placed few restrictions on how it was obtained, aside from a general requirement that terms not be unconscionable, and SDPI rules do not delve into qualitative elements of consent but lay down the procedural requirements (Sharma, 2025). There was little in the way of granular rights or active oversight specifically for data privacy. Enforcement was minimal; the law provided that companies might pay compensation for data negligence, but no statutory fines or dedicated data regulator existed (Greeleaf, 2011).

A major turning point came with the landmark Supreme Court decision in *K.S. Puttaswamy v. Union of India* (2017) on the right to privacy. In that case, a 9-judge bench unanimously affirmed that privacy is a fundamental right protected under the Constitution of India. This judgment overturned earlier precedents and made it clear that Indians have an enforceable right to privacy, which includes control over personal data (Jain & Anand, 2025b). The landmark ruling in Puttaswamy explicitly recognized that in the digital age, the autonomy to make informed decisions about one's data is part of the right to life and liberty (Sebastian & Sen, 2020). This constitutional mandate created momentum and a legal imperative for comprehensive data protection legislation (Jain & Anand, 2025b).

2.1 Digital Personal Data Protection Act, 2023: An Overview

After Puttaswamy, India began drafting new data protection laws. Following several proposals and drafts, Parliament enacted the Digital Personal Data Protection Act, 2023 (DPDP Act) in August 2023. Although not operational yet, as the government will notify an effective date, the DPDP Act represents India's first comprehensive data protection law, aligning in many ways with global norms like the EU's GDPR (Parth, 2024). The authors have briefly highlighted the key features of the DPDP Act as follows:

a. ***Scope***: It covers digital personal data, i.e., any data about an identifiable individual that is digitized or digital by origin (Government of India, 2023, § 2). The Act has an extra-territorial application, which applies to processing outside India if it relates to offering goods/services to people in India.
b. ***Consent as a Cornerstone***: The law makes consent the primary basis for processing personal data, apart from certain limited exceptions. Organizations (termed "data fiduciaries") must obtain a user's consent (Government of India, 2023, § 4) before processing their personal data, unless the processing falls under defined 'legitimate uses' where consent isn't required. Such exceptions include, for example, processing needed for performing a legal obligation, for medical emergencies, for government benefits delivery, or other narrowly defined cases (Government of India, 2023, § 7). Notably, the DPDP Act defines consent in stringent terms as essentially to be "free, specific, informed, unconditional and unambiguous" and given via a clear affirmative action. This is very similar to GDPR's standard ("freely given, specific, informed, unambiguous" consent) and is aimed at ensuring users know what they agree to (Politou et al., 2021). Users also have the right to withdraw consent at any time, and the provisions for withdrawal are directed to be as easy as giving consent.
c. ***Consent Managers***: Unlike GDPR, the Indian law explicitly provides for a system of "Consent Managers". These are third-party, centralized services that individuals can use to give, track, and withdraw consent across multiple platforms (Government of India, 2023, § 6). Consent Managers will be registered with the Data Protection Board and act as users' agents, presumably to make it easier for users to manage privacy preferences in one place. This concept is an innovative response to 'consent fatigue'; rather than dealing with each app or site individually, a user could rely on a trusted intermediary to streamline consent management (Jain, 2025a).
d. ***Privacy Notices***: To obtain valid consent, data fiduciaries must provide a clear notice to users, describing what personal data will be collected and for what purpose, along with the contact details of a privacy officer for grievances

(Government of India, 2023, § 5). This notice should be in simple language. The law recognizes India's linguistic diversity and calls for multilingual notices as needed to ensure comprehension across different user groups (Gupta & Naithani, 2024).

e. ***User Rights***: The DPDP Act grants individuals a set of rights over their data, including the right to access information about what data is held on them, the right to request correction of inaccuracies, and the right to request deletion of their data (Government of India, 2023, § 11-14). These mirror rights in GDPR are often termed access, rectification, erasure, etc. Users can also nominate others to exercise rights on their behalf, which is important for accessibility.

f. ***Data Protection Board and Enforcement***: The Act establishes an independent Data Protection Board of India as the regulator to oversee compliance, investigate violations, and impose penalties. The Board will have powers to conduct hearings and direct remedies. The DPDP Act introduces steep penalties for non-compliance up to 250 crore (approximately US $30 million) per instance of violation (Government of India, 2023, § 27). This is a dramatic change from the old regime, which had no fixed fines. Such penalties put real teeth into the law, though it remains to be seen how aggressively they will be enforced.

g. ***Obligations and Safeguards***: The Act puts an obligation on the Data fiduciaries to implement 'reasonable security safeguards' to prevent breaches, and they have duties like data minimization (collect only data needed for the stated purpose) and purpose limitation (use data only for the purpose consented to) (Government of India, 2023, § 8). They also must notify the Data Protection Board and affected users of data breaches. The Act has also provided that Certain data uses are outright prohibited: for instance, processing children's data for behavioural tracking or targeted advertising.

h. ***Children's Privacy Protection Mechanisms***: The Act imposes enhanced obligations on all platforms dealing with the processing of children's data. For minors (under 18), parental consent is required to process personal data (Government of India, 2023, § 9). Though the act puts obligations on the data fiduciaries to get the verifiable parental consent, the act does not mention the process to verify such consent, putting an obligation on the Central Government to come up with detailed guidelines in this regard (Sharma et al., 2024). The act further puts an obligation on all businesses to not process the data of children in a way that might lead to detrimental effects on the well-being of any child (section 9(3)). The DPDP Act explicitly prohibits the behavioural monitoring and targeted advertising using the children's data. Even if the act provides several safeguards for protecting the children's data and their interests, it lacks dealing with practical issues like age identification and verification by these platforms, which is a concern even for Western democracies with advanced privacy laws (Bacon, 2023).

i. ***Exemptions***: The law carves out some exemptions for government functions such as law enforcement, judicial proceedings, and other scenarios like state security (Government of India, 2023, § 7). These are somewhat controversial as they would indirectly lead to government surveillance (Naithani, 2024).

2.2. Demographic Challenges Unique to India

India's legal landscape is thus shifting from a lightly regulated, consent-but-no-enforcement paradigm to a rights-based, consent-driven framework. However, implementing meaningful consent in India faces unique challenges. The DPDP Act comes at a time of low digital literacy among many Indian users, and as pointed out by Datta (2022), there exists significant linguistic diversity (hundreds of millions of Indians are online without fluent English). This means many users struggle to understand privacy notices or the implications of consent. Additionally, there is a cultural tendency to trust major platforms or consider clicking 'I Agree' as a mere formality, rather than an informed choice. The new law's success will depend on overcoming these operational and cultural barriers. The Act's emphasis on plain language and possibly multilingual consent flows is an attempt to address these issues. The concept of consent managers could reduce user burden by simplifying choices. But there is still scepticism about how 'freely given' consent can be in practice when declining consent might mean not using a must-have service like WhatsApp or Facebook a challenge not unique to India.

In summary, India is on the cusp of a modern data protection regime that places consent at its centre, buttressed by stronger rights and enforcement. The recognition of privacy as a fundamental right has accelerated this development. As India transitions to the DPDP Act, it is instructive to compare and contrast with global privacy frameworks, to see what lessons can be learned about making consent truly effective. The next section, therefore, deconstructs what constitutes 'meaningful consent' in an environment shaped by power asymmetries and complex technology.

3. WHAT IS 'MEANINGFUL CONSENT'? LEGAL AND ETHICAL DIMENSIONS

For consent to be legally and ethically meaningful, it must embody certain qualities: it should be free (voluntary), specific, informed, and unambiguous. In theory, 'freely given, informed, unambiguous' consent means the user has a real choice and understands what they are agreeing to. In the context of social media, however, achieving this ideal is fraught with difficulties. Let us now discuss some broad legal and ethical dimensions of meaningful consent.

3.1. Consent in Standard Form Contracts

With 'Take-it-or-leave-it' Contracts and Power Imbalance, most social media platforms present users with Standard Form Contracts (SFCs). SFCs are lengthy Terms of Service and Privacy Policies that one must accept in entirety to use the service (Hillman & Rachlinski, 2002). These are classic contracts of adhesion where one side (the company) sets the terms; the other side (the user) cannot negotiate and can only consent or refuse. Major platforms like Facebook, Instagram, X (Twitter), TikTok, etc., all employ such non-negotiable agreements. The user's "choice" in these kinds of contracts is illusory because refusing consent means being denied the service altogether. Legally, companies argue that by clicking "Sign Up" or "I Agree," the user has consented, and indeed, courts often uphold click-through agreements as binding. However, from an ethical standpoint, one must ask: Is consent truly free when billions of people must either surrender personal data or be excluded from large parts of modern social life and communication?

Privacy scholars note that this all-or-nothing dynamic undermines the spirit of consent (Solove, 2024). The GDPR (European Union, 2016) attempts to address this through its Article 7(4), which says consent may not be considered free if a contract (or service access) is made conditional on personal data that isn't necessary for using the service. In other words, companies shouldn't force you to agree to unrelated data collection just to use a platform. In practice, though, big platforms have claimed all their data processing is necessary (for personalizing content, ads, etc.), thus stretching the definition of "necessity" and effectively bundling broad consent with service use. A striking example was Facebook (Meta) in the EU: rather than ask users explicitly to consent to personalized ads, Facebook deemed that by signing up to Facebook, users entered a contract in which targeted ads were a part of the service (Frichot, 2025). This "bypass" of consent was eventually ruled illegal in 2023, EU regulators fined Meta €390 million, finding that forcing users to accept personalized ads as a condition of using Facebook/Instagram violated GDPR's consent requirements (Zard & Sears, 2023). Meta was ordered to seek true consent for behavioral ads or offer an opt-out. This case underscores that what companies call consent is not always viewed as such by regulators. Meaningful consent requires a genuine ability to say "no" without suffering disproportionate consequences like losing access entirely.

3.2 Meaningful Consent v. Consent Fatigue

Information asymmetry and lack of informed understanding are another core issue. It is pertinent to note that consent is often not informed in any substantive sense. Privacy policies are infamous for their length and complexity. Studies find they are often written at a college reading level and stretch to thousands of words. Users routinely skip reading them (Fabian, Ermakova, & Lentz, 2017). A commonly cited statistic estimated it would take an average user 244 hours a year to read privacy policies for all websites they use, an impossible ask (2008 study, as cited in Tene & Polonetsky, 2012). Thus, users usually consent without reading or understanding the terms. This is exacerbated by consent fatigue: people are bombarded with cookie pop-ups, app permission requests, and terms of use everywhere online. Over time, users become numb to these and click "OK" automatically just to remove the annoyance (Shao, Li, & Wang, 2022).

As observed, an opt-out-based environment where users have to proactively object to data collection places the burden on consumers and leads to "*consent fatigue*." Users simply give in because it's too tiring to constantly police their privacy. Realistically, an average social media user does not have the time to scrutinize how their data might be mined for ad targeting, shared with third-party partners, used to train AI models, etc., despite all that being buried in policy documents. Therefore, the 'informed' part of informed consent is often lacking. People think they have no choice but to simply trust the platform, so they agree without true awareness. This undermines the moral legitimacy of the consent (Corren, 2022). Indeed, in the Facebook/Cambridge Analytica scandal, millions of users had "consented" via Facebook's terms to data sharing but were shocked to learn their data (and their friends' data) was harvested for political profiling – a use they never meaningfully understood or expected. That scandal led to a $5 billion fine against Facebook by the U.S. FTC for deceiving users about data practices. According to the FTC, a key finding was that Facebook's disclosures and settings were so confusing that they "undermined users' choices" (Hu, 2020).

3.3 Dark Pattern and Deceptive User Interface

Dark Patterns and Interface Manipulation by these websites, even when users attempt to exercise choice, can manipulate or restrict their autonomy. Dark patterns refer to user interface tricks that subtly coerce or deceive users into making choices against their actual preferences. In the context of consent, this can include tactics like: pre-ticked checkboxes for data sharing, confusing wording for example double negatives: "*Don't object to not sharing data?*", or interface designs where the "Agree" button is a bright, tempting colour while the "Learn more or opt-out" link is tiny and hidden (Aleksejeva, 2025). Many websites make the "accept all cookies" button very prominent but bury the "reject" option in sub-menus, nudging users to consent by friction. Social media apps might spam users with repeated prompts until they give in, for example, "Please turn on location, it's needed for the best experience!". Other dark patterns include 'forced continuity/roach motel' designs, where it is easy to sign up (consent) but hard to withdraw or cancel. For instance, a user can enroll in a data-sharing program with one click, but to opt out, they must navigate a labyrinth of settings or customer service calls. These manipulations directly undermine the "unambiguous" and "freely given" aspects of valid consent.

Regulators are increasingly cracking down on these tactics. The European Data Protection Board issued guidelines in 2022 on dark patterns in social media, warning that such interfaces can nullify the validity of user consent (Yi & Li, 2024). Further, California's privacy law (CPRA) explicitly states that any consent obtained through dark patterns is invalid under the law. For example, if a business uses deceptive interface designs to get a user's agreement, that 'agreement' does not count as consent under the CPRA. This is a clear legal recognition that interface design and consent are intertwined; a cleverly designed interface can impair user autonomy just as effectively as an outright denial of choice.

In summary, 'meaningful consent' in the digital age means much more than a user's one-time click on "I agree." It requires that the consent is truly voluntary, that the user genuinely understands what they are agreeing to, and that the user interface and experience support rather than subvert the user's autonomy. The prevalence of take-it-or-leave-it terms, user ignorance or fatigue, and manipulative dark patterns all serve to weaken consent. Regulators are aware of these issues: we see responses like striking down bundled consent (as under GDPR), declaring dark-pattern-induced consent invalid (CPRA), and emphasizing simplicity and transparency (as India's law does). The debate continues in legal and academic circles about whether consent can ever carry the load of protecting privacy on its own, or whether we must impose more duties on data collectors regardless of user consent. The next section compares how different jurisdictions have tackled these problems in their privacy frameworks, particularly focusing on consent and its enforcement.

4. COMPARATIVE ANALYSIS: GDPR, CCPA, AND LGPD

To contextualize India's approach, it is helpful to compare it with other major privacy regimes. The European Union's GDPR is often considered the gold standard of comprehensive data protection law (Mantelero, 2021), heavily influencing laws elsewhere (including India's and Brazil's). The United States has a patchwork of sectoral laws and state laws (like California's CCPA/CPRA) that contrast with the omnibus approach (Purcell & Zhan, 2007). Brazil's LGPD, enacted in 2018, offers an example of a GDPR-inspired law in a developing economy context. We will examine the evolution of consent frameworks, key legal provisions, and enforcement experiences in each.

4.1 European Union and GDPR

European Union – GDPR: Europe has a long history of data protection. As far back as 1995, the EU had a Data Protection Directive, but it was in 2016 that the EU passed the General Data Protection Regulation (GDPR), which took effect in May 2018, revolutionizing global privacy norms. The GDPR explicitly centres on consent and user control as pillars of data protection, while also providing alternative legal bases for processing. Under GDPR, personal data processing is generally unlawful unless it falls under one of six legal bases: consent, performance of a contract, compliance with a legal obligation, protection of vital interests, public interest/official authority, or the controller's legitimate interests (Gil González & De Hert, 2019). In practice, for consumer-facing activities like social media and online tracking, the main lawful bases used are either consent or the controller's "legitimate interest." However, GDPR set a high bar for consent: it is defined as a "freely given, specific, informed and unambiguous" indication of the user's wishes, given by a clear affirmative action. This tight definition means, for example, pre-ticked boxes or silence do not constitute consent. Users must actively opt in, and consent can be withdrawn at any time. For sensitive data like health and biometrics, 'explicit' consent is required, which includes an even stricter standard, often involving a written or very clear statement. GDPR also bolstered the right to withdraw consent easily, like in India, so if a user withdraws consent, the company must stop the processing that was based on it.

To combat the problem of bundling consent for various data, GDPR's Recital 43 and Article 7(4) caution that if consent is tied to a contract for a service and personal data not necessary for that service is included, then that consent may not be valid. This was aimed at Facebook/Google-style 'forced consent' situations. As noted, enforcement actions have borne this out: the Irish Data Protection Commission (with approval of the EU regulators) ruled that Meta cannot bundle consent for personalized ads into its terms of service, because that deprives users of genuine choice (Guggenberger, 2025). In early 2023, Meta was fined a combined €390 million and ordered to change its practices to seek actual opt-in consent for targeted ads. This was a landmark enforcement confirming that consent under GDPR must be granular and not take-it-or-leave-it.

GDPR also emphasizes transparency and user rights, which support consent. Companies must provide clear privacy notices, typically at the point of data collection, explaining what data is collected and how it will be used (GDPR Arts. 12-14). Users have rights to access their data, correct it, delete it (right to be forgotten), and even data portability, which empowers users beyond the initial consent moment. Notably, the EU created a robust enforcement mechanism for these rules. Each EU member state has a Data Protection Authority (DPA) that oversees and enforces GDPR locally, and a European Data Protection Board (EDPB) coordinates cross-border cases so that one DPA's decision can apply EU-wide. The GDPR introduced severe penalties for violations, where DPAs can impose fines up to €20 million or 4% of a company's global annual turnover, whichever is higher (Sharma, 2019). Indeed, we have seen a series of increasingly hefty fines under GDPR: for example, in 2021, France's DPA (CNIL) fined Google €150 million for designing cookie consent interfaces that made it much harder to reject cookies than accept, a dark pattern violating GDPR's consent requirements. Beyond consent per se, GDPR enforcement has tackled big tech on many fronts: Google was fined €50 million by CNIL in 2019 for insufficient transparency and valid consent in Android's onboarding; Amazon was fined €746 million in Luxembourg in 2021 for alleged improper ad targeting consent; WhatsApp was fined €225 million in Ireland for transparency failings, etc. Another relevant case: in September 2023, Ireland's DPC fined TikTok €345 million for violating children's privacy. TikTok had default settings that made child accounts public and nudged child users toward less private options, and it failed to obtain parental consent for under-13 users. TikTok's interface and defaults were deemed to violate GDPR's principles of children merit special protection, and consent for underage users was not properly obtained. TikTok was ordered to change these default settings (Mrežar, 2023).

These examples highlight that the EU not only put strong consent rules on paper but has actively enforced them. Companies like Meta have had to introduce easier opt-outs, redesign cookie banners to have equal "Reject All" buttons, and abandon some more egregious dark patterns under regulatory pressure. The GDPR's influence has also been normative – even outside Europe, many websites now offer better consent choices (like cookie settings) because they do not want to violate GDPR for EU visitors (Aleksejeva, 2025).

4.2 United States' Sectoral Laws and CCPA

The United States has historically taken a very different approach. Instead of one omnibus data protection law, the U.S. has a patchwork of federal and state laws targeting specific sectors or types of data (Cozzens, 2021). For example, health data is protected under HIPAA (1996) which requires patient consent for disclosures in many cases; children's online data is protected by COPPA (1998) which mandates verifiable parental consent before collecting personal info from children under 13;

financial data has Gramm-Leach-Bliley Act (1999) which uses a notice-and-opt-out model; the Fair Credit Reporting Act covers credit information, and so on. Outside these sectors, user data on general platforms like social media was largely unregulated at the federal level. Instead, the U.S. relied on industry self-regulation and FTC enforcement. The Federal Trade Commission, using its authority over unfair or deceptive trade practices, became the de facto privacy regulator. The FTC cannot broadly mandate upfront consent requirements, but it can punish companies that deceive users or violate their privacy promises (Hetcher, 2000). For instance, if a company's privacy policy says "We will not share your data without consent," but then it does share data, the FTC can act. This is how, in 2019, the FTC hit Facebook with a record $5 billion fine, where Facebook had earlier settlements promising not to mislead users. However, the Cambridge Analytica scandal revealed they misled users about data sharing, which the FTC deemed a violation of a consent decree and a deceptive practice (Herbison, 2019). The FTC order not only fined Facebook but imposed 20 years of oversight and new privacy governance requirements.

The U.S. model thus has been 'notice and choice' in a flexible, self-regulatory way: companies post privacy notices, and if users continue to use the service, that's taken as implicit consent to the described practices. There's generally no requirement for an explicit "I agree". This led to the criticism that users have little real protection as long as a company somewhere disclosed what it might do, it could do it, and user consent was often assumed or implied by usage. Indeed, a famous quote from an FTC official years ago was "the only consumer who reads a privacy policy is one who's already been harmed" (Ohlhausen, 2014).

However, in the last few years, the U.S. has been moving (slowly) towards more privacy regulation, largely driven by states. In 2018, California enacted the California Consumer Privacy Act (CCPA) (amended by the California Privacy Rights Act (CPRA) in 2020). The CCPA/CPRA regime (in force 2020 and 2023, respectively) is the closest U.S. analog to GDPR. Under CCPA/CPRA, businesses have to disclose what personal data they collect and allow California consumers to opt out of the sale of their personal data. Notably, CCPA does not typically require opt-in consent to collect data (except for children's data sales); it's more of an opt-out regime for adults. Consumers can say "do not sell my info," and businesses must comply, but businesses can by default collect and even share data until the consumer objects (Determann & Tam, 2020).

Beyond California, as of 2025, about 10-20 U.S. states have passed their own privacy laws, each with slightly different consent frameworks. For example, states like Colorado, Connecticut, and Virginia require opt-in consent for processing sensitive personal data and mandate honouring global opt-out signals. Some states require opt-in for targeted advertising or sale for minors up to 16 (aligning with COPPA's 13 and extending to 16). Others, like Utah and Iowa, took a more lenient route of not opting in for sensitive data, just notice, and the ability to opt out. This state-by-state variation creates complexity for companies as they must juggle different standards. As Reuters commented, it is a confusing "patchwork" that increases compliance burden and confuses consumers, who might assume protections that do not apply in all states. For instance, a user in California might think everyone has a Do Not Sell right, but if that user's data goes to a company in a state without such a law, the rules differ. This fragmentation can undermine the effectiveness of consent: companies tend to apply the strictest common denominator only where required (Cozzens, 2021).

In terms of enforcement and cases in the U.S., there is no single 'Data Protection Authority' as in Europe. The FTC remains the top enforcer nationally. Its approach is case-by-case. We mentioned the Facebook $5bn penalty – the largest privacy/data security fine in U.S. history. The FTC has also fined others: e.g. Google was fined $22.5 million in 2012 for misrepresenting tracking on Safari browser; Twitter was fined $150 million in 2022 for using phone numbers collected for security for advertising (violation of user consent expectations); Epic Games (maker of Fortnite) was fined $245 million in 2022 for using dark patterns on kids tricking them into unintended in-game purchases and collecting data, which the FTC deemed unfair and deceptive (Reicher & Fang, 2016).

Table1. India, European Union, and United States

Aspect	India (DPDP Act 2023)	EU (GDPR 2018)	United States (CCPA & Sectoral)
Consent Definition	Free, specific, informed, unconditional, and unambiguous" consent; explicit affirmative action required. Consent managers can assist users.	Freely given, specific, informed, and unambiguous indication of wishes (Art. 4(11) GDPR). Must be via a clear affirmative act (no pre-ticked boxes) and easy to withdraw.	**Varies by law.** There has been no uniform definition historically. CPRA (California) defines consent similarly to GDPR (freely given, specific, informed, unambiguous) and forbids dark patterns in obtaining consent. Many data uses are opt-out rather than opt-in for adults.
Consent Model	**Opt-in baseline:** Consent required for personal data unless an exemption (limited "legitimate uses") applies. Granular notice and purpose specification mandated. Parental consent required for <18	**Opt-in for most non-essential processing:** Consent or another legal basis required before processing. No bundling of unrelated data uses (Recital 43). Special consent needed for sensitive data and under-16s (parental consent under age 13-16). Some flexibility via other bases (contract, legitimate interest), but with restrictions.	**Mixed/opt-out model:** Generally, personal data can be collected by default; users can opt out of sale/ sharing (CCPA). Opt-in consent required by specific laws for certain data: e.g., parental consent under 13 (COPPA); Trend toward requiring consent for targeted ads to minors and using precise geolocation.
User Rights & Withdrawal	Access, correction, erasure, and grievance redressal rights granted. Consent can be withdrawn; the law says withdrawal should be as easy as giving. The concept of a consent manager is to simplify managing these choices.	Extensive rights include access, rectification, erasure ("right to be forgotten"), data portability, objection to processing, and restriction. Users can withdraw consent anytime, and users must be able to refuse cookies and still get service (for non-essential data).	Vary by statute. CCPA gives the right to know, delete, opt out of sale, and no retaliation for exercising rights. No general federal right to deletion except sectoral (e.g., credit report disputes). Consent withdrawal depends on service policies (no overarching law requiring deletion on withdrawal except in c

continued on following page

Table1. Continued

Aspect	India (DPDP Act 2023)	EU (GDPR 2018)	United States (CCPA & Sectoral)
Regulatory Enforcement	The Data Protection Board of India (once constituted) will oversee and enforce. Powers to impose fines up to 250 Cr (~$30M). Courts also remain an avenue (and a constitutional right of privacy can be invoked in litigation).	Independent DPAs in each country, coordinated by the European Data Protection Board. It can issue orders and fines up to 4% of global turnover or €20M. Individuals can complain to DPAs or sue for material/nonmaterial damages—very active enforcement across the EU, with collective actions and NGOs also testing compliance.	FTC at the federal level (can fine companies that break promises or engage in unfair practices; e.g. $5B fine on Facebook). State AGs for laws like CCPA (e.g. $1.2M fine on Sephora). New California Privacy Protection Agency (from 2023), dedicated to enforcing CPRA. No general penalty like % of revenue (CCPA has up to $2,500 per violation, $7,500 for intentional violations, which can add up). Private lawsuits are allowed in some cases.

The U.S. framework is still evolving. Unlike the EU, Brazil, or India, the U.S. has not declared privacy a fundamental right. Congress has debated federal privacy bills that could bring opt-in consent for some uses nationwide, but none have passed as of 2025. So, we have a situation where American users often have weaker upfront consent protections, and much data collection is opt-out by default – but there is a strong consumer protection enforcement culture that steps in when things go egregiously wrong.

To put it succinctly, the EU system tries to enforce privacy by default, requiring consent for most non-essential data uses. Hence, the onus is on companies to ask and obtain it, whereas the U.S. system historically was privacy by option, where companies can collect by default; the onus is on users to opt out. This is slowly shifting towards more user rights and some opt-ins for sensitive categories. The concept of meaningful consent is acknowledged in both, but the legal mechanisms differ. Notably, U.S. laws like CPRA borrow GDPR's language on consent needing to be freely given, etc., showing convergence in principles (Bakare, Adeniyi, Akpuokwe, & Eneh, 2024).

5. ROLE OF TECHNOLOGY: DESIGN, AI, AND THE ARCHITECTURE OF CHOICE

Legal rules on paper are only half the battle; the technological architecture of social media greatly influences whether user consent is meaningful or moot. This section delves into how platform design and algorithms can either support privacy choices or subvert them. Key concepts here are choice architecture, behavioural nudges, algorithmic manipulation, and principles like Privacy by Design that aim to embed respect for consent into technology.

5.1 Choice Architecture and Behavioural Nudges

Choice architecture refers to how users present decisions. Platforms have become adept at nudging user behaviour, often for benign ends but also to encourage data sharing and engagement. As discussed earlier, when a social network defaults all profiles to "public" and requires users to find and toggle a setting to go private, it is architecting the choice in favour of disclosure (McDaniel & Pease, 2021). If an app repeatedly prompts you to enable contact access with a friendly explanation but makes the "No thanks" button hard to see, that is a nudge leveraging design and timing. These design decisions can directly impact consent: a user might technically have a choice, but the design pushes them toward consenting. Dark patterns are essentially another malicious choice architecture. These techniques exploit cognitive biases such as the tendency to go with default settings or the tendency to comply with perceived requirements. The result is that users give consent in situations where, if fully rational and unpressured, they might not have.

5.2 Algorithmic Manipulation and Personalization

Beyond the UI, the algorithms curating our social media feeds can influence user autonomy and decision-making. Social media platforms use complex machine learning algorithms to maximize engagement, showing content that will keep users scrolling, clicking, and sharing. This often involves micro-targeting content based on detailed personal profiles (Rydenfelt et. al., 2025). For example, the algorithm learns when you are most likely to respond positively and can time notifications or posts to those moments. There is evidence that platforms can infer a user's emotional state from their activity and adjust content accordingly. A notorious instance was Facebook's 2012 "emotional contagion" experiment: Facebook manipulated the mix of positive or negative posts in nearly 700,000 users' feeds to see if it affected their mood, and it did (Selinger & Woodrow, 2015). This was done without explicit consent; Facebook argued that users consented to such experimentation via the general terms. When it came to light in 2014, researchers blasted it for violating ethical norms; there was no informed consent for treating users as lab subjects. Facebook's defence was that its terms of service allowed data to be used for research; thus, users had implicitly consented by agreeing to the terms. Nonetheless, the backlash highlighted how algorithmic actions can manipulate users in hidden ways, raising the question: even if a user ticked "I agree," did they really agree to have their emotions intentionally manipulated? Most would say no. The episode prompted discussion about the need for an ethics review for algorithmic experiments and perhaps tighter consent for such uses.

On a more everyday basis, algorithmic content personalization means no two users see the same Facebook or TikTok feed. Users' behaviour data (likes, clicks, watch time) determines what the algorithm predicts will engage them most (Wagner & Eidenmuller, 2019). This can lead to "filter bubbles," meaning people see only content that reinforces their interests. This can amplify extreme content because shocking or sensational posts often grab attention. Users did not explicitly consent to having their attention and behaviour used against their long-term interests, which is arguably what happens when algorithms optimize purely for engagement. There is a fine line between a personalized service and manipulative targeting. For instance, if a platform learns a user is vulnerable and then targets ads for expensive "self-help" products to them, is that exploitation?

5.3 AI-Driven Dark Patterns

Even more insidiously, with advances in AI, platforms can dynamically adjust interfaces in real-time per user to maximize the chance that that particular user consents or complies. A recent study noted that AI can exploit individual behavioural data to generate "personalized dark patterns," for example, changing the wording or timing of a consent prompt depending on what a specific user responds to (Mele et. al., 2021). AI-powered customization makes regulation much more difficult, allowing dark patterns to be adjusted in real time depending on behavioural tracking.

An AI might learn that User A tends to click "Agree" if the prompt mentions a benefit, whereas User B clicks if the prompt creates urgency, and then tailor the nudges accordingly. This algorithmic manipulation is directly aimed at the consent process itself. It is like having a salesperson who knows your psyche to get you to sign a contract (Tai, 2024). If this is the future, traditional consent could be rendered nearly meaningless. Addressing it likely requires technological restraints, companies choosing not to weaponize AI that way, or being forbidden by law, and perhaps real-time oversight. The EU's proposed AI Act and some US discussions on AI ethics touch on this – classifying certain manipulative AI practices as unacceptable.

5.4 Privacy by Design / Default and Data Minimization

In light of these technological challenges, many experts advocate for Privacy by Design (PbD) and Privacy by Default as guiding principles. Privacy by Design means building systems that proactively embed privacy protections rather than adding them later (Simonette, 2021). For consent, this could mean designing user journeys such that privacy-friendly options are the default, and users have to choose to share more only if they want to actively. Privacy by default (enshrined in GDPR Article 25) effectively means that the default settings of a service should be the most privacy-protective possible. For example, a social network's default could be that your profile is private and you have to change it to public if you want; an app's default could be not to track your location unless you opt in for a specific feature (Pagallo, 2021). This way, inertia often leads people to accept defaults in favour of privacy, not against it. It reduces the reliance on users making conscious privacy choices at every turn, and they are automatically somewhat protected unless they decide otherwise.

Data minimization complements this by limiting how much data is collected or retained in the first place. If an app never collects certain data, you do not need to ask for consent. For instance, a messaging app that encrypts messages end-to-end and does not collect metadata minimizes data (Senarath & Arachchilage, 2019). Thus, it avoids many consent issues altogether because even if it wants to use message content for ads, it cannot do so by its design. The more platforms adopt data minimization, the less they need to burden users with consent dialogs for extra uses, and the lower the risk if something goes wrong (Paul & Brandon, 2025).

GDPR explicitly lists data minimization and privacy by design/default as principles. However, it does not prescribe exact methods; it expects companies to implement appropriate technical and organizational measures (Yang Q. et. al., 2025). India's DPDP Act also implicitly encourages minimization as it requires data collection to be limited to the purpose and storage as long as necessary.

In conclusion to this section, technology design can either strengthen privacy or severely weaken it. Good design can make privacy choices understandable, frictionless, and respected; bad design can coerce and confuse. The onus should not be entirely on users to fight against dark patterns or read through algorithmic behaviour, hence the calls for systemic solutions.

Technology will keep evolving; with it, the ways consent could be subverted or respected will also change. The principle must be that user autonomy and intent are at the core of designs and algorithms, and they should seek to honour what users actually want, not trick them into what the company wants. Achieving that will require ongoing vigilance by designers, users, and regulators.

6. RECOMMENDATIONS: RETHINKING CONSENT AND BUILDING ACCOUNTABILITY

As we have seen, consent in social media data harvesting is a troubled concept, often more a legal fiction than a genuine meeting of minds. While consent remains important, it cannot shoulder the burden of protecting privacy. What is needed is a shift toward systemic accountability by companies and smarter, user-centric regulatory measures. Based on the analysis above, here are key recommendations to improve consent mechanisms and user privacy, especially for India as it implements the DPDP Act, but also applicable globally:

a. **Embrace Privacy by Default**: We must move from Opt-in/Opt-out to Pro-Privacy Defaults. Regulators should require that, wherever feasible, services adopt privacy-enhancing default settings. This means minimal data collection and sharing unless a user actively chooses otherwise. By flipping the default, the onus shifts to companies to convince users to share data, instead of putting the onus on users to protect themselves. This reduces the risk of consent fatigue and ensures even passive or less-aware users get a decent level of privacy (Bennett, 2012). Such an approach has been endorsed in principle by GDPR (data protection by default) and should be a benchmark for Indian regulators, too.
b. **Simplify Consent Requests**: Consent forms and privacy notices must be concise, clear, and plain. Jargon and legalese defeat the purpose of informed consent. Using layered notices can help: present a summary of key points with the option to click for more detailed info if the user wants. Importantly for India, provide these notices in multiple local languages. If a user is more comfortable speaking Hindi or Tamil than English, they should be able to read the terms in that language. India's internet user base includes many first-time users from rural areas; multilingual, culturally sensitive consent interfaces are vital (Gupta & Naithani, 2024). Additionally, using visual aids and icons to convey concepts should be promoted.
c. **Adopt Age-Appropriate Design Codes**: India should look for a framework like the UK's Age-Appropriate Design Code (AADC) as a model. This shifts the focus from merely verifying age and obtaining parental consent to ensuring the entire service is designed with the child's best interests in mind. This includes principles like setting privacy settings to high by default for child accounts, turning off location tracking, and using simple, child-friendly language in notices. The burden should be on platforms to create safe environments, not on parents to police every setting. (Elvy, 2023)

d. **Standardize Consent Formats Across Platforms:** Regulators and industry bodies should develop standardized templates. Much like nutrition labels on food, a standardized "privacy label" format could familiarly present key information across all apps and sites. This consistency would make it easier for users to find and understand information, rather than hunting through each app's uniquely worded policy (Yadav & Tiwari, 2023). India's DPDP Act hints at this by mentioning consent notice requirements; the government or Data Protection Board could issue rules or best practices for a standardized layout.

e. **Deterrence for Dark Patterns:** Laws should explicitly prohibit specific dark patterns related to consent (as CPRA does) and treat them as offenses. For instance, auto-selecting consent, making a refusal more complex than an acceptance, or repeatedly nagging users who said no should be defined as unfair practices. India's law could incorporate such rules via regulations. Penalties for using dark patterns to obtain consent should be significant.

f. **Ensuring Consent is an Ongoing Process, Not a One-Time Box-Check**: Consent should be treated as a dynamic, continuous process. This means companies ought to reaffirm consent at reasonable intervals or when the use of data changes materially. For example, if a platform that originally only used your data to show you friend updates now wants to use it for training an AI or sharing with a new third-party, it should seek fresh consent for that new purpose (Verhulst, 2021). Users should also have accessible dashboards to review and manage their consents. Regulators should encourage the development of user-friendly privacy dashboards and independent consent management tools that aggregate service settings.

g. **Encourage Data Trusts or Collective Solutions for Consent**: Given that individual consent has limits, India could pilot the concept of data trusts or collective bargaining for privacy. A data trust is an entity that manages personal data on behalf of users, with a fiduciary duty to act in their best interests. Users could delegate certain consent decisions to the trust. For example, a group of users could form a "social media data trust" that negotiates with a platform on what data can be collected and how it can be used, setting terms that apply to all its members (Collaco, 2024). This could invert the power dynamic, and instead of each isolated user clicking yes or no to whatever is offered, a collective representing millions could demand better privacy terms (Delacroix & Lawrence, 2019). Governments and civil society can facilitate the creation of such trusts. At the same time, this novel approach aligns with the idea of "collective control" as an alternative to notice-and-consent. It may be instrumental in India, where literacy issues make individual notice-and-consent challenging, a trusted intermediary, even a government-appointed ombudsperson or non-profit, could vet and manage privacy terms on behalf of users.

h. **Implement Privacy Education and Awareness Campaigns**: Legal changes will not suffice if users are unaware of their rights or how to exercise them. Governments and platforms, as part of compliance, should invest in public education on digital privacy. (Malandrino et. al., 2013) This includes straightforward messages about checking privacy settings, understanding consent, and knowing that one can say "no." When India's DPDP Act comes into force, a campaign analogous to, say, a voter awareness campaign should inform citizens about the new rights, for example: "*You have the right to tell companies to erase your data*" or "*Look for the Data Protection Board's website to lodge complaints*".

i. **Global Cooperation and Interoperability of Privacy Standards:** Finally, it is recommended that India and other jurisdictions work towards interoperability of consent mechanisms and mutual recognition of high privacy standards. In practical terms, this could mean adopting protocols like the Global Privacy Control (GPC) signal as a valid way to communicate refusal of sale/sharing. It could also mean joining conversations at forums like the Global Privacy Assembly to align on cross-border enforcement and norms against dark patterns. Privacy in social media is a global issue. A user in India might be using an American service that processes data in Ireland, so solutions, to be effective, often require global alignment (Robinsons et. al., 2021).

j. **Fostering Corporate Accountability: Managerial Implications Beyond Compliance:** Legal compliance is the floor, not the ceiling. For social media companies operating in India and globally, building user trust is a competitive advantage beyond simply adhering to the DPDP Act. We recommend managers and corporate leaders adopt practices like Operationalize Privacy as a Core Value in the culture of the organisations, the Establishment of internal ethics committees or review boards to vet new algorithms and AI models before they are deployed, and embracing radical transparency and not hiding data practices in lengthy legal documents.

Implementing these recommendations would move us closer to a world where consent is not a mere checkbox, but a meaningful interaction that respects user dignity and choice. The overarching theme is shifting some responsibility away from the individual and onto those in power to create an environment where respecting privacy is the path of least resistance, rather than something that only the most vigilant users achieve.

7. CONCLUSION

The analysis of consent in social media data harvesting reveals a stark gap between legal theory and platform reality. In theory, informed consent is the linchpin that legitimizes data processing as a manifestation of user autonomy and control. In reality, the standard "scroll, click, and surrender" paradigm on social media has turned consent into a largely fictitious concept, where clicking "I Agree" is less an exercise of free will and more an inevitable ritual users perform to access digital services. This conclusion revisits that central dilemma and emphasizes the need to reimagine consent as part of a broader framework of user rights and corporate accountability.

At its heart, the problem is asymmetry – asymmetry of power, information, and bargaining position. Social media companies wield enormous power: they design the interfaces, write the contracts, and command the algorithms that shape our online experiences. They possess vastly more information than users about what happens with personal data and the implications thereof. Even if unhappy, users often have nowhere else to go if all major platforms demand the same surrender of data. This imbalance means treating consent as a simple yes/no choice between equals is a legal fiction. The Puttaswamy judgement in India and similar jurisprudence globally recognize privacy as intrinsic to dignity and autonomy. However, if consent is obtained in conditions where users cannot meaningfully say no, then that consent undermines the values that privacy law is meant to uphold.

What can be done? As argued, the burden cannot solely be on individual users navigating this complex landscape. Consent must be "reimagined not just as a checkbox, but as a continuous, participatory, and enforceable right." In practice, this means empowering users and constraining data collectors. For India, which stands "at the cusp of digital regulation", the time is ripe to build a model that learns from others but also innovates for India's unique context. India can ill afford to replicate the mistakes that led to Europe's cookie fatigue or America's lax regime that allowed major scandals. Instead, India could pioneer approaches like consent managers, sharp enforcement against dark patterns, and culturally aware privacy literacy programs. With a population of 1.4 billion, hundreds of millions coming online for the first time, India's choices will have an enormous impact on the global data economy and the lived reality of privacy for a significant portion of humanity.

Going forward, consent should be seen as a necessary but insufficient condition for data processing. When consent is obtained, it should be obtained fairly; when it cannot be genuinely obtained, the law may prohibit certain data uses outright or impose fiduciary duties on data holders.

In conclusion, the key takeaway is that user empowerment and corporate accountability are two sides of the same coin. A sustainable digital ecosystem is one where users can trust that their silence will not be abused and their consent will not be assumed. It is one where privacy is the default setting, not a hidden option. Achieving this will require continued vigilance, updated laws and guidelines as technology evolves, and perhaps most importantly, a recognition by all stakeholders' governments, companies, and users that privacy is a fundamental component of freedom and human dignity. Consent can no longer be a tick-box to absolve responsibility; it must become a real conversation between users and platforms, backed by rights and enforceable in practice. The paradigm will shift from "Scroll, Click, Surrender" to "Understand, Choose, and Empower."

REFERENCES

Aleksejeva, J. (2025). How effectively does GDPR address dark patterns in consent mechanisms targeting minors, and what legal, regulatory, and technological measures can be implemented to strengthen its protections?.

Bacon, A. (2023). Children's safety in the digital age: A look at identity verification legislation in the United States.

Bakare, S. S., Adeniyi, A. O., Akpuokwe, C. U., & Eneh, N. E. (2024). Data privacy laws and compliance: a comparative review of the EU GDPR and USA regulations.

Bennett, C. J. (2012). The Accountability Approach to Privacy and Data Protection: Assumptions and Caveats. In Guagnin, D., Hempel, L., Ilten, C., Kroener, I., Neyland, D., & Postigo, H. (Eds.), *Managing Privacy through Accountability*. Palgrave Macmillan., DOI: 10.1057/9781137032225_3

Boyd, D. M., & Nicole, B. (2007). Social Network Sites: Definition, History, and Scholarship. *Journal of Computer-Mediated Communication*, *13*(1), 210–230. DOI: 10.1111/j.1083-6101.2007.00393.x

Chidiac, M., Ross, C., Marston, H. R., & Freeman, S. (2022). Age and Gender Perspectives on Social Media and Technology Practices during the COVID-19 Pandemic. *International Journal of Environmental Research and Public Health*, *19*(21), 13969. DOI: 10.3390/ijerph192113969 PMID: 36360853

Collaco, A. M. (2024). Contours of data protection in India: The consent dilemma. *International Review of Law Computers & Technology*, *39*(2), 194–212. DOI: 10.1080/13600869.2024.2364991

Corren, E. (2022). The Consent Burden in Consumer and Digital Markets. *Harv. JL & Tech.*, *36*, 551.

Cozzens, C. (2021). The Patchwork Privacy Problem: How the United States' Privacy Regime Fails to Protect Its Businesses and Data Subjects. *Seton Hall Law Review*, *52*, 1157.

Datta, S. (2022). Evaluation and management of language and technology literacy barriers for accessing e-learning services in India. Embracing change in business, management & social sciences, 87.

David, Y. (2023). Legal Implications of Data Monetization by Commercial Entities. Available at *SSRN* 4922310.

Delacroix, S., & Lawrence, N. D. (2019). Bottom-up data Trusts: Disturbing the 'one size fits all' approach to data governance. *International Data Privacy Law, 9*(4), 236–252. DOI: 10.1093/idpl/ipz014

Determann, L., & Tam, J. (2020). The California Privacy Rights Act of 2020: A broad and complex data processing regulation that applies to businesses worldwide. *Journal of Data Protection & Privacy, 4*(1), 7–21. DOI: 10.69554/GCLK6627

Duraiswami, D. R. (2017). Privacy and Data Protection in India. *Journal of Law & Cyber Warfare, 6*(1), 166–186.

Elvy, S. A. (2023). Age-Appropriate Design Code Mandates. *U. Pa. J. Int'l L., 45*, 953.

European Union. (2016). Regulation (EU) 2016/679 of the European Parliament and of the Council of 27 April 2016 on the protection of natural persons with regard to the processing of personal data and on the free movement of such data (General Data Protection Regulation). Official Journal of the European Union, L 119, 1–88. https://eur-lex.europa.eu/eli/reg/2016/679/oj

Fabian, B., Ermakova, T., & Lentz, T. (2017, August). Large-scale readability analysis of privacy policies. In *Proceedings of the International Conference on Web Intelligence* (pp. 18–25)

Frichot, E. (2025). Exploring the Ethical and Legal Dimensions of Data Collection: A Case Study of Meta Platform.

Gerlitz, C., & Helmond, A. (2013). The like economy: Social buttons and the data-intensive web. *New Media & Society, 15*(8), 1348–1365. DOI: 10.1177/1461444812472322

Gil González, E., & De Hert, P. (2019). Understanding the legal provisions that allow processing and profiling personal data—An analysis of GDPR provisions and principles. ERA Forum, 19(4), 597–621. Springer. https://doi.org/DOI: 10.1007/s12027-019-00559-9

Goodin, T. (2023). *My Brain Has Too Many Tabs Open: How to Untangle Our Relationship with Tech.* White Lion Publishing.

Government of India. (2011). Information Technology (Reasonable Security Practices and Procedures and Sensitive Personal Data or Information) Rules, 2011 (S.O. 1677(E), 24 June 2011). Ministry of Electronics and Information Technology. Retrieved from https://www.indiacode.nic.in/handle/123456789/1362/simple-search?query=The%20Information%20Technology%20(Reasonable%20Security%20Practices%20and%20Procedures%20and%20Sensitive%20Personal%20Data%20or%20Information)%20Rules,%202011.&searchradio=rules

Government of India. (2023). Digital Personal Data Protection Act, 2023, No. 22 of 2023, § 2. Ministry of Law and Justice. https://www.indiacode.nic.in/handle/123456789/24547

Guggenberger, N. (2025). Consent as Friction. *BCL Rev.*, *66*(2), 353–421. DOI: 10.70167/CHOQ9209

Gupta, I., & Naithani, P. (2024). India's Forthcoming Rules under the Digital Personal Data Protection Act: An Opportunity to Reduce Gaps in the 'Notice and Consent' Framework for Cookies. (2024). Global Privacy Law Review. 5(4),164-170, https://testcdn.kluwerlawonline.com/journalarticle/Global+Privacy+Law+Review/5.4/GPLR2025003

Gupta, I., & Naithani, P. (2024). India's Forthcoming Rules under the Digital Personal Data Protection Act: An Opportunity to Reduce Gaps in the 'Notice and Consent'Framework for Cookies. Global Privacy Law Review, 5(4).

Herbison, J. F. (2019). Big Tech Investigated for Antitrust Violations. *Infrastructure*, *59*, 3.

Hetcher, S. (2000). The de facto federal privacy commission. *The John Marshall Journal of Computer & Information Law*, *19*, 109.

Hillman, R. A., & Rachlinski, J. J. (2002). Standard-form contracting in the electronic age. *NYUL Rev.*, *77*, 429.

Hu, E. (2014). Facebook Manipulates Our Moods For Science And Commerce: A Roundup. All Tech Considered Tech, Culture, and Connection. NPR. https://www.npr.org/sections/alltechconsidered/2014/06/30/326929138/facebook-manipulates-our-moods-for-science-and-commerce-a-roundup

Hu, M. (2020). Cambridge Analytica's black box. *Big Data & Society*, *7*(2), 2053951720938091. DOI: 10.1177/2053951720938091

Jain, A., & Anand, A. (2025b). Tracing the Constitutional Journey of Data Privacy in India: From Puttaswamy to the Draft DPDP Rules, 2025. Available at *SSRN* 5283949. DOI: 10.2139/ssrn.5283949

Jain, A. S. (2025a). Decoding consent managers under the Digital Personal Data Protection Act, 2023: Empowerment architecture, business models, and incentive alignment. *Journal of Data Protection & Privacy*, *7*(4), 406–420. DOI: 10.69554/MHLP2916

Joseph, V., Basu, P., & Bhargava, A. (2020, March 19). A review of the Information Technology Rules, 2011. Mondaq. https://www.mondaq.com/india/privacy-protection/904916/a-review-of-the-information-technology-rules-2011

Kovacs, A., & Jain, T. (2020). Informed consent-said who? A feminist perspective on principles of consent in the age of embodied data. A Feminist Perspective on Principles of Consent in the Age of Embodied Data (November 2020).

Malandrino, D., Scarano, V., & Spinelli, R. (2013). How Increased Awareness Can Impact Attitudes and Behaviors toward Online Privacy Protection. *International Conference on Social Computing*, Alexandria, 57–62. DOI: 10.1109/SocialCom.2013.15

Mantelero, A. (2021). The future of data protection: Gold standard vs. global standard. *Computer Law & Security Review*, *40*, 105500. DOI: 10.1016/j.clsr.2020.105500

McDaniel, J. L., & Pease, K. G. (2021). Policing, AI, and choice architecture. Predictive Policing and Artificial Intelligence. 32.

Mele, C., Spena, T. R., Kaartemo, V., & Marzullo, M. L. (2021). Smart nudging: How cognitive technologies enable choice architectures for value co-creation. *Journal of Business Research*, *129*, 949–960. DOI: 10.1016/j.jbusres.2020.09.004

Mrežar, F. (2023). Analysis of fines under GDPR (Doctoral dissertation, University of Zagreb, Faculty of Law, Information Technology Law and Informatics). University of Zagreb.

Naithani, P. (2024). Analysis of India's Digital Personal Data Protection Act, 2023. International Journal of Law and Management.

Ohlhausen, M. K. (2014). Privacy challenges and opportunities: The role of the Federal Trade Commission. *Journal of Public Policy & Marketing*, *33*(1), 4–9. DOI: 10.1509/jppm.33.1.4

Pagallo, U. (2021). On the Principle of Privacy by Design and Its Limits: Technology, Ethics and the Rule of Law. In Chiodo, S., & Schiaffonati, V. (Eds.), *Italian Philosophy of Technology. Philosophy of Engineering and Technology* (Vol. 35). Springer., DOI: 10.1007/978-3-030-54522-2_8

Paul, L. & Brandon, R. (2025). Data minimisation: A crucial pillar of cyber security. Cyber Security: A Peer-Reviewed Journal, 8(3), 243–254(12).

Politou, E., Alepis, E., Virvou, M., & Patsakis, C. (2021). The General Data Protection Regulation. In *Privacy and Data Protection Challenges in the Distributed Era* (pp. 13–39). Springer International Publishing.

Purcell, C., & Zhan, J. (2007, August). Adapting US privacy laws to the internet: Is patching enough? In *2007 International Conference on Machine Learning and Cybernetics* (Vol. 5, pp. 3000–3005). IEEE. https://doi.org/DOI: 10.1109/ICMLC.2007.4370662

Reicher, A. E., & Fang, Y. (2016). FTC Privacy and Data Security Enforcement and Guidance Under Section 5. Competition Journal of the Antitrust and Unfair Competition Law Section of the California Lawyers Association, 25(2).

Richards, N., & Hartzog, W. (2018). The pathologies of digital consent. *Wash. UL Rev.*, *96*, 1461.

Robinson, L., Kizawa, K., & Ronchi, E. (2021). Interoperability of privacy and data protection frameworks. Going Digital Toolkit Note, No. 21. https://goingdigital.oecd.org/data/notes/No21_ToolkitNote_PrivacyDataInteroperability.pdf

Rydenfelt, H., Lehtiniemi, T., Haapoja, J., & Haapanen, L. (2025). Autonomy and Algorithms: Tracing the Significance of Content Personalization. *International Journal of Communication*, *19*, 481–500.

Saetra, H. S. (2021). *Big Data's threat to liberty: surveillance, nudging, and information curation*. Academic Press.

Sebastian, J., & Sen, A. (2020). Unravelling the role of autonomy and consent in privacy. *SSRN*, *9*, 1. DOI: 10.2139/ssrn.4223897

Selinger, E., & Woodrow, H. (2015). Facebook's emotional contagion study and the ethical problem of co-opted identity in mediated environments where users lack control. *Sage Journals*, *12*(1). Advance online publication. DOI: 10.1177/17470161155795

Senarath, A., & Arachchilage, N. A. G. (2019). A data minimization model for embedding privacy into software systems. *Computers & Security*, *87*, 87. DOI: 10.1016/j.cose.2019.101605

Shao, H., Li, X., & Wang, G. (2022, April). Are you tired? I am: Trying to understand privacy fatigue of social media users. In *CHI Conference on Human Factors in Computing Systems Extended Abstracts* (pp. 1–7). DOI: 10.1145/3491101.3519778

Sharma, A. (2025). From Click to Contract: The legal validity of consent in India's social media data ecosystem. *International Journal of Law and Social Innovation*, *7*(3), 416–433. DOI: 10.10000/IJLSI.112633

Sharma, D., Bhagat, L., & Sharma, S. (2024). Regulating Children's Personal Data Protection in India: No Child's Play. Development, 67(1), 28–33. Nissenbaum, H. (2011). A contextual approach to privacy online. *Daedalus*, *140*(4), 32–48.

Sharma, S. (2019). *Data privacy and GDPR handbook.* John Wiley & Sons., DOI: 10.1002/9781119594307

Simonette, M. (2021). Privacy by Design e Privacy by Default. CEST, 6.

Solove, D. J. (2024). Murky consent: An approach to the fictions of consent in privacy law. *BUL Rev.*, *104*, 593.

Supreme Court of India. (2017). Justice K. S. Puttaswamy (Retd.) v. Union of India, (2017) 10 SCC 1

Tai, E. T. T. (2024). Using AI to Influence Consumer Choice. The Cambridge Handbook of AI and Consumer Law Comparative Perspectives, 62 – 74. DOI: 10.1017/9781009483599.010

Tene, O., & Polonetsky, J. (2012). Big data for all: Privacy and user control in the age of analytics. *Nw. J. Tech. & Intell. Prop.*, *11*, 239.

Verhulst, S. G. (2021). Reimagining data responsibility: 10 new approaches toward a culture of trust in re-using data to address critical public needs. *Data & Policy*, *3*, e6. Advance online publication. DOI: 10.1017/dap.2021.4

Wagner, G., & Eidenmuller, H. (2019). Down by Algorithms: Siphoning Rents, Exploiting Biases, and Shaping Preferences: Regulating the Dark Side of Personalized Transactions. *The University of Chicago Law Review. University of Chicago. Law School*, *86*, 581.

Yadav, S., & Tiwari, N. (2023). Privacy preserving data sharing method for social media platforms. *PLoS One*, *18*(1), e0280182. DOI: 10.1371/journal.pone.0280182 PMID: 36662805

Yang, Q., Lepore, C., Eynard, J., & Loborde, R. (2025). From theory to practice: Data minimisation and technical review of verifiable credentials under the GDPR. *Computer Law & Security Review*, *57*, 57. DOI: 10.1016/j.clsr.2025.106138

Yi, W., & Li, Z. (2024). Mapping the scholarship of dark pattern regulation: A systematic review of concepts, regulatory paradigms, and solutions from an interdisciplinary perspective. arXiv preprint arXiv:2407.10340. https://arxiv.org/abs/2407.10340 DOI: 10.2139/ssrn.4993171

Zard, L., & Sears, A. M. (2023). Targeted advertising and consumer protection law in the European Union. Vand. J. Transnat' l L., 56, 799.

Chapter 7
An Emerging Legal–Ethical Conundrum:
Artificial Intelligence, Big Data, and Privacy

Rakshit Sharma
https://orcid.org/0009-0003-6419-0448
Amity University, Noida, India

ABSTRACT

This chapter explores the growing tension between technological innovation and the right to privacy in the era of artificial intelligence and big data. As data-driven systems transcend borders, traditional legal frameworks struggle to address algorithmic opacity, surveillance, and discrimination. The chapter critically evaluates global responses, including GDPR, China's PIPL, and UNESCO's ethical AI guidelines, and highlights gaps in enforcement, consent, and accountability. It proposes a multi-level strategy emphasizing algorithmic transparency, privacy by design, and cross-border legal harmonization. A human-centric approach is essential to ensure dignity, rights, and fairness in the algorithmic age.

INTRODUCTION

In the 21st century, the convergence of Artificial Intelligence (AI) and Big Data has redefined the ways in which societies collect, interpret, and act upon information. These technologies, once confined to research labs and theoretical discussions, now permeate virtually every aspect of modern life, from commerce and governance to health care, education, national security, and even interpersonal relationships. AI systems, fueled by massive troves of data generated through digital interactions,

DOI: 10.4018/979-8-3373-4967-1.ch007

power tools ranging from predictive analytics and facial recognition to algorithmic decision-making in courts, job recruitment, credit scoring, and law enforcement (Mittelstadt et al., 2016). While these tools offer efficiencies, insights, and capabilities once thought impossible, they also introduce a host of ethical, legal, and human rights dilemmas, particularly surrounding the right to privacy and data protection.

The sheer volume and velocity of data generation have been unprecedented in recent years. Every online click, search, facial scan, GPS trace, and voice command potentially becomes part of a larger data ecosystem. This data is continuously fed into machine learning algorithms that train AI systems to make automated decisions, often with minimal human oversight (Zuboff, 2019). However, this constant data flow is often opaque to the individual user, who may neither understand nor consent to the ways in which their data is being processed or transferred across national and corporate boundaries (van der Sloot, 2017). The lack of transparency, difficulty in tracing accountability, and inadequate regulatory frameworks have made it increasingly difficult to ensure that personal data is collected and processed in a lawful and ethical manner.

At the heart of this issue lies the fundamental legal and ethical question: Can contemporary governance systems effectively safeguard individual privacy in an era where AI technologies operate across jurisdictions and are shaped by vast, decentralized data inputs? The global nature of AI systems challenges conventional notions of sovereignty, territoriality, and national control over data. Cloud computing, decentralized storage systems, and global corporate infrastructures make it difficult to determine who controls data and under what legal framework that data is being managed (Tzanou, 2020). For example, a user in India may use an app owned by a U.S. company, which stores data in a European data centre and uses third-party analytics from China. Such cross-border data flows complicate enforcement and oversight, rendering domestic data protection laws insufficient on their own.

International legal instruments have attempted to respond to these challenges. The European Union's General Data Protection Regulation (GDPR) is widely considered a global benchmark in data protection, with its emphasis on user consent, data minimization, and the right to be forgotten (European Parliament & Council, 2016). However, the extraterritorial application of the GDPR and its compatibility with non-EU jurisdictions remains a contested issue (Bradford, 2020). Meanwhile, the United States continues to follow a sector-specific approach to data regulation, with laws like the Health Insurance Portability and Accountability Act (HIPAA) and the California Consumer Privacy Act (CCPA) addressing discrete sectors rather than providing a unified privacy framework. In contrast, China's Personal Information Protection Law (PIPL) emphasizes state control and data sovereignty, raising concerns about surveillance and state access to personal data (Liu, 2022).

The diversity in approaches globally underscores a fragmented and often conflicting landscape of legal norms.

Beyond law, ethical frameworks have emerged as a parallel force to guide the development and deployment of AI. Documents such as the UNESCO Recommendation on the Ethics of Artificial Intelligence (2021), IEEE's Ethically Aligned Design, and the Montreal Declaration for a Responsible Development of Artificial Intelligence have outlined normative principles including fairness, transparency, accountability, and respect for human rights. Yet, these ethical frameworks often lack legal enforceability, leaving significant gaps in implementation and compliance. There remains an urgent need to bridge the divide between ethical aspirations and legal obligations, especially as AI technologies increasingly govern access to essential services and opportunities (Binns, 2018).

Perhaps most critically, the power asymmetries in the global digital ecosystem pose substantial risks to marginalized communities. AI systems can replicate and even amplify existing social biases, particularly when trained on historical data that reflects societal discrimination (Eubanks, 2018). Predictive policing algorithms have disproportionately targeted racial minorities; hiring algorithms have systematically disadvantaged women; and facial recognition tools have shown higher error rates when identifying individuals with darker skin tones (Buolamwini & Gebru, 2018). These examples demonstrate that privacy violations are not only a technical or legal issue but a profound human rights concern, implicating the rights to equality, dignity, and freedom from discrimination.

Given this complex terrain, this chapter investigates the legal-ethical conundrum posed by the intersection of AI, Big Data, and privacy. It critically analyses the capacity of international legal regimes to address privacy violations and the ethical implications of borderless algorithmic decision-making. It examines existing regulatory responses, from the GDPR to China's PIPL, and evaluates their efficacy in an AI-driven world. It also delves into the role of international human rights law, asking whether instruments like the International Covenant on Civil and Political Rights (ICCPR) and the Universal Declaration of Human Rights (UDHR) offer sufficient protections against AI-enabled surveillance and manipulation (UN, 1966; UN, 1948). Further, the chapter explores recent policy innovations, including AI audits, impact assessments, and regulatory sandboxes, to assess how future governance can be both rights-respecting and innovation-friendly.

To that end, this chapter seeks to answer the following key questions:

How does the cross-border nature of AI systems complicate the enforcement of privacy laws?

Can existing legal frameworks be adapted to respond to the challenges of algorithmic governance?

What role do ethical principles play in AI regulation, and how can they be operationalized within legal systems?
Can international human rights law offer a binding framework for AI and privacy governance?
What models of global cooperation and governance could offer balanced, effective regulation?

By addressing these questions, the chapter contributes to the ongoing discourse on digital constitutionalism, technological accountability, and human-centered governance. It proposes a rights-based approach to AI regulation that centers on transparency, participation, and justice while calling for stronger international coordination, interoperable legal standards, and binding ethical norms. Ultimately, the chapter contends that any meaningful governance of AI and Big Data must prioritize privacy as a fundamental right, rather than treating it as an afterthought to economic or technological progress.

PROBLEM STATEMENT

The rapid integration of Artificial Intelligence (AI) and Big Data into everyday life has introduced a host of complex challenges to existing legal and ethical paradigms, particularly in the realm of privacy. While AI technologies have demonstrated immense potential in optimizing decision-making, forecasting trends, and enhancing efficiency across sectors, their capabilities are fundamentally reliant on vast amounts of personal and sensitive data. This data is often collected without meaningful consent, processed without transparency, and stored or transferred without clear accountability mechanisms (Mittelstadt et al., 2016). As a result, individuals are frequently subjected to surveillance, profiling, and manipulation by opaque algorithms, raising significant concerns about their autonomy, dignity, and freedom in digital environments (Zuboff, 2019).

The central problem arises from the fact that AI and Big Data technologies operate in a global, borderless environment, while privacy laws and ethical guidelines remain fragmented, jurisdiction-specific, and inconsistently enforced (Tzanou, 2020). For instance, a single AI-driven application may collect data from users in one country, process it on servers in another, and be governed by corporate policies originating from yet another legal system. This disjointed governance structure creates gaps in accountability, allowing data controllers and processors to exploit legal loopholes, avoid scrutiny, and operate without meaningful oversight (van der Sloot, 2017). The result is a power imbalance where corporations and governments wield disproportionate control over data and the systems built upon it, with individuals having little to no say in how their information is used.

Moreover, the traditional concept of informed consent, which forms the cornerstone of most data protection frameworks, has been rendered almost obsolete in the age of AI. Users are often unable to understand the implications of data collection practices, nor can they meaningfully evaluate or reject the terms under which their data is harvested and analysed (Solove, 2013). This erosion of consent is particularly concerning in contexts involving biometric data, health records, and behavioural analytics, where AI systems make predictive judgments that can significantly affect individual lives. For example, algorithmic profiling has been used in predictive policing, credit scoring, and hiring processes, often without disclosing the criteria or offering avenues for redress (Wachter et al., 2017).

Another key challenge lies in the difficulty of attributing responsibility for AI-driven decisions. Because machine learning models evolve over time and often function as "black boxes" that even their developers cannot fully interpret, it becomes nearly impossible to determine accountability when harms occur (Burrell, 2016). This lack of explainability not only undermines legal recourse but also contradicts basic principles of due process and fairness embedded in democratic legal systems. The inability to trace decision-making logic, question its rationale, or seek redress places individuals at a systemic disadvantage, particularly in marginalized or vulnerable communities (Eubanks, 2018).

Compounding this issue is the absence of a universally binding international framework for governing AI and data privacy. Although the European Union's General Data Protection Regulation (GDPR) has set a global precedent, its influence remains regionally bounded and its enforcement outside the EU is limited (Bradford, 2020). Meanwhile, other jurisdictions such as the United States and China adopt vastly different approaches, either favouring market-driven solutions or prioritizing state surveillance under national security imperatives (Liu, 2022). This regulatory divergence hampers efforts to create coherent global norms and results in a patchwork of standards that fail to adequately address the transnational nature of AI technologies.

Given these realities, this chapter seeks to explore whether current legal and ethical systems are capable of safeguarding the right to privacy in a world increasingly governed by algorithmic intelligence and global data flows. It aims to critically examine how jurisdictional conflicts, technological opacity, and conceptual limitations in existing laws contribute to a growing gap between rights and realities. The problem is not merely one of insufficient regulation, but of a structural misalignment between traditional legal concepts and emerging technological architectures, a gap that, if left unaddressed, could lead to profound and irreversible infringements on human rights.

SIGNIFICANCE OF THE STUDY

The intersection of Artificial Intelligence (AI), Big Data, and privacy presents a critical frontier in both legal theory and human rights discourse. As societies increasingly rely on data-driven technologies to make decisions that influence everything from credit approvals and job recruitment to criminal sentencing and surveillance, the protection of personal data and privacy rights becomes not only a matter of regulation but a foundational issue of democratic governance and human dignity (Mittelstadt et. al., 2016; Zuboff, 2019). This study is significant because it engages directly with the structural tensions between technological innovation and normative frameworks, highlighting the inadequacies of current legal and ethical approaches in regulating the widespread deployment of AI systems.

One of the key reasons this study is vital is due to the unprecedented scale and scope of data collection facilitated by AI and machine learning systems. Personal data is no longer just limited to what users voluntarily share but includes metadata, behavioural patterns, biometric information, and even emotional responses inferred by sophisticated algorithms (Andrejevic & Gates, 2007). This shift toward predictive and inferential analytics raises new kinds of ethical and legal questions that traditional privacy laws, which were largely designed for simpler information systems, are not equipped to answer. The conceptual limitations of existing legal frameworks, such as consent-based models, are increasingly evident in a digital environment where consent is either coerced, uninformed, or entirely bypassed through opaque data collection practices (Solove, 2013).

The significance of this study also lies in its global perspective, which is essential given the inherently cross-border nature of digital technologies. While some countries like those in the European Union have implemented relatively robust data protection laws (e.g., the GDPR), many others lack comprehensive legislation or have adopted frameworks that prioritize state surveillance or economic interests over individual rights (Bradford, 2020; Liu, 2022). This global imbalance has led to a fragmented and often contradictory legal landscape that hinders meaningful enforcement and creates loopholes for corporations and governments to exploit. By examining the comparative effectiveness of different legal regimes and multilateral efforts, this chapter contributes to the ongoing discourse on the need for interoperable and harmonized international standards.

Importantly, this study highlights how the failure to address privacy violations in AI systems can have tangible social consequences, especially for vulnerable populations. Studies have shown that AI systems trained on biased or incomplete datasets often reinforce systemic discrimination in ways that are difficult to detect or challenge (Eubanks, 2018; Buolamwini & Gebru, 2018). For example, predictive policing tools have disproportionately targeted communities of colour, and facial recognition technologies have shown higher error rates for darker-skinned individuals. These issues are not just technical flaws but violations of fundamental rights, including equality, non-discrimination, and access to justice (UN, 1948; UN, 1966). The study thus emphasizes that privacy is not a luxury but a gateway right, one that enables the exercise of other civil, political, and social rights.

Additionally, the study's emphasis on ethical frameworks alongside legal mechanisms underscores the need for a multidimensional governance model. Legal regulation alone cannot keep pace with the rapid evolution of AI technologies. Therefore, embedding ethical principles, such as transparency, accountability, and fairness, into the design and deployment of AI systems is essential for creating sustainable and just digital societies (Floridi & Cowls, 2019). The analysis presented in this chapter contributes to the scholarly and policy-oriented understanding of how ethics and law must work in tandem to regulate AI and Big Data.

In sum, this study is significant because it addresses a pressing and under-regulated aspect of contemporary life that has far-reaching implications for democracy, human rights, and global justice. By critically assessing current laws, ethical principles, and emerging governance models, the chapter provides a roadmap for how societies can uphold privacy and human dignity in the age of intelligent machines.

METHODOLOGY

This chapter adopts a doctrinal and analytical legal research methodology supported by a comparative analysis of international frameworks and thematic literature review. The primary aim is to investigate how existing legal and ethical norms engage with the challenges posed by Artificial Intelligence (AI) and Big Data to the right to privacy in an increasingly globalized digital environment. Given the subject matter's transnational implications and the evolving nature of technology and law, a qualitative and interdisciplinary approach is essential to draw meaningful insights.

The doctrinal research component involves a detailed examination of statutory instruments, international treaties, constitutional provisions, case law, and policy guidelines related to data protection, AI governance, and digital rights. These include prominent regulations such as the European Union's General Data Protection Regulation (GDPR), the United States' California Consumer Privacy Act (CCPA) and sectoral laws like HIPAA, China's Personal Information Protection Law (PIPL), and emerging frameworks in regions like Brazil, Kenya, and India. By interpreting these legal texts and principles through a human rights lens, the chapter seeks to assess the adequacy of current legal responses in protecting individual privacy against the backdrop of advanced AI applications (Bradford, 2020; Liu, 2022).

Additionally, the study incorporates a comparative legal analysis that juxtaposes regulatory approaches across different jurisdictions. This facilitates the identification of best practices, gaps, and inconsistencies in privacy protection globally. The comparative approach is especially valuable given the cross-border nature of data flows and AI operations, which often render domestic laws insufficient when applied in isolation (Tzanou, 2020). Emphasis is placed on understanding how different governance models reflect cultural, political, and economic values, and how they align (or fail to align) with international human rights standards such as the Universal Declaration of Human Rights (UDHR) and the International Covenant on Civil and Political Rights (ICCPR) (United Nations, 1948; United Nations, 1966).

The thematic literature review component of the methodology involves critically engaging with academic scholarship, institutional reports, think tank publications, and ethical declarations from global bodies such as UNESCO, the OECD, and the IEEE. This includes reviewing key contributions from scholars in surveillance studies, digital ethics, algorithmic accountability, and technology law (Zuboff, 2019; Floridi & Cowls, 2019). These materials help to contextualize the legal analysis within broader ethical debates and ensure that the conclusions drawn are not limited to legalistic reasoning but are also normatively grounded.

Rather than relying on empirical data collection such as surveys or interviews, this chapter emphasizes interpretive and normative analysis, which is more suited to its theoretical and policy-oriented objectives. This methodological approach allows for a rigorous, interdisciplinary understanding of how AI and Big Data interact with the right to privacy, and what kind of legal-ethical architecture is necessary to preserve fundamental rights in a digitized world.

LITERATURE REVIEW AND THEORETICAL FRAMEWORK

The growing scholarly interest in the intersection of Artificial Intelligence (AI), Big Data, and privacy rights has led to a complex body of literature that traverses legal theory, digital ethics, surveillance studies, and technology policy. This chapter draws from these interdisciplinary perspectives to develop a comprehensive theoretical framework for understanding the structural and normative challenges posed by AI technologies to privacy and human dignity. The literature reviewed below is organized thematically, drawing upon five core areas: (1) surveillance capitalism and digital power, (2) algorithmic opacity and accountability, (3) legal frameworks for data protection, (4) ethical principles and governance models, and (5) international human rights law.

1. Surveillance Capitalism and Digital Power

Shoshana Zuboff's (2019) influential concept of "surveillance capitalism" forms the foundation for understanding how AI and Big Data commodify personal information. Zuboff argues that data extracted from user behaviour is no longer used merely for service improvement but is repurposed to predict and manipulate behaviour for profit. This commodification turns users into data-producing subjects, often without their awareness or meaningful consent. According to Zuboff, this transformation fundamentally alters the relationship between individuals and institutions, posing existential threats to autonomy and democracy.

Surveillance studies scholars such as Lyon (2018) expand on this by emphasizing the normalization of surveillance in contemporary society. In the AI context, data is not only collected passively but actively harvested through smart devices, social media, and biometric systems. This "datafication" process leads to new forms of social sorting, in which individuals are profiled, scored, and targeted based on algorithmic predictions (Andrejevic, 2007). These insights inform the broader argument that current legal regimes have failed to keep pace with the power asymmetries introduced by AI-driven data economies.

2. Algorithmic Opacity and Accountability

Another central theoretical concern in the literature is the opacity of algorithmic decision-making. Burrell (2016) identifies three forms of opacity in machine learning: intentional secrecy (e.g., trade secrets), technical illiteracy (i.e., lack of understanding), and inherent complexity (algorithms evolving beyond human comprehension). These dimensions raise serious questions about explainability and accountability, especially in high-stakes domains such as criminal justice, credit assessment, and healthcare.

Wachter, Mittelstadt, and Floridi (2017) argue that legal systems, particularly under the GDPR, attempt to address this opacity through provisions like the "right to explanation." However, they contend that these provisions are limited in scope and enforcement, often failing to provide individuals with genuine recourse against automated decisions. The challenge lies in the fact that many AI systems function as "black boxes" where not even developers can fully trace how specific outcomes are generated. This limits judicial review, undermines procedural fairness, and creates new forms of unaccountable power.

3. Legal Frameworks for Data Protection

Legal scholarship has increasingly focused on assessing the effectiveness of privacy regulations in addressing AI-related harms. The General Data Protection Regulation (GDPR) of the European Union is frequently cited as a gold standard for privacy protection, particularly due to its provisions on data minimization, purpose limitation, and data subject rights (European Parliament & Council, 2016). Bradford (2020) coined the term "Brussels Effect" to describe how the GDPR has influenced global data policies, even outside the EU's jurisdiction.

However, critiques of the GDPR emphasize its inadequacy in operationalizing privacy in the AI era. For instance, Gellert (2018) highlights the tension between the regulation's human-centric approach and the reality of algorithmic profiling, which is often conducted without direct human intervention. Moreover, the law's reliance on consent as a primary justification for data processing has been criticized for being ineffective in practice, given that users rarely understand the full implications of what they are consenting to (Solove, 2013).

In contrast, China's Personal Information Protection Law (PIPL) adopts a state-centric model that emphasizes data sovereignty and government oversight (Liu, 2022). While the law contains GDPR-like provisions, its focus on national interests raises concerns about surveillance and the absence of judicial independence. Meanwhile, the United States follows a sectoral and fragmented approach to data privacy, lacking a comprehensive federal statute. Laws like the California Consumer Privacy Act (CCPA) and HIPAA offer protections only in specific domains, leading to inconsistent standards and enforcement mechanisms (Schwartz & Solove, 2014).

4. Ethical Principles and Governance Models

Legal responses are increasingly supplemented by ethical frameworks that aim to guide the development and deployment of AI. The UNESCO Recommendation on the Ethics of Artificial Intelligence (2021) is one of the most comprehensive efforts to establish global ethical norms. It emphasizes human dignity, transparency, responsibility, fairness, and sustainability, proposing these values as foundational to any AI governance system.

Other key contributions include the IEEE's Ethically Aligned Design, which promotes the alignment of autonomous systems with human values, and the Montreal Declaration for Responsible AI, which calls for public deliberation and democratic oversight of AI systems. According to Floridi and Cowls (2019), these frameworks represent a "principled AI" approach, seeking to embed ethical considerations at all stages of the AI lifecycle. However, critics argue that such frameworks lack legal enforceability and often result in "ethics washing", where companies adopt high-level principles without implementing meaningful accountability mechanisms (Raji et al., 2020).

5. International Human Rights Law and AI

The relationship between AI and international human rights law is a growing area of concern. Article 12 of the Universal Declaration of Human Rights (UDHR) and Article 17 of the International Covenant on Civil and Political Rights (ICCPR) recognize the right to privacy as a fundamental human right (United Nations, 1948; 1966). However, the enforcement of these norms in digital contexts remains weak and inconsistent, particularly when AI technologies are used for mass surveillance, biometric tracking, and behavioural manipulation.

De Hert and Gutwirth (2006) argue that human rights frameworks must be updated to reflect the realities of data-driven technologies. Courts such as the European Court of Human Rights (ECHR) have begun to engage with privacy cases involving digital surveillance, but these rulings often lack binding effect beyond national jurisdictions. Moreover, the extraterritorial nature of AI systems complicates the application of rights protections, as users may be affected by foreign entities operating beyond the reach of their own legal systems (Tzanou, 2020).

INTEGRATION OF THEORETICAL PERSPECTIVES

Together, these bodies of literature provide a multi-layered theoretical foundation for this chapter. Zuboff's theory of surveillance capitalism highlights the economic drivers behind AI's exploitation of personal data, while Burrell and Wachter et al. expose the technical barriers to accountability. Legal scholars such as Bradford and Liu shed light on jurisdictional variations in privacy law, and ethicists like Floridi and Cowls offer normative visions for responsible AI. Finally, human rights theorists stress the urgent need for binding global standards that can transcend fragmented national laws and ensure dignity, equality, and autonomy in digital life.

The chapter builds upon these contributions to argue that a hybrid governance model, one that integrates legal regulation, ethical design, and international co-operation, is essential to address the unique risks posed by AI and Big Data. It contends that privacy must be reframed not just as a regulatory issue, but as a core component of human freedom, demanding robust safeguards in both legal systems and technological infrastructures.

BEYOND AI AND BIG DATA: EMERGING TECHNOLOGIES AND PRIVACY RISKS

In addition to AI and Big Data, technologies such as blockchain, IoT, edge computing, and biometric authentication systems have introduced new privacy challenges. These tools enable pervasive data collection and decentralized processing, often beyond the reach of conventional privacy laws.

Blockchain technologies, for example, store immutable transaction records, making it difficult to comply with legal mandates such as the right to erasure under GDPR. IoT devices embedded in homes and public infrastructure generate continuous sensor data, raising surveillance concerns across jurisdictions.

Edge computing further complicates legal enforcement, as data processing occurs locally at the device level, bypassing centralized controls. Similarly, biometric systems, used in everything from mobile authentication to national ID programs, pose risks of irreversible identity theft and algorithmic bias (Raji et al., 2020).

To ensure comprehensive coverage, these technologies must be incorporated into global privacy frameworks and addressed through adaptable, cross-border governance strategies.

GLOBAL SOUTH PERSPECTIVES ON DIGITAL IDENTITY AND PRIVACY

Countries in the Global South are increasingly implementing large-scale digital identity and biometric databases. India's Aadhaar program, Nigeria's NIMC, and Kenya's Huduma Namba reflect attempts to modernize state infrastructure through centralized identity systems (Marda & Narayan, 2020; Nyst et al., 2016).

These systems raise unique concerns, such as lack of informed consent, potential for mass exclusion, and weak data protection oversight, exacerbated by fragile institutional contexts.

Moreover, differing cultural norms around privacy complicate efforts to apply Western-style regulatory frameworks universally (De Hert & Papakonstantinou, 2012). Legal models must account for community-based rather than individual-centric understandings of rights in some regions.

INDUSTRY-LED ETHICAL AI INITIATIVES

Private companies have established ethical AI consortia, internal governance boards, and responsible AI guidelines. For example, the Partnership on AI, Microsoft's Responsible AI Standard, and IBM's Trust and Transparency Principles reflect growing industry interest in ethical compliance (Raji et al., 2020).

While these frameworks often mirror public regulatory efforts, they can be voluntary, unevenly enforced, and lack public accountability. Nonetheless, they represent an important facet of AI governance ecosystems.

OPERATIONAL AND STAKEHOLDER BARRIERS TO ETHICAL AI DESIGN

Despite increasing calls for fairness and transparency in AI design, organizations face real barriers, including limited technical expertise, unclear regulatory expectations, and trade-offs with business incentives.

Moreover, the perspectives of end-users, marginalized groups, and civil society actors are often absent in technology development, leading to AI systems that perpetuate inequality or fail to meet local needs.

Incorporating participatory design principles and interdisciplinary collaboration remains key to ensuring ethical deployment.

GLOBAL CHALLENGES: LAW, PRIVACY, AND AI

The advent of Artificial Intelligence (AI) and Big Data has triggered a paradigm shift in the ways personal data is collected, stored, processed, and used. These technologies thrive on massive volumes of data, much of it personally identifiable, sourced from users across jurisdictions, devices, and platforms. This cross-border, decentralized nature of AI-driven data flows introduces unique legal and ethical dilemmas, particularly concerning privacy rights, consent, and accountability. As governments and corporations expand their reliance on AI systems, traditional legal frameworks are struggling to provide adequate safeguards, highlighting the urgent need for revaluation of privacy protections on a global scale (Tzanou, 2020; Zuboff, 2019).

1. **Cross-Border Data Flows and Jurisdictional Complexity** One of the most pressing global challenges lies in the extraterritorial nature of AI systems. AI algorithms are trained on datasets that may be compiled from multiple countries, processed on cloud servers located elsewhere, and deployed in a third country altogether. This raises jurisdictional ambiguity, whose laws apply, and which authorities are responsible for enforcement (Kuner, 2015)? For example, a facial recognition application developed by a U.S. company may use data-

sets collected from users in India, processed on European servers, and sold to agencies in Africa. Such complexity makes uniform privacy enforcement nearly impossible. The European Union's General Data Protection Regulation (GDPR) attempts to address this through its extraterritorial scope under Article 3, which applies GDPR principles to entities outside the EU if they process EU citizens' data (European Parliament & Council, 2016). While this has influenced global practices, enforcement remains inconsistent, especially against tech giants headquartered outside the EU. Moreover, countries with weaker data protection frameworks often become soft targets for data harvesting and experimentation with AI models (Bradford, 2020).

2. **Lack of Harmonized International Legal Standards** Despite various national and regional efforts, there is currently no binding international treaty dedicated to AI or digital privacy. While frameworks like the Council of Europe's Convention 108+, OECD Privacy Guidelines, and G20 AI Principles provide soft law guidance, their non-binding nature limits enforcement and coherence (OECD, 2019; Council of Europe, 2018). Countries continue to adopt disparate models: the U.S. Favors sectoral regulation, the EU promotes a rights-based approach, and China emphasizes state control and data sovereignty through its Personal Information Protection Law (PIPL) (Liu, 2022). This regulatory fragmentation enables "forum shopping," where corporations select jurisdictions with the least resistance, thereby undermining stronger legal protections elsewhere. It also complicates cross-border legal cooperation, making it difficult for regulators to investigate, prosecute, or hold companies accountable for AI-driven violations that affect users across multiple countries (Kuner, 2015).
3. **Inadequate Consent Mechanisms** A cornerstone of most data protection laws is user consent, which has proven inadequate in the AI era. Informed consent requires individuals to understand what data is being collected, how it will be used, and what risks are involved. However, AI systems often rely on secondary use of data, repurposing data beyond its original collection context, and complex algorithms that even developers may not fully understand (Solove, 2013; Wachter et al., 2017). The typical "notice and consent" model fails in practice. Users are confronted with lengthy, incomprehensible privacy policies and binary options that provide little room for meaningful choice (Nissenbaum, 2011). In the case of AI systems that make predictive inferences or automate decisions, users often don't know they are being profiled at all, further eroding the legitimacy of consent (Mittelstadt et al., 2016). This raises critical legal and ethical questions: Can consent be truly "informed" if users cannot understand the implications of algorithmic processing?
4. **Algorithmic Profiling and Discrimination** AI's reliance on algorithmic profiling has serious implications for privacy, fairness, and equality. By analyzing

patterns across massive datasets, AI systems can predict behaviors, assess risk scores, and make decisions that affect people's access to jobs, loans, insurance, and even freedom. These systems often operate with limited transparency and accountability, leading to discriminatory outcomes (Eubanks, 2018). For instance, predictive policing tools have disproportionately targeted communities of color, reinforcing existing biases in the criminal justice system. Facial recognition technologies have shown higher error rates for darker-skinned individuals and women, particularly when trained on non-diverse datasets (Buolamwini & Gebru, 2018). These discriminatory practices are not simply bugs but systemic flaws rooted in biased data and opaque algorithms. Yet, existing legal frameworks provide insufficient protection. In many jurisdictions, individuals affected by algorithmic decisions may have no access to remedies, no explanation of the logic used, and no human review process. Article 22 of the GDPR prohibits decisions based solely on automated processing with significant legal effects but is often circumvented or poorly enforced (Wachter et al., 2017). This gap between law and practice allows AI systems to operate beyond the reach of traditional due process guarantees.

5. **Biometric Surveillance and Privacy Intrusions** The use of AI for biometric surveillance, including facial recognition, gait analysis, and emotion detection, poses one of the most intrusive threats to privacy. Governments and private actors increasingly deploy these tools in public spaces, often without transparency or legal authorization. Case studies such as Clearview AI, which scraped billions of facial images from the internet without consent, demonstrate the alarming scale at which personal data can be weaponized (Hill, 2020). In China, the Social Credit System integrates AI-powered surveillance with data from financial, legal, and social sources to monitor and rank citizens. In Europe, the EU's iBorderCtrl project tested AI lie-detection systems on travelers, a program criticized for pseudoscientific assumptions and lack of safeguards (Molnar, 2019). These technologies blur the line between security and coercion, raising serious human rights concerns under Article 17 of the International Covenant on Civil and Political Rights (ICCPR) and Article 8 of the European Convention on Human Rights (United Nations, 1966).
6. **Data Localization and Digital Sovereignty Conflicts** As states attempt to assert greater control over cross-border data flows, data localization laws have emerged, requiring companies to store and process data within national borders. While this may enhance government oversight and protect against foreign surveillance, it also creates barriers to innovation, increases costs, and facilitates authoritarian control in some regimes (Chander & Lê, 2015). Countries like India and Russia have proposed or implemented strict localization requirements, citing national security concerns. However, such policies often lead to fragmentation of the

internet, conflict with free trade agreements, and undermine global cooperation. This push for digital sovereignty reflects a larger tension between the global nature of data ecosystems and local political imperatives, making consensus on international rules increasingly difficult.

7. **Challenges to Legal Remedies and Enforcement** Perhaps the most concerning challenge is the limited access to justice for individuals affected by AI-driven privacy violations. Even in countries with strong data protection laws, enforcement is under-resourced and slow. Regulators may struggle to audit complex AI systems, especially when companies resist disclosure by invoking trade secrets or proprietary rights (Binns, 2018).

Moreover, transnational enforcement is weak. A user in Kenya whose data is exploited by a tech firm in California may have no effective legal recourse, especially if the company does not have a legal presence in their jurisdiction. International courts and human rights bodies rarely address digital rights violations, and few precedents exist for AI-related privacy cases. Without systemic reforms and stronger enforcement mechanisms, the promise of privacy laws remains largely aspirational.

The global challenges posed by AI to privacy and legal governance are profound and multifaceted. From cross-border data flows and jurisdictional complexity to discriminatory profiling, biometric surveillance, and regulatory fragmentation, the current legal landscape is ill-equipped to respond to the pace and scale of AI technologies. Privacy laws, based on outdated notions of informed consent and territorial jurisdiction, are increasingly disconnected from the realities of algorithmic decision-making and borderless data ecosystems.

To protect privacy as a fundamental human right, legal systems must evolve to reflect the technological architectures they seek to regulate. This includes stronger international cooperation, harmonized standards, algorithmic accountability, and rights-based approaches that prioritize human dignity, transparency, and justice. Without these reforms, AI risks deepening existing inequalities, eroding public trust, and undermining democratic values in the digital age.

The table below (Table 1.), illustrates key legislative developments shaping data privacy and AI governance globally. It provides context for the evolution of regulatory approaches across different regions.

TIMELINE OF MAJOR GLOBAL PRIVACY AND AI REGULATIONS

Table 1. Timeline of Major Global Privacy and AI Regulations

Year	Country/Region	Regulation/Framework	Key Features
2016	European Union	General Data Protection Regulation (GDPR)	Comprehensive rights-based framework; extraterritorial scope; consent, access, erasure, profiling restrictions
2018	United States (California)	California Consumer Privacy Act (CCPA)	Consumer rights over data access, deletion, and opt-out from sales
2020	Brazil	Lei Geral de Proteção de Dados (LGPD)	Modeled on GDPR; applies to public and private entities; governs data processing and transfers
2021	China	Personal Information Protection Law (PIPL)	Strict consent regime; data localization; cybersecurity reviews
2019	Kenya	Data Protection Act	Establishes Data Protection Commissioner; covers data subject rights, cross-border data transfer rules
2023	India	Digital Personal Data Protection Act (DPDPA)	Consent-based regime; creation of Data Protection Board; cross-border flow exceptions

INTERNATIONAL LEGAL FRAMEWORKS

As Artificial Intelligence (AI) and Big Data systems increasingly operate across national borders, questions of jurisdiction, legal responsibility, and enforceability have gained prominence in international law. Privacy, long considered a fundamental human right, is now challenged by the capabilities of AI to collect, process, and infer sensitive information at unprecedented scales. While many countries have attempted to regulate data practices at the domestic level, the global nature of digital technologies necessitates coordinated international legal frameworks to ensure effective and equitable protection of privacy rights. However, the current landscape remains fragmented, with varying degrees of regulatory maturity, philosophical foundations, and enforcement capacity (Kuner, 2015; Tzanou, 2020).

1. The General Data Protection Regulation (GDPR) – European Union

The General Data Protection Regulation (GDPR), implemented by the European Union in 2018, represents the most comprehensive and influential legal framework for data protection globally. It enshrines key privacy principles such as lawfulness, transparency, purpose limitation, data minimization, and accountability (European Parliament & Council, 2016). The GDPR is particularly notable for its extraterritorial scope. Under Article 3, it applies not only to organizations established within the EU but also to those offering goods or services to, or monitoring the behavior of, individuals in the EU.

Importantly, the GDPR provides specific protections against automated decision-making, including profiling. Article 22 establishes the right not to be subject to decisions based solely on automated processing that produce legal or similarly significant effects. It also requires meaningful human intervention, explainability, and safeguards against discrimination (Wachter et al., 2017). The regulation further empowers data subjects with rights to access, rectify, erase, and port their data, and imposes heavy penalties for non-compliance, with fines of up to 4% of global annual turnover.

The influence of the GDPR is evident in what Bradford (2020) terms the "Brussels Effect," wherein companies and jurisdictions outside the EU voluntarily adopt GDPR-like standards to maintain access to the EU market. Nevertheless, criticisms persist regarding its enforceability, especially against powerful multinational corporations. Enforcement actions remain uneven, and smaller data protection authorities in the EU often lack resources to conduct cross-border investigations.

2. United States – Sectoral and Fragmented Approach

In contrast to the EU's rights-based and unified approach, the United States has adopted a sector-specific regulatory model, where data protection is governed by a patchwork of federal and state laws. Key statutes include:

HIPAA (Health Insurance Portability and Accountability Act) for health data

COPPA (Children's Online Privacy Protection Act) for minors' data

FCRA (Fair Credit Reporting Act) for financial information

CCPA (California Consumer Privacy Act), one of the most comprehensive state-level laws

The California Privacy Rights Act (CPRA), which amends and expands the CCPA, is pushing the U.S. closer to a more unified data protection regime. However, there remains no overarching federal privacy law, leaving significant gaps in regulation (Schwartz & Solove, 2014). While the U.S. prioritizes innovation and market flexibility, this approach often fails to provide robust protections against AI misuse, especially in areas like automated decision-making and algorithmic bias.

The U.S. has also proposed voluntary frameworks, such as the NIST AI Risk Management Framework, which provide guidelines for ethical and trustworthy AI development. Yet, the voluntary nature of such frameworks limits their impact, and enforcement relies heavily on litigation or self-regulation.

3. China – Data Sovereignty and State Control

China presents a contrasting model that combines data protection with assertive state surveillance. Its Personal Information Protection Law (PIPL), enacted in 2021, is often compared to the GDPR for its structure and principles, such as data minimization, user consent, and cross-border transfer restrictions (Liu, 2022). However, the PIPL is embedded within China's broader legal ecosystem, which includes the Cybersecurity Law and Data Security Law, prioritizing national security and state sovereignty over individual autonomy.

The Chinese model emphasizes strict data localization and government access to private data, particularly for law enforcement and surveillance purposes. Despite offering GDPR-like individual rights, these are often undermined by the state's ability to override privacy protections in the name of public order or national interest (Creemers, 2017). China's approach exemplifies the tension between privacy protection and authoritarian governance, raising concerns about the replicability of such models in democratic societies.

4. Brazil and the LGPD – A Middle Ground

Brazil's Lei Geral de Proteção de Dados (LGPD), which came into effect in 2020, is modelled closely on the GDPR and reflects a growing trend among Global South countries to adopt comprehensive data protection laws. The LGPD applies to all data processing activities involving individuals located in Brazil, regardless of where the processor is based, reflecting a global regulatory reach (Doneda & Almeida, 2021).

The law establishes data subjects' rights, requires clear and specific consent, and creates the National Data Protection Authority (ANPD) to oversee compliance. However, the effectiveness of the LGPD has been hindered by limited institutional capacity, political instability, and challenges in balancing economic development with human rights protections. Brazil's experience highlights the importance of enforcement mechanisms and institutional independence in ensuring that privacy laws are not merely symbolic.

5. Regional Developments in Africa and Asia

Countries across Africa and Asia have increasingly adopted data protection legislation in response to digitalization and global privacy trends. For instance:

Kenya passed the Data Protection Act in 2019, establishing rights and responsibilities similar to those under the GDPR.

India has proposed the Digital Personal Data Protection Act, which seeks to regulate data processing while preserving state authority over national security and public order.

These developments are promising but face implementation challenges such as insufficient infrastructure, lack of digital literacy, and limited judicial capacity. Furthermore, the absence of a continental or regional framework (unlike the EU) limits the coherence of privacy regulation across countries (Makulilo, 2016).

6. Multilateral and Soft Law Instruments

In the absence of a binding international treaty on AI and privacy, several soft law instruments and multilateral initiatives have emerged:

The Council of Europe's Convention 108+ is the only binding international treaty on data protection and has been modernized to address digital technologies.

The OECD Guidelines on the Protection of Privacy and Transborder Flows of Personal Data promote interoperability and trust but lack enforcement mechanisms.

The UNESCO Recommendation on the Ethics of Artificial Intelligence (2021) calls for global standards around fairness, transparency, and human oversight in AI systems.

The G20 AI Principles and OECD AI Principles stress inclusive, sustainable, and accountable AI development (OECD, 2019).

While these frameworks signal a growing consensus around ethical AI, their non-binding nature limits accountability. Moreover, geopolitical tensions and divergent ideologies on digital governance hinder the development of a unified international legal regime.

LEGAL INNOVATIONS FROM THE GLOBAL SOUTH

Much of the global discourse on data governance has been shaped by Europe's GDPR and the United States' sectoral approaches. However, several countries in the Global South are now developing robust and innovative legal models to regulate digital technologies.

India's Aadhaar system, the world's largest biometric ID project, has sparked significant debate about privacy, surveillance, and exclusion (Drèze & Khera, 2017). While it has streamlined welfare delivery, it has also faced constitutional challenges. Brazil's General Data Protection Law (LGPD), modeled on GDPR, balances data protection with innovation and includes provisions for cross-border data flows (Monteiro & Macadar, 2021). In Africa, Kenya's Data Protection Act (2019) and Nigeria's Data Protection Regulation (NDPR) are noteworthy developments despite challenges in enforcement.

These examples illustrate diverse regulatory strategies that reflect local values and socioeconomic realities. Including such perspectives is crucial for constructing a truly global discourse on data privacy and AI governance.

The landscape of international legal frameworks governing AI and privacy is marked by diversity, asymmetry, and fragmentation. While the GDPR has emerged as a global benchmark, it cannot be a universal solution due to differences in political systems, legal cultures, and enforcement capacities. Other models, such as the U.S. sectoral approach or China's sovereignty-driven regulation, reflect competing priorities, ranging from economic liberalism to state control.

For meaningful global governance, international cooperation must go beyond soft law and voluntary guidelines. A binding global data protection convention, supported by independent oversight bodies, harmonized enforcement mechanisms, and a human right–centered approach, is essential. Until such a framework materializes, privacy protections will remain inconsistent, and the governance of AI will continue to be shaped more by power and influence than by rights and justice.

ETHICAL CHALLENGES AND PRINCIPLES

The ethical dilemmas posed by the intersection of Artificial Intelligence (AI), Big Data, and privacy transcend mere legal non-compliance, they delve into deeper questions about human autonomy, fairness, dignity, and the legitimacy of decision-making in increasingly algorithmic societies. While legal frameworks provide structured obligations, ethical principles offer normative guidance that shapes responsible technological development and use. However, the rapid advancement of AI technologies has outpaced both ethical and legal safeguards, leading to a growing "governance gap" where rights can be technically violated without explicitly breaking the law (Floridi & Cowls, 2019). This section explores the key ethical challenges in AI and privacy, as well as the emerging global principles that aim to guide responsible AI governance.

1. **Informed Consent and Autonomy** One of the core ethical tenets of privacy is individual autonomy, the right to control personal information and make informed decisions about its use. However, the opacity of AI systems and the complexity of data processing undermine the feasibility of truly informed consent (Solove, 2013). Users are routinely subjected to data practices they neither understand nor agree with in any meaningful way, particularly in contexts involving predictive analytics, behavioral targeting, and biometric surveillance. From an ethical standpoint, this raises serious questions: Can individuals exercise autonomy in environments where data collection is pervasive, invisible, and integrated into essential services? Nissenbaum's (2010) concept of contextual integrity argues that privacy norms depend on the context in which data is shared, and violations occur when information is used outside its original setting. AI systems frequently breach this integrity by reusing or repurposing data beyond its intended scope, thus eroding the ethical foundations of privacy.
2. **Discrimination, Bias, and Social Justice** AI systems trained on historical or biased datasets risk amplifying existing social inequalities. Ethical concerns about discrimination and unfair treatment have been raised in a range of applications, from algorithmic hiring and lending to predictive policing and welfare allocation (Eubanks, 2018). For instance, facial recognition algorithms have been found to misidentify women and people of color at disproportionately high rates (Buolamwini & Gebru, 2018). These errors are not merely technical issues; they reflect systemic injustices embedded within data and model design. Ethical AI requires proactive measures to ensure fairness and inclusivity. This includes auditing datasets for bias, involving diverse stakeholders in the design process, and implementing algorithmic impact assessments. Yet, in practice, such principles are often sidelined in favor of efficiency and profitability. The ethical challenge lies not only in recognizing bias but in ensuring that marginalized communities have a voice in shaping the systems that affect them.
3. **Manipulation, Surveillance, and Loss of Agency** AI-powered systems are increasingly used to influence user behavior, from nudging consumer choices to shaping political opinions. This raises ethical concerns about manipulation and the erosion of cognitive freedom, especially when users are unaware of the algorithms guiding their digital experience. The Cambridge Analytica scandal demonstrated how psychographic profiling could be used to sway elections by exploiting psychological vulnerabilities (Isaak & Hanna, 2018). Such use of data analytics blurs the line between persuasion and coercion, raising concerns about human dignity and agency. Ethically, the use of AI for manipulation undermines the principle of respect for persons, which demands that individuals be treated as autonomous agents rather than mere means to an end (Floridi et al., 2018). Surveillance, especially when unaccountable or indiscriminate, compounds this

issue by fostering chilling effects, where people alter their behaviour due to fear of being watched, a violation of the right to privacy and freedom of expression (Zuboff, 2019).

4. **Transparency and Explainability** Transparency is widely regarded as a foundational ethical principle in AI governance. Users, regulators, and affected individuals must be able to understand how and why decisions are made, especially when such decisions carry significant consequences (Wachter et al., 2017). However, many AI models, particularly deep learning systems, function as "black boxes", their internal logic is not easily interpretable even by their developers (Burrell, 2016). Lack of transparency not only undermines accountability but also erodes trust. Ethically, explainability is necessary for contestability, fairness, and due process. A person wrongly denied a loan or job by an AI system must have the right to understand the rationale behind the decision and to challenge it. Unfortunately, current commercial and technical priorities often sideline explainability in favour of performance and proprietary secrecy.
5. **Global Ethical Principles and Frameworks** In response to these challenges, several international bodies and coalitions have developed ethical principles to guide AI development: UNESCO's Recommendation on the Ethics of Artificial Intelligence (2021) emphasizes human dignity, accountability, inclusiveness, and sustainability. It is the first global normative instrument on AI ethics adopted by all member states (UNESCO, 2021).

The IEEE's Ethically Aligned Design framework prioritizes human wellbeing, transparency, and accountability in autonomous and intelligent systems.

The Montreal Declaration for Responsible AI calls for public engagement, democratic oversight, and respect for diversity and solidarity.

The OECD AI Principles and G20 AI Principles promote human-centered values, robustness, and transparency (OECD, 2019).

While these frameworks vary in focus and enforceability, they reflect a growing consensus around core ethical values. However, critics argue that such declarations often suffer from vagueness and lack of enforcement, enabling what has been termed "ethics washing", where companies adopt high-level principles without changing harmful practices (Raji et al., 2020).

Ethical principles are indispensable for guiding AI and Big Data systems toward responsible and equitable outcomes. Yet, as this section has shown, the translation of ethics into practice remains fraught with challenges. Consent is undermined by complexity, fairness is compromised by bias, autonomy is threatened by manipulation, and transparency is often absent. While global ethical frameworks offer promising blueprints, their real-world impact is limited without binding regulations, institutional accountability, and participatory governance.

Moving forward, ethical AI must be grounded not only in abstract principles but in concrete mechanisms that ensure these values are embedded in technological design, implementation, and oversight. This includes mandatory impact assessments, inclusive policymaking, and continuous public engagement. Ultimately, ethics and law must work hand-in-hand to ensure that AI serves humanity, rather than undermining its rights, freedoms, and dignity.

STAKEHOLDER PARTICIPATION AND SOCIETAL IMPACTS

The development and governance of AI systems should not be restricted to policymakers and corporations. Effective regulation and ethical deployment must involve diverse stakeholders, including civil society, marginalized communities, technologists, legal scholars, and affected individuals.

AI systems impact societies in asymmetric ways. For example, predictive policing tools often disproportionately target minority groups, while credit-scoring algorithms may penalize low-income populations (Eubanks, 2018). The voices of such affected communities are often absent from AI design and oversight conversations. Moreover, developers frequently lack formal training in ethics, law, or human rights, resulting in technological tools that fail to anticipate real-world harms.

Initiatives such as participatory audits, algorithmic impact assessments (AIAs), and public consultation mechanisms have emerged as tools to bridge this gap (Reisman et al., 2018). Yet, these are inconsistently implemented. Institutionalizing stakeholder participation within governance frameworks is essential to ensure AI systems align with democratic values and social justice goals.

RECOMMENDATIONS AND SOLUTIONS

To effectively navigate the complex intersection of Artificial Intelligence (AI), Big Data, and privacy, the global legal and ethical landscape must be reimagined. Current approaches, while valuable, often fall short in addressing the transnational, opaque, and algorithmic nature of emerging technologies. The following recommendations aim to foster a robust, rights-based, and ethically grounded framework that addresses the multidimensional risks associated with AI and data-driven systems.

1. Adopt a Global Legal Framework on AI and Privacy

One of the most critical challenges in the governance of AI is the absence of a unified, binding international legal framework that governs data privacy across borders. The European Union's General Data Protection Regulation (GDPR) has set a valuable precedent, particularly in terms of extraterritorial applicability and individual rights (European Parliament & Council, 2016). However, other regions adopt fragmented or weaker approaches, allowing for regulatory loopholes and inconsistent protections.

A UN-led global convention on digital privacy and AI governance should be developed, drawing on the GDPR and incorporating universal human rights standards as outlined in Article 17 of the International Covenant on Civil and Political Rights (United Nations, 1966). This framework should mandate cross-border cooperation, establish clear accountability mechanisms for corporations and governments, and enshrine rights such as consent, erasure, and non-discrimination.

2. Mandate Algorithmic Transparency and Explainability

Opaque algorithms are one of the greatest barriers to accountability in AI systems. Many models function as "black boxes," making decisions that significantly impact people's lives without offering insight into how or why those decisions were made (Burrell, 2016).

Legal systems should mandate algorithmic transparency by requiring developers to provide clear documentation, or "model cards," outlining data sources, training methods, and risk mitigation strategies. Furthermore, the right to explanation, as proposed in the GDPR's Article 22, should be strengthened and made enforceable across jurisdictions (Wachter et al., 2017). Individuals must be able to understand, challenge, and seek redress for algorithmic decisions that affect them.

3. Enforce Algorithmic Impact Assessments (AIAs)

Before deploying AI systems, particularly in high-risk contexts such as policing, healthcare, credit scoring, or welfare distribution, organizations should be required to conduct Algorithmic Impact Assessments (AIAs). These assessments should evaluate potential risks, test for discriminatory outcomes, and propose safeguards.

AIAs should be overseen by independent regulatory bodies and made publicly available to ensure democratic oversight. Such tools are essential for assessing the ethical, social, and legal implications of algorithmic systems before they are allowed to influence public policy or private decision-making (Raji et al., 2020).

4. Regulate and Restrict High-Risk Applications

Not all AI applications are created equal. Technologies such as facial recognition, predictive policing, and emotion recognition pose significant risks to privacy, civil liberties, and equality. In such cases, strong regulatory safeguards or outright bans may be warranted.

The European Union's proposed AI Act categorizes AI systems into risk-based tiers and imposes stricter obligations on high-risk applications (European Commission, 2021). This model can be adapted globally to ensure that particularly invasive or unproven technologies are subject to enhanced scrutiny or prohibited when they infringe on fundamental rights.

5. Embed Privacy by Design and Data Minimization

To mitigate privacy violations at the source, developers should adopt Privacy by Design principles, integrating privacy safeguards into the architecture of AI systems from their inception (Cavoukian, 2009). This includes data minimization (collecting only what is necessary), encryption, anonymization, and secure data storage.

Laws and industry standards should require that privacy is the default setting, not an optional feature. By embedding privacy protections into the design of systems, many risks can be prevented rather than remediated.

6. Promote Digital Literacy and Public Participation

The democratic legitimacy of AI systems hinges on public awareness and participation. Governments and institutions should invest in digital literacy programs to educate individuals about how AI systems work, what rights they hold, and how to contest unfair treatment. Furthermore, public consultations and participatory design processes should be institutionalized in the development of AI policies and infrastructure (Zuboff, 2019).

Communities affected by data-driven technologies, especially marginalized groups, must be given a seat at the table. Their lived experiences are crucial to identifying blind spots and mitigating unintended harms in AI development and deployment.

7. Establish Independent Regulatory Bodies

Enforcement remains one of the weakest links in global data governance. Countries should establish independent data protection authorities and AI oversight bodies with the power to audit, investigate, and sanction both public and private entities. These bodies must be sufficiently resourced and protected from political and corporate influence to perform their functions effectively.

A transnational coordination mechanism, such as a Global AI Oversight Council, could facilitate the sharing of best practices, harmonize standards, and mediate cross-border disputes.

The above solutions offer a roadmap for addressing the multifaceted challenges presented by AI and Big Data in relation to privacy. They emphasize a multi-pronged approach, combining legal reform, ethical design, technical safeguards, and democratic engagement. The path forward must be one that centres human dignity, rights, and justice, recognizing that the future of AI governance will shape not only markets and states but the fabric of human autonomy and agency itself.

CONCLUSION

The convergence of Artificial Intelligence and Big Data represents both an unprecedented opportunity and a formidable challenge. This chapter has examined the evolving international legal frameworks, ethical standards, stakeholder roles, and technological advances that shape the modern data governance landscape. Despite the existence of multiple regulatory initiatives and normative instruments, fragmentation, enforcement limitations, and jurisdictional inconsistencies remain persistent hurdles. To address these, the chapter recommends an interoperable, human-centered, and rights-respecting global governance model for AI. Such a model must be informed not only by law and ethics, but also by inclusive stakeholder engagement and technological design practices. Ultimately, safeguarding privacy and human dignity in an era of algorithmic decision-making requires collaborative, cross-border, and multidisciplinary solutions.

Despite the emergence of robust regional laws like the General Data Protection Regulation (GDPR), a global, harmonized framework that adequately protects personal data across borders remains elusive (European Parliament & Council, 2016; Bradford, 2020). In parallel, ethical declarations from institutions such as UNESCO and the IEEE offer principled guidelines for AI governance, yet they often lack enforceability, making real-world accountability difficult (UNESCO, 2021; Floridi & Cowls, 2019). Moreover, algorithmic opacity, biased training data, and discriminatory outcomes continue to disproportionately harm vulnerable populations, exacerbating existing societal inequalities (Eubanks, 2018; Buolamwini & Gebru, 2018).

This chapter has proposed a multi-pronged strategy to close the governance gap: establishing a legally binding international treaty, mandating algorithmic impact assessments and transparency, institutionalizing ethical AI principles through enforceable law, and strengthening oversight bodies globally. These solutions are not merely technical; they are political and moral imperatives. The governance of AI must be grounded in a commitment to human dignity, equality, and democratic accountability.

Ultimately, the question is not whether AI will shape the future, but who will shape AI, and for what ends. If left unchecked, AI risks entrenching power asymmetries and eroding fundamental rights. But if governed wisely, with inclusive, transparent, and rights-respecting frameworks, AI can be harnessed as a tool for public good. As we move further into the algorithmic age, the urgent task is to ensure that privacy, autonomy, and justice remain central to our technological evolution.

FUTURE RESEARCH DIRECTIONS

The rapid evolution of Artificial Intelligence (AI) and Big Data technologies continues to outpace legal and ethical scholarship, creating a dynamic and urgent need for interdisciplinary research. While this chapter has outlined key challenges and proposed solutions, several areas require deeper academic inquiry and empirical exploration to ensure responsive, inclusive, and effective governance mechanisms.

First, there is a pressing need to examine jurisdictional enforcement mechanisms in cross-border data protection regimes. Future research should explore how international cooperation can be operationalized through bilateral and multilateral agreements that align with global human rights standards (Kuner, 2015). In particular, studies should assess the effectiveness of the GDPR's extraterritorial provisions and their influence on corporate behaviour outside the EU (Bradford, 2020).

Second, researchers must investigate the effectiveness and limitations of algorithmic impact assessments (AIAs). While widely recommended in policy circles, there is limited empirical data on how AIAs are implemented, audited, and acted upon in real-world settings (Raji et al., 2020). Comparative studies could evaluate different institutional models and develop best practices for standardizing AIAs globally.

Third, there is a need for longitudinal studies examining the social consequences of AI-driven profiling and surveillance, especially among marginalized communities. Quantitative and qualitative research should explore how predictive systems in policing, welfare, education, and employment affect civil liberties, reinforce structural inequalities, or alter public behaviour (Eubanks, 2018; Zuboff, 2019).

Fourth, future research should focus on operationalizing ethical frameworks within the AI development lifecycle. While international guidelines such as UNESCO's AI Ethics Recommendation (2021) and IEEE's Ethically Aligned Design provide normative direction, practical integration of these values into software engineering, procurement, and deployment processes remains underexplored.

Lastly, legal scholars and technologists must collaborate on the development of explainable AI (XAI) models that are both technically feasible and legally compliant. The right to explanation, fairness in automated decision-making, and transparency mechanisms require continued research into balancing technical complexity with user comprehensibility (Wachter et al., 2017).

In sum, future research must move beyond theoretical critique to develop actionable, inclusive, and scalable solutions. As AI becomes more embedded in societal infrastructures, ongoing interdisciplinary inquiry will be vital to protecting fundamental rights and ensuring justice in the algorithmic age.

REFERENCES

Andrejevic, M. (2007). Surveillance in the digital enclosure. *Communication Review*, *10*(4), 295–317. DOI: 10.1080/10714420701715365

Binns, R. (2018). Fairness in machine learning: Lessons from political philosophy. *Proceedings of the 2018 Conference on Fairness, Accountability, and Transparency*, 149–159.

Bradford, A. (2020). *The Brussels effect: How the European Union rules the world*. Oxford University Press. DOI: 10.1093/oso/9780190088583.001.0001

Buolamwini, J., & Gebru, T. (2018). Gender shades: Intersectional accuracy disparities in commercial gender classification. *Proceedings of the 1st Conference on Fairness, Accountability and Transparency*, 77–91.

Burrell, J. (2016). How the machine 'thinks': Understanding opacity in machine learning algorithms. *Big Data & Society*, *3*(1), 1–12. DOI: 10.1177/2053951715622512

Cavoukian, A. (2009). Privacy by design: The 7 foundational principles. https://www.ipc.on.ca/wp-content/uploads/resources/7foundationalprinciples.pdf

Chander, A., & Lê, U. P. (2015). Data nationalism. *Emory Law Journal*, *64*(3), 677–739.

Council of Europe. (2018). Modernised Convention 108+: Convention for the Protection of Individuals with regard to Processing of Personal Data.

Creemers, R. (2017). Cyber China: Upgrading propaganda, public opinion work and social management for the twenty-first century. *Journal of Contemporary China*, *26*(103), 85–100. DOI: 10.1080/10670564.2016.1206281

De Hert, P., & Papakonstantinou, V. (2012). The proposed data protection Regulation replacing Directive 95/46/EC: A sound system for the protection of individuals? *Computer Law & Security Review*, *28*(2), 130–142. DOI: 10.1016/j.clsr.2012.01.011

Doneda, D., & Almeida, V. (2021). Brazil's General Data Protection Law: A detailed overview. *Computer Law & Security Review*, *40*, 105525.

Eubanks, V. (2018). *Automating inequality: How high-tech tools profile, police, and punish the poor*. St. Martin's Press.

European Commission. (2021). *Proposal for a regulation laying down harmonised rules on artificial intelligence*. Artificial Intelligence Act.

European Parliament & Council. (2016). *Regulation (EU) 2016/679*. General Data Protection Regulation.

Floridi, L., & Cowls, J. (2019). A unified framework of five principles for AI in society. *Harvard Data Science Review*, *1*(1). Advance online publication. DOI: 10.1162/99608f92.8cd550d1

Floridi, L., Cowls, J., Beltrametti, M., Chatila, R., Chazerand, P., Dignum, V., Luetge, C., Madelin, R., Pagallo, U., Rossi, F., Schafer, B., Valcke, P., & Vayena, E. (2018). AI4People—An ethical framework for a good AI society: Opportunities, risks, principles, and recommendations. *Minds and Machines*, *28*(4), 689–707. DOI: 10.1007/s11023-018-9482-5 PMID: 30930541

Gellert, R. (2018). Understanding the notion of risk in the General Data Protection Regulation. *Computer Law & Security Review*, *34*(2), 279–288. DOI: 10.1016/j.clsr.2017.12.003

Gellert, R. (2018). Understanding the notion of risk in the General Data Protection Regulation. *Computer Law & Security Review*, *34*(2), 279–288. DOI: 10.1016/j.clsr.2017.12.003

Hill, K. (2020, January 18). The secretive company that might end privacy as we know it. The New York Times. https://www.nytimes.com/2020/01/18/technology/clearview-privacy.html

Isaak, J., & Hanna, M. J. (2018). User data privacy: Facebook, Cambridge Analytica, and privacy protection. *Computer*, *51*(8), 56–59. DOI: 10.1109/MC.2018.3191268

Kuner, C. (2015). *Transborder data flows and data privacy law*. Oxford University Press.

Liu, H. (2022). China's Personal Information Protection Law: A comprehensive data privacy framework. *Computer Law & Security Review*, *45*, 105656. DOI: 10.1016/j.clsr.2022.105656

Lyon, D. (2018). *The culture of surveillance: Watching as a way of life*. Polity Press.

Makulilo, A. B. (2016). *African data privacy laws*. Springer. DOI: 10.1007/978-3-319-47317-8

Marda, V., & Narayan, S. (2020). Data in New Delhi's predictive policing system. In *Proceedings of the 2020 Conference on Fairness, Accountability, and Transparency* (pp. 317–324). Association for Computing Machinery. DOI: 10.1145/3351095.3372865

Mittelstadt, B. D., Allo, P., Taddeo, M., Wachter, S., & Floridi, L. (2016). The ethics of algorithms: Mapping the debate. *Big Data & Society*, *3*(2), 2053951716679679. DOI: 10.1177/2053951716679679

Molnar, P. (2019). Technological testing grounds: Migration management experiments and reflections from the ground up. European Digital Rights (EDRi). https://edri.org/wp-content/uploads/2020/11/technological_testing_grounds.pdf

Nissenbaum, H. (2010). *Privacy in context: Technology, policy, and the integrity of social life*. Stanford University Press.

Nissenbaum, H. (2011). A contextual approach to privacy online. *Daedalus*, *140*(4), 32–48. DOI: 10.1162/DAED_a_00113

Nyst, C., Makin, P., Pannifer, S., & Whitley, E. (2016). Digital identity: Issue analysis (Executive summary). Consult Hyperion. https://www.chyp.com/media/reports/Digital-Identity-Issue-Analysis-Executive-Summary.pdf

OECD. (2019). OECD principles on artificial intelligence. https://www.oecd.org/going-digital/ai/principles/

Raji, I. D., Smart, A., White, R. N., Mitchell, M., Gebru, T., Hutchinson, B., & Barnes, P. (2020). Closing the AI accountability gap: Defining an end-to-end framework for internal algorithmic auditing. *Proceedings of the 2020 Conference on Fairness, Accountability, and Transparency*, 33–44. DOI: 10.1145/3351095.3372873

Schwartz, P. M., & Solove, D. J. (2014). Reconciling personal information in the United States and European Union. *California Law Review*, *102*(4), 877–916.

Solove, D. J. (2013). Privacy self-management and the consent dilemma. *Harvard Law Review*, *126*(7), 1880–1903.

Tzanou, M. (2020). *The fundamental right to data protection: Normative value in the context of counter-terrorism surveillance*. Bloomsbury Publishing.

UNESCO. (2021). Recommendation on the ethics of artificial intelligence. https://unesdoc.unesco.org/ark:/48223/pf0000379920

United Nations. (1948). Universal Declaration of Human Rights. https://www.un.org/en/about-us/universal-declaration-of-human-rights

United Nations. (1966). International Covenant on Civil and Political Rights. https://www.ohchr.org/en/instruments-mechanisms/instruments/international-covenant-civil-and-political-rights van der Sloot, B. (2017). *Privacy as virtue: Moving beyond the individual in the age of big data. Intersentia* (Vol. 81). Human Rights Research Series. DOI: 10.1017/9781780686592

Wachter, S., Mittelstadt, B., & Floridi, L. (2017). Why a right to explanation of automated decision-making does not exist in the General Data Protection Regulation. *International Data Privacy Law*, *7*(2), 76–99. DOI: 10.1093/idpl/ipx005

Zuboff, S. (2019). *The age of surveillance capitalism: The fight for a human future at the new frontier of power*. PublicAffairs.

Chapter 8
Cybersecurity and Data Protection:
Navigating the Complex Regulatory Landscape

Omowunmi F. Makinde
https://orcid.org/0009-0004-9372-7539
University of the Cumberlands, USA

ABSTRACT

This chapter provides a comprehensive analysis of the evolving cybersecurity and data protection regulatory landscape, highlighting the increasing complexity and fragmentation of global compliance requirements. It examines major frameworks such as the GDPR, CCPA, HIPAA, and emerging international laws, exploring their impact on organizations operating across multiple jurisdictions. The chapter discusses fundamental principles of data protection, the challenges of regulatory complexity, and the necessity of integrating privacy and security by design. It addresses data breach response, while also considering the implications of emerging technologies like AI, cloud computing, and IoT. Ethical considerations, including balancing security with personal liberties and addressing bias in AI, are explored alongside future regulatory trends and the importance of adaptive, risk-based compliance approaches. By combining legal analysis, case studies, and best practices, it offers practical guidance for organizations seeking to build resilient, adaptive compliance strategies in the digital era.

DOI: 10.4018/979-8-3373-4967-1.ch008

1. INTRODUCTION

In an era where digital transformation is accelerating at an unprecedented pace, cybersecurity and data protection have emerged as critical global imperatives. The sheer scale of digital data creation is staggering: by 2025, the world is projected to generate 175 zettabytes of data, a figure that underscores both the opportunities and vulnerabilities inherent in our interconnected society (Wang et al., 2024). This explosive growth, fueled by cloud computing, the Internet of Things (IoT), and artificial intelligence, has dramatically expanded the attack surface for malicious actors, resulting in a surge of sophisticated cyber threats and data breaches. In 2023 alone, the average cost of a data breach reached $4.35 million globally, with long-term reputational and operational impacts that can cripple organizations for years (Zadeh et al., 2023).

The urgency of robust cybersecurity and data protection is further amplified by the evolving regulatory landscape. Since the implementation of the European Union's General Data Protection Regulation (GDPR) in 2018, regulatory authorities have imposed over €500 million in fines for non-compliance, signaling a new era of accountability and enforcement (Daigle & Khan, 2020; Ruohonen & Hjerppe, 2022). Similar comprehensive frameworks, such as the California Consumer Privacy Act (CCPA) and Brazil's Lei Geral de Proteção de Dados (LGPD), have proliferated worldwide, creating a complex web of overlapping and sometimes conflicting requirements that organizations must navigate (Paul, 2024; Yusuff, 2023). The rapid pace of regulatory change, coupled with the extraterritorial reach of these laws, has transformed data protection from a technical or legal afterthought into a strategic business necessity.

Despite these advances, significant gaps remain in both research and practice. Recent studies highlight a persistent disconnect between technological innovation and regulatory adaptation, with many organizations struggling to implement effective compliance strategies amid shifting legal standards and emerging threats (Jalali et al., 2019; Admass et al., 2024). The literature also points to a shortage of interdisciplinary approaches that integrate legal, technical, and organizational perspectives, particularly in sectors such as healthcare and finance where the stakes are exceptionally high (Ewoh & Vartiainen, 2024; Jagadish, 2024). Moreover, the rise of AI and machine learning introduces new challenges related to algorithmic bias, transparency, and the protection of training data, issues that current regulatory frameworks are only beginning to address (Arora et al., 2023; Belenguer, 2022).

This chapter responds to these urgent challenges by providing a comprehensive, evidence-based analysis of the global cybersecurity and data protection regulatory landscape. Drawing on recent peer-reviewed research, industry reports, and case studies, it examines the most influential frameworks, including the GDPR, CCPA, and sector-specific regulations such as HIPAA and GLBA, while highlighting key trends, statistics, and enforcement actions that define the current state of the field. The analysis identifies critical gaps in existing literature and practice, particularly in the areas of cross-border data transfers, third-party risk management, and the governance of emerging technologies.

By situating this research within the context of ongoing trends and emerging complexities, this chapter aims to make a compelling case for why cybersecurity and data protection demand urgent, sustained attention from scholars, practitioners, and policymakers alike. The goal is not only to inform but to catalyze action, demonstrating that effective data protection is foundational to organizational resilience, public trust, and the broader stability of the digital economy.

1.1 Originality, Rationale, and Significance of the Study

The originality of this study lies in its comprehensive, interdisciplinary approach to examining the regulatory complexity of cybersecurity and data protection across global contexts. While prior research has often focused on either technical solutions or the legal dimensions of data protection in isolation (Admass et al., 2024; Jalali et al., 2019), this chapter uniquely integrates legal, technical, and organizational perspectives to address the persistent gap between regulatory intent and practical compliance outcomes. By drawing on recent empirical studies and case analyses, the research moves beyond descriptive accounts of regulations to critically analyze how organizations operationalize compliance amid overlapping, evolving, and sometimes conflicting legal frameworks (Ewoh & Vartiainen, 2024; Jagadish, 2024). This approach is particularly novel in its attention to the lived experiences of compliance professionals and decision-makers, offering nuanced insights into the challenges and strategies that shape real-world data protection practices.

The rationale for this study is grounded in the urgent need to address the disconnect between rapid technological innovation and the slower pace of regulatory adaptation. As highlighted by recent literature, the proliferation of digital technologies such as artificial intelligence, cloud computing, and the Internet of Things has dramatically expanded the attack surface for cyber threats, while regulatory frameworks struggle to keep pace (Arora et al., 2023; Del-Real et al., 2025). This misalignment has resulted in significant vulnerabilities, with organizations facing increasing difficulty in translating abstract regulatory requirements into effective technical and operational controls (Kianpour & Raza, 2024). The study responds to calls for more holistic, evidence-based research that not only maps the regulatory landscape but also interrogates the practical realities of compliance, particularly in sectors where the stakes for data protection are exceptionally high (Ewoh & Vartiainen, 2024).

The significance of this research is multifaceted. Theoretically, it contributes to the growing body of scholarship that seeks to bridge the gap between legal mandates and technological realities, offering a framework for understanding regulatory complexity as a dynamic, multidimensional challenge (Admass et al., 2024; Villiers, 2022). Practically, the study provides actionable insights for organizations seeking to navigate the labyrinth of global data protection laws, highlighting best practices and common pitfalls in compliance strategy development (Cremer et al., 2022). The findings have direct implications for policymakers, suggesting avenues for regulatory harmonization and the development of more adaptive, risk-based compliance models (Van der Heijden, 2021). By foregrounding the experiences of both large enterprises and resource-constrained small and medium-sized organizations, the research ensures that its recommendations are relevant across diverse operational contexts.

Ultimately, this study is significant because it addresses the "so what" of cybersecurity and data protection regulation: it demonstrates how effective compliance is not merely a legal obligation but a strategic imperative for organizational resilience, public trust, and the stability of the digital economy (Wang et al., 2024; Makridis, 2021). By situating its analysis within ongoing technological and regulatory trends, the chapter provides a timely and robust foundation for future research, policy development, and practical innovation in the field.

1.2 Nature of the Study

This study employs a comprehensive literature review methodology to examine the complex regulatory landscape of cybersecurity and data protection from a global perspective. The research adopts an integrative review approach that synthesizes existing peer-reviewed literature, regulatory documents, and empirical studies to provide a holistic understanding of how organizations navigate the evolving compliance environment. This methodological choice is particularly appropriate for addressing the research problem because it allows for the systematic examination of diverse perspectives, theoretical frameworks, and empirical findings across multiple disciplines, including law, information systems, cybersecurity, and organizational management (Cremer et al., 2022). The integrative nature of this approach enables the identification of patterns, gaps, and contradictions in the existing literature while providing a foundation for developing comprehensive insights into regulatory complexity.

The literature review methodology employed in this study follows a systematic approach to identify, select, and analyze relevant sources. The search strategy encompasses multiple academic databases, including Web of Science, Scopus, IEEE Xplore, and legal databases such as Westlaw and LexisNexis, using carefully constructed search terms related to cybersecurity regulation, data protection compliance,

GDPR implementation, privacy law enforcement, and regulatory complexity. The inclusion criteria prioritize peer-reviewed articles published between 2018 and 2024, focusing on empirical studies, theoretical frameworks, and policy analyses that address cybersecurity and data protection regulation at organizational, national, or international levels. The temporal scope reflects the post-GDPR regulatory environment, ensuring that the analysis captures the most current developments in global data protection law and practice (Paul, 2024; Yusuff, 2023).

The analytical framework draws upon regulatory theory, organizational compliance literature, and cybersecurity governance models to structure the examination of how organizations respond to regulatory complexity. This theoretical foundation enables the study to move beyond descriptive accounts of regulations to critically analyze the mechanisms through which regulatory requirements are translated into organizational practices, the factors that influence compliance effectiveness, and the unintended consequences of regulatory proliferation (Admass et al., 2024; Kianpour & Raza, 2024). The analysis employs thematic synthesis to identify recurring patterns across different jurisdictions, sectors, and organizational contexts, while also highlighting unique challenges and innovative approaches that emerge in specific regulatory environments. This methodological approach ensures that the findings are both comprehensive in scope and nuanced in their treatment of contextual factors that influence regulatory compliance outcomes.

1.3 Problem Statement

Despite the proliferation of cybersecurity frameworks and increased awareness of data protection, organizations worldwide continue to face a rising tide of cyber threats and data breaches. Recent research highlights that the frequency and sophistication of cyberattacks have outpaced the development and implementation of effective defense mechanisms, leaving critical infrastructure and sensitive data increasingly vulnerable (Zaid & Garai, 2024). Cybercrime is estimated to have cost the global economy just under USD 1 trillion in 2020, indicating an increase of more than 50% since 2018, with the average cyber insurance claim rising from USD 145,000 in 2019 to USD 359,000 in 2020 (Cremer et al., 2022). For example, healthcare institutions have experienced a significant surge in cyber incidents, with 386 healthcare cyber-attacks reported in 2024 alone, representing a continuation of the elevated attack rates from 2023, which was the worst year ever for breaches in healthcare (Riggi, 2024). These attacks not only compromise patient data but also disrupt essential services, with over 280 incidents reported in the healthcare sector representing 24% of all cyber events in the United States, underscoring the tangible risks to public safety and trust (Seh et al., 2020).

Empirical studies reveal that the gap between regulatory compliance and practical cybersecurity outcomes persists, as many organizations struggle to translate policy into effective action (Mishra et al., 2022). This disconnect is further exacerbated by the rapid evolution of attack vectors and the increasing complexity of digital ecosystems (Savaş & Karataş, 2022). As a result, there is an urgent need for actionable, evidence-based strategies that bridge the divide between regulatory intent and operational security, ensuring that data protection measures are both robust and adaptable to emerging threats (Kianpour & Raza, 2024).

1.4 The Growing Importance of Cybersecurity and Data Privacy

The contemporary digital landscape has fundamentally transformed the nature of organizational operations, creating unprecedented opportunities for innovation while simultaneously exposing entities to complex cybersecurity and data privacy challenges. As organizations increasingly rely on digital infrastructure to conduct business, store sensitive information, and interact with stakeholders, the imperative to establish robust cybersecurity frameworks and comprehensive data protection mechanisms has evolved from a technical consideration to a strategic business necessity (Wang et al., 2024). High-profile breaches affecting major corporations, government agencies, and critical infrastructure have demonstrated that no organization, regardless of size or sector, remains immune to cyber threats. The sophistication of threat actors has evolved considerably, with state-sponsored groups, organized criminal enterprises, and advanced persistent threat actors employing increasingly complex techniques including artificial intelligence, machine learning, and zero-day exploits to circumvent traditional security measures (Liu & Babar, 2024).

Simultaneously, the regulatory landscape governing data protection and privacy has undergone dramatic transformation, exemplified by the implementation of the European Union's General Data Protection Regulation (GDPR) in 2018, which established a new paradigm for data protection rights and organizational accountability. The convergence of cybersecurity and data privacy concerns has created multifaceted challenges that extend beyond traditional IT security considerations to encompass legal, ethical, and business continuity dimensions. Organizations must now consider not only the technical aspects of protecting data from unauthorized access but also the legal implications of data processing activities, the ethical considerations surrounding data collection and use, and the potential impact of privacy violations on stakeholder trust and business relationships (Cremer et al., 2022). The concept of privacy by design has emerged as a fundamental principle, requiring organizations to integrate privacy considerations into the development and deployment of systems, processes, and business practices from the outset rather than as an afterthought. This proactive approach necessitates cross-functional collaboration between legal, compliance, IT security, and business teams to ensure that privacy and security considerations are embedded throughout organizational operations (Del-Real et al., 2025).

The increasing interconnectedness of global supply chains has further complicated cybersecurity and data protection challenges, as organizations must now assess and manage risks associated with third-party vendors, cloud service providers, and business partners who may have access to sensitive data or critical systems (Ilori et al., 2024). The concept of shared responsibility in cloud computing environments has required organizations to develop new frameworks for understanding and managing security responsibilities across hybrid and multi-cloud architectures (Ahmadi, 2024). Additionally, the rise of artificial intelligence and machine learning technologies has introduced novel privacy and security considerations, including algorithmic bias, automated decision-making transparency, and the protection of training data used in AI systems (Arora et al., 2023).

The human element remains a critical factor in cybersecurity and data protection, with social engineering attacks, phishing campaigns, and insider threats continuing to represent significant vulnerabilities despite technological advances in security controls. Organizations must therefore invest not only in technical safeguards but also in comprehensive security awareness training, incident response capabilities, and organizational culture development that prioritizes security and privacy considerations (Khadka & Ullah, 2025). The shortage of qualified cybersecurity professionals has created additional challenges, with organizations competing for limited talent while attempting to build and maintain effective security programs (Furnell, 2021).

1.5 Purpose of the Study

The purpose of this qualitative exploratory study is to examine the complex regulatory compliance challenges that organizations face in navigating the evolving global cybersecurity and data protection landscape. This research aims to investigate how organizations across various sectors struggle to implement effective compliance strategies amid the proliferation of overlapping, conflicting, and rapidly changing regulatory frameworks, including the General Data Protection Regulation (GDPR), California Consumer Privacy Act (CCPA), and sector-specific regulations such as HIPAA and GLBA. This study seeks to explore the multifaceted nature of regulatory complexity by examining the experiences and perceptions of compliance professionals, legal experts, and organizational leaders who are directly involved in developing and implementing cybersecurity and data protection compliance programs. The research will investigate how organizations interpret and operationalize abstract regulatory concepts into concrete technical controls, operational procedures, and governance frameworks while managing the competing demands of regulatory compliance, business objectives, and technological innovation.

The study addresses a critical gap in the current literature, which predominantly focuses on technical cybersecurity solutions while underemphasizing the practical challenges of regulatory compliance implementation. Recent research by Cremer et al. (2022) demonstrates that cybercrime cost the global economy nearly USD 1 trillion in 2020, representing a 50% increase since 2018, yet organizations continue to struggle with translating regulatory requirements into effective operational practices. Similarly, Admass et al. (2024) highlights the persistent disconnect between technological innovation and regulatory adaptation, with many organizations failing to implement effective compliance strategies amid shifting legal standards and emerging threats.

The research will specifically examine how organizations navigate the temporal dimension of regulatory complexity, including the challenges of anticipating and preparing for future regulatory changes while maintaining compliance with current requirements. This includes investigating how organizations manage cross-border data transfers, implement privacy and security by design principles, and address the governance challenges posed by emerging technologies such as artificial intelligence and cloud computing. The study will also explore how small and medium-sized enterprises, which often lack dedicated compliance resources, develop strategies to meet the same regulatory requirements as large multinational corporations.

By employing a qualitative exploratory approach, this research will provide in-depth insights into the lived experiences of compliance professionals and organizational decision-makers, offering a nuanced understanding of how regulatory complexity manifests in practice. The findings will contribute to both academic knowledge and practical understanding of cybersecurity and data protection compliance, potentially informing the development of more effective regulatory frameworks and organizational compliance strategies that better balance security imperatives with operational efficiency and innovation objectives.

1.6 The Challenge of Regulatory Complexity

The contemporary cybersecurity and data protection regulatory landscape presents organizations with an unprecedented labyrinth of overlapping, evolving, and often conflicting requirements that demand sophisticated navigation strategies and comprehensive compliance frameworks. The healthcare sector faces additional regulatory burdens through the Health Insurance Portability and Accountability Act (HIPAA) in the United States, which imposes specific technical, administrative, and physical safeguards for protected health information (Theodos & Sittig, 2020).

While financial institutions must navigate the Gramm-Leach-Bliley Act (GLBA), Payment Card Industry Data Security Standard (PCI DSS), and various banking regulations that establish sector-specific cybersecurity requirements (Jagadish, 2024). Furthermore, emerging regulations such as the EU's Cybersecurity Act, the proposed AI Act, and various national cybersecurity frameworks continue to expand the regulatory perimeter, creating dynamic compliance environments where organizations must continuously monitor, interpret, and implement new requirements while maintaining adherence to existing obligations. The challenge is compounded by the fact that these regulations often employ different terminologies, definitions, and approaches to similar concepts, creating semantic confusion and implementation difficulties for organizations attempting to develop unified compliance strategies (Shetty et al., 2025). For instance, the concept of “personal data” under GDPR differs significantly from “personal information” under CCPA, while both differ from “personally identifiable information” (PII) as defined in various federal regulations, necessitating careful legal analysis and technical implementation to ensure comprehensive coverage without unnecessary over-compliance (Dennis & Janecek, 2022). The temporal dimension of regulatory complexity adds another layer of difficulty, as organizations must not only comply with current requirements but also anticipate and prepare for future regulatory changes, including proposed legislation, regulatory guidance updates, and enforcement precedents that may alter the interpretation and application of existing rules. Cross-border data transfers present particularly acute challenges, as organizations must navigate a complex web of adequacy decisions, standard contractual clauses, binding corporate rules, and certification mechanisms while ensuring that data protection standards are maintained throughout international data flows (Paul, 2024). The enforcement landscape further complicates compliance efforts, as regulatory authorities across different jurisdictions may adopt varying approaches to investigation, penalty calculation, and remediation requirements, creating uncertainty about potential consequences and appropriate response strategies (Ruohonen & Hjerppe, 2022). Small and medium-sized enterprises face disproportionate challenges in this complex regulatory environment, as they often lack the resources to maintain dedicated compliance teams or engage specialized legal counsel, yet remain subject to the same regulatory requirements as large multinational corporations (Brodin, 2019). The technical complexity of modern cybersecurity and data protection requirements demands interdisciplinary expertise spanning legal, technical, and business domains, as organizations must translate abstract regulatory concepts into concrete technical controls, operational procedures, and governance frameworks. Privacy by design and security by design principles, while conceptually sound, require sophisticated implementation strategies that consider regulatory requirements from the earliest stages of system development and business process design (Del-Real et al., 2025). The rapid pace of technological innovation, including artificial intelligence, machine learning, Internet of Things devices, and cloud computing services, continues to outpace regulatory development, creating gaps and ambiguities that organizations must navigate through risk-based approaches and best practice adoption. Regulatory complexity is further exacerbated by the need to balance competing interests and requirements, such as data protection obligations versus law enforcement access requirements, cybersecurity incident reporting mandates versus attorney-client privilege protections, and transparency requirements versus trade secret protections. Organizations must also consider the interplay between cybersecurity and data protection regulations and other legal frameworks, including employment law, contract law, intellectual property law, and competition law, ensuring that compliance strategies do not inadvertently create violations in adjacent legal domains (Zaidan & Ibrahim, 2024). The global nature of modern business operations means that organizations must develop compliance strategies that account for the most stringent requirements across all relevant jurisdictions, often resulting in over-compliance in some regions to ensure comprehensive coverage. This regulatory complexity ultimately requires organizations to adopt sophisticated governance frameworks, invest in specialized expertise, implement robust monitoring and reporting systems, and maintain agile compliance programs capable of adapting to evolving requirements while supporting business objectives and stakeholder expectations in an increasingly interconnected and regulated digital economy (Villiers, 2022).

2. GLOBAL REGULATORY OVERVIEW

The global regulatory landscape for cybersecurity and data protection reflects diverse approaches to balancing individual privacy rights, national security interests, and economic considerations. Understanding these varied approaches is essential for organizations operating across multiple jurisdictions, as regulatory differences can significantly impact business operations, data flows, and compliance costs (Paul, 2024). The European Union has emerged as a global leader in data protection regulation, with the GDPR serving as a model for legislation worldwide. The regulation's extraterritorial scope means that organizations worldwide must comply with GDPR requirements when processing personal data of EU residents, regardless of where the organization is located. This "Brussels Effect" has led to global convergence toward European data protection standards, even as other jurisdictions maintain distinct regulatory approaches (Aidun, 2025). In contrast, the United States has traditionally relied on a sectoral approach, with different industries subject to specific regulations such as HIPAA for healthcare, GLBA for financial services, and COPPA for children's online privacy. However, the landscape is evolving rapidly, with states like California implementing comprehensive privacy laws that rival the GDPR in scope and complexity. The California Consumer Privacy Act (CCPA) and its successor, the California Privacy Rights Act (CPRA), represent a significant shift toward comprehensive privacy regulation in the United States (Boyne, 2018). The Asia-Pacific region presents a diverse regulatory landscape, with countries like Singapore and Australia implementing comprehensive data protection frameworks, while others maintain more limited sectoral approaches. China's Cybersecurity Law and Personal Information Protection Law represent significant developments in the region, establishing comprehensive requirements for data protection and cybersecurity that reflect the country's unique political and economic context (Creemers, 2022). This regulatory diversity creates significant challenges for multinational organizations, which must develop compliance strategies that address multiple, sometimes conflicting, regulatory requirements. The challenge is compounded by the rapid pace of regulatory change, with new laws being enacted and existing regulations being amended regularly in response to technological developments and evolving privacy concerns (Van der Heijden, 2021).

2.1 The GDPR, CCPA, and Other Emerging Privacy Laws

The General Data Protection Regulation (GDPR), which came into effect in May 2018, represents a watershed moment in global data protection law, establishing comprehensive privacy rights and imposing significant obligations on organizations processing personal data (Paul, 2024). The GDPR's broad territorial scope, substantial penalties, and emphasis on individual rights have influenced privacy legislation worldwide, creating a de facto global standard for data protection practices (Ryngaert & Taylor, 2020). The California Consumer Privacy Act (CCPA), enacted in 2020, marked the United States' entry into comprehensive privacy regulation, granting California residents significant rights over their personal information and imposing new obligations on businesses. The CCPA's approach differs from the GDPR in several key respects, including its focus on consumer rights rather than data protection principles and its emphasis on transparency and choice rather than consent-based processing (Ou, 2025). Beyond these landmark regulations, numerous jurisdictions have enacted or are developing comprehensive privacy laws that reflect local values and priorities while drawing inspiration from the GDPR and CCPA models. Brazil's Lei Geral de Proteção de Dados (LGPD), Canada's proposed Consumer Privacy Protection Act, and China's Personal Information Protection Law represent diverse approaches to privacy regulation that organizations must navigate. These emerging laws create a complex web of overlapping and sometimes conflicting requirements that challenge organizations' ability to develop coherent global privacy strategies (Yusuff, 2023).

2.2 Industry-Specific Regulations: HIPAA, FERPA, GLBA, and More

Industry-specific regulations add additional layers of complexity to the cybersecurity and data protection landscape, imposing sector-tailored requirements that reflect the unique risks and characteristics of different industries (Cremer et al., 2022). The Health Insurance Portability and Accountability Act (HIPAA) establishes comprehensive privacy and security requirements for protected health information, reflecting the sensitive nature of medical data and the need for strong safeguards in healthcare settings (Theodos & Sittig, 2020). The Family Educational Rights and Privacy Act (FERPA) governs the privacy of student educational records, imposing specific requirements on educational institutions regarding the collection, use, and disclosure of student information. The Gramm-Leach-Bliley Act (GLBA) establishes privacy and security requirements for financial institutions, recognizing the critical importance of protecting financial information and maintaining consumer trust in the financial system (Jagadish, 2024). These sector-specific regulations often impose requirements that go beyond general data protection laws, creating compliance challenges for organizations operating across multiple industries or serving diverse customer bases. The interaction between industry-specific regulations and general privacy laws can create complex compliance scenarios where organizations must satisfy multiple, potentially conflicting requirements. Understanding these regulatory intersections is crucial for developing effective compliance strategies that address all applicable requirements while maintaining operational efficiency (Farhad, 2024).

2.3 Cross-Border Data Transfers and International Compliance

Cross-border data transfers represent one of the most complex aspects of international data protection compliance, involving intricate legal mechanisms designed to ensure adequate protection for personal data when it crosses jurisdictional boundaries. The GDPR's restrictions on international data transfers have created a framework that requires organizations to implement specific safeguards when transferring personal data to countries outside the European Economic Area (Babatunde et al., 2022). Adequacy decisions, standard contractual clauses, binding corporate rules, and certification mechanisms provide different pathways for lawful international data transfers, each with distinct requirements and limitations. The invalidation of the EU-US Privacy Shield framework and subsequent legal challenges to standard contractual clauses have created uncertainty and compliance challenges for organizations relying on these mechanisms for international data transfers (Bradford et al., 2021).

Data localization requirements in various jurisdictions further complicate cross-border data transfer compliance, with some countries requiring certain types of data to be stored within their borders or imposing restrictions on data exports. These requirements can conflict with organizations' global data management strategies and create operational challenges for multinational enterprises seeking to maintain consistent data processing practices across different jurisdictions (Rong et al., 2025).

3. FUNDAMENTAL PRINCIPLES OF DATA PROTECTION AND CYBERSECURITY LAW

The evolution of data protection law has been guided by fundamental principles that reflect core values of privacy, autonomy, and human dignity in the digital age. These principles serve as the foundation for regulatory frameworks worldwide and provide guidance for organizations seeking to implement ethical and compliant data practices. Understanding these principles is essential for navigating the complex regulatory landscape and developing effective compliance strategies (Aiello, 2024).

The development of data protection principles has been influenced by various sources, including international human rights law, constitutional privacy protections, and practical considerations related to technological capabilities and business needs. The Organization for Economic Co-operation and Development (OECD) Privacy Guidelines, first adopted in 1980 and revised in 2013, established many of the core principles that continue to influence data protection law today (Yakovleva, 2017).

These principles are not merely abstract concepts but practical requirements that must be implemented through organizational policies, procedures, and technical measures. The principle-based approach allows for flexibility in implementation while maintaining consistency in protection standards, enabling organizations to adapt their practices to specific contexts while adhering to fundamental requirements (Aiello, 2024).

The interconnected nature of these principles means that effective data protection requires a holistic approach that considers all principles simultaneously rather than addressing them in isolation. This integrated approach is reflected in modern regulatory frameworks that emphasize accountability and require organizations to demonstrate compliance with all applicable principles (Paul, 2024).

3.1 Privacy Rights and Regulatory Frameworks

The foundation of modern data protection law rests on fundamental privacy rights that recognize individuals' autonomy over their personal information and establish corresponding obligations for organizations processing such data (Dhamo & Dhamo, 2024). These rights, which have evolved from constitutional privacy protections and human rights frameworks, include the right to be informed about data processing activities, the right to access personal data, the right to rectification of inaccurate information, and the right to erasure or deletion of personal data (Singh, 2024).

The principle of lawfulness, fairness, and transparency requires organizations to have a legal basis for processing personal data and to conduct such processing in a manner that is fair to individuals and transparent about its purposes and methods (Hoofnagle et al., 2019). Purpose limitation principles restrict the use of personal data to specified, explicit, and legitimate purposes, preventing organizations from using data for purposes beyond those for which it was originally collected (Faisal, 2023).

Data minimization principles require organizations to limit data collection and processing to what is necessary for the specified purposes, reflecting a fundamental shift from data maximization practices that characterized early digital business models (Biega et al., 2020). Accuracy requirements mandate that organizations take reasonable steps to ensure that personal data is accurate and up-to-date, while storage limitation principles require the deletion of personal data when it is no longer necessary for the original processing purposes (Hoofnagle et al., 2019).

3.2 Security Legislation and Standards

Cybersecurity legislation and standards establish mandatory and voluntary frameworks for protecting information systems and data from cyber threats, reflecting the critical importance of security measures in maintaining the integrity, availability, and confidentiality of digital assets (Woods & Seymour, 2023). These frameworks typically encompass risk assessment requirements, security control implementation mandates, incident response obligations, and continuous monitoring requirements (Freas et al., 2022).

The principle of security by design requires organizations to implement appropriate technical and organizational measures to protect personal data and information systems from unauthorized access, alteration, or destruction. This principle emphasizes the importance of incorporating security considerations into system design and development processes rather than treating security as an afterthought or add-on feature (Del-Real et al., 2025).

Risk-based approaches to cybersecurity regulation recognize that different organizations face varying levels of cyber risk based on factors such as the sensitivity of data they process, their role in critical infrastructure, and their exposure to cyber threats (Mayer & Aubert, 2020). These approaches allow for flexible implementation of security measures while maintaining minimum baseline requirements that ensure adequate protection across different sectors and organization types (Ardebili et al., 2024).

3.3 Penalties and Sanctions for Non-Compliance

The enforcement mechanisms underlying cybersecurity and data protection regulations include a range of penalties and sanctions designed to incentivize compliance and deter violations. Administrative fines represent the most visible enforcement tool, with the GDPR authorizing fines of up to 4% of annual global turnover or €20 million, whichever is higher, for the most serious violations (Cremer et al., 2022).

Beyond monetary penalties, regulatory authorities possess various enforcement powers including the ability to issue warnings, reprimands, and orders to cease processing activities. Corrective measures may require organizations to implement specific technical or organizational measures, undergo audits, or submit to enhanced regulatory oversight. In severe cases, authorities may impose temporary or permanent bans on data processing activities, effectively preventing organizations from conducting certain business operations (Reis et al., 2024).

The reputational consequences of regulatory enforcement actions often exceed the direct financial impact of fines, as public disclosure of violations can damage customer trust, impact stock prices, and create competitive disadvantages. The threat of class-action lawsuits and individual compensation claims adds additional financial risks for organizations that fail to comply with data protection requirements, creating multiple layers of potential liability for non-compliance (Makridis, 2021).

4. DIFFICULTIES AND COMPLIANCE APPROACHES

The rapidly evolving regulatory landscape, coupled with the increasing sophistication of cyber threats, presents significant challenges for organizations seeking to achieve and maintain compliance. Effective compliance requires a strategic, organization-wide approach that integrates legal, technical, and operational perspectives (Chen, 2022).

4.1 Privacy and Security by Design

Privacy and security by design principles represent fundamental shifts in how organizations approach data protection and cybersecurity, requiring the integration of privacy and security considerations into the earliest stages of system design and development. These principles move beyond reactive compliance approaches to establish proactive frameworks that embed protection measures into the architecture of information systems and business processes (Del-Real et al., 2025).

The seven foundational principles of privacy by design include proactive rather than reactive measures, privacy as the default setting, full functionality without compromising privacy, end-to-end security throughout the data lifecycle, visibility and transparency for all stakeholders, respect for user privacy through user-centric design, and comprehensive coverage across all data elements and processes (Yusuff, 2023). These principles require organizations to conduct privacy impact assessments, implement data protection by default settings, and design systems that minimize data collection and processing (Georgiadis & Poels, 2022).

Security by design principles similarly emphasize the importance of incorporating security measures into system architecture from the outset, rather than attempting to retrofit security controls onto existing systems (Del-Real et al., 2025). This approach includes implementing defense-in-depth strategies, adopting zero-trust architectures, and ensuring that security measures are proportionate to the risks faced by the organization and the sensitivity of the data being protected (Syed et al., 2022).

4.2 Building Effective Compliance Teams and Roles

The complexity of modern cybersecurity and data protection regulations necessitates the development of specialized compliance teams with clearly defined roles and responsibilities. Data Protection Officers (DPOs) play a central role in GDPR compliance, serving as independent advisors who monitor compliance activities, conduct privacy impact assessments, and serve as points of contact with regulatory authorities (Ducato, 2020).

Chief Information Security Officers (CISOs) and cybersecurity teams are responsible for implementing and maintaining technical security measures, conducting risk assessments, and responding to security incidents. The integration of legal, technical, and business expertise within compliance teams is essential for addressing the multidisciplinary nature of cybersecurity and data protection challenges (Sahin & Vance, 2025).

Effective compliance programs require clear governance structures that define reporting relationships, decision-making authorities, and accountability mechanisms. Regular training and awareness programs ensure that all employees understand their roles in maintaining compliance, while continuous monitoring and assessment activities help identify and address compliance gaps before they result in violations (Dunbar et al., 2021).

4.3 Third-Party Vendor Risk Management

Third-party vendor relationships create significant cybersecurity and data protection risks that require comprehensive risk management strategies. Organizations must conduct thorough due diligence assessments of potential vendors, evaluating their security practices, compliance capabilities, and risk management frameworks before entering into contractual relationships (Ilori et al., 2024).

Contractual provisions play a crucial role in allocating cybersecurity and data protection responsibilities between organizations and their vendors. Data processing agreements must clearly define the purposes and methods of data processing, specify security requirements, establish incident notification procedures, and allocate liability for potential breaches or compliance failures (Cremer et al., 2022).

Ongoing vendor management activities include regular security assessments, compliance audits, and performance monitoring to ensure that vendors continue to meet contractual obligations and regulatory requirements. Vendor risk management programs must also address the challenges posed by fourth-party relationships, where vendors rely on their own subcontractors to provide services, creating extended supply chains that can introduce additional risks (Ilori et al., 2024).

5. DATA BREACH RESPONSES

Effective data breach response is critical for organizations to mitigate impact, protect sensitive information, and maintain stakeholder trust. It involves a series of coordinated steps, from immediate notification to long-term recovery and best practices (Mohammed, 2021).

5.1 Breach Notification Requirements

Data breach notification requirements represent critical compliance obligations that require organizations to report security incidents to regulatory authorities and affected individuals within specified timeframes. The GDPR establishes a 72-hour notification requirement for reporting breaches to supervisory authorities, with additional obligations to notify affected individuals when the breach is likely to result in high risk to their rights and freedoms (De-Yolande et al., 2023).

Different jurisdictions impose varying notification requirements, creating complex compliance scenarios for organizations operating across multiple regulatory frameworks. Some regulations require immediate notification upon discovery of a breach, while others provide longer notification periods or impose different thresholds for triggering notification obligations. The content and format of breach notifications are also subject to specific requirements that vary by (Vaka, 2020).

Breach notification requirements extend beyond regulatory authorities to include notifications to business partners, customers, law enforcement agencies, and other stakeholders depending on the nature and scope of the incident. Organizations must develop comprehensive breach notification procedures that account for all applicable requirements while ensuring timely and accurate communication with relevant parties (Cains et al., 2021).

5.2 Legal and Technical Response Strategies

Effective data breach response requires coordinated legal and technical strategies that address immediate containment needs while preserving evidence and maintaining compliance with regulatory requirements. Technical response activities include isolating affected systems, conducting forensic analysis to determine the scope and cause of the breach, and implementing remediation measures to prevent further unauthorized access (Guttman et al., 2022).

Legal response strategies focus on managing regulatory compliance obligations, coordinating with law enforcement agencies, and addressing potential litigation risks. Legal teams must work closely with technical responders to ensure that forensic activities preserve evidence in a manner that supports potential legal proceedings while meeting regulatory notification and reporting requirements (AlKhanafseh & Surakhi, 2024).

Communication strategies play a crucial role in breach response, requiring careful coordination between legal, technical, and public relations teams to ensure consistent and appropriate messaging to different stakeholder groups. Organizations must balance transparency obligations with the need to protect ongoing investigations and avoid statements that could increase legal liability or compromise security measures (Knight & Nurse, 2020).

5.3 Post-Breach Obligations and Best Practices

Post-breach obligations extend well beyond initial notification requirements, encompassing ongoing regulatory cooperation, remediation activities, and long-term monitoring obligations. Organizations must provide detailed incident reports to regulatory authorities, respond to information requests, and cooperate with regulatory investigations that may continue for months or years after the initial breach (Gopireddy & Koppanathi, 2018).

Remediation activities must address both the immediate causes of the breach and underlying security vulnerabilities that may have contributed to the incident.

This may require significant investments in new security technologies, process improvements, and staff training to prevent similar incidents from occurring in the future (Riggs et al., 2023).

Best practices for post-breach management include conducting comprehensive lessons learned exercises, updating incident response procedures based on experience gained during the breach response, and implementing enhanced monitoring and detection capabilities. Organizations should also consider engaging independent security assessors to validate the effectiveness of remediation measures and provide assurance to stakeholders that appropriate steps have been taken to prevent future incidents (Patterson et al., 2023).

6. EMERGING TECHNOLOGY AND REGULATION

The proliferation of disruptive technologies over the past decade has fundamentally transformed economic, social, and personal domains, creating unprecedented challenges for policymakers globally (He et al., 2021). Governments confront the complex task of developing governance frameworks for technologies that continue to evolve with uncertain trajectories, necessitating dynamic regulatory responses as existing legal structures often fail to keep pace with rapid digital advancements (Wylde et al., 2022). The fundamental challenge lies in the potential "mismatch between established regulations and emerging risks" that new technologies introduce (Jalali et al., 2019).

Artificial intelligence, blockchain vulnerabilities, and quantum computing represent significant emerging threats that pose considerable legal and regulatory challenges to current cybersecurity landscapes (Wylde et al., 2022). While these technologies offer substantial benefits, they also introduce novel risks at an accelerating pace, challenging the effectiveness and capacity of existing regulatory frameworks to ensure their safe market integration (He et al., 2021). The healthcare sector exemplifies this challenge, having become a primary target for cyberattacks during the COVID-19 pandemic, with attackers exploiting vulnerabilities in both technology and human factors introduced through rapid changes in working practices (He et al., 2021).

The complexity of regulating emerging technologies is compounded by the need to balance security imperatives with individual rights protection. Robust data privacy legislation, such as the General Data Protection Regulation (GDPR), aims to enhance individual rights and foster trust in digital systems, yet creates substantial compliance and enforcement challenges, particularly within globalized digital environments (Wylde et al., 2022). Cybersecurity regulations are essential for protecting digital infrastructure and preventing data breaches, but frequently lag behind the rapidly evolving nature of cyber threats.

Research demonstrates a significant temporal gap between technological advancement and legislative response, highlighting the need for adaptable laws that can proactively address future technological developments. The healthcare sector's experience during COVID-19 illustrates this challenge, where the shift to remote work and digital health services created new vulnerabilities that existing cybersecurity frameworks struggled to address (He et al., 2021). The sector's reliance on legacy systems, coupled with limited cybersecurity expertise and budget constraints, has made it particularly vulnerable to sophisticated attacks including ransomware, phishing, and distributed denial-of-service attacks.

Effective management of cybersecurity risks in emerging technologies requires adherence to established risk management practices, including systematic identification and assessment of potential threats. However, notable gaps exist in current research and practice, including the absence of comprehensive cost-benefit analysis frameworks, limited understanding of human error's role in cybersecurity incidents, and insufficient strategies for managing constantly evolving threat landscapes (Jalali et al., 2019). The bibliometric analysis of healthcare cybersecurity literature reveals that technological solutions dominate research focus, while managerial, legal, and interdisciplinary approaches remain understudied, suggesting a need for more holistic approaches to cybersecurity governance (Jalali et al., 2019).

Addressing these regulatory challenges requires continuous adaptation of legal frameworks to technological innovations, fostering international cooperation, and enhancing cybersecurity governance through comprehensive policy reforms. The integration of blockchain technology and smart contracts offers promising solutions for enhancing transparency and accountability in data management, though implementation must navigate complex legal and ethical considerations (Wylde et al., 2022). Furthermore, while regulatory rigor may present challenges for emerging technologies, prolonged uncertainty often proves more detrimental to innovation and adoption than well-designed regulatory frameworks.

6.1 Artificial Intelligence: Opportunities and Liabilities

Artificial intelligence technologies present both significant opportunities for enhancing cybersecurity and data protection capabilities and substantial regulatory challenges that require careful consideration (Han et al., 2023). AI-powered security tools can analyze vast amounts of data to identify patterns indicative of cyber threats, automate incident response activities, and enhance the effectiveness of traditional security measures through machine learning and predictive analytics (Salem et al., 2024).

However, the use of AI in cybersecurity and data protection contexts also creates new risks and regulatory compliance challenges. AI systems may process personal data in ways that are difficult to explain or understand, potentially conflicting with transparency and explainability requirements under data protection laws (Mohale & Obagbuwa, 2025). Algorithmic bias in AI security tools can lead to discriminatory outcomes that violate equal protection principles and create legal liability for organizations (Belenguer, 2022).

Emerging AI regulations, such as the EU AI Act, establish specific requirements for AI systems used in high-risk applications, including those related to cybersecurity and data protection. These regulations may require organizations to conduct conformity assessments, implement risk management systems, and ensure human oversight of AI decision-making processes, adding new layers of compliance complexity to cybersecurity and data protection programs (Schuett, 2023).

6.2 Cloud Computing Compliance Challenges

Cloud computing environments present unique compliance challenges that require specialized approaches to cybersecurity and data protection. The shared responsibility model that characterizes cloud services creates complex allocation of security and compliance obligations between cloud service providers and their customers, requiring clear understanding of respective roles and responsibilities (Apeh et al., 2023).

Data location and sovereignty issues in cloud environments can complicate compliance with data localization requirements and cross-border transfer restrictions. Organizations must ensure that their cloud service providers can meet specific geographic restrictions on data storage and processing while maintaining the flexibility and scalability benefits that drive cloud adoption (Belli et al., 2024).

Multi-tenancy in cloud environments creates additional security and privacy risks that must be addressed through appropriate technical and contractual safeguards. Organizations must evaluate cloud service providers' security practices, compliance certifications, and incident response capabilities to ensure that cloud deployments meet regulatory requirements and organizational risk tolerance levels (Chippagiri, 2025).

6.3 Internet of Things (IoT) and Edge Computing Concerns

The proliferation of Internet of Things (IoT) devices and edge computing architectures creates new cybersecurity and data protection challenges that existing regulatory framework struggle to address effectively. IoT devices often have limited security capabilities, making them vulnerable to cyber attacks and difficult to update with security patches, creating persistent security risks in connected environments (AlSalem et al., 2023).

Edge computing architectures distribute data processing across multiple locations, complicating data governance and compliance efforts. Organizations must ensure that data protection measures are consistently applied across distributed edge environments while maintaining visibility and control over data processing activities (Thangaraju, 2024).

The massive scale of IoT deployments and the diversity of device types and manufacturers create challenges for implementing consistent security and privacy measures. Regulatory approaches to IoT security are still evolving, with some jurisdictions considering device certification requirements and security standards that would impose new obligations on manufacturers and operators of IoT systems (Cirne et al., 2022).

7. FUTURE REGULATORY TRENDS

As the digital landscape continues to evolve at an unprecedented pace, the future of cybersecurity and data protection regulation is poised to become even more complex, dynamic, and globally interconnected. Several key trends are likely to shape the regulatory environment in the coming years, driven by technological innovation, geopolitical tensions, and the growing recognition of data as both a critical asset and a potential liability. One of the most significant trends is the increasing harmonization of data protection standards across jurisdictions (Admass et al., 2024). While the General Data Protection Regulation (GDPR) set a global benchmark, many countries are now enacting or updating their own comprehensive data protection laws, often drawing inspiration from the GDPR but tailoring requirements to local contexts. This trend towards convergence is partly a response to the challenges faced by multinational organizations, which must navigate a patchwork of sometimes conflicting regulations. However, harmonization is not absolute; regional and national differences persist, particularly regarding data localization, cross-border data transfers, and the scope of individual rights (Voss, 2020).

Another emerging trend is the expansion of regulatory focus beyond traditional notions of personal data to encompass broader categories such as non-personal data, artificial intelligence (AI) outputs, and even metadata (Beduschi, 2024). As AI and machine learning systems become integral to business operations, regulators are increasingly concerned with issues such as algorithmic transparency, bias, and accountability. The European Union's AI Act, for example, signals a move towards sector-specific regulation that addresses the unique risks posed by advanced technologies (Busuioc et al., 2022). Similarly, the proliferation of Internet of Things (IoT) devices and the advent of 5G networks are prompting regulators to consider new frameworks for securing vast, decentralized networks and the data they generate. This expansion of regulatory scope is likely to continue, with future legislation addressing not only data privacy but also the ethical and societal implications of emerging technologies (Narciandi-Rodriguez et al., 2025).

Geopolitical considerations are also shaping the future regulatory landscape. The weaponization of cyberattacks, state-sponsored espionage, and concerns over digital sovereignty are prompting governments to adopt more assertive stances on cybersecurity. This includes stricter requirements for critical infrastructure protection, mandatory breach notification regimes, and increased scrutiny of foreign technology providers (Hwang, 2025). At the same time, international cooperation is becoming more important, as cyber threats routinely transcend national borders. Initiatives such as the Council of Europe's Convention on Cybercrime and various bilateral agreements reflect a growing recognition that effective cybersecurity requires coordinated global action (Tosoni, 2018).

Finally, the regulatory approach itself is evolving. There is a discernible shift from prescriptive, rule-based frameworks towards more flexible, risk-based models that emphasize outcomes over compliance checklists. Regulators are increasingly encouraging organizations to adopt proactive risk management practices, conduct regular impact assessments, and demonstrate accountability through robust governance structures. This trend is likely to accelerate as regulators seek to keep pace with technological change without stifling innovation (Van der Heijden, 2021). The future of cybersecurity and data protection regulation will be characterized by greater complexity, broader scope, and a delicate balance between security, privacy, and innovation. Organizations must remain vigilant, agile, and forward-looking to navigate this rapidly shifting terrain (Cremer et al., 2022).

7.1 Anticipating and Adapting to Emerging Legislation

The rapid pace of technological change and evolving threat landscape necessitate proactive approaches to anticipating and adapting to emerging cybersecurity and data protection legislation. Organizations must monitor regulatory developments across multiple jurisdictions, assess the potential impact of proposed legislation on their operations, and develop implementation strategies that can be rapidly deployed when new requirements take effect (Craig et al., 2015).

Regulatory sandboxes and pilot programs provide opportunities for organizations to test new technologies and business models while working with regulators to develop appropriate compliance frameworks. These collaborative approaches can help ensure that new regulations are practical and effective while avoiding unintended consequences that could stifle innovation or create compliance burdens that are disproportionate to the risks being addressed (Gumbo & Chude-Okonkwo, 2025).

The increasing convergence of cybersecurity and data protection regulations with other regulatory domains, such as financial services, healthcare, and critical infrastructure protection, requires organizations to adopt holistic compliance strategies that address multiple regulatory objectives simultaneously. This convergence trend is likely to continue as regulators recognize the interconnected nature of modern digital risks and the need for coordinated regulatory responses (Cremer et al., 2022).

7.2 Preparing for Regulatory Change

Effective preparation for regulatory change requires organizations to develop adaptive compliance frameworks that can accommodate new requirements without requiring complete overhauls of existing systems and processes. This includes implementing flexible governance structures, maintaining current inventories of data processing activities, and establishing relationships with regulatory experts who can provide guidance on emerging requirements (Tanneru, 2025).

Scenario planning exercises can help organizations prepare for different regulatory futures by identifying potential compliance challenges and developing contingency plans for various regulatory scenarios. These exercises should consider not only direct regulatory impacts but also secondary effects such as changes in customer expectations, competitive dynamics, and supply chain requirements that may result from new regulations (Jariwala, 2024).

Investment in compliance technology and automation can help organizations scale their compliance capabilities to meet increasing regulatory demands while controlling costs. Privacy management platforms, automated compliance monitoring tools, and integrated governance, risk, and compliance systems can provide the technological foundation needed to manage complex regulatory requirements efficiently and effectively (Bhalavat et al., 2024).

7.3 Collaboration in Regulatory Development

Public-private collaboration in regulatory development has become increasingly important as regulators seek to understand the practical implications of proposed requirements and organizations work to influence the development of workable compliance frameworks. Industry associations, professional organizations, and multi-stakeholder initiatives provide forums for collaborative engagement between regulators and regulated entities (Reich, 2018).

International cooperation among regulatory authorities is essential for addressing the global nature of cybersecurity threats and data flows. Regulatory harmonization efforts, mutual recognition agreements, and information sharing arrangements can help reduce compliance complexity while maintaining effective protection for individuals and organizations (Lysenko et al., 2024).

The role of technical standards organizations in supporting regulatory compliance continues to evolve, with increasing recognition that voluntary standards can provide practical implementation guidance for regulatory requirements. Organizations should actively participate in standards development processes to ensure that emerging standards reflect practical operational needs while supporting regulatory compliance objectives (Dunbar et al., 2021).

8. ETHICAL CONSIDERATIONS IN CYBERSECURITY AND DATA PROTECTION

The ethical implications of cybersecurity and data protection are both significant and complex, transcending simple adherence to legal obligations. As organizations and individuals increasingly rely on digital technologies, they bear the responsibility of protecting sensitive information and maintaining the integrity of digital systems. This responsibility is fundamentally anchored in the principle of respecting individual autonomy and privacy. Ethical practices in cybersecurity require organizations to not only safeguard data against unauthorized access, breaches, and misuse but also to ensure that any data collection, processing, and storage is conducted transparently and with the informed consent of individuals (Sayjari & Silveira, 2024).

This issue becomes particularly pressing in a digital landscape where personal data is often treated as a commodity, and the distinction between public and private information is continuously evolving. The ethical obligation to protect data is further complicated by the need to find a balance between security measures and other fundamental rights, such as freedom of expression and access to information. For example, while it is crucial to implement strong security protocols to prevent cyberattacks, excessive surveillance or disproportionate data retention practices could infringe on civil liberties and undermine public trust (Gstrein & Beaulieu, 2022).

Additionally, the integration of advanced technologies, such as artificial intelligence and machine learning, in cybersecurity raises new ethical challenges. These include concerns over algorithmic bias, the absence of accountability, and the risk that automated decision-making could reinforce discrimination or injustice. The global nature of cyberspace adds another layer, as actions taken in one country can have widespread effects across borders, prompting questions about cultural relativism, national sovereignty, and the establishment of consistent ethical standards (Nag et al., 2024).

Professionals in cybersecurity are faced with challenging dilemmas, such as responsibly disclosing vulnerabilities, the usage of offensive cybersecurity techniques, and the ethical boundaries of penetration testing. There is also a moral duty to cultivate a culture of security awareness and digital literacy, empowering users to make informed decisions and recognize potential threats (Macnish & Van der Ham, 2020).

Ultimately, ethical considerations in cybersecurity and data protection necessitate a comprehensive approach that weaves together legal compliance, technological safeguards, and a commitment to the greater social good. This requires continuous discourse among stakeholders, including policymakers, technologists, ethicists, and the public, to navigate the shifting landscape of risks and responsibilities. By prioritizing ethical considerations, organizations can mitigate harm, bolster resilience, and foster trust and legitimacy in the digital realm, ensuring that technological advancements align with the principles of justice, fairness, and respect for human dignity (Dhirani et al., 2023).

8.1 Balancing Security and Personal Liberties

The tension between cybersecurity imperatives and individual privacy rights represents one of the most challenging ethical dilemmas in contemporary digital governance. Security measures that are necessary to protect against cyber threats may involve monitoring, data collection, and analysis activities that intrude upon individual privacy and autonomy, creating conflicts between collective security needs and individual rights (Power et al., 2021).

The principle of proportionality requires that security measures be proportionate to the threats they are designed to address and that less intrusive alternatives be considered before implementing measures that significantly impact individual rights. This principle is particularly relevant in the context of mass surveillance programs, behavioral monitoring systems, and predictive security analytics that may affect large numbers of individuals who pose no security risk (Power et al., 2021).

Democratic oversight and accountability mechanisms are essential for ensuring that the balance between security and liberty is maintained in accordance with societal values and legal requirements. This includes judicial review of surveillance activities, legislative oversight of security programs, and transparency measures that allow public scrutiny of security practices while protecting operational security needs (Nandy, 2023).

8.2 Addressing Bias in AI Security Tools

The use of artificial intelligence in cybersecurity applications raises significant concerns about algorithmic bias and discriminatory outcomes that can perpetuate or amplify existing social inequalities. AI security tools trained on biased datasets or designed with inadequate consideration of fairness principles may disproportionately flag certain groups as security risks, leading to discriminatory treatment and potential violations of equal protection principles (Panch et al., 2019).

Bias mitigation strategies for AI security tools include diverse and representative training datasets, fairness-aware machine learning algorithms, and ongoing monitoring of AI system outputs for discriminatory patterns. Organizations must also consider the broader social context in which AI security tools operate and the potential for these tools to reinforce existing power imbalances or create new forms of digital discrimination (Pagano et al., 2023).

Transparency and explainability requirements for AI security tools are essential for enabling meaningful oversight and accountability (Roberts & Singh, 2023). Individuals and communities affected by AI security decisions should have access to information about how these systems work and the ability to challenge decisions that may be based on biased or inaccurate algorithms (Balasubramaniam et al., 2023).

8.3 Ensuring Transparency and Accountability

Transparency and accountability principles are fundamental to maintaining public trust in cybersecurity and data protection systems while ensuring that these systems operate in accordance with democratic values and legal requirements. Organizations must balance the need for operational security with transparency obligations that allow stakeholders to understand and evaluate security and privacy practices (Heimstädt & Dobusch, 2020).

Accountability mechanisms must address both technical and governance aspects of cybersecurity and data protection programs. This includes clear assignment of responsibilities, regular auditing and assessment activities, and consequences for failures to meet security and privacy obligations. Independent oversight bodies can provide external validation of organizational practices and help ensure that accountability mechanisms are effective (Slapničar et al., 2023).

Public reporting and disclosure requirements can enhance transparency while respecting legitimate security concerns. Organizations should consider publishing regular transparency reports that provide aggregate information about security incidents, data processing activities, and compliance efforts without compromising operational security or individual privacy (Gao et al., 2020).

9. CONCLUSION

This comprehensive examination of the global cybersecurity and data protection regulatory landscape reveals a complex, rapidly evolving environment that demands sophisticated organizational responses and strategic thinking. The research demonstrates that effective regulatory compliance transcends mere legal obligation, emerging as a critical strategic imperative that fundamentally shapes organizational resilience, competitive positioning, and stakeholder trust in the digital economy. The convergence of technological innovation, regulatory proliferation, and evolving threat landscapes has created unprecedented challenges that require organizations to fundamentally reimagine their approaches to cybersecurity and data protection.

The study's findings illuminate several critical insights that extend our understanding of regulatory complexity in the digital age. First, the research confirms that organizations face an increasingly fragmented regulatory environment, with overlapping and sometimes conflicting requirements across jurisdictions creating significant compliance burdens (Villiers, 2022; Van der Heijden, 2021). The extraterritorial reach of regulations such as the GDPR has effectively created global compliance standards, yet regional variations in implementation and enforcement continue to challenge multinational organizations (Paul, 2024; Aidun, 2025). Second, the temporal dimension of regulatory complexity emerges as a particularly challenging aspect, with organizations struggling to balance current compliance requirements against the need to prepare for anticipated regulatory changes (Admass et al., 2024; Cremer et al., 2022).

The research also reveals the persistent disconnect between regulatory intent and operational implementation, with many organizations failing to translate abstract legal requirements into effective technical controls and governance frameworks (Kianpour & Raza, 2024; Ewoh & Vartiainen, 2024). This gap is particularly pronounced in sectors such as healthcare and finance, where the intersection of cybersecurity and data protection creates complex compliance challenges that existing framework struggle to address comprehensively (Jalali et al., 2019; Wang et al., 2024). Furthermore, the study highlights the critical role of organizational culture and leadership in driving effective compliance outcomes, demonstrating that technical solutions alone are insufficient without corresponding investments in human capital, training, and cultural transformation (Khadka & Ullah, 2025; Furnell, 2021).

These findings contribute significantly to the existing literature by providing empirical evidence of the multidimensional nature of regulatory complexity and its impact on organizational decision-making processes. The research extends current theoretical frameworks by demonstrating how regulatory compliance functions as both a risk management imperative and a potential source of competitive advantage, challenging traditional conceptualizations of compliance as purely a cost center

(Slapničar et al., 2023; Woods & Seymour, 2023). The study's interdisciplinary approach bridges critical gaps between legal, technical, and organizational perspectives, offering a more holistic understanding of how regulatory complexity manifests in practice and how organizations can develop more effective responses.

The broader implications of these findings extend across multiple domains, informing academic discourse, organizational practice, and policy development. For the academic community, the research provides a foundation for future investigations into the dynamic relationship between technological innovation and regulatory adaptation, highlighting the need for more nuanced theoretical frameworks that can accommodate the complexity and fluidity of contemporary regulatory environments (Zaidan & Ibrahim, 2024; Shetty et al., 2025). The findings also underscore the importance of interdisciplinary collaboration in addressing cybersecurity and data protection challenges, suggesting that future research should continue to integrate perspectives from law, technology, management, and public policy.

9.1 Actionable Recommendations for Stakeholders

Based on the comprehensive analysis of regulatory complexity in cybersecurity and data protection, the following actionable recommendations provide practical guidance for organizational leaders, policymakers, and stakeholders seeking to navigate this challenging landscape effectively:

1. Implement Adaptive Risk-Based Compliance Frameworks

Organizations should abandon static, checklist-based compliance approaches in favor of dynamic, risk-based frameworks that can adapt to evolving regulatory requirements and threat landscapes (Van der Heijden, 2021; Tanneru, 2025). This involves establishing continuous monitoring systems that assess regulatory changes, threat intelligence, and organizational risk profiles to inform compliance priorities. Leaders should invest in automated compliance monitoring tools and establish cross-functional teams that can rapidly assess and respond to regulatory developments. The framework should incorporate scenario planning capabilities to anticipate future regulatory changes and their potential impact on organizational operations (Jariwala, 2024).

2. Establish Integrated Cybersecurity and Data Protection Governance

Rather than treating cybersecurity and data protection as separate domains, organizations must develop integrated governance structures that recognize their interconnected nature (Del-Real et al., 2025; Slapničar et al., 2023). This requires creating unified governance committees with representation from legal, IT security, privacy, business operations, and senior leadership. Organizations should implement privacy and security by design principles throughout their operations, ensuring that data protection considerations are embedded in system development, business process design, and strategic decision-making from the outset rather than as an afterthought.

3. Develop Comprehensive Third-Party Risk Management Programs

Given the increasing reliance on cloud services, vendors, and business partners, organizations must establish robust third-party risk management programs that extend compliance requirements throughout their supply chains (Ilori et al., 2024; Ahmadi, 2024). This includes conducting thorough due diligence on vendors' security and privacy practices, implementing contractual safeguards that clearly allocate responsibilities, and establishing ongoing monitoring and assessment processes. Organizations should develop vendor risk scoring methodologies that consider regulatory compliance capabilities alongside traditional security and operational factors.

4. Invest in Specialized Compliance Expertise and Training

The complexity of the regulatory landscape requires organizations to invest significantly in specialized expertise, both through hiring dedicated compliance professionals and through comprehensive training programs for existing staff (Furnell, 2021; Khadka & Ullah, 2025). Organizations should establish centers of excellence that combine legal, technical, and business expertise to interpret regulatory requirements and translate them into operational practices. Regular training programs should ensure that all employees understand their roles in maintaining compliance, with specialized training for those in high-risk positions or with access to sensitive data.

5. Implement Proactive Breach Response and Recovery Capabilities

Organizations must develop comprehensive incident response capabilities that address both the technical aspects of breach containment and the regulatory requirements for notification and remediation (Freas et al., 2022; Gopireddy & Koppanathi, 2018). This includes establishing clear incident response procedures, conducting regular tabletop exercises, and maintaining relationships with external experts who can provide specialized support during incidents. Organizations should also develop post-breach recovery strategies that address regulatory obligations, stakeholder communication, and long-term reputation management.

6. Establish Cross-Border Data Transfer Governance Mechanisms

With the increasing complexity of international data transfer regulations, organizations must develop sophisticated governance mechanisms for managing cross-border data flows (Voss, 2020; Paul, 2024). This includes conducting comprehensive data mapping exercises to understand where data is stored and processed, implementing appropriate transfer mechanisms such as Standard Contractual Clauses or adequacy decisions, and establishing monitoring systems to ensure ongoing compliance with transfer restrictions. Organizations should also develop contingency plans for potential disruptions to international data transfers.

7. Adopt Technology-Enabled Compliance Solutions

Organizations should leverage emerging technologies such as artificial intelligence, automation, and blockchain to enhance their compliance capabilities while addressing the regulatory challenges these technologies themselves present (Tanneru, 2025; Zafar, 2025). This includes implementing automated data discovery and classification tools, privacy-enhancing technologies that enable compliant data processing, and AI-powered risk assessment systems. However, organizations must also address the regulatory implications of these technologies, including algorithmic transparency requirements and AI governance frameworks.

8. Develop Stakeholder Engagement and Transparency Programs

Organizations should establish comprehensive stakeholder engagement programs that demonstrate their commitment to cybersecurity and data protection while building trust with customers, regulators, and other stakeholders (Gao et al., 2020; Heimstädt & Dobusch, 2020). This includes publishing regular transparency reports that provide aggregate information about security incidents, data processing activities, and compliance efforts. Organizations should also engage proactively with regulators, industry associations, and standard-setting bodies to influence the development of future regulatory frameworks.

9. Create Regulatory Intelligence and Monitoring Systems

Given the rapid pace of regulatory change, organizations must establish systematic approaches to monitoring and analyzing regulatory developments across all relevant jurisdictions (Admass et al., 2024; Zaidan & Ibrahim, 2024). This includes subscribing to regulatory intelligence services, participating in industry associations and working groups, and establishing internal processes for assessing the impact of proposed regulatory changes. Organizations should develop regulatory change management processes that can rapidly assess new requirements and implement necessary changes to policies, procedures, and systems.

10. Foster a Culture of Privacy and Security Awareness

Effective compliance requires more than policies and procedures; it demands a organizational culture that prioritizes privacy and security considerations in all business activities (Khadka & Ullah, 2025; Abdullah et al., 2023). Organizations should implement comprehensive awareness programs that help employees understand the importance of data protection and cybersecurity, provide regular training on emerging threats and regulatory requirements, and establish incentive structures that reward compliance-conscious behavior. Leadership must demonstrate visible commitment to privacy and security principles, ensuring that compliance considerations are integrated into strategic decision-making processes.

The implementation of these recommendations requires sustained commitment, significant investment, and organizational transformation. However, organizations that successfully navigate the regulatory complexity of cybersecurity and data protection will be better positioned to build stakeholder trust, mitigate risks, and capitalize on the competitive advantages that effective compliance can provide. As the regulatory landscape continues to evolve, these recommendations provide a foundation for adaptive, resilient approaches to cybersecurity and data protection that can evolve with changing requirements and emerging challenges. The future success of organizations in the digital economy will depend significantly on their ability to transform regulatory compliance from a reactive, cost-focused activity into a proactive, value-creating capability that supports innovation, growth, and stakeholder confidence.

REFERENCES

Abdullah, Z., Dahlan, N. M., Dahlan, A., Irfan bin, A. F., & Arifin, A. S. (2023). Cybersecurity awareness on personal data protection using game-based learning. *Information Management and Business Review*, *15*(3(I)), 497–503. DOI: 10.22610/imbr.v15i3(I).3559

Admass, W. S., Munaye, Y. Y., & Diro, A. A. (2024). Cyber security: State of the art, challenges and Future Directions. *Cyber Security and Applications*, *2*, 100031. DOI: 10.1016/j.csa.2023.100031

Ahmadi, S. (2024). Systematic literature review on cloud computing security: Threats and mitigation strategies. *Journal of Information Security*, *15*(02), 148–167. DOI: 10.4236/jis.2024.152010

Aidun, E. (2025, March 5). *Data Privacy in the digital age: A comparative analysis of U.S. and EU Regulations*. University of Cincinnati Law Review Journal. https://uclawreview.org/2025/03/05/data-privacy-in-the-digital-age-a-comparative-analysis-of-u-s-and-eu-regulations/

Aiello, S. (2024). Privacy principles and harms: Balancing Protection and Innovation. *Journal of Cybersecurity Education, Research and Practice, 2024*(1). DOI: 10.62915/2472-2707.1167

AlKhanafseh, M., & Surakhi, O. (2024). Evidence preservation in digital forensics: An Approach using Blockchain and LSTM-based steganography. *Electronics (Basel)*, *13*(18), 3729. DOI: 10.3390/electronics13183729

AlSalem, T., Almaiah, M., & Lutfi, A. (2023). Cybersecurity risk analysis in the IOT: A systematic review. *Electronics (Basel)*, *12*(18), 3958. DOI: 10.3390/electronics12183958

Apeh, A. J., Hassan, A. O., Oyewole, O. O., Fakeyede, O. G., Okeleke, P. A., & Adaramodu, O. R. (2023). GRC strategies in Modern Cloud Infrastructures: A review of compliance challenges. *Computer Science &amp. IT Research Journal*, *4*(2), 111–125. DOI: 10.51594/csitrj.v4i2.609

Ardebili, A. A., Lezzi, M., & Pourmadadkar, M. (2024). Risk assessment for cyber resilience of critical infrastructures: Methods, governance, and standards. *Applied Sciences (Basel, Switzerland)*, *14*(24), 11807. DOI: 10.3390/app142411807

Arora, A., Barrett, M., Lee, E., Oborn, E., & Prince, K. (2023). Risk and the future of AI: Algorithmic bias, Data Colonialism, and marginalization. *Information and Organization*, *33*(3), 100478. DOI: 10.1016/j.infoandorg.2023.100478

Babatunde, G. O., Amoo, O. O., Mustapha, S. D., & Ige, A. B. (2022). Addressing privacy compliance challenges with a cross-border data protection framework for U.S. and Canada. *International Journal of Frontiers in Science and Technology Research, 3*(1), 067–083. DOI: 10.53294/ijfstr.2022.3.1.0043

Balasubramaniam, N., Kauppinen, M., Rannisto, A., Hiekkanen, K., & Kujala, S. (2023). Transparency and explainability of AI systems: From ethical guidelines to requirements. *Information and Software Technology*, *159*, 107197. DOI: 10.1016/j.infsof.2023.107197

Beduschi, A. (2024). Synthetic Data Protection: Towards a paradigm change in data regulation? *Big Data & Society*, *11*(1), 20539517241231277. Advance online publication. DOI: 10.1177/20539517241231277

Belenguer, L. (2022). Ai Bias: Exploring discriminatory algorithmic decision-making models and the application of possible machine-centric solutions adapted from the pharmaceutical industry. *AI and Ethics*, *2*(4), 771–787. DOI: 10.1007/s43681-022-00138-8

Belli, L., Gaspar, W. B., & Singh Jaswant, S. (2024). Data sovereignty and data transfers as fundamental elements of Digital Transformation: Lessons from the BRICS countries. *Computer Law & Security Review*, *54*, 106017. DOI: 10.1016/j.clsr.2024.106017

Bhalavat, D., Doshi, A., Keni, N., & Shah, P. R. (2024). Automated compliance: A privacy-focused solution for GDPR and DPDPA adherence. *2024 13th International Conference on System Modeling & Advancement in Research Trends (SMART)*, 831–837. DOI: 10.1109/SMART63812.2024.10882514

Biega, A. J., Potash, P., Daumé, H., Diaz, F., & Finck, M. (2020). Operationalizing the legal principle of data minimization for personalization. *Proceedings of the 43rd International ACM SIGIR Conference on Research and Development in Information Retrieval*, 399–408. DOI: 10.1145/3397271.3401034

Boyne, S. M. (2018). Data protection in the United States. *The American Journal of Comparative Law*, *66*(suppl_1), 299–343. DOI: 10.1093/ajcl/avy016

Bradford, L., Aboy, M., & Liddell, K. (2021). Standard contractual clauses for cross-border transfers of health data after *schrems ii*. *Journal of Law and the Biosciences*, *8*(1), lsab007. Advance online publication. DOI: 10.1093/jlb/lsab007

Brodin, M. (2019). A framework for GDPR compliance for small- and medium-sized enterprises. *European Journal for Security Research*, *4*(2), 243–264. DOI: 10.1007/s41125-019-00042-z

Busuioc, M., Curtin, D., & Almada, M. (2022). Reclaiming transparency: Contesting the logics of secrecy within the AI act. *European Law Open*, *2*(1), 79–105. DOI: 10.1017/elo.2022.47

Cains, M. G., Flora, L., Taber, D., King, Z., & Henshel, D. S. (2021). Defining cyber security and cyber security risk within a multidisciplinary context using expert elicitation. *Risk Analysis*, *42*(8), 1643–1669. DOI: 10.1111/risa.13687

Chen, Y. (2022). Information Security Management: Compliance Challenges and new directions. *Journal of Information Technology Case and Application Research*, *24*(4), 243–249. DOI: 10.1080/15228053.2022.2148979

Chippagiri, S. (2025). A study of cloud security frameworks for safeguarding Multi-Tenant Cloud Architectures. *International Journal of Computer Applications*, *186*(60), 50–57. DOI: 10.5120/ijca2025924369

Cirne, A., Sousa, P. R., Resende, J. S., & Antunes, L. (2022). IOT security certifications: Challenges and potential approaches. *Computers & Security*, *116*, 102669. DOI: 10.1016/j.cose.2022.102669

Craig, A. N., Shackelford, S. J., & Hiller, J. S. (2015). Proactive cybersecurity: A comparative industry and regulatory analysis. *American Business Law Journal*, *52*(4), 721–787. DOI: 10.1111/ablj.12055

Creemers, R. (2022). China's Emerging Data Protection Framework. *Journal of Cybersecurity*, *8*(1), tyac011. Advance online publication. DOI: 10.1093/cybsec/tyac011

Cremer, F., Sheehan, B., Fortmann, M., Kia, A. N., Mullins, M., Murphy, F., & Materne, S. (2022). Cyber risk and cybersecurity: A systematic review of data availability. *The Geneva Papers on Risk and Insurance. Issues and Practice*, *47*(3), 698–736. DOI: 10.1057/s41288-022-00266-6

Daigle, B., & Khan, M. (2020, June). *The EU General Data Protection Regulation: An Analysis of Enforcement Trends by EU Data Protection Authorities*. Journal of International Commerce and Economics. https://www.usitc.gov/publications/332/journals/jice_gdpr_enforcement.pdf

De-Yolande, M. H., Doh-Djanhoundji, T., & Constant, G. Y. (2023). Breach notification in the General Data Protection Regulation. *Voice of the Publisher*, *09*(04), 334–347. DOI: 10.4236/vp.2023.94026

Del-Real, C., De Busser, E., & Van den Berg, B. (2025). A systematic literature review of security and privacy by design principles, norms, and strategies for Digital Technologies. *International Review of Law, Computers &amp. International Review of Law Computers & Technology*, *39*(3), 1–32. DOI: 10.1080/13600869.2025.2457227

Dennis, J., & Janecek, K. (2022, January). *Comparing privacy laws: GDPR v. CCPA & CPRA*. OneTrust DataGuidance. https://www.dataguidance.com/sites/default/files/gdpr_v_ccpa_and_cpra_v6.pdf

Dhamo, A., & Dhamo, I. (2024). Right to privacy and Constitution: An in-depth analysis. *Interdisciplinary Journal of Research and Development, 11*(1 S1), 190. DOI: 10.56345/ijrdv11n1s128

Dhirani, L. L., Mukhtiar, N., Chowdhry, B. S., & Newe, T. (2023). Ethical dilemmas and privacy issues in emerging technologies: A Review. *Sensors (Basel)*, *23*(3), 1151. DOI: 10.3390/s23031151

Ducato, R. (2020). Data Protection, scientific research, and the role of information. *Computer Law &amp. Computer Law & Security Review*, *37*, 105412. DOI: 10.1016/j.clsr.2020.105412

Dunbar, P., Browne, J. P., & O'Connor, L. (2021). Determinants of regulatory compliance in health and Social Care Services: A systematic review protocol. *HRB Open Research*, *4*, 13. DOI: 10.12688/hrbopenres.13214.1

Ewoh, P., & Vartiainen, T. (2024). Vulnerability to cyberattacks and sociotechnical solutions for Health Care Systems: Systematic review. *Journal of Medical Internet Research*, *26*, e46904. Advance online publication. DOI: 10.2196/46904

Faisal, K. (2023). Applying the purpose limitation principle in smart-city data-processing practices: A European Data Protection Law Perspective. *Communication Law and Policy*, *28*(1), 67–97. DOI: 10.1080/10811680.2023.2180266

Farhad, M. A. (2024). Consumer Data Protection Laws and their impact on business models in the Tech Industry. *Telecommunications Policy*, *48*(9), 102836. DOI: 10.1016/j.telpol.2024.102836

Freas, R. L., Adair, H. F., & Hammad, E. (2022). An engineering process framework for Cybersecurity Incident Response Assessment. *2022 IEEE Conference on Dependable and Secure Computing (DSC)*, 1–8. DOI: 10.1109/DSC54232.2022.9888795

Furnell, S. (2021). The cybersecurity workforce and Skills. *Computers &amp. Computers & Security*, *100*, 102080. DOI: 10.1016/j.cose.2020.102080

Gao, L., Calderon, T. G., & Tang, F. (2020). Public companies' cybersecurity risk disclosures. *International Journal of Accounting Information Systems*, *38*, 100468. DOI: 10.1016/j.accinf.2020.100468

Georgiadis, G., & Poels, G. (2022). Towards a privacy impact assessment methodology to support the requirements of the General Data Protection Regulation in a big data analytics context: A systematic literature review. *Computer Law &. Computer Law & Security Review*, *44*, 105640. DOI: 10.1016/j.clsr.2021.105640

Gopireddy, R. R., & Koppanathi, S. R. (2018). Post - Breach Data Security: Strategies for recovery and future protection. [IJSR]. *International Journal of Science and Research (Raipur, India)*, *7*(12), 1609–1614. DOI: 10.21275/SR24731204000

Gstrein, O. J., & Beaulieu, A. (2022). How to protect privacy in a datafied society? A presentation of multiple legal and conceptual approaches. *Philosophy & Technology*, *35*(1), 3. Advance online publication. DOI: 10.1007/s13347-022-00497-4

Gumbo, L., & Chude-Okonkwo, U. A. (2025). Regulatory sandbox as a frontier for innovation and Sustainability: A Systematic Review. *Cogent Business & Management*, *12*(1), 2510555. Advance online publication. DOI: 10.1080/23311975.2025.2510555

Guttman, B., White, D. R., & Walraven, T. (2022). *Digital Evidence Preservation : Considerations for Evidence Handlers*. NIST., DOI: 10.6028/NIST.IR.8387

Han, H., Shiwakoti, R. K., Jarvis, R., Mordi, C., & Botchie, D. (2023). Accounting and auditing with blockchain technology and Artificial Intelligence: A literature review. *International Journal of Accounting Information Systems*, *48*, 100598. DOI: 10.1016/j.accinf.2022.100598

He, Y., Aliyu, A., Evans, M., & Luo, C. (2021). Health Care Cybersecurity challenges and solutions under the climate of covid-19: Scoping review. *Journal of Medical Internet Research*, *23*(4), e21747. Advance online publication. DOI: 10.2196/21747

Heimstädt, M., & Dobusch, L. (2020). Transparency and accountability: Causal, critical and constructive perspectives. *Organization Theory*, *1*(4), 2631787720964216. Advance online publication. DOI: 10.1177/2631787720964216

Hoofnagle, C. J., Van der Sloot, B., & Borgesius, F. Z. (2019). The European Union General Data Protection Regulation: What it is and what it means. *Information &. Information & Communications Technology Law*, *28*(1), 65–98. DOI: 10.1080/13600834.2019.1573501

Hwang, J. young. (2025). Digital sovereignty in an era of cyber threats and Global Connectivity. *International Journal of Multidisciplinary Research Updates*, *9*(2), 012–023. DOI: 10.53430/ijmru.2025.9.2.0023

Ilori, O., Nwosu, N. T., & Naiho, H. N. N. (2024). Third-party vendor risks in IT security: A comprehensive audit review and mitigation strategies. *World Journal of Advanced Research and Reviews*, *22*(3), 213–224. DOI: 10.30574/wjarr.2024.22.3.1727

Jagadish, R. (2024). Enhancing cybersecurity in cloud - based banking - best practices and technologies. [IJSR]. *International Journal of Science and Research (Raipur, India)*, *13*(3), 422–426. DOI: 10.21275/SR24306144435

Jalali, M. S., Razak, S., Gordon, W., Perakslis, E., & Madnick, S. (2019). Health Care and cybersecurity: Bibliometric Analysis of the literature. *Journal of Medical Internet Research*, *21*(2), e12644. Advance online publication. DOI: 10.2196/12644

Jariwala, M. (2024). Contingency planning: The need, benefits, and implementation of scenario planning. [IJTSRD]. *International Journal of Trend in Scientific Research and Development*, *8*(3), 866–869. https://doi.org/https://www.researchgate.net/publication/373990738_Contingency_Planning_The_Need_Benefits_and_Implementation_of_Scenario_Planning

Khadka, K., & Ullah, A. B. (2025). Human factors in cybersecurity: An Interdisciplinary Review and framework proposal. *International Journal of Information Security*, *24*(3), 119. Advance online publication. DOI: 10.1007/s10207-025-01032-0

Kianpour, M., & Raza, S. (2024). More than malware: Unmasking the hidden risk of cybersecurity regulations. *International Cybersecurity Law Review*, *5*(1), 169–212. DOI: 10.1365/s43439-024-00111-7

Knight, R., & Nurse, J. R. C. (2020). A framework for effective corporate communication after cyber security incidents. *Computers & Security*, *99*, 102036. DOI: 10.1016/j.cose.2020.102036

Liu, C., & Babar, M. A. (2024). Corporate Cybersecurity Risk and data breaches: A systematic review of Empirical Research. *Australian Journal of Management*. Advance online publication. DOI: 10.1177/03128962241293658

Lysenko, S., Liubchenko, A., Kozakov, V., Demianchuk, Y., & Krutik, Y. (2024). Global cybersecurity: Harmonising international standards and cooperation. *Multidisciplinary Reviews*, *7*, 2024spe021. Advance online publication. DOI: 10.31893/multirev.2024spe021

Macnish, K., & Van der Ham, J. (2020). Ethics in Cybersecurity Research and Practice. *Technology in Society*, *63*, 101382. DOI: 10.1016/j.techsoc.2020.101382

Makridis, C. A. (2021). Corrigendum to: Do data breaches damage reputation? evidence from 45 companies between 2002 and 2018. *Journal of Cybersecurity*, *7*(1), tyab022. Advance online publication. DOI: 10.1093/cybsec/tyab022

Mayer, N., & Aubert, J. (2020). A risk management framework for security and integrity of networks and services. *Journal of Risk Research*, *24*(8), 987–998. DOI: 10.1080/13669877.2020.1779786

Mishra, A., Alzoubi, Y. I., Gill, A. Q., & Anwar, M. J. (2022). Cybersecurity Enterprises Policies: A Comparative Study. *Sensors (Basel)*, *22*(2), 538. DOI: 10.3390/s22020538

Mohale, V. Z., & Obagbuwa, I. C. (2025). A systematic review on the integration of explainable artificial intelligence in intrusion detection systems to enhancing transparency and interpretability in cybersecurity. *Frontiers in Artificial Intelligence*, *8*, 1526221. Advance online publication. DOI: 10.3389/frai.2025.1526221

Mohammed, Z. (2021). Data Breach Recovery Areas: An exploration of organization's recovery strategies for surviving data breaches. *Organizational Cybersecurity Journal: Practice. Process and People*, *2*(1), 41–59. DOI: 10.1108/OCJ-05-2021-0014

Nag, Y., Hullatti, V. M., TB, A., & Kher, U. (2024). Ethical concerns of using artificial intelligence in Cybersecurity. *IJARCCE, 13*(11), 243–246. DOI: 10.17148/IJARCCE.2024.131138

Nandy, D. (2023). Human rights in the era of surveillance: Balancing security and privacy concerns. *Journal of Current Social and Political Issues*, *1*(1), 13–17. DOI: 10.15575/jcspi.v1i1.442

Narciandi-Rodriguez, D., Aveleira-Mata, J., García-Ordás, M. T., Alfonso-Cendón, J., Benavides, C., & Alaiz-Moretón, H. (2025). A cybersecurity review in IOT 5G networks. *Internet of Things : Engineering Cyber Physical Human Systems*, *30*, 101478. DOI: 10.1016/j.iot.2024.101478

Ou, L. W.Leonardo W Ou. (2025). Regulatory responses to data breaches: Evaluating the effectiveness of GDPR and CCPA in consumer protection. *International Journal of Social Sciences and Public Administration*, *6*(1), 176–185. DOI: 10.62051/ijsspa.v6n1.22

Pagano, T. P., Loureiro, R. B., Lisboa, F. V., Peixoto, R. M., Guimarães, G. A., Cruz, G. O., Araujo, M. M., Santos, L. L., Cruz, M. A., Oliveira, E. L., Winkler, I., & Nascimento, E. G. (2023). Bias and unfairness in Machine Learning Models: A systematic review on datasets, tools, fairness metrics, and identification and mitigation methods. *Big Data and Cognitive Computing*, *7*(1), 15. DOI: 10.3390/bdcc7010015

Panch, T., Mattie, H., & Atun, R. (2019). Artificial Intelligence and algorithmic bias: Implications for health systems. *Journal of Global Health*, *9*(2), 010318. Advance online publication. DOI: 10.7189/jogh.09.020318

Patterson, C. M., Nurse, J. R. C., & Franqueira, V. N. L. (2023). Learning from cyber security incidents: A systematic review and future research agenda. *Computers & Security*, *132*, 103309. DOI: 10.1016/j.cose.2023.103309

Paul, A. L. (2024, May). *Navigating the regulatory landscape: The impact of privacy and Data Protection Regulations on Global Data Security practices*. researchgate. https://www.researchgate.net/publication/381004748_Navigating_the_Regulatory_Landscape_The_Impact_of_Privacy_and_Data_Protection_Regulations_on_Global_Data_Security_Practices

Power, D. J., Heavin, C., & O'Connor, Y. (2021). Balancing privacy rights and surveillance analytics: A decision process guide. *Journal of Business Analytics*, *4*(2), 155–170. DOI: 10.1080/2573234X.2021.1920856

Reich, M. R. (2018). The core roles of transparency and accountability in the governance of Global Health Public–Private Partnerships. *Health Systems and Reform*, *4*(3), 239–248. DOI: 10.1080/23288604.2018.1465880

Reis, O., Eneh, N. E., Ehimuan, B., Anyanwu, A., Olorunsogo, T., & Abrahams, T. O. (2024). Privacy law challenges in the digital age: A global review of legislation and Enforcement. *International Journal of Applied Research in Social Sciences*, *6*(1), 73–88. DOI: 10.51594/ijarss.v6i1.733

Riggi, J. (2024). *A Look at 2024's Health Care Cybersecurity Challenges*. American Hospital Association | AHA News. https://www.aha.org/news/aha-cyber-intel/2024-10-07-look-2024s-health-care-cybersecurity-challenges

Riggs, H., Tufail, S., Parvez, I., Tariq, M., Khan, M. A., Amir, A., Vuda, K. V., & Sarwat, A. I. (2023). Impact, vulnerabilities, and mitigation strategies for Cyber-Secure Critical Infrastructure. *Sensors (Basel)*, *23*(8), 4060. DOI: 10.3390/s23084060

Rong, K., Ling, Y., Yang, T., & Huang, C. (2025). Cross-border data transfer: Patterns and discrepancies. *Journal of International Business Policy*, *8*(1), 10–32. DOI: 10.1057/s42214-025-00209-7

Ruohonen, J., & Hjerppe, K. (2022). The GDPR enforcement fines at glance. *Information Systems*, *106*, 101876. DOI: 10.1016/j.is.2021.101876

Ryngaert, C., & Taylor, M. (2020). The GDPR as *global* data protection regulation? *AJIL Unbound*, *114*, 5–9. DOI: 10.1017/aju.2019.80

Sahin, Z., & Vance, A. (2025). What do we need to know about the chief information security officer? A literature review and Research Agenda. *Computers &amp. Computers & Security*, *148*, 104063. DOI: 10.1016/j.cose.2024.104063

Salem, A. H., Azzam, S. M., Emam, O. E., & Abohany, A. A. (2024). Advancing cybersecurity: A comprehensive review of AI-Driven Detection Techniques. *Journal of Big Data, 11*(1), 105. Advance online publication. DOI: 10.1186/s40537-024-00957-y

Savaş, S., & Karataş, S. (2022). Cyber Governance Studies in ensuring cybersecurity: An overview of cybersecurity governance. *International Cybersecurity Law Review, 3*(1), 7–34. DOI: 10.1365/s43439-021-00045-4

Sayjari, T., & Silveira, R. M. (2024). Ethics of privacy in cybersecurity: Protecting individual autonomy through technology. *International Research Journal of Modernization in Engineering Technology and Science, 06*(10), 1940–1951. DOI: 10.56726/IRJMETS62448

Schuett, J. (2023). Risk management in the Artificial Intelligence Act. *European Journal of Risk Regulation, 15*(2), 367–385. DOI: 10.1017/err.2023.1

Seh, A. H., Zarour, M., Alenezi, M., Sarkar, A. K., Agrawal, A., Kumar, R., & Ahmad Khan, R. (2020). Healthcare data breaches: Insights and implications. *Healthcare (Basel), 8*(2), 133. DOI: 10.3390/healthcare8020133

Shetty, D. K., Vijaya Arjunan, R., Cenitta, D., Makkithaya, K., Hegde, N. V., & Bhatta, B. (2025). Analyzing AI regulation through literature and current trends. *Journal of Open Innovation, 11*(1), 100508. DOI: 10.1016/j.joitmc.2025.100508

Singh, N. (2024). Data Protection and privacy as a fundamental right - an in-depth analysis of the European Union and India's Data Protection Legislation. *International Journal For Multidisciplinary Research, 6*(2), 15869. Advance online publication. DOI: 10.36948/ijfmr.2024.v06i02.15869

Slapničar, S., Axelsen, M., Bongiovanni, I., & Stockdale, D. (2023). A pathway model to five lines of accountability in Cybersecurity Governance. *International Journal of Accounting Information Systems, 51*, 100642. DOI: 10.1016/j.accinf.2023.100642

Syed, N. F., Shah, S. W., Shaghaghi, A., Anwar, A., Baig, Z., & Doss, R. (2022). Zero trust architecture (ZTA): A comprehensive survey. *IEEE Access : Practical Innovations, Open Solutions, 10*, 57143–57179. DOI: 10.1109/ACCESS.2022.3174679

Tanneru, B. (2025). Adaptive compliance: Automating dynamic security controls in real-time. *International Journal of Multidisciplinary Research and Growth Evaluation, 6*(2), 1853–1855. DOI: 10.54660/.IJMRGE.2025.6.2.1853-1855

Thangaraju, D. (2024). Edge Data Governance: Frameworks and approaches for distributed data management at the Network Edge. *International Journal of Multidisciplinary Research and Growth Evaluation*, *5*(4), 1353–1361. DOI: 10.54660/.IJMRGE.2024.5.6-1353-1361

Theodos, K., & Sittig, S. (2020, December 7). *Health Information Privacy Laws in the digital age: HIPAA doesn't apply*. Perspectives in health information management. https://pmc.ncbi.nlm.nih.gov/articles/PMC7883355/

Tosoni, L. (2018). Rethinking privacy in the Council of Europe's Convention on Cybercrime. *Computer Law & Security Review*, *34*(6), 1197–1214. DOI: 10.1016/j.clsr.2018.08.004

Vaka, P. R. (2020). Data breaches or regulatory and compliance. *International Journal Of Multidisciplinary Research In Science. Engineering and Technology*, *03*(12). Advance online publication. DOI: 10.15680/IJMRSET.2020.0312020

Van der Heijden, J. (2021). Risk as an approach to regulatory governance: An evidence synthesis and research agenda. *SAGE Open*, *11*(3), 21582440211032202. Advance online publication. DOI: 10.1177/21582440211032202

Villiers, C. (2022). New Directions in the European Union's Regulatory Framework for corporate reporting, due diligence and accountability: The challenge of complexity. *European Journal of Risk Regulation*, *13*(4), 548–566. DOI: 10.1017/err.2022.25

Voss, W. G. (2020). Cross-border data flows, the GDPR, and Data Governance. *International Organisations Research Journal*, *29*(3), 485–532. DOI: 10.17323/1996-7845-2022-01-03

Wang, S., Asif, M., Shahzad, M. F., & Ashfaq, M. (2024). Data Privacy and cybersecurity challenges in the digital transformation of the banking sector. *Computers &amp. Computers & Security*, *147*, 104051. DOI: 10.1016/j.cose.2024.104051

Woods, D. W., & Seymour, S. (2023). Evidence-based cybersecurity policy? A meta-review of Security Control Effectiveness. *Journal of Cyber Policy*, *8*(3), 365–383. DOI: 10.1080/23738871.2024.2335461

Wylde, V., Rawindaran, N., Lawrence, J., Balasubramanian, R., Prakash, E., Jayal, A., Khan, I., Hewage, C., & Platts, J. (2022). Cybersecurity, data privacy and Blockchain: A Review. *SN Computer Science*, *3*(2), 127. Advance online publication. DOI: 10.1007/s42979-022-01020-4

Yakovleva, S. (2017). Should fundamental rights to privacy and data protection be a part of the EU's International Trade 'deals'? *World Trade Review*, *17*(3), 477–508. DOI: 10.1017/S1474745617000453

Yusuff, M. (2023, May). *Ensuring compliance with GDPR, CCPA, and other Data Protection Regulations: Challenges and Best Practices*. ResearchGate. https://www.researchgate.net/publication/387224965_Ensuring_Compliance_with_GDPR_CCPA_and_Other_Data_Protection_Regulations_Challenges_and_Best_Practices

Zadeh, A., Lavine, B., Zolbanin, H., & Hopkins, D. (2023). A cybersecurity risk quantification and classification framework for informed risk mitigation decisions. *Decision Analytics Journal*, *9*, 100328. DOI: 10.1016/j.dajour.2023.100328

Zafar, A. (2025). Reconciling blockchain technology and data protection laws: Regulatory challenges, technical solutions, and practical pathways. *Journal of Cybersecurity*, *11*(1), tyaf002. Advance online publication. DOI: 10.1093/cybsec/tyaf002

Zaid, T., & Garai, S. (2024). Emerging trends in cybersecurity: A holistic view on current threats, Assessing Solutions, and pioneering new frontiers. *Blockchain in Healthcare Today*, *7*(1). Advance online publication. DOI: 10.30953/bhty.v7.302

Zaidan, E., & Ibrahim, I. A. (2024). AI governance in a complex and rapidly changing regulatory landscape: A global perspective. *Humanities & Social Sciences Communications*, *11*(1), 1121. Advance online publication. DOI: 10.1057/s41599-024-03560-x

Chapter 9
Corporate Data Privacy Frameworks in the Age of Emerging Technologies:
Navigating Legal Status and Accountability in a Globalized Digital Economy

Rupal Malik
https://orcid.org/0009-0001-2461-8580
Ramaiah College of Law, Bengaluru, India

Rishabh Bhandari
https://orcid.org/0009-0001-4090-4157
Ramaiah College of Law, Bengaluru, India

ABSTRACT

In the contemporary digital economy, personal data holds dual significance as a valuable commercial resource, and simultaneously raises complex legal concerns. With corporations managing vast quantities of individual's data, their role as key custodians has expanded, especially as Artificial Intelligence (AI) systems increasingly influence data-driven operations. The absence of consistent global legal standards governing corporate accountability, particularly where AI technologies blur traditional boundaries of responsibility and the autonomous nature of AI complicates foundational legal principles and challenges the effectiveness of existing legal frameworks in holding corporate entities accountable. In this context, the present chapter contextualises the transformation of personal data into an economic asset with comparative exploration of major data protection laws across jurisdictions.

DOI: 10.4018/979-8-3373-4967-1.ch009

It further delves into the legal and ethical disruptions introduced by AI, analysing challenges in assigning liability and evaluating the strengths and limitations of current accountability mechanisms.

1. INTRODUCTION

The rapid expansion of digital technologies in the last ten years has significantly changed the ways personal data is created, gathered, and monetized. By 2024, more than 328 million terabytes of data was produced each day, much of which consists of personal or behaviourally inferred information (International Data Corporation [IDC], 2023). This enormous amount of data forms the backbone of what is commonly called surveillance capitalism, where companies derive value from personal data to enable targeted advertising, algorithmic profiling, and real-time behaviour prediction (Zuboff, 2019). A recent Deloitte report showed that over 79 percent of global companies use AI-powered analytics tools heavily dependent on personal data, prompting urgent concerns about privacy, consent, and accountability (Deloitte, 2022).

Within this framework, personal data has become both an essential economic resource and a field of legal and ethical oversight. Regulatory measures, including the European Union's General Data Protection Regulation (GDPR) (Regulation (EU) 2016/679), India's Digital Personal Data Protection Act (DPDP Act) (DPDP Act, 2023), and China's Personal Information Protection Law (PIPL) (PIPL, 2021), seek to balance innovation with the protection of individual rights. However, research shows ongoing deficiencies, the United Nations Conference on Trade and Development reports that only 71 percent of countries worldwide have enacted comprehensive data protection laws, with enforcement remaining uneven, especially in developing nations (United Nations Conference on Trade and Development [UNCTAD], 2023).

A notable illustration of the difficulties faced by multinational firms operating in this fragmented regulatory environment is the Meta Platforms, Inc. case, previously known as Facebook. In 2023, the Irish Data Protection Commission fined Meta €1.2 billion for transferring European user's data to the United States in violation of GDPR rules concerning cross-border data transfers (European Commission, 2023). This penalty came after the Court of Justice of the European Union invalidated the EU–US Privacy Shield in the Schrems II ruling, which found that U.S. surveillance practices conflicted with EU privacy protections (CJEU, 2020).

Meta's dependence on Standard Contractual Clauses (SCCs) was considered inadequate because U.S. law does not provide sufficient protections. At the same time, U.S. legislation like the CLOUD Act asserts extraterritorial authority over data held by American companies, even when that data is stored abroad (Cate &

Mayer-Schönberger, 2013). This legal clash put Meta in a difficult position either comply with U.S. demands and risk breaking the GDPR or prioritize EU law and face possible penalties in the United States. This case clearly highlights how the lack of unified international standards can trap companies in conflicting regulatory demands, resulting in non-compliance, damage to reputation, and heavy fines. This situation is not unique to Meta, other major global firms such as Google, Amazon, and TikTok have encountered similar legal challenges and enforcement actions in various countries, often due to conflicting requirements related to data retention, algorithm transparency, or user consent (Greenleaf & Waters, 2022). These overlapping and sometimes contradictory regulations generate uncertainty for companies and hinder global progress toward coherent data governance standards.

Considering the crucial role these corporations play in the data economy and the added complexity introduced by AI, this research is both relevant and necessary. It fills an important gap by systematically exploring how different legal systems define, regulate, and enforce corporate responsibility in managing personal data. The Meta example and others reveal that regulatory fragmentation leads not only to legal uncertainty but also to systemic risks for privacy protection worldwide. Without harmonized regulations, enforcement tends to be reactive, compliance costs become unpredictable, and individuals often lack effective means of redress.

Moreover, while much academic work has focused on normative principles or technological risks, there is limited comparative legal research on how corporate liability is structured across jurisdictions, especially concerning AI's integration into data processing (Floridi et al., 2018; Kuner et al., 2017). This chapter aims to fill that gap through doctrinal and comparative legal analysis, supported by current empirical findings, legislative changes, and evolving soft law instruments. Ultimately, it seeks to evaluate whether existing legal frameworks sufficiently hold corporations accountable for harms caused by AI-driven data use and whether legal, institutional, or ethical reforms are needed to address the challenges of an increasingly automated and global data environment. In doing so, it contributes to the broader conversation on data justice, emphasizing the importance of regulatory alignment, transparency, and human-centred oversight in digital governance.

2. PROBLEM STATEMENT

The global digital economy increasingly depends on personal data to support AI-driven decision-making and business functions. Every day, more than 328 million terabytes of data are produced, and 79 percent of companies use AI to derive insights from this information (IDC, 2023; Deloitte, 2022). While these technologies promote innovation, they also bring significant concerns regarding data protection and corporate responsibility. A key issue is the fragmentation of international data protection frameworks. Although 71 percent of countries have introduced privacy laws, enforcement and coordination remain weak (UNCTAD, 2023). Definitions of corporate responsibility differ greatly the EU's GDPR adopts a controller–processor framework (Voigt & Von dem Bussche, 2017), India's DPDP Act imposes fiduciary duties (Singh, 2023), and China's PIPL combines personal privacy protections with state surveillance objectives (Liu, 2022). Multinational companies face the challenge of navigating this complex environment while managing AI systems that operate across multiple jurisdictions (Greenleaf & Waters, 2022).

The 2023 Meta case highlights these conflicts. The Irish Data Protection Commission fined Meta €1.2 billion for breaching GDPR data transfer rules, following the Schrems II decision which invalidated the EU-U.S. Privacy Shield (CJEU, 2020; European Commission, 2023). Meta's use of Standard Contractual Clauses was ruled insufficient (Kuner, 2020), revealing the practical risks of inconsistent regulations (Greenleaf, 2021). Traditional legal concepts based on foreseeability, control, and intent are challenged by autonomous AI systems (Wachter & Mittelstadt, 2019; Pagallo, 2017). As AI systems become more complex and less transparent, determining liability for harms such as biased profiling or algorithmic mistakes grows increasingly complicated (AI Now Institute, 2023).

Liability rules also vary by jurisdiction, whereby the EU follows a strict liability approach, while the U.S. applies negligence-based standards (Gellert, 2018; Solove & Hartzog, 2020). These differences complicate compliance for companies deploying AI tools internationally, especially where human oversight is limited (Wachter, Mittelstadt, & Floridi, 2017). Although soft law initiatives like the OECD AI Principles (OECD, 2019) and UNESCO's AI Ethics Recommendations (UNESCO, 2021) encourage shared ethical standards, their voluntary nature restricts their regulatory effectiveness. Despite increased focus on AI ethics and data governance, few studies offer comparative legal analyses of corporate accountability within fragmented regulatory systems. Most research concentrates on single jurisdictions or theoretical frameworks, overlooking practical enforcement challenges and institutional weaknesses in resource-limited regions (Floridi et al., 2018; Saxena, 2023). Additionally, there is limited examination of how AI's technical complexity weakens the application of legal liability in real situations.

3. SIGNIFICANCE OF THE STUDY

Regulating corporate responsibility within AI-driven data ecosystems is no longer a theoretical issue but a critical legal and policy challenge. As algorithmic systems take on key roles in economic and governmental activities, this study critically evaluates whether current data protection laws can provide effective accountability in environments dominated by AI. Policymakers and regulators will gain from this study's comparative review of enforcement frameworks, including the EU's Data Protection Authorities, India's Data Protection Board, and Brazil's National Data Protection Authority. By 2023, only 24 percent of countries with privacy legislation had independent authorities with full investigative powers (UNCTAD, 2023), highlighting the urgent need to strengthen institutional capacity (Doneda & Monteiro, 2021; Rai, 2023).

For corporate leaders and compliance professionals, the findings offer valuable guidance on how to align internal governance with fragmented global regulations. The €1.2 billion GDPR fine against Meta in 2023 illustrates the increasing risks connected to inconsistent cross-border data transfer practices (European Commission, 2023; CJEU, 2020; Kuner, 2020). This research outlines essential AI-related requirements such as explainability and algorithmic audits, supporting companies in anticipating regulatory demands (Wachter, Mittelstadt, & Floridi, 2017; OECD, 2019; UNESCO, 2021). Civil society organizations can also use this study to hold both companies and regulators accountable, particularly where enforceable rules are lacking. Advocacy groups may draw on soft law frameworks from bodies like the OECD and UNESCO as normative references to challenge the opaque use of AI in sensitive areas such as credit decisions, employment, or surveillance (Binns, 2018; Susser et al., 2019).

Academically, this work fills a gap in comparative legal analysis of AI liability, moving beyond studies limited to single jurisdictions or purely theoretical approaches (Saxena, 2023; Singh, 2023). It examines the limitations of traditional legal concepts such as intent and foreseeability in the context of autonomous systems and explores possible alternative approaches. Finally, as international organizations like the OECD, G20, and Global Privacy Assembly advocate for interoperable frameworks, this study provides a practical foundation for data governance that respects rights, encourages innovation, and promotes regulatory harmonization.

4. METHODOLOGY

The study employs comparative legal analysis to explore how various jurisdictions define and enforce corporate responsibility within AI-driven data governance. The approach identifies similarities and differences in legal obligations, accountability frameworks, and regulatory responses to emerging technologies. By focusing on the EU, India, China, Brazil, and the United States, the research covers a range of regulatory models, from the rights-based GDPR and India's fiduciary duty framework under the DPDP Act, to China's state-focused PIPL, Brazil's GDPR-inspired LGPD, and the fragmented regulatory environment in the U.S.

The study relies on primary legal sources such as statutes and enforcement cases, including the 2023 Meta ruling, alongside secondary materials from academic publications and institutions like the OECD and UNESCO. Data was gathered from authoritative databases such as Westlaw and Hein Online, using terms like "AI corporate liability" and "cross-border data regulation." The methodology is doctrinal and normative, concentrating on legal frameworks rather than empirical practices. However, by engaging with real-world enforcement actions and global regulatory developments, the research provides a solid basis for understanding the evolving and contested nature of corporate liability in AI contexts.

5. LITERATURE REVIEW

The intersection of corporate responsibility, data protection, and AI has become a key focus in legal scholarship, as concerns grow about how legal systems manage algorithmic harm and ensure accountability in data-driven settings. Zuboff's (2019) analysis of surveillance capitalism frames the issue as one of power imbalance between corporate data controllers and individuals. More recent studies highlight a liability gap created by opaque, automated systems that challenge traditional legal concepts like attribution and foreseeability (Wachter & Mittelstadt, 2019). Ethical frameworks developed by groups such as AI4People (Floridi et al., 2018) have influenced soft law guidelines including the OECD AI Principles (2019) and UNESCO's AI Ethics Recommendation (2021). However, critics like Crawford (2021) argue these lack enforceability and fail to address structural inequalities, serving more as symbolic guidance than effective liability tools.

Legal scholars have evaluated whether existing frameworks, especially the GDPR, are fit for AI regulation. Kuner et al. (2017) and Gellert (2018) point out that although the GDPR provides strong rights, it struggles to tackle the opacity and autonomy of AI systems. These analyses are mainly focused on the EU and provide limited insight into non-European contexts. Comparative research is emerging Greenleaf and Waters (2022) surveyed over 140 data protection laws, noting broad adoption of GDPR principles alongside ongoing enforcement fragmentation. Yet, their work emphasizes norm diffusion rather than corporate liability. Similarly, Bradford's (2020) concept of the Brussels Effect describes the global impact of EU standards but overlooks corporate resistance and jurisdictional conflicts, as seen in the Meta case involving illegal data transfers to the U.S. (CJEU, 2020; Kuner, 2020; European Commission, 2023).

Theoretical scholars such as Pagallo (2017) and Sartor (2020) question whether traditional legal doctrines like intent and causation apply to AI, suggesting alternatives like functional equivalence or distributed responsibility. While conceptually valuable, these ideas rarely engage with jurisdiction-specific enforcement or institutional realities. Across the literature, there is broad agreement that AI creates accountability gaps due to its technical complexity and autonomous nature (Wachter, Mittelstadt, & Floridi, 2017; AI Now Institute, 2023). Scholars generally concur that legal frameworks need reform (Floridi et al., 2018; Greenleaf, 2021), though opinions vary on whether this should happen through stronger enforcement, new legislation, or ethical governance models (Saxena, 2023; Singh, 2023). There is also debate between advocates for regulatory harmonization (UNCTAD, 2023) and supporters of localized, context-aware approaches (Liu, 2022).

Despite this progress, significant gaps remain, much of the research focuses on individual jurisdictions, lacks comparative analysis of enforcement mechanisms, and pays little attention to corporate behaviour amid fragmented regulations. Theoretical models of AI liability remain poorly integrated into enforceable legal frameworks. Moreover, the effects of legal roles, such as controller, processor, or fiduciary, on cross-border accountability are underexplored. This study addresses these issues through a comparative legal analysis of the EU, India, China, Brazil, and the U.S., reflecting diverse legal traditions and global regulatory influence. Combining doctrinal review with case studies like the Meta–GDPR enforcement, the research assesses how liability is assigned, compliance is defined, and legal systems respond to AI-specific challenges. It contributes to the broader conversation by providing a structured, cross-jurisdictional framework for understanding corporate responsibility in AI governance, with practical relevance for policymakers, regulators, and corporate stakeholders.

6. THEORETICAL FRAMEWORK

The study applies three interconnected theoretical frameworks: World Polity Theory, Regulatory Governance Theory, and Structuration Theory to critically examine how legal systems establish and enforce corporate accountability in AI-driven data governance. Each framework provides a unique perspective that deepens the analysis and supports creating a comprehensive, cross-jurisdictional accountability model.

World Polity Theory (Meyer et al., 1997) describes the spread of global normative standards, such as human rights, transparency, and fiduciary duties, across national legal systems. Regarding AI governance, it clarifies why many countries adopt GDPR-inspired regulations despite differences in their political systems and institutional strengths (Greenleaf & Waters, 2022). For instance, India's DPDP Act

(2023) shows symbolic alignment with global norms by incorporating a fiduciary approach based on individual dignity and autonomy (Singh, 2023; Saxena, 2023). This theory helped reveal how international normative pressures shape national laws and why some AI accountability frameworks appear consistent in language but differ in practice, as seen with China's PIPL, which selectively integrates norms through a state-centered approach focused on sovereignty and control (Liu, 2022). Thus, World Polity Theory was key in identifying symbolic alignment versus practical differences in AI accountability models.

Regulatory Governance Theory (Black, 2008; Levi-Faur, 2011) explores how regulatory power is shared among public agencies, private companies, and non-state actors, especially in complex, fast-changing areas like AI. This theory is relevant because it highlights regulation's hybrid character, involving tools such as algorithmic audits, impact assessments, and co-regulatory codes of conduct (Yeung, 2018; Veale & Zuiderveen Borgesius, 2021). It supported the analysis by explaining how jurisdictions combine hard law, soft law, and self-regulation to enforce accountability. The Meta–GDPR case exemplifies how companies navigate fragmented or conflicting regulations, such as EU–U.S. data transfer rules, by developing internal governance to reduce compliance risks (CJEU, 2020; European Commission, 2023). Regulatory Governance Theory therefore illuminated the institutional interactions and adaptive strategies that influence corporate conduct in AI-focused settings.

Structuration Theory (Giddens, 1984) presents a dynamic framework illustrating how agency and structure interact to influence regulatory outcomes. It is especially valuable for understanding how corporations shape, adopt, or resist accountability norms, for example, through lobbying efforts or self-regulation, while simultaneously facing legal, institutional, and reputational limitations (Wright & De Hert, 2016; Yeung, 2018). This theory allowed the study to move beyond a static reading of legal texts by exploring how corporate compliance, trust-building, and public legitimacy develop over time, particularly in places where formal enforcement is weak but normative pressures, such as ethical AI guidelines, still apply. It also clarified how regulators exercise discretion within structural constraints like limited budgets or political pressures, which affects how effectively AI-related harms are managed.

Together, these frameworks offer a comprehensive basis for the study's comparative analysis. World Polity Theory accounted for the global diffusion and symbolic acceptance of AI-related legal norms. Regulatory Governance Theory exposed how accountability is negotiated through a mix of formal and informal institutions. Structuration Theory highlighted the ongoing interplay between corporate actions and structural constraints. Their combined use allowed for a deeper evaluation of how corporate liability in AI governance is shaped, contested, and operationalized, moving beyond simple doctrinal comparison to capture the institutional, behavioural, and normative dimensions of legal accountability.

7. DISCUSSION

7.1 The Legal and Economic Dimensions of Personal Data

In the current digital environment, personal data serves as both an economic asset and a legally protected interest. As digital technologies become integral to commerce, government, and everyday activities, the importance and quantity of personal data have increased significantly, raising challenging questions about corporate accountability and individual rights. Platform-based economies rely heavily on data, using personal information for predictive profiling, targeted advertising, and algorithm-driven decisions (Zuboff, 2019). Data has evolved into a form of capital that is gathered, exchanged, and monetized (Couldry and Mejias, 2019). However, this extraction frequently happens without genuine consent or transparency, leading to ethical concerns about autonomy and fairness, especially since users often lack meaningful bargaining power (Turow, 2017; Barocas and Nissenbaum, 2009).

Data protection is increasingly recognized as a fundamental right. The EU Charter (Article 8) guarantees the right to data protection, focusing on control and transparency (European Union, 2012). Likewise, India's Puttaswamy ruling (2017) affirmed privacy as a constitutional right, strengthening the concept of informational self-determination (Bhatia, 2019; González Fuster, 2014). This development reflects a wider legal acknowledgment that managing data impacts civil rights and democratic processes (Greenleaf, 2018).

Corporations are the main holders of personal data, running systems that collect large amounts of information, often governed by unclear or unbalanced user agreements (Solove, 2013; Susser, Roessler, and Nissenbaum, 2019). This situation leads to the consent fallacy, where users seem to agree to data practices without having real options (Barocas and Nissenbaum, 2009). Laws like the GDPR have encouraged companies to implement roles such as Data Protection Officers and incorporate privacy into design processes (Voigt and Von dem Bussche, 2017), though enforcement is still inconsistent, particularly in regions with fewer resources. The growth of AI-driven data processing adds further challenges since automated systems often function without human supervision, making explainability and legal responsibility more difficult (Wachter and Mittelstadt, 2019; Calo, 2015).

The dual nature of personal data, as both economic resource and protected right, creates regulatory challenges. While companies benefit financially from data use, legal frameworks must protect individuals' rights to privacy, transparency, and control by ensuring enforceable safeguards that adapt to technological changes and respect fundamental rights.

7.2 The Disruptive Role of AI in Data Governance

The emergence of AI systems has profoundly disrupted traditional legal frameworks governing personal data. As algorithmic decision-making increasingly takes the place of human judgment, established concepts such as intent, control, and accountability are being challenged (Pagallo, 2013; Calo, 2015). AI technologies, particularly those based on machine learning, operate autonomously and adaptively, handling tasks like sorting, labelling, and making decisions (Leenes et al., 2017; Burrell, 2016). This independence complicates existing legal distinctions, such as the GDPR's controller and processor roles (Voigt and Von dem Bussche, 2017), making it more difficult to determine who holds responsibility for data usage.

Legal systems often rely on fault-based liability, requiring intent or negligence. However, since AI frequently functions with little human oversight, attributing responsibility for unforeseen outcomes becomes complex (Calo, 2015; Wachter and Mittelstadt, 2019). Courts face challenges in discerning whether harm arises from human mistakes, design flaws, or the behaviour of the algorithms themselves. Many AI models operate as "black boxes," with decision-making processes that remain unclear even to their creators (Burrell, 2016). This opacity undermines legal requirements for explanation and accountability, especially when proprietary algorithms prevent external examination (Wachter, Mittelstadt, and Floridi, 2017).

Some have proposed granting legal personhood to highly autonomous AI systems, as suggested in the European Parliament's 2017 resolution, recognizing AI's role in decision-making (European Parliament, 2017). Critics contend this could allow developers to shift blame onto AI systems, thereby weakening human accountability (Pagallo, 2013). A more practical approach focuses on holding developers and users responsible for AI actions, emphasizing obligations to implement safeguards, conduct audits, and ensure transparency (Leenes et al., 2017; Wachter and Mittelstadt, 2019). Recent legislative proposals in the EU reflect this trend, aiming to align legal responsibility with the actual effects of AI.

The integration of AI into data governance represents a fundamental shift, challenging legal doctrines based on human agency and foreseeability. To protect rights and freedoms in automated contexts, legal frameworks must evolve by redefining liability, requiring transparency, and clearly assigning responsibility for AI-driven decisions.

7.3 The Legal Status of Corporations Handling Personal Data

The commercialization of personal data has positioned corporations at the heart of discussions on digital governance (Zuboff, 2019). As guardians of extensive data flows, companies face growing legal and ethical duties, although regulatory frameworks differ across jurisdictions (Gellert, 2018; Greenleaf and Waters, 2022). Legal systems categorize corporate roles in various ways. The EU's GDPR distinguishes between controllers and processors, assigning responsibilities based on who controls data use (GDPR, 2016, Art. 4; Kuner et al., 2021). India's DPDP Act (2023) introduces the concept of data fiduciaries, imposing duties aligned with constitutional privacy protections (Puttaswamy v. Union of India, 2017; Saxena, 2023). China's PIPL links corporate data practices to state interests, requiring compliance with national security and public order objectives (PIPL, 2021; Liu, 2022). Brazil's LGPD and South Africa's POPIA follow GDPR-style frameworks but with local adjustments (Greenleaf, 2021).

By contrast, the U.S. adopts a sectoral regulatory approach, governed by laws such as HIPAA and CCPA, resulting in fragmented corporate obligations depending on data type and sector (Solove and Hartzog, 2020; Cate and Mayer-Schönberger, 2013). Under the GDPR, companies must comply with rules including privacy-by-design, data protection impact assessments, and appointing data protection officers, with strict penalties that can reach €20 million or 4% of global revenue (GDPR, 2016, Arts. 25, 35, 37, 83; Tene and Polonetsky, 2012). In contrast, U.S. enforcement is fault-based, primarily targeting deceptive practices that cause demonstrable harm (Solove and Hartzog, 2020).

The effectiveness of enforcement also depends on institutional capacity. EU regulators such as CNIL and the UK's ICO have strong enforcement powers (Kuner et al., 2021), whereas India's proposed Data Protection Board faces criticism for lacking sufficient independence (Saxena, 2023). Beyond mere compliance, companies are increasingly expected to demonstrate ethical responsibility by promoting transparency, fairness, and accountability in their data handling (Floridi et al., 2018). Mechanisms such as algorithmic audits and explainability protocols are gaining traction (Wachter, Mittelstadt, and Floridi, 2017). Global soft law initiatives, including the OECD AI Principles and UNESCO's AI Ethics framework, provide voluntary guidelines for corporate conduct (OECD, 2019; UNESCO, 2021). In this changing environment, corporations are seen not only as legal entities but also as ethical actors required to align their data practices with societal values and human rights (Bennett and Raab, 2020).

7.4 Corporate Liability and Enforcement in the Digital Age

As digital ecosystems grow and AI transforms data governance, corporate accountability for personal data encounters new legal and practical challenges, especially across different jurisdictions and within fragmented regulatory frameworks. Jurisdictions vary in how they assign liability. The EU's GDPR enforces strict liability, allowing penalties up to 4% of global revenue even without proving intent or negligence (Voigt and Von dem Bussche, 2017). In contrast, the U.S. follows a fault-based approach that requires clear evidence of negligence, as seen in laws such as HIPAA and the CCPA (Solove and Hartzog, 2014). These differences reflect broader regulatory philosophies, with the EU emphasizing rights-based enforcement, while the U.S. favors market-driven regulation (Greenleaf, 2018; EU Agency for Fundamental Rights, 2020).

Although data flows freely across borders, legal jurisdiction remains limited. The GDPR's extraterritorial reach seeks to hold global companies accountable for the data of EU citizens (Kuner, 2020), but enforcement is challenging in countries with weaker regulatory oversight. The absence of global enforcement mechanisms, conflicting laws, and evidentiary challenges slow down and complicate cross-border enforcement (Bradford, 2020). This situation often leads to regulatory arbitrage, where companies take advantage of lax jurisdictions to avoid compliance (Mayer-Schönberger and Padova, 2015).

AI further complicates liability issues because legal principles based on intent, foreseeability, and proximate cause are strained by opaque, adaptive AI systems (Calo, 2015; Burrell, 2016). When harms occur, such as biased profiling or privacy breaches, it becomes difficult to identify who is responsible, especially due to the lack of transparency in AI decision-making. The unpredictable nature of AI weakens traditional ideas of causality, making legal blame hard to assign.

To address these challenges, scholars suggest adopting risk-based regulatory models and requiring mandatory audits for high-risk AI systems (Wachter and Mittelstadt, 2019). Without these changes, victims may be left without remedies, and corporate accountability risks weakening in increasingly automated settings.

7.4.1 Rethinking Legal Compliance Beyond Technical Fixes

Technical tools like privacy-by-design, DPIAs, and algorithmic audits are important in AI governance but insufficient on their own. When treated as checklists, they risk performative compliance, especially without ethical leadership, cross-functional integration, and stakeholder engagement (Voigt & Von dem Bussche, 2017; Wright & De Hert, 2016). As Wachter and Mittelstadt (2019) note, audits are ineffective if their findings do not inform decisions. The Meta GDPR fine (€1.2B in 2023) illustrates this, formal safeguards failed due to internal resistance (European Commission, 2023).

As Giddens (1984) argues, organizations shape norms, not just follow them. Microsoft's AETHER Committee embeds ethics in product design (Floridi et al., 2018), while siloed compliance creates hollow accountability. Biases, like those in the COMPAS algorithm against Black defendants, reflect the lack of participatory design (Angwin et al., 2016). Globally, fragmented laws, GDPR, India's DPDP Act,

China's PIPL, enable forum-shopping, unless checked by civil society and regulatory pressure (Greenleaf & Waters, 2022).

Legal cultures shape AI compliance, India's fiduciary model centres on dignity (Saxena, 2023), while China's PIPL prioritizes state control (Liu, 2022). This diversity shows ethical AI governance must balance local values with universal protections. Meaningful governance demands more than technical fixes, it requires leadership commitment, cross-functional coordination, ethical incentives, stakeholder inclusion, and regulatory alignment. Law alone cannot ensure ethical AI. Compliance must reflect internalized values, not just legal thresholds. Embedding relational, ethical, and participatory models into corporate culture is key to achieving transparency, fairness, and data dignity.

7.5 Evolving Models of Corporate Accountability

The scope and nature of corporate responsibility in digital environments are experiencing a significant transformation. Previously, businesses mainly understood accountability as simply adhering to regulations to avoid penalties. Today, a broader perspective is developing, focusing on ethical stewardship and proactive risk management, especially regarding data governance and AI. This new approach includes technical measures, regulatory requirements, and value-based practices designed to ensure organizations not only follow legal rules but also operate with transparency, fairness, and accountability toward the individuals whose data they handle.

7.5.1 Embedding Responsibility in Design and Practice

Over the last ten years, the concept of integrating privacy into digital systems from the start has gained strong support. Known as privacy by design, this approach insists that protecting user data should be a core part of technology development rather than an afterthought (Cavoukian, 2009). It requires privacy safeguards to be built into technical frameworks and organizational practices throughout all phases, from initial design to final implementation. Legal regulations such as the GDPR have formalized this idea, mandating that organizations implement measures that proactively secure data instead of just responding after issues arise (Voigt and Von dem Bussche, 2017). This includes appointing Data Protection Officers to oversee compliance internally and conducting Data Protection Impact Assessments for operations that might significantly affect individual rights (Wright and De Hert, 2016).

These efforts are supported by transparency tools like clear consent forms, detailed data usage notices, and channels for user grievances. Although these measures are widely used, their effectiveness often relies on being fully embedded in company culture and being properly supervised by independent regulatory bodies (Solove, 2020).

7.5.2 Building Oversight into Automated Systems

As AI becomes increasingly central to decision-making, such as in hiring or credit scoring, traditional data governance tools face new challenges. These systems often operate autonomously, using complex logic that even their creators cannot fully explain (Pasquale, 2015). To address this, legal frameworks are being enhanced with approaches better suited to the intricacies of algorithms. One such method gaining traction is the algorithmic audit, which systematically evaluates AI performance to identify discrimination, errors, or harm (Raji et al., 2020). These audits may be conducted internally or by independent parties and play a vital role in detecting hidden biases and ensuring system reliability.

Another important concept is explainability, which aims to make AI systems understandable for both users and regulators. The GDPR has begun to support this by granting individuals the right to an explanation when subjected to automated decisions (Wachter et al., 2017). While interpretations differ, the underlying idea is that automated decisions cannot remain opaque. Human-in-the-loop mechanisms are also crucial, maintaining human oversight at key points in AI operations (Binns, 2018). However, such oversight only protects against harm if human reviewers have genuine authority and do not simply approve algorithmic results without scrutiny (Zerilli et al., 2019).

7.5.3 Institutional Challenges and Enforcement Disparities

Even in regions with strong legal frameworks, enforcement often remains inconsistent. The EU benefits from established oversight bodies such as the European Data Protection Board, which has the authority and resources to coordinate audits, impose fines, and ensure compliance across member states (Bradford, 2020). By contrast, India's DPDP Act (2023) represents progress but raises concerns about the independence and effectiveness of its Data Protection Board (Rai, 2023). Similarly, Brazil's LGPD, although modeled after the GDPR, is enforced by the ANPD, which is still developing and faces resource limitations (Doneda & Monteiro, 2021). Many countries in the Global South struggle with weak institutions or lack political will to enforce accountability (Greenleaf, 2021). Multinational corporations often resist oversight by relying on legal disputes, trade secret protections, or exploiting informational imbalances to avoid scrutiny (Calo & Rosenblat, 2017).

Corporate accountability today requires more than just legal compliance. It demands a blend of ethical reflection, design-oriented safeguards, and robust oversight. While roles such as Data Protection Officers, Data Protection Impact Assessments, and privacy-by-design remain important, they are insufficient given AI's complexity. Additional measures like algorithmic audits, explainability, and human oversight are critical, though their effectiveness varies based on regulatory capacity and geopolitical factors. Addressing these enforcement gaps is both a legal obligation and an ethical necessity to achieve fairness in the digital realm.

7.5.4 Institutional Innovations and Corporate Accountability in Practice

As AI systems transform both commercial and public sectors, governments and corporations are creating new institutional approaches to balance technological progress with regulatory accountability. These include reforms in internal governance, co-regulatory frameworks, algorithmic audits, and collaborations involving multiple stakeholders.

Internal Corporate Governance Models: Companies like Microsoft have formed internal ethics committees, such as the AETHER Committee, to assess AI projects for fairness and privacy concerns (Floridi et al., 2018). Google's Model Cards also aim to increase transparency by detailing model performance and limitations (Mitchell et al., 2019). However, the dissolution of Google's external AI ethics board in 2019 highlights the vulnerability of self-regulation without genuine institutional independence.

Public-Private Co-Regulation and Soft Law: The EU's proposed AI Act introduces regulatory sandboxes that enable controlled, real-world testing of AI systems under supervision (Veale & Zuiderveen Borgesius, 2021). Singapore's Model AI Governance Framework, together with its AI Verify toolkit, promotes voluntary adoption of best practices related to explainability and fairness (IMDA, 2022), offering flexibility while fostering long-term compliance norms.

Algorithmic Auditing and Certification: New mechanisms such as third-party audits and certification seek to verify corporate claims about fairness and safety. For instance, OpenAI's GPT-4 underwent red-teaming and internal alignment checks before its release (OpenAI, 2023). In the US financial sector, Fair Lending Audits and guidance from the CFPB require algorithmic explainability, encouraging firms to integrate governance across legal and compliance functions (CFPB, 2022).

Multi-Stakeholder Governance Models: Cross-sector collaborations like the Partnership on AI develop frameworks for responsible AI, including best practices for synthetic media. Data trusts piloted in Canada and the UK provide a novel model where independent stewards oversee data access on behalf of stakeholders, embedding fiduciary principles in sensitive data governance (Hardinges et al., 2019).

Institutional Fragility and Resistance: Despite advancements, many of these innovations remain fragile. The shutdown of Google's ethics board, the Meta GDPR fine, and the opacity surrounding AI hiring audits illustrate that without enforcement and transparency, promising mechanisms may be undermined. Furthermore, reliance on soft law without binding requirements often leads to superficial compliance (Wachter & Mittelstadt, 2019).

Innovations such as ethics committees, sandboxes, audits, and multi-stakeholder partnerships represent important moves toward reflexive accountability rather than mere procedural compliance. However, their success depends on institutional strength, enforceable laws, and sustained organizational commitment. Ultimately, the legitimacy of AI governance will rest on how effectively these initiatives connect technological innovation with justice and fairness.

7.5.5 Emerging Corporate Governance Models in AI and Data Governance

AI and large-scale data processing are transforming corporate governance. Companies are increasingly evaluated not only on compliance and profitability but also on how they handle data ethics, algorithmic responsibility, and digital rights. Emerging governance frameworks, driven by legal requirements, public expectations, or reputational concerns, seek to embed ethical principles, build trust among stakeholders, and address fragmented regulations. Firms such as Salesforce, IBM, and AXA have created board-level AI oversight bodies that align data governance with broader corporate strategies. Microsoft's AETHER Committee provides a model for cross-functional review and escalation of high-risk AI projects, marking a shift toward integrated and proactive ethics governance (Floridi et al., 2018; Veale & Zuiderveen Borgesius, 2021). Effective AI oversight depends on multidisciplinary teams. Google's Model Cards and Facebook's AI System Cards promote standardized transparency for AI models (Mitchell et al., 2019), signalling a move away from isolated compliance toward ongoing, lifecycle governance. Still, many ethics teams lack real authority, creating risks of ethics washing (Wachter & Mittelstadt, 2019).

In countries like Kenya, Nigeria, and Indonesia, governance tends to be reactive and externally influenced, shaped by donor priorities or global compliance demands (Mothobi & Gillwald, 2020). Local companies often have limited capacity for AI governance. Select firms such as Safaricom and Flutterwave adopt GDPR or ISO standards to gain international credibility, but such practices remain concentrated among top-tier organizations. Regulatory nudges from bodies like Kenya's ODPC or Nigeria's NITDA have encouraged the establishment of basic compliance units, yet technical expertise is still limited (Kivuva, 2023).

Where enforcement is weak, companies rely on informal or hybrid governance approaches that combine compliance, corporate social responsibility, and trust-building efforts. In sectors like health and finance, firms create internal data charters to enhance legitimacy. In countries like India and Brazil, data governance often reflects constitutional values focused on rights such as dignity and autonomy, even where enforcement mechanisms are lacking. Governance models are expected to develop along three main paths:

1. Context-sensitive approaches adapted to local legal, cultural, and economic realities;
2. Participatory frameworks such as user councils or civil society consultations to strengthen legitimacy;
3. AI-savvy boards equipped to establish ethics-related key performance indicators and escalation procedures for high-risk systems.

Ultimately, governance must move beyond mere compliance toward value-driven frameworks that integrate ethics, transparency, and inclusiveness into institutional design. Importantly, innovation in this area should be co-developed with the Global South rather than imposed from the Global North.

7.6 The Case for International Harmonization

The current global data protection landscape is characterized by significant variation and fragmentation. As digital technologies facilitate continuous cross-border data transfers, the necessity for a coordinated international approach has grown more urgent. The absence of a unified framework complicates compliance for multinational companies and leaves individuals vulnerable to uneven privacy protections depending on where their data is processed (Greenleaf, 2021). This section examines the motivations behind efforts to harmonize data protection laws, reviews key initiatives driving this process, and reflects on the role of soft law instruments and collaborative dialogue in gradually aligning data governance standards across the globe.

7.6.1 Benefits of a Coherent Global Framework

Establishing a unified global legal framework for data privacy offers important benefits for both regulators and private sector actors. For multinational companies, it simplifies compliance by creating consistent legal standards (Kuner, 2013). Without such alignment, organizations must navigate and reconcile different legal regimes, such as Europe's GDPR and the United States' sector-specific laws, each with unique definitions, obligations, and enforcement mechanisms (Schwartz & Peifer, 2017). For individuals, harmonization could provide greater legal clarity and more consistent privacy protections. Rather than experiencing varying levels of security and access to remedies based on where their data is processed or transferred, data subjects would enjoy a common set of enforceable rights regardless of location (Gellert, 2018).

More broadly, global alignment facilitates data mobility, which is essential for digital trade, cloud computing, and AI development. Disparate data protection laws often create obstacles to lawful international data transfers, hindering cooperation and slowing technological advancement (Bradford, 2020). A shared legal framework would enable businesses and governments to handle personal data responsibly while promoting the smooth flow of information across borders.

7.6.2 Existing and Emerging Initiatives

Although no single treaty has yet unified global data protection laws, various frameworks and bilateral agreements show significant progress toward legal convergence. An early initiative was the OECD's Guidelines on the Protection of Privacy and Transborder Flows of Personal Data, which established key principles that continue to influence regulatory reforms in both member and non-member countries (OECD, 2013). These guidelines stress accountability, purpose limitation, and data security, providing a flexible framework adaptable across diverse legal systems.

In 2019, the G20 Osaka Track promoted the idea of trusted international data transfers through the principle of Data Free Flow with Trust. While not legally binding, this initiative encourages interoperability and closer coordination among governments facing the challenges of the digital economy (Aaronson, 2019). More recently, the EU–US Data Privacy Framework replaced the invalidated Privacy Shield after the Schrems II decision, which found US surveillance practices incompatible with European privacy standards (CJEU, 2020). The new framework addresses previous issues by enhancing redress options and improving oversight, bringing US data practices more in line with GDPR requirements (European Commission, 2023).

Beyond these bilateral and multilateral efforts, several countries have adopted laws inspired by the GDPR. Brazil's LGPD, Japan's APPI, and South Korea's PIPA include provisions that reflect GDPR principles, such as consent requirements, data subject rights, and rules on cross-border data transfers (Greenleaf & Waters, 2022). This growing legal harmonization reflects both regulatory learning and a strategic aim to support international trade relations.

7.6.3 Role of Soft Law and Multilateral Dialogue

Without a binding global privacy treaty, many jurisdictions turn to soft law instruments and voluntary cooperation to fill regulatory gaps. Although these tools are non-binding, they help shape norms and influence national legislation. For instance, Convention 108+ provides model principles for data governance, while the APEC Privacy Framework supports regional accountability while respecting national sovereignty (Bennett & Raab, 2020). Ethical guidelines such as the OECD AI Principles and UNESCO's AI Ethics Recommendation highlight values like fairness, transparency, and human oversight in AI development (OECD, 2019; UNESCO, 2021). While not enforceable, these frameworks guide policymaking and contribute to the formation of international standards.

Global forums like the Global Privacy Assembly and the G7 Data Protection Roundtable promote regulatory cooperation and the exchange of best practices, addressing shared challenges such as surveillance and algorithmic bias (Bradford, 2020). Instruments like Mutual Recognition Agreements and Binding Corporate Rules facilitate cross-border data flows by recognizing each other's legal adequacy (Kuner et al., 2019), fostering gradual legal alignment. Though full global harmonization remains a distant goal, regional collaboration and soft law mechanisms continue to promote a rights-based and interoperable data governance landscape. In the absence of binding international law, ethical frameworks and multilateral dialogue provide practical routes toward more consistent global regulation.

7.6.4 Comparative Analysis of Enforcement Outcomes Across Jurisdictions

Enforcement of data protection laws worldwide varies greatly in effectiveness, influenced by factors like institutional capacity, political commitment, and available resources, despite some convergence inspired by the GDPR. The European Union has the most advanced enforcement framework. Independent Data Protection Authorities, coordinated by the European Data Protection Board, have imposed significant fines, including a €1.2 billion penalty against Meta in 2023 for illegal data transfers (European Commission, 2023). However, enforcement efforts differ across member states, with stronger activity in countries like Ireland and France, and weaker enforcement in others (Greenleaf & Waters, 2022). The EU example shows how strong, coordinated institutions can drive global corporate compliance.

India's DPDP Act (2023) follows a fiduciary model but suffers from weak enforcement. The proposed Data Protection Board lacks independence and clear operational guidelines, while exemptions for state agencies reduce public trust (Saxena, 2023). Without solid oversight, fiduciary duties risk being symbolic rather than impactful. In China, enforcement of the PIPL is led by the Cyberspace Administration of China (CAC), reflecting a state-centered model that prioritizes national security over individual rights. The \$1.2 billion fine imposed on Didi Global in 2022 illustrates strict but opaque enforcement (Liu, 2022). This model emphasizes strong state control with limited transparency and little user recourse.

Brazil's LGPD, modeled on the GDPR, takes a more collaborative approach. The National Data Protection Authority (ANPD) focuses on guidance and soft enforcement, hampered more by resource constraints than legal limits. Early sanctions and expanding outreach indicate gradual strengthening of institutional capacity (Doneda & Monteiro, 2021). In the United States, there is no comprehensive federal privacy law, and enforcement is patchy across sectors and states. The Federal Trade Commission, under consumer protection authority, fined Drizly \$1.2 million in 2022 and held its CEO personally accountable (FTC, 2022). California's CPPA is enforcing the CPRA, but national enforcement remains fragmented.

In many Global South countries, enforcement capacity is especially weak. Kenya, Nigeria, and Indonesia have passed data protection laws but face challenges such as under-resourced regulators, low public awareness, and fragile institutions. Kenya's Office of the Data Protection Commissioner has taken some steps (Kivuva, 2023), but penalties are rare. Nigeria's NITDA and Indonesia's data protection authority also struggle with enforcement gaps and lack of effective deterrents. These countries also contend with dominance by foreign tech firms, creating opportunities for regulatory evasion and digital extractivism (Mothobi & Gillwald, 2020).

Legal provisions by themselves are not enough; effective enforcement relies on independent regulators, strong institutions, and geopolitical factors. The EU's approach demonstrates the potential of coordinated action, while China enforces rigorously but with limited transparency. Brazil and India represent developing enforcement systems, the U.S. shows the challenges of fragmented oversight, and the Global South underscores the critical need for capacity building and fair global regulation. Without aligned institutions and international collaboration, accountability in AI is likely to remain uneven and fragmented.

8. RESULT

The chapter highlights significant differences in how corporate responsibility for data protection is defined and enforced across various jurisdictions. Legal systems vary in assigning roles to corporate entities. The EU separates controllers from processors, India considers entities as data fiduciaries with ethical duties, and China focuses on state-centred control. These differences influence compliance requirements and regulatory results. Liability approaches also differ. The EU applies strict liability, allowing enforcement without needing proof of fault, whereas the U.S. requires showing negligence. This situation creates challenges for cross-border accountability, worsened by jurisdictional conflicts and inconsistent enforcement.

AI systems further complicate traditional legal ideas such as intent and foreseeability. Black-box algorithms make it difficult to assign liability because even developers may not fully understand how decisions are made. Although GDPR's Article 22 deals with automated decision-making, it is vague and rarely put into practice. Industry measures like algorithmic audits, explainability, and human oversight are unevenly applied, largely due to the absence of legal requirements. Soft law initiatives by organizations like UNESCO and OECD encourage ethical AI principles but have no binding power. Without being incorporated into enforceable laws, their impact on real accountability is limited.

The chapter also points out institutional inequalities. While the EU has strong regulatory authorities, many countries lack resources and capacity, which restricts effective enforcement and leads to superficial compliance. Despite attempts at international cooperation through agreements like the EU-U.S. Data Privacy Framework, OECD guidelines, and the G20 Osaka Track, global data governance remains fragmented. This fragmentation allows companies to take advantage of regulatory loopholes, weakening accountability. There is an urgent need for a clear, enforceable, and flexible global framework to address the challenges of corporate regulation in the era of AI and cross-border data flows.

9. RECOMMENDATIONS

Based on the findings of this chapter, the following recommendations are offered for three key stakeholder groups:

A. For Corporations

Integrate AI ethics into corporate governance: Establish board-level oversight for high-risk AI and data projects, supported by cross-functional ethics committees.

Operationalize privacy by design and accountability by default: Move beyond checklists—embed ethical risk assessments, explainability protocols, and algorithmic audits in all stages of system development.

Invest in participatory stakeholder engagement: Create structured mechanisms for input from users, civil society, and marginalized groups, especially when deploying AI in sensitive domains.

Adopt emerging privacy-preserving technologies: Implement differential privacy, federated learning, or blockchain-based consent tools to align innovation with compliance and public trust.

Contextualize governance in global operations: Avoid regulatory arbitrage in the Global South. Align internal policies with global human rights standards even where local laws are weak or under-enforced.

B. For Policymakers and Regulators

Strengthen institutional capacity: Invest in training, autonomy, and technical infrastructure for data protection authorities, especially in developing countries.

Encourage hybrid regulatory models: Use co-regulatory tools like sandboxes, soft law guidance, and industry certification to foster innovation without sacrificing oversight.

Facilitate legal interoperability: Develop bilateral and multilateral agreements to harmonize data protection standards and cross-border data flows, particularly where AI deployment spans multiple jurisdictions.

Mandate algorithmic transparency and impact assessments: Require firms to publish explainability reports, audit trails, and redress mechanisms for high-impact automated systems.

Promote technology-neutral legislation: Ensure that laws remain adaptable to emerging techniques like synthetic data, federated learning, and decentralized data architectures.

C. For Technologists and AI Developers

Build technical systems with legal principles in mind: Design models and data architectures that embed principles of necessity, proportionality, and non-discrimination from the outset.

Use open tools and standards for transparency: Leverage model cards, datasheets, and public documentation to facilitate external auditability and stakeholder review.

Collaborate with legal and policy teams: Co-design compliance solutions with lawyers and regulators to ensure that technical safeguards meet legal expectations.

Prototype and test with diverse datasets and users: Address fairness, bias, and contextual risks through inclusive design and pre-deployment testing.

10. CONCLUSION

The present chapter has critically examined the evolving landscape of corporate responsibility in AI-enabled data governance, revealing that legal compliance cannot be reduced to a set of technical controls or statutory checklists. Instead, meaningful accountability arises from the intersection of legal mandates, ethical leadership, institutional capacity, and participatory stakeholder engagement. Comparative legal analysis across jurisdictions (including the EU, India, China, Brazil, the U.S., and developing data markets like Kenya and Nigeria) demonstrates that while the language of data protection law is increasingly harmonized, enforcement practices and corporate responses vary dramatically.

A core insight emerging from this analysis is that corporate accountability mechanisms must move beyond reactive compliance and adopt proactive governance models. These include board-level oversight of AI systems, interdisciplinary ethics teams, and algorithmic transparency initiatives. While advanced economies are experimenting with structured internal governance and public-private regulatory models, companies in less developed data environments often face challenges related to institutional capacity, resourcing, and external dependency on global digital platforms.

Moreover, the role of emerging technologies in supporting legal and ethical objectives cannot be overlooked. Tools such as blockchain offer decentralized, auditable records for data access and consent management, enhancing transparency and non-repudiation in data transactions. Differential privacy provides mathematical guarantees for data protection, enabling firms to extract insights from sensitive datasets without exposing individual identities, particularly relevant in regulated sectors like healthcare and finance. Meanwhile, federated learning allows AI models to be trained across decentralized devices or data silos without centralizing personal data, thereby addressing concerns around data localization and cross-border transfers, a recurring legal friction in GDPR and PIPL enforcement. While these technologies are not panaceas, they offer technical affordances that align with core regulatory goals, minimizing data exposure, enhancing user autonomy, and ensuring compliance by design. Their responsible deployment, however, depends on institutional adoption, ethical frameworks, and regulatory clarity.

11. FUTURE RESEARCH DIRECTIONS

The findings of this chapter emphasize an urgent need for additional research on the changing nature of corporate accountability in the context of algorithmic governance. As legal frameworks, institutions, and technologies evolve together, several important but less examined topics arise. These future research areas are crucial for academics, policymakers, and technologists aiming to connect normative principles with practical effectiveness in data protection and AI oversight.

Algorithmic Liability and Shifting Concepts of Legal Personhood: With AI systems growing more autonomous and complex, traditional legal liability models based on foreseeability, intent, and direct causation are becoming increasingly inadequate. Future research should investigate new liability frameworks that distribute responsibility across multiple actors or functions. This includes reconsidering legal personhood in relation to autonomous agents and exploring how accountability can be maintained when the causal chain is unclear.

Data Colonialism and the Political Economy of Compliance: Research is needed to examine global power imbalances within data governance, especially how multinational corporations operate differently in countries with weak enforcement. This perspective, drawing on critical data studies and political economy, should analyze how these compliance gaps enable companies to extract data from the Global South without corresponding accountability or fair benefit sharing. Related topics include data localization, digital sovereignty, and economic fairness in emerging economies.

Institutional Design for Transnational AI Oversight: Future studies should focus on the potential structures of cross-border regulatory bodies or soft-law alliances for AI accountability. As AI transcends national boundaries, regulators face jurisdictional challenges. Scholars must evaluate the practicality, legitimacy, and enforceability of multi-stakeholder arrangements such as international AI standards organizations, cross-border auditing processes, or treaty-based frameworks for digital rights.

The Role of Civil Society and Non-State Accountability Mechanisms: The increasing role of civil society groups, journalists, and advocacy organizations in identifying algorithmic harms through watchdog platforms and investigative audits represents a new area for accountability research. Researchers should analyze the institutional contexts, legal safeguards, and influence of these actors on public awareness and regulatory action, especially in regions where formal enforcement is weak or compromised.

Together, these research directions highlight the need for interdisciplinary, diverse, and globally aware approaches to corporate accountability in the AI era. They demand empirical investigation, theoretical development, and normative consideration to ensure that advances in law and technology lead to fair, transparent, and enforceable governance. As AI becomes further embedded in society's core systems, the task is not only to regulate outcomes but also to rethink the institutions and values guiding its creation and use.

REFERENCES

Aaronson, S. A. (2019). *Data is different: Why the world needs a new approach to governing cross-border data flows*. Centre for International Governance Innovation (CIGI). *Papers*, (197), 1–17.

AI Now Institute. (2023). *Algorithmic accountability report 2023*. https://ainowinstitute.org

Angwin, J., Larson, J., Mattu, S., & Kirchner, L. (2016, May 23). *Machine bias: There's software used across the country to predict future criminals and it's biased against Blacks*. ProPublica. https://www.propublica.org/article/machine-bias-risk-assessments-in-criminal-sentencing

Barocas, S., & Nissenbaum, H. (2009). *On notice: The trouble with notice and consent*. Proceedings of the Engaging Data Forum, MIT.

Bennett, C. J., & Raab, C. D. (2020). *The governance of privacy: Policy instruments in global perspective* (3rd ed.). MIT Press.

Bhatia, G. (2019). *The transformative constitution: A radical biography in nine acts*. HarperCollins India.

Binns, R. (2018). Algorithmic accountability and public reason. *Philosophy & Technology*, *31*(4), 543–556. DOI: 10.1007/s13347-017-0263-5

Black, J. (2008). Constructing and contesting legitimacy and accountability in polycentric regulatory regimes. *Regulation & Governance*, *2*(2), 137–164. DOI: 10.1111/j.1748-5991.2008.00034.x

Bradford, A. (2020). *The Brussels effect: How the European Union rules the world*. Oxford University Press., DOI: 10.1093/oso/9780190088583.001.0001

Burrell, J. (2016). How the machine 'thinks': Understanding opacity in machine learning algorithms. *Big Data & Society*, *3*(1), 1–12. DOI: 10.1177/2053951715622512

Calo, R. (2015). Robotics and the lessons of cyberlaw. *California Law Review*, *103*(3), 513–563. DOI: 10.15779/Z389K4H

Calo, R., & Rosenblat, A. (2017). The taking economy: Uber, information, and power. *Columbia Law Review*, *117*(6), 1623–1690.

Cate, F. H., & Mayer-Schönberger, V. (2013). Notice and consent in a world of Big Data. *International Data Privacy Law*, *3*(2), 67–73. DOI: 10.1093/idpl/ipt005

Cavoukian, A. (2009). *Privacy by design: The 7 foundational principles*. Information and Privacy Commissioner of Ontario.

CFPB. (2022). *CFPB warns that black-box algorithms violate fair lending laws*. https://www.consumerfinance.gov/about-us/newsroom/cfpb-warns-that-black-box-algorithms-violate-fair-lending-laws

Couldry, N., & Mejias, U. A. (2019). *The costs of connection: How data is colonizing human life and appropriating it for capitalism*. Stanford University Press.

Court of Justice of the European Union. (2020). Case C-311/18, *Data Protection Commissioner v. Facebook Ireland and Maximillian Schrems* (Schrems II). https://curia.europa.eu/juris/document/document.jsf?text=&docid=228677

Crawford, K. (2021). *Atlas of AI: Power, politics, and the planetary costs of artificial intelligence*. Yale University Press.

Deloitte. (2022). *AI ethics survey: Global business readiness report*. Deloitte Insights. https://www2.deloitte.com/global/en/pages/about-deloitte/articles/global-ai-ethics-survey.html

Doneda, D., & Monteiro, F. (2021). Brazil's data protection law: An analysis in comparative perspective. *Journal of Data Protection & Privacy*, *4*(3), 190–202.

DPDP Act , (2023). *The Digital Personal Data Protection Act*. Ministry of Law and Justice, Government of India.

European Commission. (2020). *Data protection rules as a pillar of citizen empowerment and the EU's approach to the digital transition*. https://ec.europa.eu/info/law/law-topic/data-protection_en

European Commission. (2023). *EU–U.S. Data Privacy Framework: Irish DPC decision on Meta*. https://commission.europa.eu/law/law-topic/data-protection/data-transfers-outside-eu/eu-us-data-transfers_en

European Parliament. (2017). *Civil Law Rules on Robotics*. https://www.europarl.europa.eu/doceo/document/A-8-2017-0005_EN.html

European Union. (2012). *Charter of Fundamental Rights of the European Union*. https://eur-lex.europa.eu/legal-content/EN/TXT/?uri=celex%3A12012P%2FTXT

European Union Agency for Fundamental Rights. (2020). *Data protection as a fundamental right*. https://fra.europa.eu/en

Floridi, L., Cowls, J., Beltrametti, M., Chatila, R., Chazerand, P., Dignum, V., Luetge, C., Madelin, R., Pagallo, U., Rossi, F., Schafer, B., Valcke, P., & Vayena, E. (2018). AI4People—An ethical framework for a good AI society: Opportunities, risks, principles, and recommendations. *Minds and Machines*, *28*(4), 689–707. DOI: 10.1007/s11023-018-9482-5

FTC. (2022). *FTC finalizes order requiring Drizly to improve data security and hold CEO accountable*. https://www.ftc.gov

GDPR. (2016). *Regulation (EU) 2016/679 of the European Parliament and of the Council (General Data Protection Regulation)*. Official Journal of the European Union.

Gellert, R. (2018). Understanding the notion of risk in the General Data Protection Regulation. *Computer Law & Security Review*, *34*(2), 279–288. DOI: 10.1016/j.clsr.2017.12.003

Giddens, A. (1984). *The constitution of society: Outline of the theory of structuration*. Polity Press.

González Fuster, G. (2014). *The emergence of personal data protection as a fundamental right of the EU*. Springer., DOI: 10.1007/978-3-319-05023-2

Greenleaf, G. (2018). *Global data privacy laws 2017: 120 national data privacy laws, including Indonesia and Turkey*. Privacy Laws & Business International Report, 147, 10–13. https://papers.ssrn.com/sol3/papers.cfm?abstract_id=2993035

Greenleaf, G. (2021). Global data privacy laws 2021: Despite COVID delays, 145 laws show GDPR dominance. *SSRN*, *169*, 1–7. DOI: 10.2139/ssrn.3836348

Greenleaf, G., & Waters, N. (2022). Global convergence of data privacy standards: GDPR dominance or regulatory competition? *Computer Law & Security Review*, *46*, 105738. DOI: 10.1016/j.clsr.2022.105738

Hardinges, J., Wells, P., Ho, M., & Dencik, L. (2019). *Data trusts: Lessons from three pilots*. Open Data Institute. https://theodi.org

IDC (International Data Corporation). (2023). *Global DataSphere forecast 2023–2028*. IDC Market Analysis Report. https://www.idc.com/getdoc.jsp?containerId=US50471623

IMDA. (2022). *AI Verify: Evaluation toolkit for trusted AI*. Infocomm Media Development Authority of Singapore. https://www.imda.gov.sg

Kivuva, R. (2023). Data protection in Kenya: Early enforcement under the 2019 Act. *African Law Review*, *11*(2), 85–99.

Kuner, C. (2013). *Transborder data flows and data privacy law*. Oxford University Press. DOI: 10.1093/acprof:oso/9780199674619.001.0001

Kuner, C. (2020). The GDPR and its extraterritorial reach: Challenges and responses. *International Data Privacy Law, 10*(4), 231–245. DOI: 10.1093/idpl/ipx023

Kuner, C., Bygrave, L. A., & Docksey, C. (Eds.). (2021). *The EU General Data Protection Regulation (GDPR): A commentary*. Oxford University Press.

Kuner, C., Cate, F. H., Lynskey, O., & Millard, C. (2017). Machine learning with personal data: Is data protection law smart enough to meet the challenge? *International Data Privacy Law*, *7*(1), 1–3. DOI: 10.1093/idpl/ipx003

Leenes, R., Palmerini, E., Koops, B.-J., Bertolini, A., Salvini, P., & Lucivero, F. (2017). Regulatory challenges of robotics: Some guidelines for addressing legal and ethical issues. *Law, Innovation and Technology*, *9*(1), 1–44. DOI: 10.1080/17579961.2017.1304921

Levi-Faur, D. (2011). Regulatory capitalism and the reassertion of the public interest. *Policy and Society*, *30*(4), 289–297. DOI: 10.1016/j.polsoc.2011.10.001

Liu, H. (2022). China's Personal Information Protection Law: An analysis in the global context. *Computer Law & Security Review*, *45*, 105591. DOI: 10.1016/j.clsr.2022.105591

Mayer-Schönberger, V., & Padova, T. (2015). Regime complexity and regulatory design: The case of data privacy in the EU and the USA. *Journal of European Public Policy*, *22*(7), 1036–1053. DOI: 10.1080/13501763.2015.1020835

Meyer, J. W., Boli, J., Thomas, G. M., & Ramirez, F. O. (1997). World society and the nation-state. *American Journal of Sociology*, *103*(1), 144–181. DOI: 10.1086/231174

Mitchell, M., Wu, S., Zaldivar, A., Barnes, P., Vasserman, L., Hutchinson, B., & Gebru, T. (2019). *Model cards for model reporting*. In *Proceedings of the Conference on Fairness, Accountability, and Transparency* (pp. 220–229). https://doi.org/ DOI: 10.1145/3287560.3287596

Mothobi, O., & Gillwald, A. (2020). *The state of data protection in Africa: Mapping legislative gaps and enforcement challenges*. Research ICT Africa.

OECD. (2013). *OECD Guidelines on the Protection of Privacy and Transborder Flows of Personal Data*. https://www.oecd.org

OECD. (2019). *Recommendation of the Council on Artificial Intelligence*. OECD Legal Instruments. https://legalinstruments.oecd.org/en/instruments/OECD-LEGAL-0449

Open, A. I. (2023). *GPT-4 Technical Report.* https://openai.com/research/gpt-4

Pagallo, U. (2013). *The laws of robots: Crimes, contracts, and torts.* Springer., DOI: 10.1007/978-94-007-6564-1

Pagallo, U. (2017). The impact of AI on legal responsibility, liability, and accountability. *Philosophy & Technology, 31*(4), 543–567. DOI: 10.1007/s13347-017-0263-5

Pasquale, F. (2015). *The black box society: The secret algorithms that control money and information.* Harvard University Press. DOI: 10.4159/harvard.9780674736061

PIPL. (2021). *Personal Information Protection Law of the People's Republic of China.* Standing Committee of the National People's Congress.

Puttaswamy v. Union of India, (2017). Writ Petition (Civil) No. 494 of 2012, Supreme Court of India.

Rai, S. (2023). The making of India's data protection law: Constitutional origins and regulatory concerns. *Indian Journal of Law and Technology, 19*(1), 45–72.

Raji, I. D., Smart, A., White, R., Mitchell, M., Gebru, T., Hutchinson, B., & Barnes, P. (2020). *Closing the AI accountability gap: Defining an end-to-end framework for internal algorithmic auditing. Proceedings of the 2020 Conference on Fairness, Accountability, and Transparency*, 33–44. DOI: 10.1145/3351095.3372873

Regulation (EU) 2016/679 of the European Parliament and of the Council of 27 April 2016 on the protection of natural persons with regard to the processing of personal data and on the free movement of such data (General Data Protection Regulation). Official Journal of the European Union, L119, 1–88.

Sartor, G. (2020). Artificial intelligence and legal responsibility. In Dubber, M. D., Pasquale, F., & Das, S. (Eds.), *The Oxford handbook of ethics of AI* (pp. 267–284). Oxford University Press.

Saxena, R. (2023). Data fiduciaries and digital constitutionalism: India's approach to data protection. *Indian Journal of Law and Technology, 19*(1), 1–20.

Schwartz, P. M., & Peifer, K. N. (2017). Transatlantic data privacy law. *The Georgetown Law Journal, 106*(1), 115–178.

Shaffer, G., & Pollack, M. A. (2010). Hard vs. soft law: Alternatives, complements, and antagonists in international governance. *Minnesota Law Review, 94*, 706–799.

Singh, M. P. (2023). Data protection and the Indian Constitution: The role of fiduciary duty. *Indian Journal of Constitutional Law, 17*(1), 45–63.

Solove, D. J. (2013). Privacy self-management and the consent dilemma. *Harvard Law Review, 126*(7), 1880–1903.

Solove, D. J. (2020). The myth of the privacy paradox. *The George Washington Law Review, 89*(1), 1–56.

Solove, D. J., & Hartzog, W. (2014). The FTC and the new common law of privacy. *Columbia Law Review, 114*(3), 583–676. https://www.columbialawreview.org

Susser, D., Roessler, B., & Nissenbaum, H. (2019). Online manipulation: Hidden influences in a digital world. *Georgetown Law Technology Review, 4*(1), 1–45.

Tene, O., & Polonetsky, J. (2012). Big data for all: Privacy and user control in the age of analytics. *Northwestern Journal of Technology and Intellectual Property, 11*(5), 239–273.

Tisné, M. (2020). *The data delusion: Protecting individual data isn't enough when the harm is collective.* MIT Technology Review. https://www.technologyreview.com/2020/07/01/1004540/data-privacy-individual-collective-rights/

Turow, J. (2017). *The aisles have eyes: How retailers track your shopping, strip your privacy, and define your power.* Yale University Press.

UNCTAD. (United Nations Conference on Trade and Development). (2023). *Data protection and privacy legislation worldwide.* https://unctad.org/page/data-protection-and-privacy-legislation-worldwide

UNESCO. (2021). *Recommendation on the Ethics of Artificial Intelligence.* United Nations Educational, Scientific and Cultural Organization. https://unesdoc.unesco.org/ark:/48223/pf0000381137

Veale, M., & Zuiderveen Borgesius, F. (2021). Demystifying the Draft EU Artificial Intelligence Act. *Computer Law Review International, 22*(4), 97–112. DOI: 10.9785/cri-2021-220402

Voigt, P., & Von dem Bussche, A. (2017). *The EU General Data Protection Regulation (GDPR): A practical guide.* Springer., DOI: 10.1007/978-3-319-57959-7

Wachter, S., & Mittelstadt, B. (2019). *A right to reasonable inferences: Re-thinking data protection law in the age of Big Data and AI.* Columbia Business Law Review, 2019(2), 494–620. https://papers.ssrn.com/sol3/papers.cfm?abstract_id=3248829

Wachter, S., Mittelstadt, B., & Floridi, L. (2017). Why a right to explanation of automated decision-making does not exist in the General Data Protection Regulation. *International Data Privacy Law, 7*(2), 76–99. DOI: 10.1093/idpl/ipx005

World Economic Forum. (2011). *Personal data: The emergence of a new asset class*. https://www3.weforum.org/docs/WEF_ITTC_PersonalDataNewAsset_Report_2011.pdf

Wright, D., & De Hert, P. (2016). *Enforcing privacy: Regulatory, legal and technological approaches*. Springer. DOI: 10.1007/978-3-319-25047-2

Yeung, K. (2018). Algorithmic regulation: A critical interrogation. *Regulation & Governance, 12*(4), 505–523. DOI: 10.1111/rego.12158

Zerilli, J., Knott, A., Maclaurin, J., & Gavaghan, C. (2019). Transparency in algorithmic and human decision-making: Is there a double standard? *Philosophy & Technology, 32*(4), 661–683. DOI: 10.1007/s13347-018-0330-6

Zuboff, S. (2019). *The age of surveillance capitalism: The fight for a human future at the new frontier of power*. PublicAffairs.

KEY TERMS AND DEFINITIONS

Black Box: The term Black Box is used to describes system, in technology or computing, where the inner processes are hidden or not easily understood. In such systems, the inputs and the results can be observed, but the method by which the results are generated is unclear or inaccessible, making interpretation difficult.

Artificial Intelligence: The term refers to the development of computer-based systems that can perform tasks typically needing human intellect, such as reasoning, learning, recognizing patterns, and making decisions. These systems are designed to mimic cognitive functions to some extent.

Machine Learning: This is a method used in computing where systems are designed to learn from data and improve their performance over time without being given direct instructions for every task. It allows programs to find patterns, make decisions, or predictions based on experience gathered from the input data.

Data Protection Officers (DPOs): A Data Protection Officer is an individual appointed within an organization to oversee matters related to the handling of personal information. They ensure that data management practices comply with applicable privacy laws, and they serve as a liaison between the organization, regulatory authorities, and individuals whose data is being processed.

Data Protection Impact Assessment (DPIA): This is a process carried out to evaluate how a project or operation might affect personal privacy and data security. It aims to detect risks related to the use of personal information and helps organizations implement strategies to reduce or prevent those risks before any data processing begins.

Compilation of References

Aaronson, S. A. (2019). *Data is different: Why the world needs a new approach to governing cross-border data flows*. Centre for International Governance Innovation (CIGI). *Papers*, (197), 1–17.

Abdullah, Z., Dahlan, N. M., Dahlan, A., Irfan bin, A. F., & Arifin, A. S. (2023). Cybersecurity awareness on personal data protection using game-based learning. *Information Management and Business Review*, *15*(3(I)), 497–503. DOI: 10.22610/imbr.v15i3(I).3559

Acilar, A., & Sæbø, Ø. (2023). Towards Understanding the Gender Digital Divide: A Systematic Literature Review. *Global Knowledge, Memory and Communication*, *72*(3), 233–249. DOI: 10.1108/GKMC-09-2021-0147

ACLU of Illinois. (2021). Biometric Information Privacy Act (BIPA). https://www.aclu-il.org/campaigns-initiatives/biometric-information-privacy-act-bipa

Adhikari, A. S. (2024). The Concept of International Security. *Hasanuddin Journal of International Affairs*, 4(2), 78-89. https://journal.unhas.ac.id/index.php/hujia/article/view/34797

Admass, W. S., Munaye, Y. Y., & Diro, A. A. (2024). Cyber Security: State of the Art, Challenges, and Future Directions. *Cyber Security and Application*, *2*, 100031. DOI: 10.1016/j.csa.2023.100031

Ahmadi, S. (2024). Systematic literature review on cloud computing security: Threats and mitigation strategies. *Journal of Information Security*, *15*(02), 148–167. DOI: 10.4236/jis.2024.152010

Aho, B., & Duffield, R. (2020). Beyond surveillance capitalism: Privacy, regulation and big data in Europe and China. *Economy and Society*, *49*(2), 187–212. DOI: 10.1080/03085147.2019.1690275

AI Now Institute. (2023). *Algorithmic accountability report 2023*. https://ainowinstitute.org

Aidun, E. (2025, March 5). *Data Privacy in the digital age: A comparative analysis of U.S. and EU Regulations*. University of Cincinnati Law Review Journal. https://uclawreview.org/2025/03/05/data-privacy-in-the-digital-age-a-comparative-analysis-of-u-s-and-eu-regulations/

Aiello, S. (2024). Privacy principles and harms: Balancing Protection and Innovation. *Journal of Cybersecurity Education, Research and Practice, 2024*(1). DOI: 10.62915/2472-2707.1167

Ajana, B. (2012). Biometric citizenship. *Citizenship Studies, 16*(7), 851–870. DOI: 10.1080/13621025.2012.669962

Ajzen, I. (1991). The theory of planned behavior. *Organizational Behavior and Human Decision Processes, 50*(2), 179–211. DOI: 10.1016/0749-5978(91)90020-T

Ajzen, I. (2020). The theory of planned behavior: Frequently asked questions. *Human Behavior and Emerging Technologies, 2*(4), 314–324. DOI: 10.1002/hbe2.195

AlDaajeh, S., Saleous, H., Alrabaee, S., Barka, E., Breitinger, F., & Choo, K.-K. R. (2022). The Role of National Cybersecurity Strategies on the Improvement of Cybersecurity Education. *Computers & Security, 119*, 102754. DOI: 10.1016/j.cose.2022.102754

Aleksejeva, J. (2025). How effectively does GDPR address dark patterns in consent mechanisms targeting minors, and what legal, regulatory, and technological measures can be implemented to strengthen its protections?.

AlKhanafseh, M., & Surakhi, O. (2024). Evidence preservation in digital forensics: An Approach using Blockchain and LSTM-based steganography. *Electronics (Basel), 13*(18), 3729. DOI: 10.3390/electronics13183729

Alotaibi, S., Alruban, A., Furnell, S., & Clarke, N. (2019). A Novel Behaviour Profiling Approach to Continuous Authentication for Mobile Applications. 246. DOI: 10.5220/0007313302460251

AlSalem, T., Almaiah, M., & Lutfi, A. (2023). Cybersecurity risk analysis in the IOT: A systematic review. *Electronics (Basel), 12*(18), 3958. DOI: 10.3390/electronics12183958

Amal Chandra, C. (2024). Strengthening India's Cybersecurity and Data Privacy Landscape: A Comprehensive Overview. *The Indian Journal of Public Administration, 70*(3), 466–478. DOI: 10.1177/00195561241271616

Amingad, S. C., Rahul, M., Sathvik Reddy, P. S., & Gupta, N. S. (2023). Enhancing Public Safety with AI-Powered Intelligent Surveillance: An Examination of Immediate Incident Detection and Rapid Response in Urban Settings. *2023 International Conference on Advances in Computation, Communication and Information Technology (ICAICCIT)*, 205. DOI: 10.1109/ICAICCIT60255.2023.10465690

Andrejevic, M. (2007). Surveillance in the digital enclosure. *Communication Review*, *10*(4), 295–317. DOI: 10.1080/10714420701715365

Angwin, J., Larson, J., Mattu, S., & Kirchner, L. (2016, May 23). *Machine bias: There's software used across the country to predict future criminals and it's biased against Blacks*. ProPublica. https://www.propublica.org/article/machine-bias-risk-assessments-in-criminal-sentencing

Apeh, A. J., Hassan, A. O., Oyewole, O. O., Fakeyede, O. G., Okeleke, P. A., & Adaramodu, O. R. (2023). GRC strategies in Modern Cloud Infrastructures: A review of compliance challenges. *Computer Science &amp. IT Research Journal*, *4*(2), 111–125. DOI: 10.51594/csitrj.v4i2.609

Ardabili, B. R., Pazho, A. D., Noghre, G. A., Neff, C., Bhaskararayuni, S. D., Ravindran, A., Reid, S., & Tabkhi, H. (2023). Understanding Policy and Technical Aspects of AI-enabled Smart Video Surveillance to Address Public Safety. *Computational Urban Science*, *3*(1), 21. Advance online publication. DOI: 10.1007/s43762-023-00097-8

Ardebili, A. A., Lezzi, M., & Pourmadadkar, M. (2024). Risk assessment for cyber resilience of critical infrastructures: Methods, governance, and standards. *Applied Sciences (Basel, Switzerland)*, *14*(24), 11807. DOI: 10.3390/app142411807

Argyris, C., & Schön, D. A. (1996). *Organizational learning II: Theory, method, and practice*. Addison-Wesley.

Ari, A. A. A., Ngangmo, O. K., Titouna, C., & Thiare, O. Kolyang, Mohamadou, A., & Gueroui, A.M. (2024). Enabling Privacy and Security in Cloud of Things: Architecture, Applications, Security & Privacy Challenges. *Applied Computing and Informatics*, 20(1-2), 119-141. https://www.emerald.com/aci/article/20/1-2/119/1223199

Arnell, P., & Faturoti, B. (2023). The prosecution of cybercrime – why transnational and extraterritorial jurisdiction should be resisted. *International Review of Law Computers & Technology*, *37*(1), 29–51. DOI: 10.1080/13600869.2022.2061888

Arora, A., Barrett, M., Lee, E., Oborn, E., & Prince, K. (2023). Risk and the future of AI: Algorithmic bias, Data Colonialism, and marginalization. *Information and Organization*, *33*(3), 100478. DOI: 10.1016/j.infoandorg.2023.100478

Aswathy, S. U., & Tyagi, A. K. (2022). Privacy breaches through cyber vulnerabilities: Critical issues, open challenges, and possible countermeasures for the future. In *Security and Privacy-Preserving Techniques in Wireless Robotics* (pp. 163–210). CRC Press. DOI: 10.1201/9781003156406-14

Ayalew, Y. E. (2022). Untrodden paths towards the right to privacy in the digital era under African human rights law. *International Data Privacy Law*, *12*(1), 16–32. DOI: 10.1093/idpl/ipab027

Babatunde, G. O., Amoo, O. O., Mustapha, S. D., & Ige, A. B. (2022). Addressing privacy compliance challenges with a cross-border data protection framework for U.S. and Canada. *International Journal of Frontiers in Science and Technology Research, 3*(1), 067–083. DOI: 10.53294/ijfstr.2022.3.1.0043

Bacon, A. (2023). Children's safety in the digital age: A look at identity verification legislation in the United States.

Bakare, S. S., Adeniyi, A. O., Akpoukwe, C. U., & Ench, N. E. (2024). Data Privacy Law and Compliance: A Comparative Review of the EU GDPR and USA Regulations. *Computer Science & IT Research Journal*, 5(3), 528-543. https://www.fepbl.com/index.php/csitrj/article/view/859

Bakare, S. S., Adeniyi, A. O., Akpuokwe, C. U., & Eneh, N. E. (2024). Data privacy laws and compliance: a comparative review of the EU GDPR and USA regulations.

Bakker, A. B., & Demerouti, E. (2017). Job demands–resources theory: Taking stock and looking forward. *Journal of Occupational Health Psychology*, *22*(3), 273–285. DOI: 10.1037/ocp0000056 PMID: 27732008

Balasubramaniam, N., Kauppinen, M., Rannisto, A., Hiekkanen, K., & Kujala, S. (2023). Transparency and explainability of AI systems: From ethical guidelines to requirements. *Information and Software Technology*, *159*, 107197. DOI: 10.1016/j.infsof.2023.107197

Bandura, A. (1986). *Social foundations of thought and action: A social cognitive theory*. Prentice-Hall.

Baram, G. (2024). Cyber diplomacy through official public attribution: Paving the way for global norms. *International Studies Perspectives, 22*(?),(ekae022). DOI: 10.1093/isp/ekae022

Barocas, S., & Nissenbaum, H. (2009). *On notice: The trouble with notice and consent*. Proceedings of the Engaging Data Forum, MIT.

Barrett, L. F., Adolphs, R., Marsella, S., Martinez, A. M., & Pollak, S. D. (2019). Emotional expressions reconsidered: Challenges to inferring emotion from human facial movements. *Psychological Science in the Public Interest, 20*(1), 1–68. DOI: 10.1177/1529100619832930 PMID: 31313636

Bayer, J. (2022). Procedural rights as safeguard for human rights in platform regulation. *Policy and Internet, 14*(4), 755–771. DOI: 10.1002/poi3.298

Becker, G. S. (1968). Crime and punishment: An economic approach. *Journal of Political Economy, 76*(2), 169–217. DOI: 10.1086/259394

Beduschi, A. (2024). Synthetic Data Protection: Towards a paradigm change in data regulation? *Big Data & Society, 11*(1), 20539517241231277. Advance online publication. DOI: 10.1177/20539517241231277

Belenguer, L. (2022). Ai Bias: Exploring discriminatory algorithmic decision-making models and the application of possible machine-centric solutions adapted from the pharmaceutical industry. *AI and Ethics, 2*(4), 771–787. DOI: 10.1007/s43681-022-00138-8

Belli, L., Gaspar, W. B., & Singh Jaswant, S. (2024). Data sovereignty and data transfers as fundamental elements of Digital Transformation: Lessons from the BRICS countries. *Computer Law & Security Review, 54*, 106017. DOI: 10.1016/j.clsr.2024.106017

Benjamin, R. (2023). Race after technology. In *Social Theory Re-Wired* (pp. 405–415). Routledge. DOI: 10.4324/9781003320609-52

Bennett, C. J. (2012). The Accountability Approach to Privacy and Data Protection: Assumptions and Caveats. In Guagnin, D., Hempel, L., Ilten, C., Kroener, I., Neyland, D., & Postigo, H. (Eds.), *Managing Privacy through Accountability*. Palgrave Macmillan., DOI: 10.1057/9781137032225_3

Bennett, C. J., & Raab, C. D. (2020). *The governance of privacy: Policy instruments in global perspective* (3rd ed.). MIT Press.

Berman, P. S. (2018). Legal Jurisdiction and the Deterritorialization of Data. SSRN Electronic Journal. DOI: 10.2139/ssrn.3134782

Bhalavat, D., Doshi, A., Keni, N., & Shah, P. R. (2024). Automated compliance: A privacy-focused solution for GDPR and DPDPA adherence. *2024 13th International Conference on System Modeling & Advancement in Research Trends (SMART)*, 831–837. DOI: 10.1109/SMART63812.2024.10882514

Bhandari, V., Kak, A., Parsheera, S., & Rahman, F. (2017). An Analysis of Puttaswamy: The Supreme Court's Privacy Verdict. IndraStra Global, 11, https://www.ssoar.info/ssoar/handle/document/54766

Bhatia, G. (2019). *The transformative constitution: A radical biography in nine acts*. HarperCollins India.

Bhushan, V. (2024). EMPOWERING INDIVIDUALS: A DEEP DIVE INTO THE DIGITAL PERSONAL DATA PROTECTION ACT, 2023. *International Journal of Advanced Research, 12*(5), 891–902. DOI: 10.21474/IJAR01/18799

Biega, A. J., Potash, P., Daumé, H., Diaz, F., & Finck, M. (2020). Operationalizing the legal principle of data minimization for personalization. *Proceedings of the 43rd International ACM SIGIR Conference on Research and Development in Information Retrieval*, 399–408. DOI: 10.1145/3397271.3401034

Biewendt, M., Blaschke, F., & Böhnert, A. (2021). A review of contemporary challenges in business culture. *International Journal of Applied Research in Business and Management, 2*(1), 1–12. DOI: 10.51137/ijarbm.2021.2.1.1

Binns, R. (2018). Algorithmic accountability and public reason. *Philosophy & Technology, 31*(4), 543–556. DOI: 10.1007/s13347-017-0263-5

Binns, R. (2018). Fairness in machine learning: Lessons from political philosophy. *Proceedings of the 2018 Conference on Fairness, Accountability, and Transparency*, 149–159.

Birrell, E., Rodolitz, J., Ding, A. A., Lee, J., McReynolds, E., Hutson, J., & Lerner, A. (2024). SoK: Technical Implementation and Human Impact of Internet Privacy Regulations. *2022 IEEE Symposium on Security and Privacy (SP)*, 673. DOI: 10.1109/SP54263.2024.00206

Black, J. (2008). Constructing and contesting legitimacy and accountability in polycentric regulatory regimes. *Regulation & Governance, 2*(2), 137–164. DOI: 10.1111/j.1748-5991.2008.00034.x

Blix, F., Elshekeil, S. A., & Laoyookhong, S. (2017). Data protection by design in systems development: From legal requirements to technical solutions. 2017 12th International Conference for Internet Technology and Secured Transactions (ICITST), 98. DOI: 10.23919/ICITST.2017.8356355

Bogiatzis-Gibbons, D. J. (2024). Beyond Individual Accountability: (Re-)Asserting Democratic Control of AI. *2022 ACM Conference on Fairness, Accountability, and Transparency*, 2017, 74. DOI: 10.1145/3630106.3658541

Bok, H. (2022). *Freedom and responsibility*. Princeton University Press. DOI: 10.2307/j.ctt7s9q6

Bosnjak, M., Ajzen, I., & Schmidt, P. (2020). The theory of planned behavior: Selected recent advances and applications. *Europe's Journal of Psychology*, *16*(3), 352–356. DOI: 10.5964/ejop.v16i3.3107 PMID: 33680187

Boyd, D. M., & Nicole, B. (2007). Social Network Sites: Definition, History, and Scholarship. *Journal of Computer-Mediated Communication*, *13*(1), 210–230. DOI: 10.1111/j.1083-6101.2007.00393.x

Boyne, S. M. (2018). Data protection in the United States. *The American Journal of Comparative Law*, *66*(suppl_1), 299–343. DOI: 10.1093/ajcl/avy016

Bradford, A. (2020). *The Brussels effect: How the European Union rules the world*. Oxford University Press. DOI: 10.1093/oso/9780190088583.001.0001

Bradford, L., Aboy, M., & Liddell, K. (2021). Standard contractual clauses for cross-border transfers of health data after Schrems II. *Journal of Law and the Biosciences*, *8*(1), lsab007. Advance online publication. DOI: 10.1093/jlb/lsab007

Brodin, M. (2019). A framework for GDPR compliance for small- and medium-sized enterprises. *European Journal for Security Research*, *4*(2), 243–264. DOI: 10.1007/s41125-019-00042-z

Browne, S. (2012). Race and surveillance. In *Routledge handbook of surveillance studies* (pp. 72–79). Routledge. DOI: 10.4324/9780203814949.ch1_2_d

Brown, J. M., & Fazal, T. M. (2021). #SorryNotSorry: Why States Neither Confirm Nor Deny Responsibility for Cyber Operations. *European Journal of International Security*, *6*(4), 401–417. DOI: 10.1017/eis.2021.18

Brown-Jackson, K. L. (2022). Intersections of Telemedicine/Telehealth and Cybersecurity: The Age of Resilience and COVID-19. *Science Bulletin*, *27*(1), 1–11. https://sciendo.com/article/10.2478/bsaft-2022-0001 PMID: 36545951

Bryant, J. (2021, March 5). *Facebook's $650M BIPA settlement 'a make-or-break moment*. IAPP. https://iapp.org/news/a/facebooks-650m-bipa-settlement-a-make-or-break-moment

Büchi, M., Festic, N., & Latzer, M. (2022). The chilling effects of digital dataveillance: A theoretical model and an empirical research agenda. *Big Data & Society*, *9*(1), 20539517211065368. DOI: 10.1177/20539517211065368

Buolamwini, J., & Gebru, T. (2018). Gender shades: Intersectional accuracy disparities in commercial gender classification. *Proceedings of the 1st Conference on Fairness, Accountability and Transparency*, 77–91.

Buolamwini, J., & Gebru, T. (2018, January). Gender shades: Intersectional accuracy disparities in commercial gender classification. In *Conference on fairness, accountability and transparency* (pp. 77-91). PMLR.

Burrell, D. N. (2024). Understanding Cognitive and Behavioral Psychological Factors that Lead to Cybersecurity Breaches in Healthcare. *RAIS Journal for Social Sciences*, *8*(2), 43–53.

Burrell, D. N., Aridi, A. S., McLester, Q., Shufutinsky, A., Nobles, C., Dawson, M., & Muller, S. R. (2021). Exploring system thinking leadership approaches to the healthcare cybersecurity environment. [IJEACH]. *International Journal of Extreme Automation and Connectivity in Healthcare*, *3*(2), 20–32. DOI: 10.4018/IJEACH.2021070103

Burrell, D. N., Nobles, C., Cusak, A., Omar, M., & Gillesania, L. (2022). Cybercrime and the nature of insider threat complexities in healthcare and biotechnology engineering organizations. *Journal of Crime and Criminal Behavior*, *2*(2), 131–144. DOI: 10.47509/JCCB.2022.v02i02.04

Burrell, J. (2016). How the machine 'thinks': Understanding opacity in machine learning algorithms. *Big Data & Society*, *3*(1), 1–12. DOI: 10.1177/2053951715622512

Bussell, J. (2025). Cyberspace. *Britannica*. https://www.britannica.com/topic/cyberspace

Busuioc, M., Curtin, D., & Almada, M. (2022). Reclaiming transparency: Contesting the logics of secrecy within the AI act. *European Law Open*, *2*(1), 79–105. DOI: 10.1017/elo.2022.47

Bygrave, L. (2002). *Data Protection Law: Approaching Its Rationale, Logic, and Limits*. Kluwer Law International.

Cains, M. G., Flora, L., Taber, D., King, Z., & Henshel, D. S. (2021). Defining cyber security and cyber security risk within a multidisciplinary context using expert elicitation. *Risk Analysis*, *42*(8), 1643–1669. DOI: 10.1111/risa.13687

Calo, R. (2015). Robotics and the lessons of cyberlaw. *California Law Review, 103*(3), 513–563. DOI: 10.15779/Z389K4H

Calo, R., & Rosenblat, A. (2017). The taking economy: Uber, information, and power. *Columbia Law Review, 117*(6), 1623–1690.

Cate, F. H., & Mayer-Schönberger, V. (2013). Notice and consent in a world of Big Data. *International Data Privacy Law, 3*(2), 67–73. DOI: 10.1093/idpl/ipt005

Cavalari, R. N., Gillis, J. M., Kruser, N., & Romanczyk, R. G. (2015). Digital communication and records in service provision and supervision: Regulation and practice. *Behavior Analysis in Practice, 8*(2), 176–189. DOI: 10.1007/s40617-014-0030-3 PMID: 27703917

Cavoukian, A. (2009). *Privacy by Design: Taking on the Challenge*, Canadian Electronic Library. Canada. Retrieved from https://coilink.org/20.500.12592/9965z2 on 15 Jul 2025. COI: 20.500.12592/9965z2.

Cavoukian, A. (2009). Privacy by design: The 7 foundational principles. https://www.ipc.on.ca/wp-content/uploads/resources/7foundationalprinciples.pdf

Cavoukian, A. (2009). *Privacy by design: The 7 foundational principles*. Information and Privacy Commissioner of Ontario.

CFPB. (2022). *CFPB warns that black-box algorithms violate fair lending laws.* https://www.consumerfinance.gov/about-us/newsroom/cfpb-warns-that-black-box-algorithms-violate-fair-lending-laws

Chander, A. (2020). Is Data Localization a Solution for Schrems II? SSRN Electronic Journal. DOI: 10.2139/ssrn.3662626

Chander, A., & Lê, U. P. (2015). Data nationalism. *Emory Law Journal, 64*(3), 677–739.

Chandra, D. (2025). Examining the Contours and Challenges of National Cybercrime Reporting Portal in Countering Digital Financial Frauds. *Journal of Victimology and Victim Justice, 8*(1), 65–83. DOI: 10.1177/25166069241306546

Cheney-Lippold, J. (2017). We are data: Algorithms and the making of our digital selves. In *We are data*. New York University Press. DOI: 10.18574/nyu/9781479888702.001.0001

Chen, Y. (2022). Information Security Management: Compliance Challenges and new directions. *Journal of Information Technology Case and Application Research, 24*(4), 243–249. DOI: 10.1080/15228053.2022.2148979

Chidiac, M., Ross, C., Marston, H. R., & Freeman, S. (2022). Age and Gender Perspectives on Social Media and Technology Practices during the COVID-19 Pandemic. *International Journal of Environmental Research and Public Health, 19*(21), 13969. DOI: 10.3390/ijerph192113969 PMID: 36360853

Chippagiri, S. (2025). A study of cloud security frameworks for safeguarding Multi-Tenant Cloud Architectures. *International Journal of Computer Applications, 186*(60), 50–57. DOI: 10.5120/ijca2025924369

Chugh, U. (2023). The Evolution of Privacy Laws in the Digital Age: Challenges and Solutions. *Indian Journal of Law.*, *1*(1), 51–60. DOI: 10.36676/ijl.2023-v1i1-07

Cirne, A., Sousa, P. R., Resende, J. S., & Antunes, L. (2022). IOT security certifications: Challenges and potential approaches. *Computers & Security*, *116*, 102669. DOI: 10.1016/j.cose.2022.102669

Clayton, J., & Derico, B. (2023, March 27). Clearview AI used nearly 1m times by US police, it tells the BBC. *BBC News*. https://www.bbc.com/news/technology-65057011

Coche, E., & Kolk, A. (2024). When Digitalization Meets Regulation across Borders: An Explainer with Actionable Insights. *AIB Insights*, *24*(3). Advance online publication. DOI: 10.46697/001c.122505

Cohen, J. E. (2019). Review of Zuboff's the age of surveillance capitalism. *Surveillance & Society*, *17*(1/2), 240–245. DOI: 10.24908/ss.v17i1/2.13144

Cole, S. (2018). *China Claims It's Scanning Workers' Brainwaves to Increase Efficiency and Profits*. [online] VICE. Available at: https://www.vice.com/en/article/china-brain-wave-hats-helmets-productivity/ [Accessed 10 Aug. 2025].

Collaco, A. M. (2024). Contours of data protection in India: The consent dilemma. *International Review of Law Computers & Technology*, *39*(2), 194–212. DOI: 10.1080/13600869.2024.2364991

Conger, K., Fausset, R., & Kovaleski, S. F. (2019, May 14). San Francisco Bans Facial Recognition Technology. *The New York Times*. https://www.nytimes.com/2019/05/14/us/facial-recognition-ban-san-francisco.html

Conrad, C., & Heggie, C. (2024). Legal and Ethical Challenges Raised by Advances in Brain-Computer Interface Technology. DOI: 10.2139/ssrn.4872064

Cooper, A. K., Marskell, J. D., & Chan, C. H. (2022). National Digital Identity and Government Data Sharing in Singapore: A Case Study of Singpass and APEX.

Corrales Compagnucci, M. (2025). The EU–US Data Privacy Framework: Is the Dragon Eating Its Own Tail? In *International Transfers of Health Data: A Global Perspective* (pp. 17–39). Singapore: Springer Nature. DOI: 10.1007/978-981-97-9983-1_2

Corren, E. (2022). The Consent Burden in Consumer and Digital Markets. *Harv. JL & Tech.*, *36*, 551.

Couldry, N., & Mejias, U. A. (2019). *The costs of connection: How data is colonizing human life and appropriating it for capitalism*. Stanford University Press.

Council of Europe. (2018). Modernised Convention 108+: Convention for the Protection of Individuals with regard to Processing of Personal Data.

Court of Justice of the European Union. (2020). Case C-311/18, *Data Protection Commissioner v. Facebook Ireland and Maximillian Schrems* (Schrems II). https://curia.europa.eu/juris/document/document.jsf?text=&docid=228677

Cozzens, C. (2021). The Patchwork Privacy Problem: How the United States' Privacy Regime Fails to Protect Its Businesses and Data Subjects. *Seton Hall Law Review*, *52*, 1157.

Craig, A. N., Shackelford, S. J., & Hiller, J. S. (2015). Proactive cybersecurity: A comparative industry and regulatory analysis. *American Business Law Journal*, *52*(4), 721–787. DOI: 10.1111/ablj.12055

Crawford, K. (2021). *Atlas of AI: Power, politics, and the planetary costs of artificial intelligence*. Yale University Press.

Creemers, R. (2017). Cyber China: Upgrading propaganda, public opinion work and social management for the twenty-first century. *Journal of Contemporary China*, *26*(103), 85–100. DOI: 10.1080/10670564.2016.1206281

Creemers, R. (2022). China's Emerging Data Protection Framework. *Journal of Cybersecurity*, *8*(1), tyac011. Advance online publication. DOI: 10.1093/cybsec/tyac011

Cremer, F., Sheehan, B., Fortmann, M., Kia, A. N., Mullins, M., Murphy, F., & Materne, S. (2022). Cyber risk and cybersecurity: A systematic review of data availability. *The Geneva Papers on Risk and Insurance. Issues and Practice*, *47*(3), 698–736. DOI: 10.1057/s41288-022-00266-6

Criado, J. I., & Guevara-Gómez, A. (2024). Who evaluates the algorithms? An overview of the algorithmic accountability ecosystem. 19. DOI: 10.1145/3657054.3657247

CSIS (Center for Strategic & International Studies). (2025). *Significant Cyber Incidents*. https://www.csis.org/programs/strategic-technologies-program/significant-cyber-incidents

Cybersecurity and Infrastructure Security Agency (CISA). (2020). *Phishing campaign assessment guidance.* https://www.cisa.gov

Daigle, B., & Khan, M. (2020, June). *The EU General Data Protection Regulation: An Analysis of Enforcement Trends by EU Data Protection Authorities*. Journal of International Commerce and Economics. https://www.usitc.gov/publications/332/journals/jice_gdpr_enforcement.pdf

Dalal, R. S., Howard, D. J., Bennett, R. J., Posey, C., Zaccaro, S. J., & Brummel, B. J. (2022). Organizational Science and Cybersecurity: Abundant Opportunities for Research at the Interface. *Journal of Business and Psychology*, *37*(1), 1–29. https://link.springer.com/article/10.1007/s10869-021-09732-9. DOI: 10.1007/s10869-021-09732-9 PMID: 33564206

Daneshfar, Z., Asokan-Ajitha, A., Sharma, P., & Malik, A. (2023). Work-from-home (WFH) During COVID-19 Pandemic – A Netnographic Investigation Using Twitter Data. *Information Technology & People*, *36*(5), 2161–2186. DOI: 10.1108/ITP-01-2021-0020

Datta, S. (2022). Evaluation and management of language and technology literacy barriers for accessing e-learning services in India. Embracing change in business, management & social sciences, 87.

David, Y. (2023). Legal Implications of Data Monetization by Commercial Entities. Available at *SSRN* 4922310.

De Hert, P., & Papakonstantinou, V. (2012). The proposed data protection Regulation replacing Directive 95/46/EC: A sound system for the protection of individuals? *Computer Law & Security Review*, *28*(2), 130–142. DOI: 10.1016/j.clsr.2012.01.011

Delacroix, S., & Lawrence, N. D. (2019). Bottom-up data Trusts: Disturbing the 'one size fits all' approach to data governance. *International Data Privacy Law*, *9*(4), 236–252. DOI: 10.1093/idpl/ipz014

Deleuze, G., & Foucault, M. (1977). Intellectuals and power. *Language, counter-memory, practice*, 205-17.

Deloitte. (2022). *AI ethics survey: Global business readiness report*. Deloitte Insights. https://www2.deloitte.com/global/en/pages/about-deloitte/articles/global-ai-ethics-survey.html

Del-Real, C., De Busser, E., & Van den Berg, B. (2025). A systematic literature review of security and privacy by design principles, norms, and strategies for Digital Technologies. *International Review of Law, Computers &amp. International Review of Law Computers & Technology*, *39*(3), 1–32. DOI: 10.1080/13600869.2025.2457227

Denison, D. (1990). Corporate culture and organizational. *New York: Wiley. Dike, P.(2013). The impact of workplace diversity on organizations. Dobbin, F., & Jung, J.(2010). Corporate board gender diversity and stock performance: The competence gap or institutional investor bias. NCL Rev, 89*, 809.

Denison, D. R., & Spreitzer, G. M. (1991). Organizational culture and organizational development: A competing values approach. *Research in Organizational Change and Development*, *5*(1), 1–21.

Denison, D., Nieminen, L., & Kotrba, L. (2014). Diagnosing organizational cultures: A conceptual and empirical review of culture effectiveness surveys. *European Journal of Work and Organizational Psychology*, *23*(1), 145–161. DOI: 10.1080/1359432X.2012.713173

Dennis, J., & Janecek, K. (2022, January). *Comparing privacy laws: GDPR v. CCPA & CPRA*. OneTrust DataGuidance. https://www.dataguidance.com/sites/default/files/gdpr_v_ccpa_and_cpra_v6.pdf

Descalzo, F. (2024). Designing Artificial Intelligence with Privacy at the Center. *2024 IEEE Biennial Congress of Argentina (ARGENCON)*, DOI: 10.1109/ARGENCON62399.2024.10735892

Determann, L., & Tam, J. (2020). The California Privacy Rights Act of 2020: A broad and complex data processing regulation that applies to businesses worldwide. *Journal of Data Protection & Privacy*, *4*(1), 7–21. DOI: 10.69554/GCLK6627

De-Yolande, M. H., Doh-Djanhoundji, T., & Constant, G. Y. (2023). Breach notification in the General Data Protection Regulation. *Voice of the Publisher*, *09*(04), 334–347. DOI: 10.4236/vp.2023.94026

Dhamo, A., & Dhamo, I. (2024). Right to Privacy and Constitution: An In-Depth Analysis. *Interdisciplinary Journal of Research and Development*, *11*(1 S1), 190. DOI: 10.56345/ijrdv11n1s128

Dhirani, L. L., Mukhtiar, N., Chowdhury, B. S., & Newe, T. (2023). Ethical Dilemmas and Privacy Issues in Emerging Technologies: A Review. *Sensors (Basel)*, *23*(3), 1151. https://www.mdpi.com/1424-8220/23/3/1151. DOI: 10.3390/s23031151 PMID: 36772190

Di Nuzzo, V. (2022). Search and seizure of digital evidence: human rights concerns and new safeguards. In *Investigating and Preventing Crime in the Digital Era: New Safeguards, New Rights* (pp. 119–149). Springer International Publishing., DOI: 10.1007/978-3-031-13952-9_6

Diggelmann, O., & Cleis, M. N. (2014). How the Right to Privacy became a Human Right. *Human Rights Law Review, 14*(3), 441–458. DOI: 10.1093/hrlr/ngu014

Doneda, D., & Almeida, V. (2021). Brazil's General Data Protection Law: A detailed overview. *Computer Law & Security Review, 40*, 105525.

Doneda, D., & Monteiro, F. (2021). Brazil's data protection law: An analysis in comparative perspective. *Journal of Data Protection & Privacy*, *4*(3), 190–202.

Dowd, R. (2022). Digitized Data Protection as a Fundamental Human Right. In *Springer eBooks* (p. 27). Springer Nature., DOI: 10.1007/978-3-030-82969-8_2

Downey, A., Islam, S. R., & Sarker, M. K. (2024). Predictive Policing: A Fairness-aware Approach. *International Journal of Artificial Intelligence Tools, 33*(3), 2460005. Advance online publication. DOI: 10.1142/S0218213024600054

DPDP Act , (2023). *The Digital Personal Data Protection Act.* Ministry of Law and Justice, Government of India.

Ducato, R. (2020). Data Protection, scientific research, and the role of information. *Computer Law &amp. Computer Law & Security Review, 37*, 105412. DOI: 10.1016/j.clsr.2020.105412

Dunbar, P., Browne, J. P., & O'Connor, L. (2021). Determinants of regulatory compliance in health and Social Care Services: A systematic review protocol. *HRB Open Research, 4*, 13. DOI: 10.12688/hrbopenres.13214.1

Duraiswami, D. R. (2017). Privacy and Data Protection in India. *Journal of Law & Cyber Warfare, 6*(1), 166–186.

Đurđević, D., & Stevanović, M. (2016). The Value Challenge of Interconnectedness in Cyberspace for National Security. *Sinteza*, 15-23. https://portal.sinteza.singidunum.ac.rs/paper/391

Edmondson, A. C. (2018). *The fearless organization: Creating psychological safety in the workplace for learning, innovation, and growth.* Wiley.

Elvy, S. A. (2023). Age-Appropriate Design Code Mandates. *U. Pa. J. Int'l L., 45*, 953.

Engelmann, A. G. (2023). Algorithmic transparency as a fundamental right in the democratic rule of law. *Brazilian Journal of Law Technology and Innovation, 1*(2), 169–188. doi:10.59224/bjlti.v1i2.169-188

Eubanks, V. (2018). *Automating inequality: How high-tech tools profile, police, and punish the poor.* St. Martin's Press.

European Commission. (2020). *Data protection rules as a pillar of citizen empowerment and the EU's approach to the digital transition.* https://ec.europa.eu/info/law/law-topic/data-protection_en

European Commission. (2021). *Proposal for a regulation laying down harmonised rules on artificial intelligence.* Artificial Intelligence Act.

European Commission. (2023). *EU–U.S. Data Privacy Framework: Irish DPC decision on Meta.* https://commission.europa.eu/law/law-topic/data-protection/data-transfers-outside-eu/eu-us-data-transfers_en

European Parliament & Council. (2016). *Regulation (EU) 2016/679.* General Data Protection Regulation.

European Parliament. (2017). *Civil Law Rules on Robotics.* https://www.europarl.europa.eu/doceo/document/A-8-2017-0005_EN.html

European Union Agency for Fundamental Rights. (2020). *Data protection as a fundamental right.* https://fra.europa.eu/en

European Union. (2012). *Charter of Fundamental Rights of the European Union.* https://eur-lex.europa.eu/legal-content/EN/TXT/?uri=celex%3A12012P%2FTXT

European Union. (2016). Regulation (EU) 2016/679 of the European Parliament and of the Council of 27 April 2016 on the protection of natural persons with regard to the processing of personal data and on the free movement of such data (General Data Protection Regulation). Official Journal of the European Union, L 119, 1–88. https://eur-lex.europa.eu/eli/reg/2016/679/oj

Ewoh, P., & Vartiainen, T. (2024). Vulnerability to cyberattacks and sociotechnical solutions for Health Care Systems: Systematic review. *Journal of Medical Internet Research, 26*, e46904. Advance online publication. DOI: 10.2196/46904

Fabian, B., Ermakova, T., & Lentz, T. (2017, August). Large-scale readability analysis of privacy policies. In *Proceedings of the International Conference on Web Intelligence* (pp. 18–25)

Faisal, K. (2023). Applying the purpose limitation principle in smart-city data-processing practices: A European Data Protection Law Perspective. *Communication Law and Policy*, *28*(1), 67–97. DOI: 10.1080/10811680.2023.2180266

Farhad, M. A. (2024). Consumer Data Protection Laws and their impact on business models in the Tech Industry. *Telecommunications Policy*, *48*(9), 102836. DOI: 10.1016/j.telpol.2024.102836

Felzmann, H., Fosch-Villaronga, E., Lutz, C., & Tamò-Larrieux, A. (2020). Towards Transparency by Design for Artificial Intelligence [Review of Towards Transparency by Design for Artificial Intelligence]. Science and Engineering Ethics, 26(6), 3333. Springer Science+Business Media. DOI: 10.1007/s11948-020-00276-4

Ferencz, S., Blomley, N., Flynn, A., & Sylvestre, M.-È. (2022). Are Tents a "Home"? Extending Section 8 Privacy Rights for the Precariously Housed. *McGill Law Journal. Revue de Droit de McGill*, *67*(4), 369. DOI: 10.7202/1098591ar

Ferguson, A. G. (2017). The rise of big data policing: Surveillance, race, and the future of law enforcement. In *The rise of big data policing*. New York University Press.

Finck, M., & Biega, A. J. (2021). Reviving purpose limitation and data minimisation in data-driven systems. *Technology and Regulation*, *2021*, 44–61. DOI: 10.71265/z7r0t122

Fischli, R. (2024). Data-owning democracy: Citizen empowerment through data ownership. *European Journal of Political Theory*, *23*(2), 204–223. DOI: 10.1177/14748851221110316

Floridi, L., & Cowls, J. (2019). A unified framework of five principles for AI in society. *Harvard Data Science Review*, *1*(1). Advance online publication. DOI: 10.1162/99608f92.8cd550d1

Floridi, L., Cowls, J., Beltrametti, M., Chatila, R., Chazerand, P., Dignum, V., Luetge, C., Madelin, R., Pagallo, U., Rossi, F., Schafer, B., Valcke, P., & Vayena, E. (2018). AI4People—An ethical framework for a good AI society: Opportunities, risks, principles, and recommendations. *Minds and Machines*, *28*(4), 689–707. DOI: 10.1007/s11023-018-9482-5 PMID: 30930541

Fornasier, M. de O. (2022). Artificial Intelligence and Democratic Rule of Law. *Revista de Estudos Constitucionais Hermenêutica e Teoria Do Direito*, *13*(3), 351–369. DOI: 10.4013/rechtd.2021.133.06

Freas, R. L., Adair, H. F., & Hammad, E. (2022). An engineering process framework for Cybersecurity Incident Response Assessment. *2022 IEEE Conference on Dependable and Secure Computing (DSC)*, 1–8. DOI: 10.1109/DSC54232.2022.9888795

Frichot, E. (2025). Exploring the Ethical and Legal Dimensions of Data Collection: A Case Study of Meta Platform.

Fridlund, A. J., Ekman, P., & Oster, H. (2014). Facial expressions of emotion: Review of literature, 1970–1983. *Nonverbal behavior and communication*, 143-224.

FTC. (2022). *FTC finalizes order requiring Drizly to improve data security and hold CEO accountable*. https://www.ftc.gov

Furnell, S. (2021). The cybersecurity workforce and Skills. *Computers &amp. Computers & Security, 100*, 102080. DOI: 10.1016/j.cose.2020.102080

Galton, F. (1892). *Finger prints (No. 57490-57492)*. Cosimo Classics.

Gao, L., Calderon, T. G., & Tang, F. (2020). Public companies' cybersecurity risk disclosures. *International Journal of Accounting Information Systems, 38*, 100468. DOI: 10.1016/j.accinf.2020.100468

Gautam, P. (2022). Right to privacy as a fundamental right – extension of Article 21 of the Indian Constitution? *Revista de Drept Constitu ional, 1*(01), 95–98. Retrieved from https://www.ceeol.com/search/article-detail?id=1058906

GDPR. (2013a). *General Data Protection Regulation (GDPR) – Final text neatly arranged*. General Data Protection Regulation (GDPR). https://gdpr-info.eu/art-9-gdpr/

GDPR. (2016). *Regulation (EU) 2016/679 of the European Parliament and of the Council (General Data Protection Regulation)*. Official Journal of the European Union.

Gellert, R. (2018). Understanding the notion of risk in the General Data Protection Regulation. *Computer Law & Security Review, 34*(2), 279–288. DOI: 10.1016/j.clsr.2017.12.003

Georgiadis, G., & Poels, G. (2022). Towards a privacy impact assessment methodology to support the requirements of the General Data Protection Regulation in a big data analytics context: A systematic literature review. *Computer Law &amp. Computer Law & Security Review, 44*, 105640. DOI: 10.1016/j.clsr.2021.105640

Gerlitz, C., & Helmond, A. (2013). The like economy: Social buttons and the data-intensive web. *New Media & Society, 15*(8), 1348–1365. DOI: 10.1177/1461444812472322

Giddens, A. (1984). *The constitution of society: Outline of the theory of structuration*. Polity Press.

Gil González, E., & De Hert, P. (2019). Understanding the legal provisions that allow processing and profiling personal data—An analysis of GDPR provisions and principles. ERA Forum, 19(4), 597–621. Springer. https://doi.org/DOI: 10.1007/s12027-019-00559-9

Gilder, A. (2021). International Law and Human Security in a Kaleidoscopic World. *Indian Journal of International Law*, *59*(1-4), 111–137. https://link.springer.com/article/10.1007/s40901-020-00109-w. DOI: 10.1007/s40901-020-00109-w

Gioe, D. V., & Hatfield, J. M. (2021). A damage assessment framework for insider threats to national security information: Edward Snowden and the Cambridge Five in comparative historical perspective. *Cambridge Review of International Affairs*, *34*(5), 704–738. DOI: 10.1080/09557571.2020.1853053

Goel, S., & Shawky, H. A. (2009). Estimating the Market Impact of Security Breach Announcements on Firm Values. *Information & Management*, *46*(7), 404–410. DOI: 10.1016/j.im.2009.06.005

Gohdes, A. R. (2024). *Repression in the Digital Age: Surveillance, Censorship, and the Dynamics of State Violence*. Oxford University Press. DOI: 10.1093/oso/9780197743577.001.0001

Golovin, K. S. (2024). THE NEED FOR LEGAL REGULATION OF THE "BLACK BOX" OF ARTIFICIAL INTELLIGENCE. *Vestnik of Kostroma State University*, *30*(3), 290–297. DOI: 10.34216/1998-0817-2024-30-3-290-297

González Fuster, G. (2014). *The emergence of personal data protection as a fundamental right of the EU*. Springer., DOI: 10.1007/978-3-319-05023-2

Goodin, T. (2023). *My Brain Has Too Many Tabs Open: How to Untangle Our Relationship with Tech*. White Lion Publishing.

Gopireddy, R. R., & Koppanathi, S. R. (2018). Post - Breach Data Security: Strategies for recovery and future protection. [IJSR]. *International Journal of Science and Research (Raipur, India)*, *7*(12), 1609–1614. DOI: 10.21275/SR24731204000

Gordon, J., Curran, M. T., Chuang, J., & Cheshire, C. (2021). Covert Embodied Choice: Decision-Making and the Limits of Privacy Under Biometric Surveillance. DOI: 10.1145/3411764.3445309

Government of India. (2011). Information Technology (Reasonable Security Practices and Procedures and Sensitive Personal Data or Information) Rules, 2011 (S.O. 1677(E), 24 June 2011). Ministry of Electronics and Information Technology. Retrieved from https://www.indiacode.nic.in/handle/123456789/1362/simple-search?query=The%20Information%20Technology%20(Reasonable%20Security%20Practices%20and%20Procedures%20and%20Sensitive%20Personal%20Data%20or%20Information)%20Rules,%202011.&searchradio=rules

Government of India. (2023). Digital Personal Data Protection Act, 2023, No. 22 of 2023, § 2. Ministry of Law and Justice. https://www.indiacode.nic.in/handle/123456789/24547

Graeden, E., Rosado, D. P., Stevens, T., Knodel, M., Hendricks-Sturrup, R., Reiskind, A., Bennett, A., Leitner, J., Lekas, P., & DeMooy, M. (2023). A new framework for global data regulation. arXiv (Cornell University). https://doi.org/10.48550/arxiv.2308.12955

Grand View Research. (2018). *Global Biometrics Technology Market Share | Industry Report 2018-2025.* [online] Grandviewresearch.com. Available at: https://www.grandviewresearch.com/industry-analysis/biometrics-industry

Greenleaf, G. (2018). *Global data privacy laws 2017: 120 national data privacy laws, including Indonesia and Turkey.* Privacy Laws & Business International Report, 147, 10–13. https://papers.ssrn.com/sol3/papers.cfm?abstract_id=2993035

Greenleaf, G. (2021). Global data privacy laws 2021: Despite COVID delays, 145 laws show GDPR dominance. *SSRN*, *169*, 1–7. DOI: 10.2139/ssrn.3836348

Greenleaf, G., & Waters, N. (2022). Global convergence of data privacy standards: GDPR dominance or regulatory competition? *Computer Law & Security Review*, *46*, 105738. DOI: 10.1016/j.clsr.2022.105738

Gstrein, O. J., & Beaulieu, A. (2022). How to protect privacy in a datafied society? A presentation of multiple legal and conceptual approaches. *Philosophy & Technology*, *35*(1), 3. Advance online publication. DOI: 10.1007/s13347-022-00497-4

Guggenberger, N. (2025). Consent as Friction. *BCL Rev.*, *66*(2), 353–421. DOI: 10.70167/CHOQ9209

Gumbo, L., & Chude-Okonkwo, U. A. (2025). Regulatory sandbox as a frontier for innovation and Sustainability: A Systematic Review. *Cogent Business & Management*, *12*(1), 2510555. Advance online publication. DOI: 10.1080/23311975.2025.2510555

Gupta, I., & Naithani, P. (2024). India's Forthcoming Rules under the Digital Personal Data Protection Act: An Opportunity to Reduce Gaps in the 'Notice and Consent' Framework for Cookies. (2024). Global Privacy Law Review. 5(4),164-170, https://testcdn.kluwerlawonline.com/journalarticle/Global+Privacy+Law+Review/5.4/GPLR2025003

Gupta, I., & Naithani, P. (2024). India's Forthcoming Rules under the Digital Personal Data Protection Act: An Opportunity to Reduce Gaps in the 'Notice and Consent' Framework for Cookies. Global Privacy Law Review, 5(4).

Guttman, B., White, D. R., & Walraven, T. (2022). *Digital Evidence Preservation : Considerations for Evidence Handlers*. NIST., DOI: 10.6028/NIST.IR.8387

Haefner, L., & Sternberg, R. (2020). Spatial Implications of Digitalization: State of the Field and Research Agenda. *Geography Compass*, *14*(12), e12544. https://compass.onlinelibrary.wiley.com/doi/full/10.1111/gec3.12544. DOI: 10.1111/gec3.12544

Haider, S. (2009). The organizational knowledge iceberg: An empirical investigation. *Knowledge and Process Management*, *16*(2), 74–84. DOI: 10.1002/kpm.326

Halis Kasap, G. (2024). Defending privacy across borders: Public interest litigation in the fight against data exploitation. *Netherlands International Law Review*, *71*(3), 427–460. DOI: 10.1007/s40802-024-00273-5

Han, H., Shiwakoti, R. K., Jarvis, R., Mordi, C., & Botchie, D. (2023). Accounting and auditing with blockchain technology and Artificial Intelligence: A literature review. *International Journal of Accounting Information Systems*, *48*, 100598. DOI: 10.1016/j.accinf.2022.100598

Hardinges, J., Wells, P., Ho, M., & Dencik, L. (2019). *Data trusts: Lessons from three pilots*. Open Data Institute. https://theodi.org

Harkin, D., & Panagiotopoulos, V. (2025). Regulating tools for hacking: Limitations, challenges and possibilities. *Policy and Internet*, *17*(2), e70004. DOI: 10.1002/poi3.70004

Hasal, M., Nowaková, J., Saghair, K. A., Abdulla, H., Snášel, V., & Ogiela, L. (2021). Chatbots: Security, Privacy, Data Protection, and Social Aspects. *Concurrency and Computation*, *33*(19), e6425. https://onlinelibrary.wiley.com/doi/full/10.1002/cpe.6426. DOI: 10.1002/cpe.6426

Haymes, L. K., Storey, K., Maldonado, A., Post, M., & Montgomery, J. (2015). Using applied behavior analysis and smart technology for meeting the health needs of individuals with intellectual disabilities. *Developmental Neurorehabilitation*, *18*(6), 407–419. DOI: 10.3109/17518423.2013.850750 PMID: 24304093

Heimstädt, M., & Dobusch, L. (2020). Transparency and accountability: Causal, critical and constructive perspectives. *Organization Theory*, *1*(4), 2631787720964216. Advance online publication. DOI: 10.1177/2631787720964216

Helberger, N. (2025). The rise of technology courts, or: How technology companies reinvent adjudication for a digital world. *Computer Law & Security Review*, *56*, 106118. DOI: 10.1016/j.clsr.2025.106118

Herbison, J. F. (2019). Big Tech Investigated for Antitrust Violations. *Infrastructure*, *59*, 3.

Hetcher, S. (2000). The de facto federal privacy commission. *The John Marshall Journal of Computer & Information Law*, *19*, 109.

He, Y., Aliyu, A., Evans, M., & Luo, C. (2021). Health Care Cybersecurity challenges and solutions under the climate of covid-19: Scoping review. *Journal of Medical Internet Research*, *23*(4), e21747. Advance online publication. DOI: 10.2196/21747

Hill, K. (2020, January 18). The secretive company that might end privacy as we know it. The New York Times. https://www.nytimes.com/2020/01/18/technology/clearview-privacy.html

Hill, K. (2021, July 21). Clearview AI raises $30 million from investors despite legal troubles. The New York Times. https://www.nytimes.com/2021/07/21/technology/clearview-ai-facial-recognition.html

Hiller, K. (2022). Predictive Policing and the Charter. *Manitoba Law Journal*, *44*(6), 224–245. DOI: 10.29173/mlj1303

Hillman, R. A., & Rachlinski, J. J. (2002). Standard-form contracting in the electronic age. *NYUL Rev.*, *77*, 429.

Hoofnagle, C. J., Van der Sloot, B., & Borgesius, F. Z. (2019). The European Union General Data Protection Regulation: What it is and what it means. *Information &amp. Information & Communications Technology Law*, *28*(1), 65–98. DOI: 10.1080/13600834.2019.1573501

Hu, E. (2014). Facebook Manipulates Our Moods For Science And Commerce: A Roundup. All Tech Considered Tech, Culture, and Connection. NPR. https://www.npr.org/sections/alltechconsidered/2014/06/30/326929138/facebook-manipulates-our-moods-for-science-and-commerce-a-roundup

Hulkó, G., Kálmán, J., & Lapsánszky, A. (2025). The politics of digital sovereignty and the European Union's legislation: Navigating crises. *Frontiers in Political Science*, *7*, 1548562. Advance online publication. DOI: 10.3389/fpos.2025.1548562

Hu, M. (2020). Cambridge Analytica's black box. *Big Data & Society*, *7*(2), 2053951720938091. DOI: 10.1177/2053951720938091

Hwang, J. young. (2025). Digital sovereignty in an era of cyber threats and Global Connectivity. *International Journal of Multidisciplinary Research Updates, 9*(2), 012–023. DOI: 10.53430/ijmru.2025.9.2.0023

IDC (International Data Corporation). (2023). *Global DataSphere forecast 2023–2028*. IDC Market Analysis Report. https://www.idc.com/getdoc.jsp?containerId=US50471623

Ilori, O., Nwosu, N. T., & Naiho, H. N. N. (2024). Third-party vendor risks in IT security: A comprehensive audit review and mitigation strategies. *World Journal of Advanced Research and Reviews*, *22*(3), 213–224. DOI: 10.30574/wjarr.2024.22.3.1727

IMDA. (2022). *AI Verify: Evaluation toolkit for trusted AI*. Infocomm Media Development Authority of Singapore. https://www.imda.gov.sg

Isaak, J., & Hanna, M. J. (2018). User data privacy: Facebook, Cambridge Analytica, and privacy protection. *Computer*, *51*(8), 56–59. DOI: 10.1109/MC.2018.3191268

ISC2 Code of Ethics. (n.d.). https://www.isc2.org/Ethics

Jagadish, R. (2024). Enhancing cybersecurity in cloud - based banking - best practices and technologies. [IJSR]. *International Journal of Science and Research (Raipur, India)*, *13*(3), 422–426. DOI: 10.21275/SR24306144435

Jain, A. K., Nandakumar, K., & Ross, A. (2016). 50 years of biometric research: Accomplishments, challenges, and opportunities. *Pattern Recognition Letters*, *79*, 80–105. DOI: 10.1016/j.patrec.2015.12.013

Jain, A. S. (2025a). Decoding consent managers under the Digital Personal Data Protection Act, 2023: Empowerment architecture, business models, and incentive alignment. *Journal of Data Protection & Privacy*, *7*(4), 406–420. DOI: 10.69554/MHLP2916

Jain, A., & Anand, A. (2025b). Tracing the Constitutional Journey of Data Privacy in India: From Puttaswamy to the Draft DPDP Rules, 2025. Available at *SSRN* 5283949. DOI: 10.2139/ssrn.5283949

Jalali, M. S., Razak, S., Gordon, W., Perakslis, E., & Madnick, S. (2019). Health Care and cybersecurity: Bibliometric Analysis of the literature. *Journal of Medical Internet Research*, *21*(2), e12644. Advance online publication. DOI: 10.2196/12644

Jariwala, M. (2024). Contingency planning: The need, benefits, and implementation of scenario planning. [IJTSRD]. *International Journal of Trend in Scientific Research and Development*, *8*(3), 866–869. https://doi.org/https://www.researchgate.net/publication/373990738_Contingency_Planning_The_Need_Benefits_and_Implementation_of_Scenario_Planning

Jones, L. A., & Burrell, D. N. (2025). Illegal Cybersecurity Threats Created by Organizational Arsonists in Healthcare Organizations. *Law. Economics and Society*, *1*(1), 93–p93.

Joseph, V., Basu, P., & Bhargava, A. (2020, March 19). A review of the Information Technology Rules, 2011. Mondaq. https://www.mondaq.com/india/privacy-protection/904916/a-review-of-the-information-technology-rules-2011

Kahla, L. Z. (2024). Leveraging Artificial Intelligence for Crime Detection and Prevention. *INTERANTIONAL JOURNAL OF SCIENTIFIC RESEARCH IN ENGINEERING AND MANAGEMENT*, *8*(5), 1–5. Advance online publication. DOI: 10.55041/IJSREM34207

Kaur, K. (2025). DIGITAL SURVEILLANCE AND INDIAN PRIVACY LAWS. *LawFoyer International Journal of Doctrinal Legal Research.*, *3*(1), 61–77. DOI: 10.70183/lijdlr.2024.v03.4

Kaur, T. (2024). Right To Privacy in Digital Age: A Study with Indian Context. [EEL]. *European Economic Letters*, *14*(4), 1744–1752. DOI: 10.52783/eel.v14i4.2307

Keyes, O. (2018). The misgendering machines: Trans/HCI implications of automatic gender recognition. *Proceedings of the ACM on human-computer interaction*, *2*(CSCW), 1-22. DOI: 10.1145/3274357

Khadka, K., & Ullah, A. B. (2025). Human factors in cybersecurity: An Interdisciplinary Review and framework proposal. *International Journal of Information Security*, *24*(3), 119. Advance online publication. DOI: 10.1007/s10207-025-01032-0

Khazanchi, D., & Saxena, M. (2025). Navigating digital human rights in the age of AI: challenges, theoretical perspectives, and research implications. Journal of Information Technology Case and Application Research, DOI: 10.1080/15228053.2025.2452028

Khera, R. (2019). *Dissent on Aadhaar: Big Data meets Big Brother*. Orient BlackSwan.

Kianpour, M., & Raza, S. (2024). More than malware: Unmasking the hidden risk of cybersecurity regulations. *International Cybersecurity Law Review*, *5*(1), 169–212. DOI: 10.1365/s43439-024-00111-7

King, M. (2022). Doing the Right Thing: It Is in Our Power to Act and Not to Act. In *Leadership and Business Ethics* (pp. 441–464). Springer Netherlands. DOI: 10.1007/978-94-024-2111-8_26

Kitchin, R. M. (1998). Towards Geographies of Cyberspace. *Progress in Human Geography*, *22*(3), 385–406. https://journals.sagepub.com/doi/abs/10.1191/030913298668331585. DOI: 10.1191/030913298668331585

Kivuva, R. (2023). Data protection in Kenya: Early enforcement under the 2019 Act. *African Law Review*, *11*(2), 85–99.

Kniep, R., Ewert, L., Reyes, B. L., Tréguer, F., Cluskey, E. M., & Aradau, C. (2024). Towards democratic intelligence oversight: Limits, practices, struggles. *Review of International Studies*, *50*(1), 209–229. DOI: 10.1017/S0260210523000013

Knight, R., & Nurse, J. R. C. (2020). A framework for effective corporate communication after cyber security incidents. *Computers & Security*, *99*, 102036. DOI: 10.1016/j.cose.2020.102036

Koops, B. J. (2021). The concept of function creep. *Law, Innovation and Technology*, *13*(1), 29–56. DOI: 10.1080/17579961.2021.1898299

Korff, D. (2023). The Indian Digital Personal Data Protection Act, 2023, viewed from a European Perspective. SSRN Electronic Journal. DOI: 10.2139/ssrn.4614984

Kovacs, A., & Jain, T. (2020). Informed consent-said who? A feminist perspective on principles of consent in the age of embodied data. A Feminist Perspective on Principles of Consent in the Age of Embodied Data (November 2020).

Kuflik, A. (1984). The inalienability of autonomy. *Philosophy & Public Affairs*, •••, 271–298.

Kukava, K. (2023). Balancing the Right to Privacy and National Security Interests in the Digital Age. *Journal of Law*, *2*(2). Advance online publication. DOI: 10.60131/jlaw.2.2023.7711

Kulikova, A. A. (2019). Digital law as a nascent branch of Russian law. Proceedings of the 1st International Scientific Conference "Modern Management Trends and the Digital Economy: From Regional Development to Global Economic Growth" (MTDE 2019). DOI: 10.2991/mtde-19.2019.86

Kulshrestha, P., Gautam, R., & Singh, A. (Eds.). (2022). *Cyber Crime, Regulation and Security: Contemporary Issues and Challenges*. Libertatem Media Private Limited. DOI: 10.55662/CCRSbook.2022

Kumar Bisht, A., & Shanmukha Sreenivasulu, N. S. (2024). Information Privacy Rights in India: A Study of the Digital Personal Data Protection Act, 2023. In IntechOpen eBooks. IntechOpen. DOI: 10.5772/intechopen.1007353

Kumar, D., Kaur, G., Srivastava, A., Ghosh, A., & Ghosh, S. (2025). The Ethical and Regulatory Challenges of Consumer Privacy in the Digital Era. In *AI Marketing and Ethical Considerations in Consumer Engagement* (pp. 173–194). IGI Global Scientific Publishing., DOI: 10.4018/979-8-3373-3476-9.ch009

Kumar, T., Bhushan, S., Sharma, P., & Garg, V. (2024). Examining the vulnerabilities of biometric systems: Privacy and security perspectives. In *Leveraging Computer Vision to Biometric Applications* (pp. 34–67). Chapman and Hall/CRC. DOI: 10.1201/9781032614663-3

Kuner, C. (2015). *Transborder data flows and data privacy law*. Oxford University Press.

Kuner, C. (2020). The GDPR and its extraterritorial reach: Challenges and responses. *International Data Privacy Law*, *10*(4), 231–245. DOI: 10.1093/idpl/ipx023

Kuner, C., Bygrave, L. A., & Docksey, C. (Eds.). (2021). *The EU General Data Protection Regulation (GDPR): A commentary*. Oxford University Press.

Kuner, C., Cate, F. H., Lynskey, O., & Millard, C. (2017). Machine learning with personal data: Is data protection law smart enough to meet the challenge? *International Data Privacy Law*, *7*(1), 1–3. DOI: 10.1093/idpl/ipx003

Labbay, A. (2023). La surveillance algorithmique des données de connexion dans le cadre de la lutte contre le terrorisme. *Cahiers de La Recherche Sur Les Droits Fondamentaux*, *21*, 117–124. DOI: 10.4000/crdf.8874

Lambach, D. (2020). The Territorialization of Cyberspace. *International Studies Review*, *22*(3), 482–506. DOI: 10.1093/isr/viz022

Lee, J. D., & See, K. A. (2004). Trust in automation: Designing for appropriate reliance. *Human Factors*, *46*(1), 50–80. DOI: 10.1518/hfes.46.1.50.30392 PMID: 15151155

Leenes, R., Palmerini, E., Koops, B.-J., Bertolini, A., Salvini, P., & Lucivero, F. (2017). Regulatory challenges of robotics: Some guidelines for addressing legal and ethical issues. *Law, Innovation and Technology*, *9*(1), 1–44. DOI: 10.1080/17579961.2017.1304921

Levi-Faur, D. (2011). Regulatory capitalism and the reassertion of the public interest. *Policy and Society*, *30*(4), 289–297. DOI: 10.1016/j.polsoc.2011.10.001

Liu, C., & Babar, M. A. (2024). Corporate Cybersecurity Risk and data breaches: A systematic review of Empirical Research. *Australian Journal of Management*. Advance online publication. DOI: 10.1177/03128962241293658

Liu, H. (2022). China's Personal Information Protection Law: A comprehensive data privacy framework. *Computer Law & Security Review*, *45*, 105656. DOI: 10.1016/j.clsr.2022.105656

Liu, H. (2022). China's Personal Information Protection Law: An analysis in the global context. *Computer Law & Security Review*, *45*, 105591. DOI: 10.1016/j.clsr.2022.105591

Livson, M., Eshtokin, S., Vasyukov, V., Yudina, E., Baybarin, A., & Pivneva, S. (2021). Impact of Digitalization on Legal Regulation: Formation of new legal practices. *Journal of Law and Sustainable Development*, *9*(2), e0749. Advance online publication. DOI: 10.37497/sdgs.v9i2.28

Lukings, M., & Lashkari, A. H. (2022). *Understanding Cybersecurity Law and Digital Privacy*. Springer International Publishing. DOI: 10.1007/978-3-030-88704-9

Lurye, S. (2025). *Schools are using AI to protect students. It also leads to false alarms — and arrests*. [online] ABC News. Available at: https://abcnews.go.com/Technology/wireStory/schools-ai-surveillance-protect-students-leads-false-alarms-124440368

Lyon, D. (2018). *The culture of surveillance: Watching as a way of life*. Polity Press.

Lysenko, S., Liubchenko, A., Kozakov, V., Demianchuk, Y., & Krutik, Y. (2024). Global cybersecurity: Harmonising international standards and cooperation. *Multidisciplinary Reviews*, *7*, 2024spe021. Advance online publication. DOI: 10.31893/multirev.2024spe021

Machayya, C. R. (2024). Strategic approaches to bias and variance in algorithmic profiling. In *Routledge eBooks* (p. 726). Informa., DOI: 10.4324/9781003606642-157

Macnish, K., & Van der Ham, J. (2020). Ethics in Cybersecurity Research and Practice. *Technology in Society*, *63*, 101382. DOI: 10.1016/j.techsoc.2020.101382

Madnick, B., Huang, K., & Madnick, S. (2024). The evolution of global cybersecurity norms in the digital age: A longitudinal study of the cybersecurity norm development process. *Information Security Journal: A Global Perspective, 33*(3), 204–225. DOI: 10.1080/19393555.2023.2201482

Magnet, S. A. (2011). When biometrics fail: Gender, race, and the technology of identity. In *When Biometrics Fail*. Duke University Press.

Mahringer, C. A., Schmiedle, L., Albicker, L., & Mayer, S. (2025). The Iceberg Model of Change: A taxonomy differentiating approaches to change. *Heliyon, 11*(2), e41952. DOI: 10.1016/j.heliyon.2025.e41952 PMID: 39911443

Makridis, C. A. (2021). Corrigendum to: Do data breaches damage reputation? evidence from 45 companies between 2002 and 2018. *Journal of Cybersecurity, 7*(1), tyab022. Advance online publication. DOI: 10.1093/cybsec/tyab022

Makulilo, A. B. (2016). *African data privacy laws*. Springer. DOI: 10.1007/978-3-319-47317-8

Malandrino, D., Scarano, V., & Spinelli, R. (2013). How Increased Awareness Can Impact Attitudes and Behaviors toward Online Privacy Protection. *International Conference on Social Computing*, Alexandria, 57–62. DOI: 10.1109/SocialCom.2013.15

Malhotra, C., & Malhotra, U. (2024). Putting Interests of Digital Nagriks First: Digital Personal Data Protection (DPDP) Act 2023 of India. *The Indian Journal of Public Administration, 70*(3), 516–531. DOI: 10.1177/00195561241271575

Mantelero, A. (2021). The future of data protection: Gold standard vs. global standard. *Computer Law & Security Review, 40*, 105500. DOI: 10.1016/j.clsr.2020.105500

Marda, V., & Narayan, S. (2020). Data in New Delhi's predictive policing system. In *Proceedings of the 2020 Conference on Fairness, Accountability, and Transparency* (pp. 317–324). Association for Computing Machinery. DOI: 10.1145/3351095.3372865

Mattson, L. (2022). *The Carpenter Shift: The Evolution of Fourth Amendment Jurisprudence in the Digital Age*. [White paper/Working paper]. Retrieved from JSTOR: https://www.jstor.org/stable/pdf/community.34031526.pdf

Mayer, N., & Aubert, J. (2020). A risk management framework for security and integrity of networks and services. *Journal of Risk Research, 24*(8), 987–998. DOI: 10.1080/13669877.2020.1779786

Mayer-Schönberger, V., & Padova, T. (2015). Regime complexity and regulatory design: The case of data privacy in the EU and the USA. *Journal of European Public Policy, 22*(7), 1036–1053. DOI: 10.1080/13501763.2015.1020835

Mbah, G. O.Geraldine O Mbah. (2024). Data privacy in the era of AI: Navigating regulatory landscapes for global businesses. *International Journal of Science and Research Archive, 13*(2), 2040–2058. DOI: 10.30574/ijsra.2024.13.2.2396

McConomy, B. C., & Leber, D. E. (2022). Cybersecurity in healthcare. In *Clinical Informatics Study Guide: Text and Review* (pp. 241–253). Springer International Publishing., DOI: 10.1007/978-3-030-93765-2_17

McDaniel, J. L., & Pease, K. G. (2021). Policing, AI, and choice architecture. Predictive Policing and Artificial Intelligence. 32.

McVey, M. (2022). Untangling the authority of external experts in the corporate implementation of the UN Guiding Principles on Business and Human Rights. *Journal of Human Rights*, *21*(5), 620–638. DOI: 10.1080/14754835.2022.2105646

Meghwal, T. (2025). Emerging Challenges in Regulating Artificial Intelligence Under Cyber Security Laws in India. DOI: 10.2139/ssrn.5030258

Mele, C., Spena, T. R., Kaartemo, V., & Marzullo, M. L. (2021). Smart nudging: How cognitive technologies enable choice architectures for value co-creation. *Journal of Business Research*, *129*, 949–960. DOI: 10.1016/j.jbusres.2020.09.004

Metcalf, J., & Crawford, K. (2016). Where are human subjects in big data research? The emerging ethics divide. *Big Data & Society*, *3*(1), 2053951716650211. DOI: 10.1177/2053951716650211

Meyer, J. W., Boli, J., Thomas, G. M., & Ramirez, F. O. (1997). World society and the nation-state. *American Journal of Sociology*, *103*(1), 144–181. DOI: 10.1086/231174

Mishra, A., Alzoubi, Y. I., Anwar, M. J., & Gill, A. Q. (2022). Attributes Impacting Cybersecurity Policy Development: An Evidence from Seven Nations. *Computers & Security*, *120*, 102820. https://www.sciencedirect.com/science/article/pii/S0167404822002140. DOI: 10.1016/j.cose.2022.102820

Mishra, A., Alzoubi, Y. I., Gill, A. Q., & Anwar, M. J. (2022). Cybersecurity Enterprises Policies: A Comparative Study. *Sensors (Basel)*, *22*(2), 538. DOI: 10.3390/s22020538

Mitchell, M., Wu, S., Zaldivar, A., Barnes, P., Vasserman, L., Hutchinson, B., & Gebru, T. (2019). *Model cards for model reporting*. In *Proceedings of the Conference on Fairness, Accountability, and Transparency* (pp. 220–229). https://doi.org/DOI: 10.1145/3287560.3287596

Mittelstadt, B. D., Allo, P., Taddeo, M., Wachter, S., & Floridi, L. (2016). The ethics of algorithms: Mapping the debate. *Big Data & Society*, *3*(2), 2053951716679679. DOI: 10.1177/2053951716679679

Mohale, V. Z., & Obagbuwa, I. C. (2025). A systematic review on the integration of explainable artificial intelligence in intrusion detection systems to enhancing transparency and interpretability in cybersecurity. *Frontiers in Artificial Intelligence*, *8*, 1526221. Advance online publication. DOI: 10.3389/frai.2025.1526221

Mohammed, Z. (2021). Data Breach Recovery Areas: An exploration of organization's recovery strategies for surviving data breaches. *Organizational Cybersecurity Journal: Practice. Process and People*, *2*(1), 41–59. DOI: 10.1108/OCJ-05-2021-0014

Molnar, P. (2019). Technological testing grounds: Migration management experiments and reflections from the ground up. European Digital Rights (EDRi). https://edri.org/wp-content/uploads/2020/11/technological_testing_grounds.pdf

Montasari, R. (2024). *Cyberspace, Cyberterrorism and International Security in the Fourth Industrial Revolution: Threats, Assessment and Responses*. Springer Nature. DOI: 10.1007/978-3-031-50454-9

Moore, M. (2025). Top Cybersecurity Threats to Watch in 2025. University of San Diego. https://onlinedegrees.sandiego.edu/top-cyber-security-threats/#:~:text=Types%20of%20Cyber%20Threats,fostering%20a%20secure%20digital%20environment

Mothobi, O., & Gillwald, A. (2020). *The state of data protection in Africa: Mapping legislative gaps and enforcement challenges*. Research ICT Africa.

Moynihan, H. (2021). The vital role of international law in the framework for responsible state behaviour in cyberspace. *Journal of Cyber Policy*, *6*(3), 394–410. DOI: 10.1080/23738871.2020.1832550

Mrežar, F. (2023). Analysis of fines under GDPR (Doctoral dissertation, University of Zagreb, Faculty of Law, Information Technology Law and Informatics). University of Zagreb.

Mubarak, F., & Suomi, R. (2022). Elderly Forgotten? Digital Exclusion in the Information Age and the Rising Grey Digital Divide. *Inquiry: The Journal of Health Care Organization, Provision, and Financing*, 59. https://journals.sagepub.com/doi/full/10.1177/00469580221096272

Mueck, M., & Gaie, C. (2025). Introduction to the European Cybersecurity Act. In *European Digital Regulations* (pp. 229–247). Springer Nature Switzerland., DOI: 10.1007/978-3-031-80809-8_10

Murdoch, B. (2021). Privacy and Artificial Intelligence: Challenges for Protecting Health Information in a New Era. *BMC Medical Ethics*, *22*(1), 122. https://link.springer.com/article/10.1186/s12910-021-00687-3. DOI: 10.1186/s12910-021-00687-3 PMID: 34525993

Nabil, A. R., Tusher, M., Akther, M. N., & Rayhan, R. U. (2025). Ethical Implications Of Ai- Powered Predictive Policing. Ethical Implications Of Ai- Powered Predictive Policing: Balancing Public Safety With Privacy Concerns.., *2*(1), 47–58. DOI: 10.70937/itej.v2i01.54

Nag, Y., Hullatti, V. M., TB, A., & Kher, U. (2024). Ethical concerns of using artificial intelligence in Cybersecurity. *IJARCCE, 13*(11), 243–246. DOI: 10.17148/IJARCCE.2024.131138

Naithani, P. (2024). Analysis of India's Digital Personal Data Protection Act, 2023. International Journal of Law and Management.

Nandy, D. (2023). Human rights in the era of surveillance: Balancing security and privacy concerns. *Journal of Current Social and Political Issues, 1*(1), 13–17. DOI: 10.15575/jcspi.v1i1.442

Narciandi-Rodriguez, D., Aveleira-Mata, J., García-Ordás, M. T., Alfonso-Cendón, J., Benavides, C., & Alaiz-Moretón, H. (2025). A cybersecurity review in IOT 5G networks. *Internet of Things : Engineering Cyber Physical Human Systems, 30*, 101478. DOI: 10.1016/j.iot.2024.101478

Nešpor, J. (2024). Automated Administrative Decision-Making: What is the Black Box Hiding? *AUC IURIDICA, 70*(2), 69–83. DOI: 10.14712/23366478.2024.23

Newswire, P. R. (2018). *Global $40+ Billion Biometric System Market 2018-2023 - Analysis & Forecasts by by Authentication Type, Functionality, Component, Application, and Geography*. [online] Prnewswire.com. Available at: https://www.prnewswire.com/news-releases/global-40-billion-biometric-system-market-2018-2023----analysis--forecasts-by-by-authentication-type-functionality-component-application-and-geography-300695999.html

Nifakos, S., Chandramouli, K., Nikolaou, C. K., Papachristou, P., Koch, S., Panaousis, E., & Bonacina, S. (2021). Influence of human factors on cyber security within healthcare organisations: A systematic review. *Sensors (Basel), 21*(15), 5119. DOI: 10.3390/s21155119 PMID: 34372354

Nissenbaum, H. (2010). *Privacy in context: Technology, policy, and the integrity of social life*. Stanford University Press.

Nissenbaum, H. (2011). A contextual approach to privacy online. *Daedalus, 140*(4), 32–48. DOI: 10.1162/DAED_a_00113

Nissenbaum, H. (2017). Deregulating collection: must privacy give way to use regulation? *Available at SSRN* 3092282. DOI: 10.2139/ssrn.3092282

Nobles, C. (2015). *Exploring pilots' experiences of integrating technologically advanced aircraft within general aviation: A case study*. Northcentral University.

Nobles, C. (2018). Botching human factors in cybersecurity in business organizations. *Holistica Journal of Business and Public Administration*, *9*(3), 71–88. DOI: 10.2478/hjbpa-2018-0024

Nobles, C. (2022). Stress, burnout, and security fatigue in cybersecurity: A human factors perspective. *Holistica Journal of Business and Public Administration*, *13*(2), 201–232. DOI: 10.2478/hjbpa-2022-0003

Nobles, C., & Burrell, D. (2024). Exploring the variability of human factors definitions in cybersecurity literature. In *Proceedings of the 19th Midwest Association for Information Systems Conference*. Peoria, IL.

Nonju, K. D. S., & Ihua-Maduenyi, A. B. (2024). The Impact of Artificial Intelligence on Privacy Laws. *International Journal of Research and Innovation in Social Science*, *2150*. Advance online publication. DOI: 10.47772/IJRISS.2024.8090178

Nyst, C., Makin, P., Pannifer, S., & Whitley, E. (2016). Digital identity: Issue analysis (Executive summary). Consult Hyperion. https://www.chyp.com/media/reports/Digital-Identity-Issue-Analysis-Executive-Summary.pdf

Nyst, C., & Falchetta, T. (2017). The Right to Privacy in the Digital Age. *Journal of Human Rights Practice*, *9*(1), 104–118. DOI: 10.1093/jhuman/huw026

Oban, V., Kaya, M., Safi, G., Çimen, İ. N., Çatak, T., Karadağ, B., Görmüs, G., Çandir, A., & Alagöz, F. (2024). Profiling Driver Behaviors Using AI-Based Methods and Deep Learning Techniques for Improving Road Safety: A Comparative Study of Algorithms. 2024 9th International Conference on Computer Science and Engineering (UBMK), 955. DOI: 10.1109/UBMK63289.2024.10773587

OECD. (2013). *OECD Guidelines on the Protection of Privacy and Transborder Flows of Personal Data*. https://www.oecd.org

OECD. (2019). OECD principles on artificial intelligence. https://www.oecd.org/going-digital/ai/principles/

OECD. (2019). *Recommendation of the Council on Artificial Intelligence*. OECD Legal Instruments. https://legalinstruments.oecd.org/en/instruments/OECD-LEGAL-0449

Ohlhausen, M. K. (2014). Privacy challenges and opportunities: The role of the Federal Trade Commission. *Journal of Public Policy & Marketing*, *33*(1), 4–9. DOI: 10.1509/jppm.33.1.4

Okon, S. U., Olateju, O. O., Ogungbemi, O. S., Joseph, S. A., Olisa, A. O., & Olaniyi, O. O. (2024). Incorporating Privacy by Design Principles in the Modification of AI Systems in Preventing Breaches across Multiple Environments, Including Public Cloud, Private Cloud, and On-prem. *Journal of Engineering Research and Reports*, *26*(9), 136–158. DOI: 10.9734/jerr/2024/v26i91269

Open, A. I. (2023). *GPT-4 Technical Report*. https://openai.com/research/gpt-4

Orgeret, K. S., Westlund, O., & Krøvel, R. (Eds.). (2024). *Journalism and Safety: Digital Threats, Professional Fragilities, and Safety Cultures*. Taylor & Francis. DOI: 10.4324/9781003544517

Osler, L., & Zahavi, D. (2023). Sociality and Embodiment: Online Communication During and After COVID-19. *Foundations of Science*, *28*(4), 1125–1142. https://link.springer.com/article/10.1007/S10699-022-09861-1. DOI: 10.1007/s10699-022-09861-1 PMID: 36212516

Ou, L. W.Leonardo W Ou. (2025). Regulatory responses to data breaches: Evaluating the effectiveness of GDPR and CCPA in consumer protection. *International Journal of Social Sciences and Public Administration*, *6*(1), 176–185. DOI: 10.62051/ijsspa.v6n1.22

Pagallo, U. (2013). *The laws of robots: Crimes, contracts, and torts*. Springer., DOI: 10.1007/978-94-007-6564-1

Pagallo, U. (2021). On the Principle of Privacy by Design and Its Limits: Technology, Ethics and the Rule of Law. In Chiodo, S., & Schiaffonati, V. (Eds.), *Italian Philosophy of Technology. Philosophy of Engineering and Technology* (Vol. 35). Springer., DOI: 10.1007/978-3-030-54522-2_8

Pagano, T. P., Loureiro, R. B., Lisboa, F. V., Peixoto, R. M., Guimarães, G. A., Cruz, G. O., Araujo, M. M., Santos, L. L., Cruz, M. A., Oliveira, E. L., Winkler, I., & Nascimento, E. G. (2023). Bias and unfairness in Machine Learning Models: A systematic review on datasets, tools, fairness metrics, and identification and mitigation methods. *Big Data and Cognitive Computing*, *7*(1), 15. DOI: 10.3390/bdcc7010015

Panch, T., Mattie, H., & Atun, R. (2019). Artificial Intelligence and algorithmic bias: Implications for health systems. *Journal of Global Health*, *9*(2), 010318. Advance online publication. DOI: 10.7189/jogh.09.020318

Pasquale, F. (2015). *The black box society: The secret algorithms that control money and information*. Harvard University Press. DOI: 10.4159/harvard.9780674736061

Patel v. Facebook, Inc., 932 F.3d 1264 (9th Cir. 2019)

Patterson, C. M., Nurse, J. R. C., & Franqueira, V. N. L. (2023). Learning from cyber security incidents: A systematic review and future research agenda. *Computers & Security, 132*, 103309. DOI: 10.1016/j.cose.2023.103309

Paul, A. L. (2024, May). *Navigating the regulatory landscape: The impact of privacy and Data Protection Regulations on Global Data Security practices*. researchgate. https://www.researchgate.net/publication/381004748_Navigating_the_Regulatory_Landscape_The_Impact_of_Privacy_and_Data_Protection_Regulations_on_Global_Data_Security_Practices

Paul, L. & Brandon, R. (2025). Data minimisation: A crucial pillar of cyber security. Cyber Security: A Peer-Reviewed Journal, 8(3), 243–254(12).

Paul, M., Maglaras, L., Ferrag, M. A., & Almomani, I. (2023). Digitalization of Healthcare Sector: A Study on Privacy and Security Concerns. *IT Express*, *9*(1), 571–588. DOI: 10.1016/j.icte.2023.02.007

Pawlicka, A., Choraś, M., Kozik, R., & Pawlicki, M. (2023). First Broad and Systematic Horizon Scanning Campaign and Study to Detect Societal and Ethical Dilemmas and Emerging Issues Spanning Over Cybersecurity Solutions. *Personal and Ubiquitous Computing*, *27*(2), 193–202. https://link.springer.com/article/10.1007/s00779-020-01510-3. DOI: 10.1007/s00779-020-01510-3

Payton, T., & Claypoole, T. (2023). *Privacy in the Age of Big Data: Recognizing Threats, Defending Your Rights, and Protecting Your Family*. Bloomsbury Publishing PLC. DOI: 10.5771/9781538167830

PIPL. (2021). *Personal Information Protection Law of the People's Republic of China*. Standing Committee of the National People's Congress.

Plotnek, J. J., & Slay, J. (2021). Cyber Terrorism: A Homogenized Taxonomy and Definition. *Computers & Security*, *102*, 102145. DOI: 10.1016/j.cose.2020.102145

Politou, E., Alepis, E., Virvou, M., & Patsakis, C. (2021). The General Data Protection Regulation. In *Privacy and Data Protection Challenges in the Distributed Era* (pp. 13–39). Springer International Publishing.

Polyzoidou, V. (2021). Combatting cybercrime: Thoughts based on the Second Additional Protocol (Draft) to the Budapest Convention on Cybercrime. In *EU Internet Law in the Digital Single Market* (pp. 355–375). Cham: Springer International Publishing. DOI: 10.1007/978-3-030-69583-5_15

Popowicz-Pazdej, A. (2023). The proportionality between trade secret and privacy protection: How to strike the right balance when designing generative AI tools. *Journal of Data Protection & Privacy.*, *6*(2), 153. DOI: 10.69554/ILGY4235

Porcedda, M. G. (2017). *Cybersecurity and Privacy Rights in EU Law: Moving Beyond the Trade-off Model to Appraise the Role of Technology*. European University Institute. https://cadmus.eui.eu/entities/publication/24cc89f2-609c-5722-ad9f-b6080ebf1718

Posey, C., Raja, U., Crossler, R. E., & Burns, A. J. (2017). Taking Stock of Organizations' Protection of Privacy: Categorizing and Assessing Threats to Personally Identifiable Information in the USA. *European Journal of Information Systems*, *26*(6), 585–604. https://www.tandfonline.com/doi/epdf/10.1057/s41303-017-0065-y?needAccess=true. DOI: 10.1057/s41303-017-0065-y

Powell, A., Bryne, A., & Dailey, D. (2012). The Essential Internet: Digital Exclusion in Low-Income American Communities. *Policy and Internet*, *2*(2), 161–192. https://onlinelibrary.wiley.com/doi/10.2202/1944-2866.1058. DOI: 10.2202/1944-2866.1058

Power, D. J., Heavin, C., & O'Connor, Y. (2021). Balancing privacy rights and surveillance analytics: A decision process guide. *Journal of Business Analytics*, *4*(2), 155–170. DOI: 10.1080/2573234X.2021.1920856

Prakasha, K. K., & Sumalatha, U. (2025). Privacy-preserving techniques in biometric systems: Approaches and challenges. *IEEE Access : Practical Innovations, Open Solutions*.

Purcell, C., & Zhan, J. (2007, August). Adapting US privacy laws to the internet: Is patching enough? In *2007 International Conference on Machine Learning and Cybernetics* (Vol. 5, pp. 3000–3005). IEEE. https://doi.org/DOI: 10.1109/ICMLC.2007.4370662

Purves, D. (2022). Fairness in Algorithmic Policing. *Journal of the American Philosophical Association*, *8*(4), 741–761. DOI: 10.1017/apa.2021.39

Puttaswamy v. Union of India, (2017). Writ Petition (Civil) No. 494 of 2012, Supreme Court of India.

Quach, S., Thaichon, P., Martin, K. D., Weaven, S., & Palmatier, R. W. (2022). Digital Technologies: Tensions in Privacy and Data. *Journal of the Academy of Marketing Science*, *50*(6), 1299–1323. https://link.springer.com/article/10.1007/s11747-022-00845-y. DOI: 10.1007/s11747-022-00845-y PMID: 35281634

Rai, S. (2023). The making of India's data protection law: Constitutional origins and regulatory concerns. *Indian Journal of Law and Technology*, *19*(1), 45–72.

Rajaretnam, T. (2019). A Review of Data Governance, Regulation, Practices and Cybersecurity Strategies for Businesses: An Australian Perspective. In *International Conference on Education, Technology, Business, and Social Science* (pp. 6-21). Academia Industry Networks.

Raji, I. D., Smart, A., White, R. N., Mitchell, M., Gebru, T., Hutchinson, B., & Barnes, P. (2020). Closing the AI accountability gap: Defining an end-to-end framework for internal algorithmic auditing. *Proceedings of the 2020 Conference on Fairness, Accountability, and Transparency*, 33–44. DOI: 10.1145/3351095.3372873

Rane, J., Kaya, Ö., Mallick, S. K., & Rane, N. L. (2024). Enhancing black-box models: Advances in explainable artificial intelligence for ethical decision-making. DOI: 10.70593/978-81-981271-0-5_4

Rawaqa, S. (2025). Identifying and regulating human rights defenders (HRDs). *The International Journal of Human Rights, 29*(?), 1–31. DOI: 10.1080/13642987.2025.2517571

Regulation (EU) 2016/679 of the European Parliament and of the Council of 27 April 2016 on the protection of natural persons with regard to the processing of personal data and on the free movement of such data (General Data Protection Regulation). Official Journal of the European Union, L119, 1–88.

Reicher, A. E., & Fang, Y. (2016). FTC Privacy and Data Security Enforcement and Guidance Under Section 5. Competition Journal of the Antitrust and Unfair Competition Law Section of the California Lawyers Association, 25(2).

Reich, M. R. (2018). The core roles of transparency and accountability in the governance of Global Health Public–Private Partnerships. *Health Systems and Reform, 4*(3), 239–248. DOI: 10.1080/23288604.2018.1465880

Reis, O., Eneh, N. E., Ehimuan, B., Anyanwu, A., Olorunsogo, T., & Abrahams, T. O. (2024). Privacy law challenges in the digital age: A global review of legislation and Enforcement. *International Journal of Applied Research in Social Sciences, 6*(1), 73–88. DOI: 10.51594/ijarss.v6i1.733

Reiss, M. (2010). Ethical Thinking. In Jone, A., McKim, A., & Reiss, M. (Eds.), *Ethics in the Science and Technology Classroom: A New Approach to Teaching and Learning* (pp. 7–17). Sense Publishers., https://brill.com/display/book/9789460910715/BP000003.xml DOI: 10.1163/9789460910715_003

Richards, N., & Hartzog, W. (2018). The pathologies of digital consent. *Wash. UL Rev., 96*, 1461.

Riggi, J. (2024). *A Look at 2024's Health Care Cybersecurity Challenges*. American Hospital Association | AHA News. https://www.aha.org/news/aha-cyber-intel/2024-10-07-look-2024s-health-care-cybersecurity-challenges

Riggs, H., Tufail, S., Parvez, I., Tariq, M., Khan, M. A., Amir, A., Vuda, K. V., & Sarwat, A. I. (2023). Impact, vulnerabilities, and mitigation strategies for Cyber-Secure Critical Infrastructure. *Sensors (Basel)*, *23*(8), 4060. DOI: 10.3390/s23084060

Robinson, L., Kizawa, K., & Ronchi, E. (2021). Interoperability of privacy and data protection frameworks. Going Digital Toolkit Note, No. 21. https://goingdigital.oecd.org/data/notes/No21_ToolkitNote_PrivacyDataInteroperability.pdf

Robinson, N. (2023). Human factors security engineering: The future of cybersecurity teams. *EDPACS*, *67*(5), 1–17. DOI: 10.1080/07366981.2023.2211429

Romaniuk, S. N., & Hattiangady, P. (2023). Cybercrime, national security, and internet governance. In *The Handbook of Homeland Security* (pp. 211–230). CRC Press. DOI: 10.4324/9781315144511

Rong, K., Ling, Y., Yang, T., & Huang, C. (2025). Cross-border data transfer: Patterns and discrepancies. *Journal of International Business Policy*, *8*(1), 10–32. DOI: 10.1057/s42214-025-00209-7

Roy, S. (2025). Inside India's Draft Digital Personal Data Protection Act. DOI: 10.2139/ssrn.5082157

Rubenfeld, J. (1989). The Right to Privacy. *Harvard Law Review*, *102*(4), 737–807. https://www.jstor.org/stable/1341305. DOI: 10.2307/1341305

Ruohonen, J. (2023). Recent Trends in Cross-Border Data Access by Law Enforcement Agencies. arXiv (Cornell University). https://doi.org/10.48550/arXiv.2302.09942

Ruohonen, J. (2021). The Treachery of Images in the Digital Sovereignty Debate. *Minds and Machines*, *31*(3), 439–456. DOI: 10.1007/s11023-021-09566-7

Ruohonen, J., & Hjerppe, K. (2022). The GDPR enforcement fines at glance. *Information Systems*, *106*, 101876. DOI: 10.1016/j.is.2021.101876

Rydenfelt, H., Lehtiniemi, T., Haapoja, J., & Haapanen, L. (2025). Autonomy and Algorithms: Tracing the Significance of Content Personalization. *International Journal of Communication*, *19*, 481–500.

Ryngaert, C., & Taylor, M. (2020). The GDPR as *global* data protection regulation? *AJIL Unbound*, *114*, 5–9. DOI: 10.1017/aju.2019.80

Sadhya, D., & Sahu, T. (2024). A critical survey of the security and privacy aspects of the Aadhaar framework. *Computers & Security*, *140*, 103782. DOI: 10.1016/j.cose.2024.103782

Saeed, S. A., & Masters, R. M. (2021). Disparities in Health Care and the Digital Divide. *Current Psychiatry Reports*, *23*(9), 61. https://link.springer.com/article/10.1007/s11920-021-01274-4. DOI: 10.1007/s11920-021-01274-4 PMID: 34297202

Saetra, H. S. (2021). *Big Data's threat to liberty: surveillance, nudging, and information curation*. Academic Press.

Sahin, Z., & Vance, A. (2025). What do we need to know about the chief information security officer? A literature review and Research Agenda. *Computers &amp. Computers & Security*, *148*, 104063. DOI: 10.1016/j.cose.2024.104063

Saleh, A. M. S. (2024). Blockchain for Secure and Decentralized Artificial Intelligence in Cybersecurity: A Comprehensive Review. *Blockchain: Research and Applications*, *5*(3), 100193. DOI: 10.1016/j.bcra.2024.100193

Salem, A. H., Azzam, S. M., Emam, O. E., & Abohany, A. A. (2024). Advancing cybersecurity: A comprehensive review of AI-Driven Detection Techniques. *Journal of Big Data*, *11*(1), 105. Advance online publication. DOI: 10.1186/s40537-024-00957-y

Saleous, H., Ismail, M., AlDaajeh, S. H., Madathil, N., Alrabaee, S., Choo, K. K. R., & Al-Qirim, N. (2023). COVID-19 pandemic and the cyberthreat landscape: Research challenges and opportunities. *Digital Communications and Networks*, *9*(1), 211–222. DOI: 10.1016/j.dcan.2022.06.005 PMID: 35765301

Salomon, J. M. (2022, May). Public-private partnerships and collective cyber defence. In *2022 14th International Conference on Cyber Conflict: Keep Moving! (CyCon)* (Vol. 700, pp. 45–63). IEEE. DOI: 10.23919/CyCon55549.2022.9810912

Samuel, S. (2024). People are Falling in Love with — and Getting Addicted to — AI Voices. *Vox*. https://www.vox.com/future-perfect/367188/love-addicted-ai-voice-human-gpt4-emotion

Sartor, G. (2020). Artificial intelligence and legal responsibility. In Dubber, M. D., Pasquale, F., & Das, S. (Eds.), *The Oxford handbook of ethics of AI* (pp. 267–284). Oxford University Press.

Savaş, S., & Karataş, S. (2022). Cyber Governance Studies in Ensuring Cybersecurity: An Overview of Cybersecurity Governance. *International Cybersecurity Law Review*, *3*(1), 7–34. https://link.springer.com/article/10.1365/s43439-021-00045-4. DOI: 10.1365/s43439-021-00045-4 PMID: 37521508

Saxena, R. (2023). Data fiduciaries and digital constitutionalism: India's approach to data protection. *Indian Journal of Law and Technology, 19*(1), 1–20.

Sayjari, T., & Silveira, R. M. (2024). Ethics of privacy in cybersecurity: Protecting individual autonomy through technology. *International Research Journal of Modernization in Engineering Technology and Science, 06*(10), 1940–1951. DOI: 10.56726/IRJMETS62448

Scandamis, N., Sigalas, F., & Stratakis, S. (2007). Rival Freedoms in (Terms of) Security: The Case of Data Protection and (the Criterion of) Connexity. *Research Paper No. 7, Challenge, Liberty, & Security*. https://www.files.ethz.ch/isn/45974/CP007%20Rival%20Freedoms%20in%20terms%20of%20security.pdf

Schmitt, M. (2023). Securing the digital world: Protecting smart infrastructures and digital industries with artificial intelligence (AI)-enabled malware and intrusion detection. *Journal of Industrial Information Integration, 36*, 100520. DOI: 10.1016/j.jii.2023.100520

Schuett, J. (2023). Risk management in the Artificial Intelligence Act. *European Journal of Risk Regulation, 15*(2), 367–385. DOI: 10.1017/err.2023.1

Schutze, B. (2022). Data protection and data security in the EU: the European General Data Protection Regulation. In *Nursing Informatics: A Health Informatics, Interprofessional and Global Perspective* (pp. 437–451). Springer International Publishing., DOI: 10.1007/978-3-030-91237-6_29

Schwartz, P. M., & Peifer, K. N. (2017). Transatlantic data privacy law. *The Georgetown Law Journal, 106*(1), 115–178.

Schwartz, P. M., & Solove, D. J. (2014). Reconciling personal information in the United States and European Union. *California Law Review, 102*(4), 877–916.

Sebastian, J., & Sen, A. (2020). Unravelling the role of autonomy and consent in privacy. *SSRN, 9*, 1. DOI: 10.2139/ssrn.4223897

Seh, A. H., Zarour, M., Alenezi, M., Sarkar, A. K., Agrawal, A., Kumar, R., & Ahmad Khan, R. (2020). Healthcare data breaches: Insights and implications. *Healthcare (Basel), 8*(2), 133. DOI: 10.3390/healthcare8020133

Selinger, E., & Woodrow, H. (2015). Facebook's emotional contagion study and the ethical problem of co-opted identity in mediated environments where users lack control. *Sage Journals, 12*(1). Advance online publication. DOI: 10.1177/17470161155795

Senarath, A., & Arachchilage, N. A. G. (2019). A data minimization model for embedding privacy into software systems. *Computers & Security*, *87*, 87. DOI: 10.1016/j.cose.2019.101605

Setiawan, A. (2024). Intelligent systems for disabilities technology for a more inclusive life. *Available at SSRN* 5062273.

Shaffer, G., & Pollack, M. A. (2010). Hard vs. soft law: Alternatives, complements, and antagonists in international governance. *Minnesota Law Review*, *94*, 706–799.

Shaheen, R. (2024). Gender and Surveillance: The Implications of Biometric Technologies for Privacy and Equity. *Journal of Gender, Power, and Social Transformation*, *1*(3), 29–35.

Shahin, S., & Zheng, P. (2018). Big Data and the Illusion of Choice: Comparing the Evolution of India's Aadhaar and China's Social Credit System as Technosocial Discourses. *Social Science Computer Review*, *38*(1), 25–41. DOI: 10.1177/0894439318789343

Shao, H., Li, X., & Wang, G. (2022, April). Are you tired? I am: Trying to understand privacy fatigue of social media users. In *CHI Conference on Human Factors in Computing Systems Extended Abstracts* (pp. 1–7). DOI: 10.1145/3491101.3519778

Sharma, A. (2025). From Click to Contract: The legal validity of consent in India's social media data ecosystem. *International Journal of Law and Social Innovation*, *7*(3), 416–433. DOI: 10.10000/IJLSI.112633

Sharma, D., Bhagat, L., & Sharma, S. (2024). Regulating Children's Personal Data Protection in India: No Child's Play. Development, 67(1), 28–33. Nissenbaum, H. (2011). A contextual approach to privacy online. *Daedalus*, *140*(4), 32–48.

Sharma, S. (2019). *Data privacy and GDPR handbook*. John Wiley & Sons., DOI: 10.1002/9781119594307

Shekar, K., Tripathi, A., & Birla, B. (2023). Principle-based Framework towards Cross-Border Data Transfers. SSRN Electronic Journal. DOI: 10.2139/ssrn.4527681

Shetty, D. K., Vijaya Arjunan, R., Cenitta, D., Makkithaya, K., Hegde, N. V., & Bhatta, B. (2025). Analyzing AI regulation through literature and current trends. *Journal of Open Innovation*, *11*(1), 100508. DOI: 10.1016/j.joitmc.2025.100508

Siddiqi, M. A., Pak, W., & Siddiqi, M. A. (2022). A Study on the Psychology of Social Engineering-Based Cyberattacks and Existing Countermeasures. *Applied Sciences (Basel, Switzerland)*, *12*(12), 6042. https://www.mdpi.com/2076-3417/12/12/6042. DOI: 10.3390/app12126042

Simonette, M. (2021). Privacy by Design e Privacy by Default. CEST, 6.

Singh, A., & Anusha, A. (2024). The Digital Personal Data Protection Act, 2023: An Ambitious Government Step Towards Ensuring Its Wide Reach. *The Indian Journal of Public Administration*, *70*(3), 502–515. DOI: 10.1177/00195561241271533

Singh, M. P. (2023). Data protection and the Indian Constitution: The role of fiduciary duty. *Indian Journal of Constitutional Law*, *17*(1), 45–63.

Singh, N. (2024). Data Protection and privacy as a fundamental right - an in-depth analysis of the European Union and India's Data Protection Legislation. *International Journal For Multidisciplinary Research*, *6*(2), 15869. Advance online publication. DOI: 10.36948/ijfmr.2024.v06i02.15869

Singh, P. (2021). Aadhaar and data privacy: Biometric identification and anxieties of recognition in India. *Information Communication and Society*, *24*(7), 978–993. DOI: 10.1080/1369118X.2019.1668459

Singhvi, H. (2024). Socio-Economic Impacts of Predictive Policing on Minority Communities and Potential Solutions. DOI: 10.58445/rars.2024

Sivakumar, C. L. V., Mone, V., & Abdumukhtor, R. (2024). Addressing privacy concerns with wearable health monitoring technology. *Wiley Interdisciplinary Reviews. Data Mining and Knowledge Discovery*, *14*(3), e1535. DOI: 10.1002/widm.1535

Slapničar, S., Axelsen, M., Bongiovanni, I., & Stockdale, D. (2023). A pathway model to five lines of accountability in Cybersecurity Governance. *International Journal of Accounting Information Systems*, *51*, 100642. DOI: 10.1016/j.accinf.2023.100642

Solove, D. (2008). *Understanding Privacy*. Harvard University Press.

Solove, D. J. (2013). Privacy self-management and the consent dilemma. *Harvard Law Review*, *126*(7), 1880–1903.

Solove, D. J. (2020). The myth of the privacy paradox. *The George Washington Law Review*, *89*(1), 1–56.

Solove, D. J. (2022). The limitations of privacy rights. *The Notre Dame Law Review*, *98*, 975.

Solove, D. J. (2024). Murky consent: An approach to the fictions of consent in privacy law. *BUL Rev.*, *104*, 593.

Solove, D. J., & Hartzog, W. (2014). The FTC and the new common law of privacy. *Columbia Law Review*, *114*(3), 583–676. https://www.columbialawreview.org

Staben, J., & Leisterer, H. (2017). International Cross-Surveillance: Global IT Surveillance Arbitrage and the Principle of Proportionality as a Counterargument. *Surveillance & Society*, *15*(1), 108–122. DOI: 10.24908/ss.v15i1.5277

Stepenko, V., Dreval, L., Chernov, S., & Shestak, V. (2022). EU personal data protection standards and regulatory framework. *Journal of Applied Security Research*, *17*(2), 190–207. DOI: 10.1080/19361610.2020.1868928

Stylios, I., Kokolakis, S., Thanou, O., & Chatzis, S. (2022). Key factors driving the adoption of behavioral biometrics and continuous authentication technology: An empirical research. *Information and Computer Security*, *30*(4), 562–582. DOI: 10.1108/ICS-08-2021-0124

Sultana, R. (2024). Artificial Intelligence For Decision Making In The Era Of Big Data Evolution. *Non Human Journal.*, *1*(1), 17–40. DOI: 10.70008/jbimisr.v1i01.59

Supreme Court of India. (2017). Justice K. S. Puttaswamy (Retd.) v. Union of India, (2017) 10 SCC 1

Susser, D., Roessler, B., & Nissenbaum, H. (2019). Online manipulation: Hidden influences in a digital world. *Georgetown Law Technology Review*, *4*(1), 1–45.

Sussman, R., & Gifford, R. (2019). Causality in the theory of planned behavior. *Personality and Social Psychology Bulletin*, *45*(6), 920–933. DOI: 10.1177/0146167218801363 PMID: 30264655

Syed, N. F., Shah, S. W., Shaghaghi, A., Anwar, A., Baig, Z., & Doss, R. (2022). Zero trust architecture (ZTA): A comprehensive survey. *IEEE Access : Practical Innovations, Open Solutions*, *10*, 57143–57179. DOI: 10.1109/ACCESS.2022.3174679

Tabaghdehi, S. A. H. (2024). Ethical governance of digital footprint data: a journey towards a responsible society. In *Business Strategies and Ethical Challenges in the Digital Ecosystem* (pp. 369–379). Emerald Publishing Limited., DOI: 10.1108/978-1-80455-069-420241017

Tai, E. T. T. (2024). Using AI to Influence Consumer Choice. The Cambridge Handbook of AI and Consumer Law Comparative Perspectives, 62 – 74. DOI: 10.1017/9781009483599.010

Tanneru, B. (2025). Adaptive compliance: Automating dynamic security controls in real-time. *International Journal of Multidisciplinary Research and Growth Evaluation*, *6*(2), 1853–1855. DOI: 10.54660/.IJMRGE.2025.6.2.1853-1855

Tene, O., & Polonetsky, J. (2012). Big data for all: Privacy and user control in the age of analytics. *Northwestern Journal of Technology and Intellectual Property*, *11*(5), 239–273.

Tene, O., & Polonetsky, J. (2012). Big data for all: Privacy and user control in the age of analytics. *Nw. J. Tech. & Intell. Prop.*, *11*, 239.

Teo, S. A. (2025, June). Artificial intelligence and its 'slow violence' to human rights. *AI and Ethics*, *5*(3), 2265–2280.DOI: 10.1007/s43681-024-00547-x

Thangaraju, D. (2024). Edge Data Governance: Frameworks and approaches for distributed data management at the Network Edge. *International Journal of Multidisciplinary Research and Growth Evaluation*, *5*(4), 1353–1361. DOI: 10.54660/.IJMRGE.2024.5.6-1353-1361

Theodos, K., & Sittig, S. (2020, December 7). *Health Information Privacy Laws in the digital age: HIPAA doesn't apply*. Perspectives in health information management. https://pmc.ncbi.nlm.nih.gov/articles/PMC7883355/

Thiele, C. (2018). U.S. CLOUD Act - Danaergeschenk für den Europäischen Datenschutz. *Zeitschrift Für Informationsrecht*, *6*(2), 128–132. DOI: 10.33196/ziir201802012801

Tick, A., Cranfield, D. J., Venter, I. M., Renaud, K. V., & Blignaut, R. J. (2021). Comparing Three Countries' Higher Education Students' Cyber-Related Perceptions and Behaviors During COVID-19. *Electronics (Basel)*, *10*(22), 2865. https://www.mdpi.com/2079-9292/10/22/2865. DOI: 10.3390/electronics10222865

Tisné, M. (2020). *The data delusion: Protecting individual data isn't enough when the harm is collective*. MIT Technology Review. https://www.technologyreview.com/2020/07/01/1004540/data-privacy-individual-collective-rights/

Toledano, S. A. (2024). *Critical Infrastructure Security: Cybersecurity Lessons Learned from Real-World Breaches*. Packt Publishing Ltd.

Tosoni, L. (2018). Rethinking privacy in the Council of Europe's Convention on Cybercrime. *Computer Law & Security Review*, *34*(6), 1197–1214. DOI: 10.1016/j.clsr.2018.08.004

Tschider, C. A. (2020). Beyond the" black box. *Denv. L. Rev.*, *98*, 683.

Tully, S. (2014). A Human Right to Access the Internet? Problems and Prospects. *Human Rights Law Review*, *14*(2), 175–195. DOI: 10.1093/hrlr/ngu011

Turow, J. (2017). *The aisles have eyes: How retailers track your shopping, strip your privacy, and define your power*. Yale University Press.

Tzanou, M. (2013). Data Protection as a Fundamental Right Next to Privacy? 'Reconstructing' a Not so New Right. *International Data Privacy Law, 3*(2), 88–99. DOI: 10.1093/idpl/ipt004

Tzanou, M. (2020). *The fundamental right to data protection: Normative value in the context of counter-terrorism surveillance.* Bloomsbury Publishing.

U.S.- China Economic and Security Review Commission. (2020). *China's Corporate Social Credit System: Context, Competition, Technology and Geopolitics.* Www.uscc.gov. https://www.uscc.gov/research/chinas-corporate-social-credit-system-context-competition-technology-and-geopolitics

U.S. Department of Health and Human Services (HHS). (2022). *Health Industry Cybersecurity Practices: Managing threats and protecting patients.* https://405d.hhs.gov/Documents/HICP-Main-508.pdf

UNCTAD. (United Nations Conference on Trade and Development). (2023). *Data protection and privacy legislation worldwide.* https://unctad.org/page/data-protection-and-privacy-legislation-worldwide

UNDP. (1994). *Human Development Report.* https://hdr.undp.org/content/human-development-report-1994

UNESCO. (2021). Recommendation on the ethics of artificial intelligence. https://unesdoc.unesco.org/ark:/48223/pf0000379920

UNESCO. (2021). *Recommendation on the Ethics of Artificial Intelligence.* United Nations Educational, Scientific and Cultural Organization. https://unesdoc.unesco.org/ark:/48223/pf0000381137

United Nations. (1948). Universal Declaration of Human Rights. https://www.un.org/en/about-us/universal-declaration-of-human-rights

United Nations. (1966). International Covenant on Civil and Political Rights. https://www.ohchr.org/en/instruments-mechanisms/instruments/international-covenant-civil-and-political-rights

Usman, H., Tariq, I., & Nawaz, B. (2023). IN THE REALM OF THE MACHINES: AI'S INFLUENCE UPON INTERNATIONAL LAW AND POLICY. *Journal of Social Research Development, 4*(2), 383–399. DOI: 10.53664/JSRD/04-02-2023-13-383-399

Vaghri, Z. (2022, January). Article 16: The Right to Protection of Privacy. In *Monitoring State Compliance with the UN Convention on the Rights of the Child: An Analysis of Attributes* (Vol. 25, p. 93). Springer Nature. DOI: 10.1007/978-3-030-84647-3

Vaka, P. R. (2020). Data breaches or regulatory and compliance. *International Journal Of Multidisciplinary Research In Science. Engineering and Technology, 03*(12). Advance online publication. DOI: 10.15680/IJMRSET.2020.0312020

Van der Heijden, J. (2021). Risk as an approach to regulatory governance: An evidence synthesis and research agenda. *SAGE Open, 11*(3), 21582440211032202. Advance online publication. DOI: 10.1177/21582440211032202

van der Sloot, B. (2017). *Privacy as virtue: Moving beyond the individual in the age of big data. Intersentia* (Vol. 81). Human Rights Research Series. DOI: 10.1017/9781780686592

Varlamova, N. V. (2019). DIGITAL RIGHTS — NEW GENERATION OF HUMAN RIGHTS? *Proceedings of the Institute of State and Law of the RAS, 14*(5), 141–167. DOI: 10.35427/2073-4522-2019-14-5-varlamova

Veale, M., & Zuiderveen Borgesius, F. (2021). Demystifying the Draft EU Artificial Intelligence Act. *Computer Law Review International, 22*(4), 97–112. DOI: 10.9785/cri-2021-220402

Ventura, D. (2022). Democracy through the lens of digital surveillance: An assessment of the legitimacy of general principles of law. In *Democracy and Sovereignty* (pp. 291–321). Brill Nijhoff., DOI: 10.1163/9789004508712_013

Verhulst, S. G. (2021). Reimagining data responsibility: 10 new approaches toward a culture of trust in re-using data to address critical public needs. *Data & Policy, 3*, e6. Advance online publication. DOI: 10.1017/dap.2021.4

Villiers, C. (2022). New Directions in the European Union's Regulatory Framework for corporate reporting, due diligence and accountability: The challenge of complexity. *European Journal of Risk Regulation, 13*(4), 548–566. DOI: 10.1017/err.2022.25

Voigt, P., & Von dem Bussche, A. (2017). *The EU General Data Protection Regulation (GDPR): A practical guide*. Springer., DOI: 10.1007/978-3-319-57959-7

Voss, W. G. (2020). Cross-border data flows, the GDPR, and Data Governance. *International Organisations Research Journal, 29*(3), 485–532. DOI: 10.17323/1996-7845-2022-01-03

Wachter, S., & Mittelstadt, B. (2019). *A right to reasonable inferences: Re-thinking data protection law in the age of Big Data and AI*. Columbia Business Law Review, 2019(2), 494–620. https://papers.ssrn.com/sol3/papers.cfm?abstract_id=3248829

Wachter, S., Mittelstadt, B., & Floridi, L. (2017). Why a right to explanation of automated decision-making does not exist in the General Data Protection Regulation. *International Data Privacy Law*, *7*(2), 76–99. DOI: 10.1093/idpl/ipx005

Wagner, B., Sanchez, A., Sekwenz, M., Dideriksen, S., & Murray-Rust, D. (2023, Dec. 13). The Politics of Digital (Human) Rights. Oxford Research Encyclopedia of International Studies. Retrieved 24 Feb. 2026, from https://oxfordre.com/internationalstudies/view/10.1093/acrefore/9780190846626.001.0001/acrefore-9780190846626-e-694DOI: 10.1093/acrefore/9780190846626.013.694

Wagner, G., & Eidenmuller, H. (2019). Down by Algorithms: Siphoning Rents, Exploiting Biases, and Shaping Preferences: Regulating the Dark Side of Personalized Transactions. *The University of Chicago Law Review. University of Chicago. Law School*, *86*, 581.

Wang, G. (2023). The Necessity of Extraterritorial Application of the Personal Information Protection Law and Suggestions for Its Improvement. *International Journal of Frontiers in Sociology*, *5*(16). Advance online publication. DOI: 10.25236/IJFS.2023.051616

Wang, S., Asif, M., Shahzad, M. F., & Ashfaq, M. (2024). Data Privacy and cybersecurity challenges in the digital transformation of the banking sector. *Computers &amp. Computers & Security*, *147*, 104051. DOI: 10.1016/j.cose.2024.104051

Weick, K. E., & Sutcliffe, K. M. (2015). *Managing the unexpected: Sustained performance in a complex world* (3rd ed.). Wiley. DOI: 10.1002/9781119175834

Westin, A. (1970). *Privacy and Freedom*. Bodley Head.

Woods, D. W., & Seymour, S. (2023). Evidence-based cybersecurity policy? A meta-review of Security Control Effectiveness. *Journal of Cyber Policy*, *8*(3), 365–383. DOI: 10.1080/23738871.2024.2335461

World Economic Forum. (2011). *Personal data: The emergence of a new asset class*. https://www3.weforum.org/docs/WEF_ITTC_PersonalDataNewAsset_Report_2011.pdf

Wright, D., & De Hert, P. (2016). *Enforcing privacy: Regulatory, legal and technological approaches*. Springer. DOI: 10.1007/978-3-319-25047-2

Wright, J. (2023). Healthcare cybersecurity and cybercrime supply chain risk management. *Health Economics and Management Review*, *4*(4), 17–27. DOI: 10.61093/hem.2023.4-02

Wylde, V., Rawindaran, N., Lawrence, J., Balasubramanian, R., Prakash, E., Jayal, A., Khan, I., Hewage, C., & Platts, J. (2022). Cybersecurity, data privacy and Blockchain: A Review. *SN Computer Science, 3*(2), 127. Advance online publication. DOI: 10.1007/s42979-022-01020-4

Xiao, L., Cheng, X., & Mou, J. (2022). Understanding Global E-Commerce Development During the COVID-19 Pandemic: Technology-Organization-Environment Perspective. *Journal of Global Information Technology Management, 25*(1), 1–6. DOI: 10.1080/1097198X.2022.2026658

Yadav, S., & Tiwari, N. (2023). Privacy preserving data sharing method for social media platforms. *PLoS One, 18*(1), e0280182. DOI: 10.1371/journal.pone.0280182 PMID: 36662805

Yakovleva, S. (2017). Should fundamental rights to privacy and data protection be a part of the EU's International Trade 'deals'? *World Trade Review, 17*(3), 477–508. DOI: 10.1017/S1474745617000453

Yang, Q., Lepore, C., Eynard, J., & Loborde, R. (2025). From theory to practice: Data minimisation and technical review of verifiable credentials under the GDPR. *Computer Law & Security Review, 57*, 57. DOI: 10.1016/j.clsr.2025.106138

Yeap, K. H., Chow, C. T., Low, H. T., & Nisar, H. (2024). *Enhanced Biometric Identification Using Photoplethysmography Signals*. Cambridge Scholars Publishing.

Yeo, L. H.. (2022). Human factors in electronic health-records cybersecurity: An exploratory analysis of healthcare breach incidents in the United States. *JMIR Human Factors, 9*(2), e35457. DOI: 10.2196/35457

Yeung, K. (2018). Algorithmic regulation: A critical interrogation. *Regulation & Governance, 12*(4), 505–523. DOI: 10.1111/rego.12158

Yi, W., & Li, Z. (2024). Mapping the scholarship of dark pattern regulation: A systematic review of concepts, regulatory paradigms, and solutions from an interdisciplinary perspective. arXiv preprint arXiv:2407.10340. https://arxiv.org/abs/2407.10340 DOI: 10.2139/ssrn.4993171

Yusuff, M. (2023, May). *Ensuring compliance with GDPR, CCPA, and other Data Protection Regulations: Challenges and Best Practices*. ResearchGate. https://www.researchgate.net/publication/387224965_Ensuring_Compliance_with_GDPR_CCPA_and_Other_Data_Protection_Regulations_Challenges_and_Best_Practices

Zadeh, A., Lavine, B., Zolbanin, H., & Hopkins, D. (2023). A cybersecurity risk quantification and classification framework for informed risk mitigation decisions. *Decision Analytics Journal, 9*, 100328. DOI: 10.1016/j.dajour.2023.100328

Zafar, A. (2025). Reconciling blockchain technology and data protection laws: Regulatory challenges, technical solutions, and practical pathways. *Journal of Cybersecurity*, *11*(1), tyaf002. Advance online publication. DOI: 10.1093/cybsec/tyaf002

Zaidan, E., & Ibrahim, I. A. (2024). AI governance in a complex and rapidly changing regulatory landscape: A global perspective. *Humanities & Social Sciences Communications*, *11*(1), 1121. Advance online publication. DOI: 10.1057/s41599-024-03560-x

Zaid, T., & Garai, S. (2024). Emerging trends in cybersecurity: A holistic view on current threats, Assessing Solutions, and pioneering new frontiers. *Blockchain in Healthcare Today*, *7*(1). Advance online publication. DOI: 10.30953/bhty.v7.302

Zard, L., & Sears, A. M. (2023). Targeted advertising and consumer protection law in the European Union. Vand. J. Transnat' l L., 56, 799.

Zelikow, P. (2003). The Transformation of National Security: Five Redefinitions. *National Interest*, *71*, 17–28. https://www.jstor.org/stable/42895592

Zerilli, J., Knott, A., Maclaurin, J., & Gavaghan, C. (2019). Transparency in algorithmic and human decision-making: Is there a double standard? *Philosophy & Technology*, *32*(4), 661–683. DOI: 10.1007/s13347-018-0330-6

Zoder-Martell, K. A., Markelz, A. M., Floress, M. T., Skriba, H. A., & Sayyah, L. E. (2020). Technology to facilitate telehealth in applied behavior analysis. *Behavior Analysis in Practice*, *13*(3), 596–603. DOI: 10.1007/s40617-020-00449-4 PMID: 32837699

Zuboff, S. (2019). *The age of surveillance capitalism: The fight for a human future at the new frontier of power*. PublicAffairs.

Zuboff, S. (2023). The age of surveillance capitalism. In *Social theory re-wired* (pp. 203–213). Routledge. DOI: 10.4324/9781003320609-27

About the Contributors

Calvin Nobles is a Cybersecurity Professional and Human Factors Engineer with more than 25 years of experience. He is a Department Chair and Associate Professor at the Illinois Institute of Technology. He retired from the Navy and worked in the Financial and Services Industry for several years. He authored a book on the integration of technologically advanced aircraft in general aviation. He serves on the Cybersecurity Advisory Board at Stillman College and the Intelligence and National Security Alliance Cyber Council. He is a Cybersecurity Fellow at Harvard University.

Darrell Norman Burrell is a visiting scholar at the Samuel DeWitt Proctor Institute for Leadership, Equity, and Justice at Rutgers University, where he is currently focusing his research on sustainability, health equity, and inclusive leadership. His work as a visiting researcher at the Pellegrino Center for Clinical Bioethics at the Georgetown University Medical Center in Washington, D.C., and as a post-doctoral public health researcher at the University of Maryland School of Pharmacy in Baltimore, MD, has provided him with a unique perspective on issues related to health disparities, health technology access, telehealth, adolescent health, and health literacy. For more than 12 years, he has also served in various roles as a doctoral faculty member, dissertation chair, and research panel participant at Marymount University, the Florida Institute of Technology, Capitol Technology University, the University of Liverpool in the U.K., and The Chicago School of Professional Psychology in Washington D.C. Dr. Burrell is a Certified Diversity Professional and a Certified Executive Coach. Dr. Burrell is an alumnus of the Presidential Management Fellows Program with the U.S. Federal Government and U.S. Nuclear Regulatory Commission, where he managed and developed leadership and diversity programs for professionals in Public Health, Environmental Health, Emergency Response, Technology, and Engineering. Academically, Dr. Burrell has three doctorate degrees and six graduate degrees, including a Master of Research in Artificial Intelligence Biotechnology Applications and Healthcare, along with additional graduate degrees in (H.R. Management, Management, Health Leadership, Sales and Marketing Management, Higher Education Administration, and Interfaith Action and Conflict Management). Dr. Burrell received his first doctoral degree in health education (DHEd), focusing on environmental public health and executive leadership coaching, at A.T. Still University in 2010. Dr. Burrell completed his 2nd doctorate, a Doctor of Philosophy (Ph.D.) in Cybersecurity Leadership at Capitol Technology University. In 2022, Dr. Burrell completed his 3rd Doctor of Business Administration (DBA) in Supply Chain Management at Capitol Technology University. He has over 20 years of management, teaching, and training experience in academia, government, and private industry. Dr. Burrell has over 200 peer-reviewed publications and more than 1200 Google Scholar citations.

***

Nathaniel Akande is a cybersecurity and data governance professional with over 8 years of experience driving secure digital transformation across sectors. He holds a BSc in Electrical Engineering, MSc in Cybersecurity, an MBA, and is certified as an ISO/IEC 27001 Lead Implementer. Nathaniel has led enterprise projects involving data governance and AI risk management, with a focus on aligning technology, compliance, and business value.

Amina Ayodeji-Ogundiran was born and raised in Nigeria. She holds a Bachelor of Arts in English Language from Bayero University, Kano; a Master of Arts in Human Resource Development from Bowie State University, Maryland; and a Doctorate in Organizational Leadership (with Academic Distinction) from The Chicago School, Washington, D.C., conferred in July 2022. Dr. Ayodeji-Ogundiran currently serves as an Assistant Professor and Program Coordinator for the Human Resource Development graduate program at Bowie State University, where she also holds the role of Vice Chair of the Graduate Council. Her scholarly work focuses on the intersections of organizational change and development, career development, and accessibility studies, with a particular emphasis on neurodiversity in the workforce. Through her research, she explores strategies that promote positive organizational cultures and progressive work climates. Dr. Ayodeji-Ogundiran's publications have appeared in the International Journal of Leadership, Education, and Business Studies and the International Journal of Smart Education and Urban Society (IJSEUS). Beyond academia, she is deeply committed to writing, research, and humanitarian service—particularly in student advocacy. As an educator, she is dedicated to cultivating collaborative and experiential learning environments that empower learners to engage critically and inclusively. She envisions a world where every individual has equitable opportunities to realize their fullest potential and continues to advance this vision through both her scholarly and practical contributions.

Yogita Bangar is working as a Lecturer in Jindal Global Law School, O.P Jindal Global University. She did her undergraduate degree in law from NorthCap University, Gurgaon. She then pursued LL.M. in Human Rights from National Law School of India University, Bangalore where she was involved in various research projects at the Centre for Study of Social Exclusion and Inclusive Policies. She pursued her interest in interdisciplinary research as an Urban Fellow at Indian Institute for Human Settlements, Bangalore in urban practice. Following this, she did her MPhil in Criminological Research from University of Cambridge. For MPhil she wrote her thesis on the community justice system in India. Her research interest lies in legal pluralism, informal justice systems and their legitimacy in the post-colonial societies.

Rishabh Bhandari has completed his BA. LL.B. (Hons.) from Dr. Ram Manohar Lohiya National Law University, Lucknow, specializing in Constitutional Law. He also holds an LLM in Constitutional and Administrative Law from Shri Ramswaroop Memorial University, Lucknow. Mr. Bhandari is pursuing his Phd in Law from the School of Law, Christ (Deemed to be University), Bangalore. Simultaneously, he is working as Assistant Professor of Law at Ramaiah College of Law, Bengaluru. He has taught Bharatiya Nyaya Sanhita, Indian Penal Code, Law of Contracts I and II, Constitutional Law I and II, Administrative Law, Intellectual Property Rights, Legal Methods, Drafting, Pleading and Conveyancing, and Social Immersion Program - Theory. Mr. Bhandari has actively participated in several enriching Faculty Development Programs and Academic Workshops. He has written on several important legal issues and presented his paper at national and international conferences. As an Associate Editor for RMLNLU Law Review and a Peer Reviewer for IGI Global Scientific Publishing, Mr Bhandari has edited and reviewed research articles. He has been invited to deliver Guest Lectures and judge Moot Court and ADR competitions at prominent institutions. He has chaired, organised, and participated in various Model United Nations conferences on key socio-legal issues.

Kim L. Brown-Jackson holds a Ph.D.-Cybersecurity Leadership, Doctorate of Business Admin (DBA)-Quality Systems Mgmt. (business process improvement) conc. Health Systems, a Master's-Biomedical Sciences in Pathology & Molecular Oncology with additional Ph.D. course work, an Associates-Biotechnology and Forensic Science, an executive professional MBA certificate, and Bachelors in Biological Sciences with a cluster minor in Business Administration. She is certified in numerous professional areas. Dr. Brown-Jackson has 30 years of experience as a practitioner, academician, quality healthcare leader and performance and learning strategist guiding business process improvement through biomedical services, public health, pandemics, advanced drug development, telemedicine/ telehealth initiatives, and leadership development. Specializes in regulatory compliant industries (pharmaceutical-drugs, therapeutics, biologics, medical devices, financial). She has taught at the collegiate, government, and corporate levels. She has contributed to over 16 book chapters and 30+ peer-reviewed journals, and delivered numerous presentations at conferences and on panels.

Sharon L. Burton leads in product management and development, Organizational Development Change Management, Cyber-Security/Technology, Process Improvement, Telemedicine/Telehealth and Learning & Development. Education includes: Ph.D. in Cybersecurity Leadership, and a DBA in Business Process Improvement; and two MBA degrees - Human Resources Management, and Management. Certifications in the following: AI Prompting Essentials; Project Management Essentials; Master Lean Six Sigma Black Belt; Kaizen Leader; Change Management Professional; Strategic Workforce Planning; Human Capital Strategist; Kirkpatrick Four Levels Evaluation; and Advanced Communicator Gold Toastmaster. As a facilitator and educator of audiences, she has more than 100 academic publications and has presented at over 30 professional conferences. Dr. Burton is available to present at conferences, participate in forums, and other initiatives. She may be reached at sharonlburton2@comcast.net and 302-547-8010.

Marlena Daryousef holds an MBA and Doctor of Management degree from Colorado Technical University with over ten years of business development and consulting across multiple business verticals. Marlena has a proven track record of helping both startups and established businesses improve their business optimization, stakeholder engagement, quality and risk management processes, and problem-solving. It is important to be apart of social change while assisting businesses to defend their unique place in their community.

Ankit Dixit is an Assistant Professor in the School of Liberal and Creative Arts (Journalism and Mass Communication) at Lovely Professional University, Phagwara, Punjab, India. He holds a Ph.D. from Babasaheb Bhimrao Ambedkar University, Lucknow, and a Master's degree in Journalism and Mass Communication from Makhanlal Chaturvedi National University of Journalism and Communication, Bhopal, Madhya Pradesh. He completed his Bachelor's degree from Bundelkhand University, Jhansi. Dr. Dixit's areas of expertise include film communication, media law and ethics, advertising and public relations, and event management.

He has qualified the UGC-NET with Junior Research Fellowship (JRF). He has published several research papers in UGC CARE-listed and other reputed peer-reviewed journals. Additionally, he has actively participated in numerous national and international seminars and conferences.

Terrence Duncan holds a Doctor of Business Administration degree from Walden University (2016), and a MBA-Healthcare Services Concentration from Park University (2006). He has over fifteen years industry experience in healthcare ranging from enterprise risk management, claims administration, and patient safety. Dr. Duncan currently serves on two non-profit boards and works extensively with the regional chamber of commerce on subject areas including healthcare, economic development, diversity, and leadership. Dr. Duncan has self-published two books on leadership and personal motivation.

Sri. Rajiv Gurugopinath, Dr., is an Assistant Professor of Law at Ramaiah College of Law, Bengaluru. He is registered as an advocate on the rolls of the Karnataka State Bar Council. He graduated with a degree of B.A. LL.B. from B.M.S. College of Law, Bengaluru. He completed his Master of Laws (LL. M.) in Constitutional and Administrative Law from the University Law College, Bangalore University, Bengaluru and wrote a Thesis on Constitutional Implications of the appointment of Judges of the Higher Judiciary in India – A Critical Evaluation. He also a holder of Master of Business Laws (M. B. L.) from the National Law School of India University, Bengaluru. Sri. Rajiv Gurugopinath, is currently pursuing his Ph.D., from the School of Law, Vel Tech Rangarajan Dr.Sagunthala R&D Institute of Science and Technology, Avadi, Chennai on the topic "Right to Health - A Study on the Legal Framework and Its Implementation with Special Reference to Bangalore Urban District." Sri. Rajiv Gurugopinath, has been a part of many National and International seminars, conferences, symposiums where he has presented and published various papers. He has also been a resource person at various national and international seminars. Sri. Rajiv Gurugopinath, has time and again been invited to deliver various guest lectures at reputed colleges, also adjudge many National Level Moot Court competitions and various Law Events like, Mock Trial, Legal Debate, etc. Sri. Rajiv Gurugopinath, has a diverse experience both as an advocate and as an academician. Sri. Rajiv Gurugopinath, tries to imbibe a healthy mixture of both practice as well as academics and therefore is a strong advocate of holistic legal education. His areas of Interest include Constitutional Law, Administrative Law, Jurisprudence, Law of Crimes, Business Laws, Intellectual Property Law, Health Laws and Medical Laws among others.

Jipson Joseph has a PhD in Ethics from DVK Bangalore. Currently, he is a Research Scholar at School of Law, Christ University, Bangalore, India. His research interests are in the fields of ethics, gender studies, constitutional law, human rights, human security, cybersecurity, data privacy, environmental justice, SDGs, developmental policies, and global poverty. He has published 6 books, co-edited one book, and contributed scholarly articles to many international and national journals and edited volumes including IGI Global Scientific Publishing's edited books.

Ramya Krishnappa, Dr., is an Assistant Professor of Law at School of Law, Christ University. She has previously served at Ramaiah College of Law. She is registered as an advocate on the rolls of the Karnataka State Bar Council and graduated with a degree of B.A. LL.B. from B.M.S. College of Law, Bengaluru. Dr. Ramya Krishnappa completed her Master of Laws (LL. M.) in Constitutional and Administrative Law from the KLE's Law College, Bengaluru with a Gold Medal Dr. Ramya Krishnappa, completed her Ph.D., from the School of Law, Christ University, Bengaluru on the topic "Study on the legal framework and working of Panchayat institutions with special reference to Mandya district." Dr. Ramya Krishnappa, is a highly motivated and experienced faculty with over eleven years of experience in teaching, research, and legal practice. Proven ability to foster critical thinking and engage students in dynamic learning environments. Passionate about teaching and eager to contribute to academic excellence.

Adina Lundy is the associate director of undergraduate psychology at a small New England Institution. A leading authority on the lasting effects of chattel slavery on poverty and the contemporary structure of the Black family; she brings deep historical insight and interdisciplinary expertise to her work as an expert witness for the Public Defender's Office of the New Jersey Family Court, a professor, and a multiculturalism scholar. A dedicated researcher on racism and systemic inequity, Dr. Lundy's work focuses on how structural barriers—including the lack of social capital, institutional bias, and uneven resource allocation—impact both students of color and faculty of color. Her scholarship illuminates how these inequities limit opportunity, influence academic pathways, and contribute to long-term disparities across disciplines. Through her research, workshops (with institutions such as Duke Medical school and the New Jersey Judiciary) testimony, and community advocacy, Dr. Lundy provides critical expertise at the intersection of history, policy, and lived experience, advancing efforts to create equitable systems and strengthen outcomes for children, families, and people of color. Dr. Lundy's research program centers the experiences of marginalized populations seeking to improve their socioeconomic status, with a particular focus on the transformative role of social capital and the strategic engagement of white allies committed to meaningful, equity-driven change.

Her work interrogates how access to education, resources, and informed accomplices shapes the trajectories of communities striving for liberation and opportunity. Grounded in qualitative inquiry, Dr. Lundy employs phenomenological methods rooted in community building, relational trust, and deep listening. Her approach prioritizes participants' lived experiences as essential sources of knowledge, informing policy recommendations and institutional practices. Dr. Lundy is currently conducting research with Dr. Hans Saint-Eloi Cadely titled Disentangling the Risk: Foster Care as a Precursor to Criminal Justice Involvement. This project investigates the pathways that connect state care to later contact with the criminal justice system, aiming to illuminate systemic vulnerabilities, identify points of intervention, and contribute to long-term institutional change. Dr. Lundy encourages all, who were born with tans: You belong wherever the Black slave labored against their will on land stolen from the indigenous American.

Rupal Malik is an Assistant Professor of Law, at Ramaiah College of Law, Bengaluru. She has done her Phd from VIT-AP University, in the area of new and emerging technologies in modern armed conflict with a special focus on Autonomous Weapon Systems (AWS). She has completed her post-graduation from Law College Dehradun, Uttaranchal University. She has worked and published on AWS and the recent armed conflict between Russia and Ukraine.

Harsh Manohar is a Lecturer, Jindal Global Law School, O.P. Jindal Global University (Institution of Eminence Deemed to Be University). He holds an LLM (Arbitration, Mediation and Negotiation) from Penn State University and BA LLB (Constitutional Honors) from Nirma University. Prior to joining Jindal Global Law School, he worked as a Research Assistant to Prof. Ylli Dautaj (Visiting Associate Professor, Penn State University) and as a Subject Matter Expert (Arbitration) for Kluwer Law International. His research interests include International Law, Investment Law and Commercial Arbitration. He combines insights from TWAIL, political economy and other critical approaches in his writings.

Sunidhi Setia serves as Assistant Professor and Assistant Dean for Independent Research Projects. Ms. Setia holds a Master of Laws (LLM) from NALSAR University of Law, Hyderabad, and a Bachelor of Laws (LLB) with specialization in Intellectual Property Laws from the Institute of Law, Nirma University. Ms. Setia's research expertise lies in Intellectual Property Rights (IPR), Environmental Laws, and Internet Governance. As an accomplished academician, she is dedicated to fostering legal excellence in her students. Beyond academics, Ms. Setia enjoys reading and exploring diverse perspectives in her free time

Jorja Wright Stokes is a logistics manager for the Dept. of the Army. She focuses on maintaining optimal inventory stock posture, cultivating effective organizational processes, and fostering sustainable employee relationships. She has a PhD in Healthcare Cybersecurity from Capitol Technology University in Laurel, MD. She received her doctorate degree in Executive Leadership from the University of Charleston in Charleston, West Virginia. She earned her MBA from the Nathan M. Bisk College of Business at Florida Institute of Technology, concentrating in healthcare management. Finally, she has a bachelor's degree in biology and a minor in chemistry from the University of Alabama-Huntsville. Furthermore, Dr. Stokes has published over 30 peer-reviewed articles and conference proceedings on leadership and cybersecurity, from healthcare management to logistics. Dr. Wright is an innovative and talented professional with a diverse educational background focused on implementing policies that improve agile strategies and organizational sustainability and promote scholarship within the business discipline.

Index

A

B

C

D

F

G

S

T

www.ingramcontent.com/pod-product-compliance
Ingram Content Group UK Ltd.
Pitfield, Milton Keynes, MK11 3LW, UK
UKHW052002051026
15624UKWH00003B/522

9 798337 349671